The Heart of a Woman

MUSIC IN AMERICAN LIFE

A list of books in the series appears at the end of this book.

The Heart of a Woman

The Life and Music of Florence B. Price

RAE LINDA BROWN

Edited and with a Foreword
by Guthrie P. Ramsey Jr.

Afterword by Carlene J. Brown

UNIVERSITY OF
ILLINOIS PRESS
Urbana, Chicago, and Springfield

Publication of this book was supported by grants from the H. Earle Johnson Fund of the Society for American Music, the Henry and Edna Binkele Classical Music Fund, and the Women's Philharmonic Advocacy (www.wophil.org).

Note on music examples: The author's examples were first prepared around 2009, and since then several scholarly editions have appeared. The editors have silently corrected the examples originally provided to correspond to the later scholarly editions.

1 2 3 4 5 C P 5 4 3 2 1
∞ This book is printed on acid-free paper.

Library of Congress Cataloging-in-Publication Data
Names: Brown, Rae Linda, 1953– author. | Ramsey, Guthrie P, editor.
Title: The heart of a woman: the life and music of Florence B. Price / Rae Linda Brown; edited and with a foreword by Guthrie P Ramsey, Jr.; afterword by Carlene J. Brown.
Description: Urbana: University of Illinois Press, 2020. | Series: Music in American life | Includes bibliographical references and index. |
Identifiers: LCCN 2019054490 (print) | LCCN 2019054491 (ebook) | ISBN 9780252043239 (cloth) | ISBN 9780252085109 (paperback) | ISBN 9780252052118 (ebook)
Subjects: LCSH: Price, Florence, 1887–1953. | African-American women composers—Biography. | African-American composers—Biography. | Women composers—Biography. | Composers—Biography. | LCGFT: Biographies.
Classification: LCC ML410.P835 B76 2020 (print) | LCC ML410.P835 (ebook) | DDC 780.92 [B]—dc23
LC record available at https://lccn.loc.gov/2019054490
LC ebook record available at https://lccn.loc.gov/2019054491

THE HEART OF A WOMAN

By Georgia Douglas Johnson

The heart of a woman goes forth with the dawn,
As a lone bird, soft winging, so restlessly on,
Afar o'er life's turrets and vales does it roam
In the wake of those echoes the heart calls home.

The heart of a woman falls back with the night,
And enters some alien cage in its plight,
And tries to forget it has dreamed of the stars
While it breaks, breaks, breaks on the sheltering bars.

Source: *The Heart of a Woman and Other Poems*
(The Cornhill Company, 1918)

Contents

Foreword
Keep Digging
Florence Price, Rae Linda Brown, and the Art of a Woman

GUTHRIE P. RAMSEY JR.

The year was 1979. Rae Linda Brown didn't know it at the time, but fate was putting her on a course to tell another black woman musician's life story. Brown was working on a graduate degree in African American Studies at Yale University. She was doing the yeoman's work of cataloguing all the music in the James Weldon Johnson Memorial Collection of Negro Arts and Letters when she happened on an anomaly—a manuscript score written by a composer she'd never heard of and one that would change her life. The score was a symphony—Symphony No. 3 in C minor—and it was composed by a Florence Beatrice Price.

Although she was intrigued by this woman and her music, Brown continued to work dutifully in the archive. The results of her efforts became her MA thesis, which she completed in 1980. It was published in 1982 and seen immediately as an important contribution to the field. She chose this kind of reference work, perhaps, as much for practical reasons as for her own scholarly curiosities. It was a finite collection, and thus, as a cataloguing project, it had a clear endpoint. In other words, it perfectly suited an ambitious MA student with designs to move on to the PhD. The idea that she would have under her belt published research work before receiving her doctorate is telling.

At the time that Brown was embarking on her topic, the new field of African American Studies was gaining ground as a legitimate and dynamic discipline. Born of student protests in the 1960s, by the 1980s it was maturing into a bulwark of American arts and letters. Brown apparently understood that cataloging collections like the James Weldon Johnson Memorial Collection would certainly assist future researchers. More important, however, is that a thesis based on music would make a strong argument for the utility of music studies—and by extension, the expressive arts—*within* African American Studies. For all her administrative and organizational inclinations (those would bloom brilliantly later in her career), Brown could not have known that her serendipitous discovery of Price's third symphony would turn into a decade's long diligent pursuit to learn everything she could about Price and document it.

A gifted pianist, composer, and pedagogue, Florence Price was born in 1887, directly following the Reconstruction period; she died as the Civil Rights Movement was taking shape. She passed away in 1953, the year her most committed scholarly inquisitor, Rae Linda Brown, was born. Brown's research career took shape during a time in which Black Studies was gaining ground on campuses around the country. Nearly a decade after the intense activism that produced the field began, a wave of "multiculturalism" swept through and reshaped traditional Eurocentric disciplines into more expansive profiles that included black subjects. An explosion of literature energized the field, particularly in the realm of literary criticism buoyed by poststructuralist theoretical tools.

Black music studies made a slower march toward the theoretical excess of 1980s black literary studies that made black cultural study an avant-garde profession in the academy. Black music research's concerns, however, were more compensatory. And they were precisely what Rae Linda Brown's work became: the discovery of hidden figures and the providing of supporting materials that also provided context. This shared goal was pursued by an interdisciplinary phalanx of musicians, scholars, composers, and educators who combined forces to discover and document the music that had been, for the most part, ignored by the larger musicological establishment. Rae Linda pursued her quest to write Price's story within a focused scholarly and musical community with support to give. In many ways, she was the first fruit of the professionalization of black music research.

The black music studies ecology of the post–Civil Rights period into which Brown made her first forays into scholarship was filled with powerhouses. The musicologist Eileen Southern, who was also the first black woman to earn tenure at Harvard University, had written the monumental compendium *The Music of Black Americans: A History* in 1971. Widely understood as field-defining, the book's second edition would appear in 1983, a year after Brown's MA thesis was published. Librarian Dena Epstein's game-changing book, *Sinful Tunes and Spirituals*, appeared in 1977. Its research took the author nearly two decades to complete. The young folklorist and ethnomusicologist Portia Maultsby challenged her subfield to take black music research seriously—not to give only lip service and "rap sessions" but to give it deliberate, sustained scholarship that was the result of rigorous training. In the late 1970s and early 1980s, Maultsby produced a series of publications that ordered her field's approach to past and present black music making. Academic journals dedicated to black music research appeared during this period as well. Eileen Southern's *The Black Perspective in Music* began in 1973. Samuel A. Floyd Jr., founded *Black Music Research Journal* in 1980. This was all an exciting context for Brown to begin working on a figure like Price. Evidence abounded that there was, indeed, a scholarly audience for work on this musician in that moment.

Rae Linda's notable mentors and interlocutors also included performers like Willis Patterson, an operatic singer, voice teacher, and professor of music at the University of Michigan. In 1985, Patterson convened the Black American Music Symposium, which was at the time the most ambitious and significant gathering of musicians, scholars, educators, and composers to be assembled to acknowledge African American music's contributions to America. More than 600 participants (not including the 16,000 audience members) performed and spoke about a variety of topics over six days. Rae Linda Brown, who was listed as a PhD candidate in the program, served on a panel devoted to black women musicians. No doubt, she read from her dissertation-in-progress on Florence Price. Judging from her visibility at the symposium and the trajectory of her career, she was by now recognized as an important emerging voice in the field. Indeed, black music research and the larger discipline of African American Studies (both of which she claimed) were on the move, and Brown was certainly in the forefront of the mix.

From those beginnings, Rae Linda Brown completed her PhD in 1987 (coincidentally the centennial year of Price's birth) having taken a position at the University of Michigan a year prior. She joined good company there. The pioneering musicologist Richard Crawford had been working to put the study of American music of all kinds into the mainstream of musicological discourse. With both Willis Patterson and Crawford at the institution, she was spared the need to validate the importance of Price as a research topic. From this important bully pulpit—the epic center of American music study—she was clearly participating in the transformation of music studies in the United States.

Brown's treatment of Price's life and works reflected many of the personal and professional tributaries that had made her into the scholar she had become. As a musicologist trained at Yale University by Claude Palisca, a luminary in the field from whom she received support and the tools to hear through the silences of history, she told Price's compelling story. Although her chosen topic may have been "nonstandard" at that time, Brown learned that she could apply the same rigorous standards to Price that Palisca had to his own groundbreaking studies on early music. I got a bird's-eye view of Brown's exacting scholarly standards when, as her research assistant, I was instructed to find every reference to Price in *The Chicago Defender* over a thirty-year period. She wanted no stone left unturned.

As an accomplished organist, Brown's instincts were inherently, and perhaps primarily, musical. One gets the sense from *The Heart of a Woman* that she believed Price's own dedication to *music* against all odds was the sole reason for telling this story. Indeed, Rae Linda's impeccable musicianship provided her the necessary skills to prepare Price's music to be heard by contemporary ears. She worked tirelessly to edit Price's manuscripts for numerous ensembles through the years. These include the American Symphony Orchestra, the Women's Philharmonic, the Chicago String Ensemble, the Orchestra of the Plymouth Music Series, the Savannah Symphony, the Albany Symphony, the Springfield Symphony, and the Camellia Symphony. From these editions, musicians have also been able to record Price's music for posterity. With the zeal of an activist, Brown prepared these editions as if she had taken it upon herself to assure Price's string of successes would continue well into the future. In *The Heart of a Woman*, Brown's artistic empathy can be keenly felt in the ways that she framed Price's achievements, great and small. Because of her treatment, readers will want to cheer for every musical victory that Price wins, particularly when she became the first black woman composer to have a symphony performed by a major orchestra.

Clearly, Rae Linda saw this book as a statement of African American Studies and black feminism as much as it is a music studies one. Throughout it she uses intersectional frameworks—though they aren't named as such—to explain Price's family history, migrations, and class status, as well as the politics of skin color within African American communities. The arch of the story reaches from slavery through Reconstruction, the Harlem and Chicago Renaissances, the Depression, and up to the dawn of the Civil Rights Movement. We follow Price from the Deep South to New England and Chicago. Each environment carried different forms of discrimination. We learn how she navigated an abusive marriage and found the fortitude to provide for her children as a black single mother. We see how she strategically built networks of support among women (both black and white), in much the same way that Brown did in her career. And we witness the challenges faced by an African American woman who dared to view herself as a creator of art music even as she tackled various forms of structural inequalities in that art world. Price fought her entire life to be heard and seen.

Throughout her career, Rae Linda also fought in her quiet, determined way to expand opportunities and expectations for black women in the field. When she left her first faculty position at the University of Michigan for the University of California, Irvine, in 1989, she continued to show the wide scope of her abilities. As the first faculty member to hold the department's endowed chair at Irvine, she created a new jazz studies program and was ultimately awarded a prestigious teaching award for her efforts. Brown loved jazz; she dedicated her career to teaching its history and spoke often of musicians she found moving and what new music had made an impact on her. Just as she championed the Western art music of African American composers like Florence Price, she was also a strong promoter of jazz musicians in her circle. Although her scholarship was focused on concert music composers, there's no evidence that Rae Linda believed that it was somehow "better" than jazz. She, like most in the community of scholars in which she cut her teeth, rejected the hierarchies that dominated musicological discourse for decades.

While teaching at Irvine, Brown grew interested in administration, becoming chair of the Department of Music and eventually moving into upper administration as faculty assistant to the executive vice chancellor and provost and serving as dean of several interdisciplinary programs. During that time, she was elected president of the Society for American Music (1999–2001), the first African American to hold that key position. In 2008, her gifts for administration led her to become associate provost for Undergraduate Education at Loyola Marymount University, Los Angeles. When I visited campus once, I was stunned to hear her play organ for the convocation. Indeed, like Price, Rae Linda seemed to keep in touch with her performance side: she never stopped playing for a church throughout her career. I'm sure playing brought her joy, satisfaction, and balance. Her last and most impressive professional accomplishment was becoming Provost and senior vice president for Academic Affairs at Pacific Lutheran University in 2016.

Clearly, Brown tried to satisfy her numerous professional ambitions while balancing them against the demands of single motherhood. Thus, she was in a fine position to thoroughly contextualize Price's life and career, particularly with respect to being a black woman in a music field. Over the course of our friendship and professional camaraderie, Rae Linda shared with me some of the difficult instances of racism and sexism she'd encountered throughout her career. She aptly demonstrates in *The Heart of a Woman* that Price had obviously dealt with similar issues. As she traces Price's family background, childhood, training, and professional ascendance, Brown's subtle yet unflinching accounts are laced with intermittent commentary that allows readers to identify some of the insidious structural inequities the composer faced as she sought to be heard.

Although the end of Price's life was marked by heartbreaking disappointments, in Brown's telling, the entirety of Price's musical journey can only be considered a success in the history of American concert music. Brown's analysis of the Symphony No. 3, the piece she discovered in the archive as a graduate student, brings the story of these two musical women's work full circle. In

Brown's estimation, the work was a remarkable achievement of Afro-modernism in music. Such an assessment—with all its social and musical implications—is made possible by Price's mature, searching musicianship but also by Brown's lucid sonic analysis, which shows the evolution of the composer's voice throughout the book.

In the acknowledgments, Rae Linda states that her mentors Claude Palisca and Eileen Southern advised her to "keep digging" for information about Price at a time when her music had faded from public attention. She did. In 1999, the year she became president of the Society for American Music (then the Sonneck Society), Rae Linda received responses from three scholars (I was one) to what was the first full draft of this book. The present version is taken from a 2006 version, which apparently incorporated suggestions from the 1999 reports. Rae Linda continued to work toward improving her manuscript: it was marked up with handwritten notes that were obviously never intended for others' eyes. Clearly, she was still digging—scrambling to keep up with developments in Price's legacy and with the many demands of her fast-track career in college administration. Rae Linda stated near the end of her life that this book was completed and directed her sister, the music scholar Carlene Brown, to see it that it was published. This important book and the numerous performances that Rae Linda tirelessly facilitated for ensembles through the years are testaments to her devotion to Price's life and legacy.

Price's music is in vogue again and enjoying a new level of visibility because of Rae Linda's foundational and decades-long dedication. And now a new generation of scholars, musicians, and institutions are unearthing lost scores, adding new insights and the programming and recording of her compositions.[1] There's even a Facebook page providing updates about Price's work and a documentary of her life that appeared in 2015. Indeed, these are some of the compelling reasons for *The Heart of a Woman* to have its moment now—years after it was first conceived.

But there's another reason for this book's necessity today. With the rise of women as both powerful subjects of and authors of new scholarship, it's important to see Rae Linda's final scholarly statement as another example of what women can achieve both musically and intellectually despite all the obstacles placed before them. In this way, *The Heart of a Woman* can be considered a contemporary statement of black feminist thought. Indeed, this book stands as a profound testament to how far the hearts of two women—the composer and the determined scholarly devotee—could push their craft. As the poet Georgia Douglas Johnson wrote in the poem that gave this book and a Price song its title, "[t]he heart of a woman goes forth with the dawn . . . even as it breaks, breaks, breaks on the sheltering bars."

Just as Florence Price died as she was about to embark on her first European trip that would prove her international acclaim, Rae Linda Brown passed away before she could see this manuscript in book form. It will nonetheless always stand as testament to my friend, mentor, and sister's significance to the field of American music studies. Her musicianship, scholarly standards, drive, and devotion can be experienced on every page of this moving book.

Acknowledgments

My biography of Florence B. Price is very long in coming. My interest in Florence Price began while completing my master's degree at Yale University. In 1979–1980, I catalogued the music in the James Weldon Johnson Collection of Negro Arts and Letters in the Beinecke Rare Book Library.[1] It was there that I found some of Price's music, including the unpublished manuscript of the Symphony in C Minor (1940). Many years later while considering dissertation topics, I talked with the late Professor Eileen Southern who encouraged me to consider a topic in African American music. That conversation, at the annual AMS meeting in Boston in 1981, was the first of many we had over the years. How glad I am that I took her advice. My interest in and dedication to research, writing, and teaching about African American music has remained steady since.

Equally supportive very early on in my investigation of Florence Price's music was Claude Palisca, my dissertation advisor at Yale University. At a time when American music dissertations were still a novelty at some universities, Professor Palisca enthusiastically championed my topic. To the late Professor Eileen Southern and late Professor Claude Palisca, I owe my heartfelt gratitude. Their passion for research and the high standards that they set for our field have served for me all of these years as inspiration. They taught me to "keep digging" until I found what I was looking for and to never accept "it can't be found" as an excuse to give up on an important lead. Mostly, they taught me how important it is to love what you do.

During the earlier years of my research, there were numerous librarians, musicologists, and historians who helped me to gather information about Florence Price. These include Deborra Richardson (Moorland-Spingarn Research Center, Howard University), Sharon Scott, Dorothy Lyles, and Edward Manney (Vivian Harsh Research Collection of Afro-American History and Literature, Carter

G. Woodson Regional Library of the Chicago Public Library), Tom Dillard (Torreyson Library, University of Central Arkansas), Jeanne Morrow (New England Conservatory of Music Library), Marguerite L. Daly (New England Conservatory of Music), Jeanne Salathiel (Detroit Public Library), Willard B. Gatewood (University of Arkansas), Chester W. Williams (former dean, New England Conservatory of Music), and Robert Brubaker (Chicago Historical Society). I also wish to thank the reference librarians and staffs of the Detroit Public Library (which conserves the papers of the Michigan W.P.A. Symphony Orchestra); E. Azalia Hackley Memorial Collection of Negro Music, Drama, and Dance (Detroit Public Library); Chicago Public Library Music Division, Beinecke Rare Book and Manuscript Library of Yale University; Mullins Library Special Collections at the University of Arkansas; and the Music Division of the Library of Congress. I especially want to thank Suzanne Flandreau of the Center for Black Music Research, who found material even when I was not looking for it, and Wayne Shirley for his many years of expert advice and dedication to this project.

I am especially grateful to the many colleagues, friends, and students of Florence Price and their sons and daughters who shared with me her musical scores, photographs, letters, scrapbooks, and memorabilia. It is her friends who have given life to this book by sharing their memories and mementos of her with me. These include Eleanor Price (no relation), Vera Flandorf, Orrin Clayton Suthern, II, Dr. Ruth Fouché, Verna Arvey (wife of William Grant Still), Mildred Hall (wife of Dr. Frederick Hall), Bernice Hall (daughter-in-law of Dr. Frederick Hall), and Valter Poole (conductor of the Michigan W.P.A. Orchestra).[2] Special thanks go to Dr. Florence Stith, Eugenia Anderson, Bernice Skooglund, and William Duncan Allen, who gave me musical manuscripts and shared their memories of Florence Price. I am particularly indebted to Judith Anne Still (daughter of William Grant Still), Josephine Harreld Love, Helen White, and Marion Ross, all of whom spent days and days with me helping to establish a framework for Florence Price's life and career. I thank them for their time and hospitality (in Flagstaff, Los Angeles, Detroit, Chicago, and Little Rock). From them, I learned about Florence Price, the mother, wife, and friend. They gave me the photographs that appear in this book, many never before seen.

Thanks also go to Theodore Chadwick (great-grandson of George Whitefield Chadwick, director of the New England Conservatory of Music, 1897–1930), who gave me permission to use materials from Chadwick's memoirs. Special appreciation goes to Lawrence Robinson, Florence Price's grandson, who shared with me wonderful stories of his grandmother. I also wish to thank Vicki J. Taylor Hammond and Timothy J. Taylor (Florence Price's grandchildren) for their permission to publish the musical scores, letters, and other materials in this book. Without them, this book would never have come to fruition.

Over these many years, there have been numerous friends and colleagues who have helped me along the way—with suggested leads on information, thoughts about how to organize material, and general words of wisdom. Thanks go to Mildred Denby Green, Calvert Johnson, Steven Ledbetter, Doris McGinty, Josephine Wright, Maurice Wheeler, Judith Tick, Adrienne Fried Block, Marsha Heizer, Rick Powell, and Rich Crawford. A special thank you to Barbara Garvey Jackson who shared with me her initial work on Florence B. Price and was a gracious host during my visit to Arkansas.

To Leonard Brown, Dwight Andrews, Bill Banfield, Samuel A. Floyd Jr., the late Bill Brown, Olly Wilson, T. J. Anderson, Anthony Brown, Willis Patterson, Carol Oja, Vivian Perlis, Hale Smith, Althea Waites, Kei Akagi, Catherine Parsons Smith, R. Drew Smith, Angelique Walker-Smith, and my brother Guthrie Ramsey—oh, my goodness! I give you my deepest gratitude. Your encouragement (phone calls, emails, letters, visits—my house, yours, and at conference convocations), professionalism (talking about, reading, and critiquing my work), and love kept me going when I needed it most. And you always knew.

This book was supported by several fellowships and grants that I received, including a Dorothy Danforth Fellowship (Yale University), Rackham Faculty Research Grant (The University of Michigan), Ford Foundation Postdoctoral Fellowship, the Institute of American Cultures Research Grant (University of California, Los Angeles), the University of California President's Fellowship, and a University of California, Irvine Research Grant. Thank you to Jim Simmons, who transcribed all of the musical examples for the book and for never complaining about it. And thank you, Judith McCulloh, for championing this book at the University of Illinois Press from the beginning and for being a wonderful editor and friend.

Last, and most importantly, I am blessed to have a wonderful family—my sisters Carlene Brown and Helaine Teale and their families (Elvis, Ryanna, Nyah, Charles, Ileah, and Jason) who have encouraged me from graduate school to the present; my mother, Doris Brown, upon whose shoulders we all still stand; and my son William of whom I am very proud. Thank you for your love and support.

Sources

The necessary evidence required to write a detailed biography of Florence Price is surprisingly scant. She was a very private woman who preferred to reveal herself through her music rather than through correspondence and memorabilia. Since Price was a devoted single mother who also had a commanding career, she probably had precious little time to sort through and organize her scores, file press clippings, and the like. That we have any documentation of Price's career at all, outside of newspaper accounts, is due, in large part, to her daughter, Florence Price Robinson, who began to help promote her mother's career in the 1940s.

Some facts about Price's family history are revealed in archival sources. Census records from the 1840s to 1900 were used to gather information on Price's maternal grandparents (no information could be found on her paternal grandparents). This source was also used to glean information about Dr. and Mrs. Smith and the Smith household. Birth certificates (while not always accurate), marriage and death certificates, wills, property deeds, mortgages, city directories, and probate records were also useful in ascertaining information about the Smiths in Little Rock. The reader should be mindful that recorded vital statistics do not exist for all of Price's family, including her own birth certificate; Arkansas law did not require these records for blacks until the 1920s.

Shortly after Price moved to Chicago she became very active in the two Chicago branches of the National Association of Negro Musicians. The activities of this organization, on both the local and national levels, were recorded regularly in the black-owned newspaper, the *Chicago Defender*. This source proved indispensable in documenting many of Price's compositions and performances of her music, those that she and others played.

It appears that Price was very generous in sharing her scores, giving copies of her manuscripts to anyone whom she thought would seriously be interested in performing them. After her death, numerous compositions, music manuscripts, and printed scores were distributed to individuals around Chicago and in other places, including library repositories. Unfortunately, many of the manuscripts were given as memorabilia, some even as single sheets. This presents a particular problem in trying to ascertain an accurate list of Price's oeuvre since no inventory of her scores was kept. Many of these manuscripts represent the only surviving copies of a work. My research has uncovered about 300 scores or portions of scores; undoubtedly, many other compositions are now lost.

The largest single source of Price's music is located at the University of Arkansas. Established by Florence Price Robinson shortly before her death in 1975, the Florence Beatrice Smith Price Materials (Manuscript Collection 988, Mullins Library Special Collections) contains 164 items dated 1906–1953 and includes correspondence, photographs, musical programs, and miscellaneous materials.

One of the most revealing items in the Price Archive is the few extant pages from her diary. In it she wrote the most intimate thoughts about her work; melodies as they occurred to her, transcriptions of birdsongs, her career aspirations, and such mundane musings as the weather temperature. Price's diary was a way of telling her story—her solace revealing her inner self. Apparently, this diary was very detailed because she recorded conversations that she had with people regarding her compositions. Unfortunately, the complete diary does not survive. After her death, pages of it were given away as mementos to her friends.

Price and her daughter took care to make sure that Price's music was represented in the major repositories of African American history and culture. These include the James Weldon Johnson Memorial Collection of Negro Arts and Letters at Yale University, which conserves a "presentation copy" of the unpublished Symphony No. 3 in C Minor; the Moorland-Spingarn Research Center at Howard University, which was gifted one page of the Symphony No. 2 in G Minor; the E. Azalia Hackley Memorial Collection of Negro Music, Drama, and Dance (Detroit Public Library); the Vivian G. Harsh Collection of Afro-American History and Literature (Chicago Public Library); and the Schomburg Center for Research in Black Culture of the New York Public Library.

The Marian Anderson Collection, established at the University of Pennsylvania in 1977, conserves the largest collection of Price's art songs. The fifty-three songs, two spiritual arrangements, and one piano piece comprise the largest portion of music in the collection—a measure of the high esteem in which

Miss Anderson held Price's music. Indeed, Marian Anderson premiered many of Price's songs written for and dedicated to the diva.

Persistence and imagination was required in finding Price's scores located among the private collections of her friends and professional colleagues. This rich source for the investigation of Price's music, of which oral history is an integral factor, had been virtually untapped. Price's colleagues, living throughout the country, shared with me music manuscripts, correspondence, programs, and their memories of Price and her notable performances. I am grateful to concert pianist William Duncan Allen, who gave me the first known surviving copies of Price's *Piano Concerto in One Movement*. Chicago organist Eugenia Anderson had several of the missing orchestral parts for the concerto (although we still do not have a full set of orchestral parts or the full score). Organists Bernice Skooglund and Florence Stith had organ and piano manuscripts not available elsewhere. Concert singers Helen White and Mildred Hall, the widow of composer Frederick Hall, had songs and piano music.

Given the paucity of primary source material on Price herself (for example, a complete diary, letters, and the like), much of this story is told through major events in her life (for example, the first performance of her Symphony in E Minor with the Chicago Symphony). Her life is also revealed by focusing on the major institutions with which she was affiliated (the Woman's Symphony Orchestra of Chicago, the National Association of Negro Musicians, and the WPA ensembles). This approach to writing her biography accomplishes two goals: first, it sheds light on Price's aspirations, both personal and professional; and second, it allows, for the first time, these historically important institutions to be the focal point around which her creative life unfolds. To this end, the reader may miss the details of Price's personal relationships. Whenever materials were available, I have used them to glean insight into her persona.

The Heart of a Woman

Introduction

She does not know her beauty
She thinks her brown body has no glory.
If she could dance naked under palm trees
And see her image in the river
She would know.
But there are no palm trees on the street,
And dish water gives back no images.
—Waring Cuney, *No Image**

This book documents the life and work of Florence Beatrice Smith Price (1887–1953), America's first significant African American woman composer. It is intended to fill the lacunae of biographical sources of those pioneering African American composers who have contributed significantly to the rich and diversified musical heritage of black Americans. In order to place the music of Florence Price in the proper musical and historical perspective, careful consideration is given to the social, economic, and political forces that shaped American history from the mid–nineteenth century to the mid–twentieth century and had an impact on the creative endeavors of the African American.

Florence Price was the most widely known African American woman composer from the 1930s to her death in 1953. She achieved national recognition when her Symphony in E Minor was premiered by the Chicago Symphony in 1933 under the direction of Frederick Stock. The concert marked the first performance of a large-scale work by a black woman to be performed by a major American orchestra.

This book is the story of over a century and a half of African American cultural history told through the lives of one family in dramatic situations: in the deep South during the days of slavery, in the urban South during Reconstruction, in New England at the turn of the century, and in the Midwest from the 1930s. It traces Florence Price and her family from the birth of her maternal grandparents, free blacks in a slave state, to her death in Chicago in 1953. Several themes run through this book. The role of education in African American culture is a pervasive topic during Price's lifetime. Only through education could self-help be promoted and racial uplift be achieved. Issues of

American musical nationalism and the relationship between cultural identity and musical creation are also prominent. For some African American composers of the 1920s and 1930s, advancement of the race and cultural identity in musical composition were almost synonymous. Central to this book are the interrelated and often conflicting issues for Price about gender, race, and class. At least two issues unfold here—the impact of marriage and motherhood on a woman's career aspirations and the idea of difference and tension within the African American community.

I hope that through the exploration of these themes a broader and more representative view of African American culture will evolve. In many ways, this discourse may contradict stereotypical views currently in circulation, particularly of African American women. But, hopefully, the unfolding narrative will help the reader understand the "politics of respectability" in early-twentieth-century African American culture.

Price's exploration of self comes about over a long period of time and is ultimately realized through her music—as a teacher, as a performer, and through the development of her musical compositions. Marginalized in her occupation, by her gender, and by her race, Price's story is not one of defeat but one of triumph specific to African American women. As bell hooks has pointed out in *Feminist Theory: From Margin to Center*, "Black women with no institutionalized 'other' that we may discriminate against, exploit, or oppress often have a lived experience that directly challenges the prevailing classist, sexist, racist social structure and its concomitant ideology. This lived experience may shape our consciousness in such a way that our world view differs from those who have a degree of privilege (however relative within the existing system). . . . I am suggesting that we have a central role to play in the making of feminist theory and a contribution to offer that is unique and valuable."[1]

In documenting Price's life, I have tried to render visibility to this Invisible Woman by offering a peek into the private sphere of African American culture, a cultural space that receives little attention in scholarship and popular discourse. My book, while not entering aggressively into theoretical explanations of the relationship between identity, cultural politics, and musical expression, provides a necessary first step into such activity. My work will, hopefully, inspire future studies that examine the signifyin(g) value of the work of black female composers. Such studies need first to *know* about these women and, second, to understand something of the prevailing ideologies and social contexts in which they created. Only then can we move into the type of feminist criticism that has made such an impact on the field of musicology and cultural studies in recent years.

* * *

Price was born in Little Rock, Arkansas, in 1887 during post–Reconstruction. Known as the "Negro Paradise," Little Rock was the pride of the South. Florence Beatrice and her family belonged to the small, but significant, black upper class. Her father, Dr. James H. Smith, became the city's first black dentist when he moved there in 1886. Florence Irene Gulliver Smith, Price's mother, was a businesswoman and a well-trained singer and pianist.

During the Reconstruction years (1865–1877), a well-defined social structure of three distinct social classes developed within the black community. The hierarchy that emerged was comprised of a complex web of interrelated characteristics that found unique expression in the African American experience. In other words, as Willard Gatewood explains, "Much of what accounted for status and prestige in the black community had no counterpart in white society, because status and prestige among blacks were in large part bound up with their experience with slavery—their particular place in the slave system, their role in opposing it, and the extent to which their families had been free from it."[2]

The majority of Little Rock's blacks, at the base of the system, lived in poverty; they had little education and few advanced skills. Emanating from the growing number of small businesses, the black middle class formed. The upper class, the smallest in number, was an amalgam of two groups. The "old families" were all former slaves born in or around the city. They included, for example, Rev. William Wallace Andrews, taught to read and write by his master, who founded Little Rock's first black public school.

The other group within the black aristocracy, the "new families," was comprised of skilled, and often well-educated blacks, who relocated to Little Rock. Dr. Smith is counted among this group as well as Mifflin W. Gibbs, who became the first black municipal judge in the United States. The "old families," and the handful of very successful blacks who settled in Little Rock after the Civil War, combined to form the small, but powerful, black elite. Their behavior and attitudes "bore all the earmarks of gentility, super-respectability, and refinement."[3]

Common among the black elite was the importance they placed on literacy or advanced education. Many of their offspring were educated at the best black colleges in the north, as well as Harvard and Yale. They returned to Little Rock to teach the masses of black illiterate children in the public schools or in one of the city's four black colleges. Florence Beatrice's teacher, Charlotte Andrews Stephens, Rev. Andrews's daughter, was educated at Oberlin, and upon her return to Little Rock she became the first black teacher in the newly organized public school system for black children. Both Florence Beatrice and William Grant Still were taught by Mrs. Stephens in elementary school. Because of this dedicated teacher's profound sense of self and her fine education in the humanities and in music at Oberlin, she would be a tremendous influence on both of these gifted children.

For all of the social proscriptions associated with the black aristocracy, a central mission was individual and collective advancement of the race. They actively built schools, churches, and social institutions. Dr. Smith, who taught in rural Arkansas, was among many in his class who understood that only through education could the race be uplifted. These socially conscious people also built healthcare facilities where they could take care of the elderly and sick. Some doctors, like Dr. Smith, often rendered their services in-kind, receiving little or no monetary remuneration.

Within the black social structure, there existed a complex and stratified caste system. Wealth, occupation, and formal education were but part of the criteria that defined one's place within the community. In Willard Gatewood's seminal study, *Aristocrats of Color*, the author points out that the majority of the members of the upper class were light-skinned blacks or mulattos (blacks with white ancestry). Historical proscriptions as well as attitudes of superiority contributed to the association of fair complexions with the upper class. The lighter one's skin, the more likely one would be embraced by the black elite.

Light-skinned blacks were considered privileged in many ways. Considered acceptable by whites because of their Caucasian features, they were perceived to be more intelligent than blacks with darker skin. This perception often opened doors, particularly in securing employment, that were unavailable to others in the black community. This combination of artificial factors contributed to the disproportionate statistic of light-skinned blacks equated with high achievement—W. E. B. Du Bois's Talented Tenth.[4] Most blacks were more astute, however, realizing that skin color was but one factor in achieving social status.[5]

From the beginning, the Smiths were included among the upper echelon in this socially conscious city. Like most of the "aristocrats of color," the Smiths were mulattos, that is, they were of mixed racial heritage with very fair complexions and Caucasian features. Their refined manners, cultural sophistication, and appealing (from a white person's viewpoint) outward appearance all contributed to their inclusion among the black elite and their acceptance by whites.

For the Smith family, being light-skinned blacks had brought with it certain privileges before *de facto* segregation. There had been a certain amount of freedom to move about Little Rock unrestricted and opportunities to advance economically. When the "Jim Crow" laws were instituted, all blacks, regardless of their social status, became second-class citizens through arbitrary laws that stripped them of their basic human rights. By the time Florence Beatrice left for college in 1903, Little Rock was no more the "Negro Paradise" it once had been.

The New England Conservatory of Music, which Price attended after high school, was considered the proper finishing school for someone of her social background. It was here, while Price was writing her first symphony, that she began to explore her interest in the use of Negro folk materials in large-scale compositions.

If she had any serious career aspirations as a performer or as a composer, Price laid them aside after graduating from the Conservatory. Returning home to teach was little questioned by her. A sense of mission and service was deeply embedded in her, not only through her father's example of active involvement in black social causes, but by many members of the black community. Further, the ties of family and tradition were too strong. Her expectation and that of her parents after college was to marry and to have a family. It would be many years before Price set pen to paper again to pursue her innate gifts as a composer.

Between 1906 and 1912, Florence Beatrice taught music at several black colleges (then an amalgam of elementary, high school, and college) in and near Little Rock and in Atlanta. She was a formidable teacher and a beacon of light for all of her students and for the college communities. The model of the elite black woman, she was well-educated, articulate, and elegant but also shy, modest, and always reserved.

In 1912, Florence Beatrice married Thomas J. Price, a very successful attorney who had practiced first in Washington, D.C. Soon after, they started a family. When time permitted, Price took up composing again. Still not seeing herself as a serious composer, she concentrated on writing teaching pieces for piano and for violin with piano accompaniment. For a long time, Price tried to suppress her creative impulse but it was still there, still needing to find expression. There had been a significant gap, almost twenty years, between writing the symphony at the conservatory and now. Even in writing the children's pieces, she could no longer deny her passion for composing; it would soon become a way of life.

In 1927, Price and her family moved to Chicago to escape the oppressive legalized social proscriptions of the South. While she lived in Little Rock, her way of life as a Negro woman, to some extent, had been determined for her. The "Jim Crow" laws forced her to abdicate her rights, but she soon realized that no one could take away her self-esteem. The pride that was instilled in her as a black woman would be there for life.

It was in Chicago that Price's artistic impulse was liberated. She discovered a city full of vitality and an environment that was conducive to her creative energy. She had many opportunities, both in social and professional situations, to interact with other artists, among them visual artists, dancers, writers, and actors. These quite stimulating convocations hearkened back to Price's childhood, the Little Rock of old, which had been an intellectually and culturally rich one for her.

By the early 1930s, Price had developed into a serious composer whose skills were no doubt strengthened and accelerated by the many opportunities she had to hear her music performed. She wrote in all genres except opera, producing works for piano, organ, voice, chamber ensembles, orchestra, and chorus, and she arranged spirituals for voice and instrumental combinations. Her music was regularly performed by a professional coterie of friends and colleagues in Chicago as well as by some of the leading concert singers of the day, including Marian Anderson, Blanche Thebom, Roland Hayes, Abbie Mitchell, and Harry Burleigh. An accomplished pianist and organist, Price premiered many of her own piano and organ works. Her large-scale works were also being performed by the major ensembles of the Chicago area.

Price was successful professionally for many reasons, not the least of which was due to the supportive network she established shortly after her arrival in Chicago. The importance of women's musical groups in the 1930s and 1940s figured prominently. As far as can be determined Price did not belong to any black women's clubs but she retained membership in two musical organizations led by white women—the Chicago Club of Women Organists and the Musicians Club of Women. These clubs supported women as they struggled to gain hard-earned recognition in the professional fields, including that of composer.

The exclusion of women in professional organizations by men was very real. Women's support networks remained outside the purview of male-dominated organizations, and they had little or no effect on them. The Chicago Club of Women Organists, for example, who functioned independently of the national American Guild of Organists, provided opportunities for women organists to perform and for composers to have their organ, choral, and solo vocal music heard. Price greatly benefited from the exposure she received through them.

As supportive as the women's organizations were, there were disadvantages as well. Gloria T. Hull points out in *Color, Sex and Poetry* "because of women's less-advantaged status, these networks could often only amount to consolation circles for the disfranchised."[6] For many white women, these organizations served more as a much-needed social outlet than as a professional one. White women's clubs were formed because women were excluded from occupations and other activities for which their education prepared them. Their interests, however, were not with women whose lives depended upon work and making professional contacts. For many of them their associations were more of a "want" than a "need." For Price, on the other hand, these professional contacts were her lifeline.

There is little doubt that Price's light-skinned complexion was also a factor that permitted her entry and acceptance into professional circles where her darker-skinned sisters were implicitly not welcome. Of the groups who were most active in promoting her music, she was the first African American composer to be represented through the Illinois Federation of Music Clubs and the first black member of both the Chicago Club of Women Organists and the Musicians Club of Women. The fact that Price was fair enough to pass for white in no way lessens the significance of her achievements, but it attests to the key role that skin color played for Americans in attaining one's career goals. Some black musicians, like Price, were at least able to get their foot in the front door of professional opportunity; many blacks in classical music, other than singers who went abroad, weren't even getting into the back door.

Issues of gender, class, and race were ever-present for black women in the first half of the century, and the inherent conflicts that were prevalent for professional women were difficult to reconcile. For this reason, Price maintained an active involvement in the National Association of Negro Musicians (NANM). It was NANM and, by extension, the *Chicago Defender*, which covered the activities of the black community, both locally and nationally that kept Price's name before the public for the twenty-five years she resided in Chicago.

NANM boasted of equal participation by men and women. In fact, the R. Nathaniel Dett Club, the younger of Chicago's two branches, was suggested and organized by a small group of women, although already by the second meeting, men were included. Both at the local and national levels, women held the office of president and other board positions. Black people, men and women, could not negate the pivotal role that race played in American society. On some levels, black men and women *had* to work together. Locked out of many professional opportunities, there was an astute awareness of race among NANM members, many of whom were among the most talented/gifted African American musicians in the country. The attitude of the members of the Dett Club was typical. In a summary of the Club's activities in 1926, the writer notes, "There was a sense of urgency in the Club's attitude as it faced the problem of segregation in the concert halls of America." Exerting political and economic pressure where it could, "the members urged that Roland Hayes [one of the most highly paid singers in America] not appear in concert halls where Negroes were not permitted to attend."[7] Because Price was a well-respected musician, her career was certainly advanced because she was accepted by white as well as black social and professional circles.

* * *

I have told Florence Price's story in the fullest context of her life as an African American woman in the vibrant cities in which she lived—Little Rock, Boston, Atlanta, and Chicago. Only through an understanding of the social, political, and economic milieu of her time can the reader more fully appreciate Price's music and the context in which it was written.

Particular attention is given to the black classical musical tradition in these cities, which is often overshadowed by the proliferation of jazz, blues, and gospel music. This is particularly true of Chicago, which had a very active classical music scene from about 1910. The music of black composers and performers, as well as nationally known artists, regularly appeared in the city's black churches and in special concerts that took place in larger venues, including Orchestra Hall. The *Chicago Defender*, owned and edited by Robert Abbot, was an important vehicle through which information about classical music was disseminated. Because the *Defender* had both local and national editions, readers from throughout the nation could be kept apprised of the accomplishments of black classical musicians.

Shortly after Price arrived in Chicago, her life changed significantly. For the first time, she began to concentrate on her career. From 1931–1940, her whole life virtually revolved around the composition, promotion, performance, and critical reception of three major works: the Symphony in E Minor (1932), the *Piano Concerto in One Movement* (1934), and the Symphony in C Minor (1940). Although Price continued to write small-scale pieces, these works are pivotal in her oeuvre and thus I have devoted a significant portion of this book to them. Tracing the history of these three pieces reveals much about Price's development as a composer and a person.

The Symphony in E Minor is squarely in the nationalist tradition and it may be more fully considered in the context of the Harlem Renaissance and the New Negro Movement of the 1920s and 1930s. The spirit of African American folk music provides the contextual foundation for this work and other compositions written during this time period. Its formal structure is rather conservative: a sonata-allegro movement and two rondos. Only in the second movement, a chorale, does the symphony deviate somewhat from the norm.

By the time Price wrote the *Piano Concerto in One Movement*, however, it is clear that she was seeking her own voice in large-scale composition. She moved away from traditional structures in search of a musical language that was more fully expressive of herself as an individual. African American musical references become the guidepost for the unfolding of the work in both its musical content and its structure. In writing about the Concerto, traditional terminology proved to be inadequate so I have used a new term—Afro-Romantic—which better reflects the work's musical substance.[8] The approach Price uses as a composer is one in which the content of the work suggests its own form. The unfolding of a spiritual-like melody in the first section and call-and-response procedures in the second section, for example, are the essence from which the structure of the concerto emanates. Much of the concerto is free from European traditions; simultaneously, however, it still embraces the harmonic language of the past.

Price's Symphony in C Minor reveals a mature composer, completely confident in large-scale idioms. With the ideas of the nationalist movement and of the Harlem Renaissance now passé, she, as did other black artists, looked to realistic subject matter—the Great Migration, the Depression, and the adjustment to urban life—for inspiration. It is in this context of the second flowering of black artistic expression, called the Chicago Renaissance (1935–1950), that this symphony was conceived. African American musical scores are referenced more subtly and the score, overall, shows an assured grasp of contemporary musical developments.

By no means do all of Price's scores reflect her African American heritage, but its presence is celebrated in all of the large-scale works that survive. It is also in these works that her growth as a composer is so vividly revealed.

In an often-quoted essay from his 1903 classic book, *The Souls of Black Folk*, W. E. B. Du Bois poignantly examines what he perceives as the duality of black culture—a duality which has been discussed in writings about African American literature throughout the century.

> After the Egyptian and Indian, the Greek and Roman, the Teuton and Mongolian, the Negro is a sort of seventh son, born with a veil, and gifted with second-sight in this American world,—a world which yields him no true self-consciousness, but only lets him see himself through the revelation of the other world. It is a peculiar sensation, this double-consciousness, this sense of always looking at one's self through the eyes of others, of measuring one's soul by the tape of a world that looks on in amused contempt and pity. One ever feels his two-ness,—an American, a Negro; two souls, two thoughts, two unreconciled strivings; two warring ideals in one dark body, whose dogged strength alone keeps it from being torn asunder.
>
> The history of the American Negro is the history of this strife,—this longing to attain self-conscious manhood, to merge his double self into a better and truer self. In this merging he wishes neither of the older selves to be lost. He would not Africanize America, for America has too much to teach the world and Africa. He would not bleach his Negro soul in a flood of white Americanism, for he knows that Negro blood has a message for the world. He simply wishes to make it possible for a man to be both a Negro and an American, without being cursed and spit upon by his fellows, without having the doors of Opportunity closed roughly in his face.

Historically, writers have explicated musically Du Bois's "double-consciousness" by articulating the essence of the two primary traditions within African American music—one oral and one literate. These two traditions are seemingly a dichotomy. As Olly Wilson has pointed out in articles, black music in Du Bois's second tradition, the literate tradition, is, in fact, reconciled within the "veil." It is not simply the American ideal as white America envision it. It is, rather a reinterpretation of that American ideal as viewed through the prism of black American experience; it involves a unique reinterpretation of the broader American experience from a black vantage point.[9] In essence, the musical forms associated with the literate musical tradition emanate from preexistent European forms. But a transformation of these forms takes place when the dominant elements in a composition transcend European influence and can be isolated as constituents of African American tradition in American culture.

Price's compositions fuse Euro-American structures with elements from her own American cultural heritage, which creates an art music that, while utilizing European forms, affirms its integrity as an African American mode of expression. The musical synthesis she creates demonstrates how the African American composer could transcend received musical forms in articulating a unique American artistic and cultural self.

But on a deeper level, Price's life and work challenge Du Bois's famous text and, in fact, explode it, revealing their limitation in capturing the essence, complexities, and processes that are of African American culture. My study shows that there are many competing voices behind the veil. Price's life offers but one example of their multiple selves and multiple consciousness—not just double. Hers is the life story of an African American woman who worked not to achieve Du Bois's "self-conscious manhood" but who sought to quietly articulate the undeniable role that black women have played in private and public African American life and culture.

PART I

Southern Roots

1 Family Ties

Florence Beatrice had remarkable parents. Her mother, Florence Irene Gulliver Smith, was an amateur singer, accomplished pianist, and astute businesswoman. Her father, Dr. James H. Smith, a dentist, was also one of Little Rock's most esteemed community activists.

Florence Irene Gulliver was born to William Gulliver and Mary McCoy Gulliver in Indianapolis in 1854.[1] Mary McCoy, a mulatto (an African American of mixed race heritage), was born in 1835 in North Carolina.[2] She was the oldest daughter of William J. McCoy, a barber, and Margaret Chambers, both of North Carolina.[3]

The McCoys were free blacks in a state where the slave population constituted over 90 percent of the total population of blacks in 1860.[4] Everyone in the McCoy household could read and write, a rarity among blacks in the antebellum South. Most southern states passed strict laws prohibiting anyone from teaching slaves to read or write, arguing that slaves might become dissatisfied and incite rebellion. Even free blacks suffered severe punishment for violating the law. The 1830 North Carolina law states,

> That any free person, who shall hereafter teach, or attempt to teach, any slave within the State to read and write, the use of figures excepted, or shall give or sell to such slave or slaves any books or pamphlets, shall be liable to indictment in any court of record in this State having jurisdiction thereof, and upon conviction, shall, at the discretion of the court, if a white man or woman, be fined not less than one hundred dollars, nor more than two hundred dollars, or imprisoned; and if a free person of color, shall be fined, imprisoned, or whipped, at the discretion of the court, not exceeding thirty nine lashes, nor less than twenty lashes.[5]

William and Margaret McCoy had three children. After Mary, there was Laura, born in 1839 or 1841. With their two daughters, the McCoys moved to

Indianapolis during the 1840s, leaving the disparagement of living in a slave state behind them. It was here that their youngest daughter, Alice, was born in 1850.

William Gulliver, Florence Irene's father, also a mulatto, was born in Virginia in 1831. After he established a profession as barber, he moved from Virginia to Indianapolis as a young man where he met the McCoys. By 1854, he was married to Mary McCoy and in that year they became the proud parents of their daughter, Florence Irene. And by 1860 Gulliver and his father-in-law, William McCoy, had established a family barbershop.

It is possible to speculate about the time and the reason for William Gulliver's and the McCoy family's move to Indiana from the South, Virginia and South Carolina, respectively. During the 1840s and 1850s, large numbers of white immigrants settled in the South, and miscegenation, although banned in most states, was commonplace. William Gulliver and William McCoy were probably free blacks and although we cannot say for certain, slave studies suggest that, given their surnames, they may have been the children of white fathers and Negro mothers. Hence the use of the term, "mulatto." However, social and legal distinctions between mulattoes and "pure" Negroes were virtually nonexistent. As competition for jobs between free Negroes and whites became more widespread, free Negroes were constrained unduly and their few liberties became more and more restricted. Unfair labor practices were also instituted. Some southern states even began to consider expulsion, colonization, and enslavement as a drastic means of protecting jobs. Many blacks, like Gulliver and the McCoys, fled before any of these steps could be imposed. Frederick Douglass, himself an escaped slave, declared that Negroes should be prepared for more and more limited employment opportunities. In 1853 he wrote,

> The old avocations, by which colored men obtained a livelihood, are rapidly, unceasingly and inevitably passing into other hands; every hour sees the black man elbowed out of employment by some newly arrived emigrant, whose hunger and whose color are thought to give him a better title to the place; and so we believe it will continue to be until the last prop is levelled beneath us.
>
> As a black man, we say if we cannot stand up, let us fall down. We desire to be a man among men while we do live; and when we cannot, we wish to die. It is evident, painfully evident to every reflecting mind, that the means of living, for colored men, are becoming more and more precarious and limited. Employment and callings, formerly monopolized by us, are no longer.
>
> White men are becoming house-servants, cooks and stewards on vessels—at hotels.—They are becoming porters, stevedores, wood-sawyers, hod-carriers, brick-makers, white-washers and barbers, so that the blacks can scarcely find the means of subsistence—a few years ago, and a *white* barber would have been a curiosity—now their poles stand on every street. Formerly blacks were almost the exclusive coachmen in wealthy families: this is no longer; white men are now

> employed, and for aught we see, they fill their servile station with obsequiousness as profound as that of the blacks. The readiness and ease with which they adapt themselves to these conditions ought not to be lost sight of by the colored people.[6]

By virtue of their financial independence the Gullivers and the McCoys became part of Indianapolis's small middle-class black community. Consisting of free blacks and slaves who had escaped the South before the Civil War, the members of this class provided the foundation for generations of the black elite in the city. Like others in their community, the McCoys and the Gullivers established a lucrative business and provided a sound education for their children.

By all accounts, William and Mary Gulliver lived comfortably at 179 Kentucky Ave. Gulliver's successful business grew into a chain of barbershops. The family also owned considerable property.[7] By 1870, the value of their real estate was assessed at $13,000 (from $1000 in 1860) and their personal estate was valued at $500. The Gullivers had indeed become well established members of Indianapolis's black middle class.[8]

The Gullivers had a full household. Sometime before 1860 Mary's sister, Laura, a dressmaker, then in her early twenties, came to live with them. And by 1870, Mary's youngest sister, Alice, a teacher then twenty, was also living with them. Given that unmarried women rarely lived alone and that perhaps they had trouble making ends meet, the young women no doubt welcomed the open home of their sister and her husband.

Surrounded by her parents and aunts, Florence Irene grew up in a stable and comfortable environment. The Gullivers could afford a few luxuries, including piano lessons for their daughter, not uncommon for an advantaged Negro woman of her time. She had a good public school education and she was no doubt aided in her studies by her parents and her aunts, all of whom were literate.

Florence became a school teacher. Teaching was one of the few career options available to educated black women in the nineteenth century. Florence taught all courses, including music, at the New Eleventh [Elementary] School on the northwest corner of Huntington and Michigan Ave. in Indianapolis. She was probably the only Negro teacher in the almost all-white school. In 1874, two years before Florence left Indianapolis for Little Rock, the school system enrolled 18,074 white students and 1,051 "colored" pupils.[9] It was during this time that Florence Irene probably met James Smith whom she ultimately married in 1876.

* * *

Florence Price's father, James H. Smith, was born of free parents of mixed racial blood, in Camden, Delaware, December 4, 1843.[10] When he was four or five years old his parents moved just across the Delaware River to Penns Grove, New Jersey, where the family resided until his father's death.

There are no family records extant from Smith's childhood but the move from Delaware to New Jersey was no doubt precipitated by the desire to escape from slave society. Although the number of free blacks in Delaware, a slave state,[11] surpassed the slave population and constituted only 5 percent of the total population in that state, comprehensive codes of law ensured that free blacks were monitored at all times. Viewed as a threat to the institution of slavery, free blacks were kept in check. The Delaware Code of 1852 restricted residency in that state to those free blacks who were already living there; legal residence was denied to all others. To keep the numbers of free blacks from escalating, the law forbade any resident from returning to the state if he or she left for sixty days. Gatherings of blacks were also looked upon with suspicion and, as such, assemblies were strictly forbidden, particularly political rallies. A free Negro who was merely present at a political meeting was guilty of a misdemeanor and fined $20.00.[12]

New Jersey, though not the golden land of opportunity, provided some respite from the restrictive and oppressive Delaware laws. In the North, free blacks did have their personal freedom, since slavery was abolished shortly after the first quarter of the nineteenth century. Further, free blacks posed little threat to the white population because their numbers were relatively small. Like free blacks in the South, northern free blacks found their greatest challenge was securing a good job. With stiff competition from white immigrants, blacks were often limited to domestic work and common labor; few blacks held skilled jobs or became professionals. While many blacks in the North could read and write, few had education beyond this.

At the age of 15, young Smith went to New York City, where he was employed as a private secretary to a Mrs. J. Bastrop and where he continued his education. From New York City he went to Philadelphia to study dentistry with a Dr. Clark, a friend of Mrs. Bastrop and a well-known dentist in that city. Smith remained in Philadelphia for three years, preparing himself for college while working as an apprentice in the dental offices of Drs. Kennard and Longfellow.

It was during this time that the Civil War broke out. Sensing that the war would somehow make an improvement in the life of black Americans, Smith, like other free blacks, was prepared to bear arms. Along with four other Negro men, Smith petitioned Governor Seymour of New York for permission to organize a company of soldiers, but the governor refused to allow the company to be raised. In spite of their volunteer efforts, Smith and other black men were not allowed to join the Union army in the first months of the war. This decision was overturned as the war dragged on and the need for soldiers increased.

Smith was eventually to be drafted into the army, but he never served. Without his knowledge, Mrs. Bastrop, Smith's former employer, fearing the worst for him, hired a person to replace Smith for $1100, so that he could continue his dental apprenticeship. Mrs. Bastrop's fears were not unfounded. The Negro soldier faced special discrimination, including a longer enlistment than white soldiers, and worst of all, if he was caught by the Confederacy, he could face the often brutal treatment given to runaway slaves.

Smith continued his apprenticeship, all the while readying himself for college. When he applied to dental college in 1863, however, he was refused admission because of his race. It was not an unexpected turn of events. For Negroes, the quest for a college education, prior to the end of the Civil War, was arduous. Most institutions would not accept them, and if they did, the obstacles were almost overwhelming. Barred by most white colleges and having no Negro dental school available to him, Smith persevered in his pursuit of education; undaunted, his interest in dentistry remained unwavering. Smith returned to the offices of Drs. Longfellow, Kennard, and Flagg, and he was finally awarded a certificate in dentistry one year later.

Dr. Smith was truly a pioneer in the field of dentistry. Prior to 1880 there were less than one dozen legal black dentists in the country. Like Smith, most blacks were denied entrance to colleges, so they entered the profession through white offices, where they served as laboratory technicians and apprentices to white doctors who did not want to attend their black patients. Of Dr. Smith's few black colleagues, most were located in the South; a few black dentists were located in the major northern centers of black migration, including Chicago, Philadelphia, New York, and Boston.[13]

Just at the close of the Civil War, Dr. Smith was ready to set up practice. He settled first in Pittsburgh and, although he did fairly well, after one year, he moved to Chicago. The first black dentist in Chicago, Smith set up his dental offices in the heart of the city, at the corner of State and Madison, in the Loop.[14] His practice grew into a lucrative one. While in Chicago, Smith was active at the Quinn Chapel A.M.E. Church, holding the prestigious and important post of superintendent of the Sunday school. Founded in 1853, Quinn Chapel was one of the first organized black churches in Chicago. In the evenings, he attended a business college in the city.

At first Dr. Smith did well in Chicago but disaster was soon to strike. In the great fire of 1871 Smith lost everything. He knew he had to begin again but Chicago would have little to offer now. An aggregation of black Chicagoans, including Smith, headed south to southern Arkansas. Teaching would provide him with the needed income to purchase new instruments to begin again.

Dr. Smith, who was dedicated in his mission to teach the masses of illiterate black children in the South, founded several black schools and taught at night in two of the country schoolhouses. Building schools and educating blacks during Reconstruction was no easy task, especially in rural areas.[15] Dr. Smith's depressing but rewarding teaching experience was typical.

The one-room schoolhouses were located in the backwoods of Arkansas. Constructed with the materials at hand, the buildings were loosely made of logs, with "a thousand or more openings between the logs." The two schools where Dr. Smith taught were virtually identical except that one was improved by a stick chimney made of mud, dry grass, and sticks. Although enhanced by a fireplace, the rooms were drafty and cold and the log seats were hard.

Later Dr. Smith would describe such schoolhouses in his novel *Maudelle*. He wrote:

> The scenes presented in these night schools were such as to fill the human heart with sympathy too deep for expression in anything but tears. The school building was nothing more than an old log hut, twenty feet square, with no windows and only one door not high enough to admit a common-sized person without his stooping. The seats were simply logs, hewn on two sides; one of which furnished the seat, and the other, turned to the floor, kept the log in place.
>
> Into this primitive school-room sixty or seventy people crowded every night with intense eagerness for the trial of their long-neglected mentality. Many of the pupils had already grown gray in age, and misshapen in form, in the service of the white race.
>
> Night after night these old people wrestled with their letters, cheered on by the hope that they might learn to read God's word before death overtook them; and they were rewarded with that much learning and more, although many of them were between the ages of fifty and eighty years.[16]

In addition to these challenges, Dr. Smith and other black teachers faced constant threats to their life. White neighbors rarely tolerated Negro schools in their district. Believing that education for Negroes was unnecessary, whites were fearful that an educated Negro would be unruly and a menace to society. Both black and white teachers spent much of their time trying to convince them otherwise. Dr. Smith developed his or her own strategy for survival. Usually, if he could win over the most influential individual in the white community, then the Negro school was allowed to open. Smith's efforts were met with skepticism but he was allowed to continue.

Smith saved all of the little money he earned as a teacher. When he had conserved enough he moved to the big city of Little Rock where he would start his family. On November 15, 1876, Smith, then 33, and Florence Irene Gulliver, 22, whom he met sometime before his move to Little Rock, were married by Rev. W. S. Lankford, a Minister of the Gospel, in Florence's hometown of

Indianapolis.[17] The couple's marriage ceremony was expeditious; they got the license and they married on the same day.

Immediately after their marriage, the couple settled in Little Rock where they resided at 416 Sixth St. For two more years, Dr. Smith continued to teach. In 1878, seven years after moving to Arkansas, he was ready and able to resume his dental practice. The 1880 Little Rock City Directory, which lists both residences and businesses together, indicates that Smith worked out of his home. Given that many dentists in the 19th century were itinerant, this arrangement was not unusual. For a while, Mrs. Smith occupied her time teaching music.

One year after the Smiths married, their first child, Charles W. H., was born in October 1877. Soon after, a daughter, Florence Gertrude was born in January 1880. The family was prosperous and seemingly happy, but tragedy soon struck. Florence Gertrude died as a young child, probably before she was seven years old.[18] Seven long years after the birth of Florence Gertrude, the Smiths were blessed with another daughter, Florence Beatrice, born April 9, 1887.[19]

It is not known why the Smiths also named their second born daughter Florence.[20] To distinguish between mother and daughter, Florence Beatrice was known affectionately as Beatrice or Bea (sometimes spelled "Bee"). In a letter to Arkansas historian Mary Hudgins, Price's daughter later explained her mother's nickname:

> There were three children and mother is the youngest. You would not be aware of the fact, however, because the article stated Beatrice [referring to the 1889 Goodspeed article about her grandfather, Dr. Smith]. This is the name she was always known by. The name you [Hudgins] know is her professional name. She was always referred to affectionately as BEE. Many who claimed to know her well would say, "Florence and I have been friends for years." Then others would know this was not the case because no close friend ever called her Florence. My grandmother was known as Flo and it was easier to distinguish between the two in this manner. It was a middle name that she always went by. Florence Beatrice Smith Price.[21]

Although Florence Beatrice was a "blue baby,"[22] born with a heart condition that was to plague her on and off throughout her life, she was a special child and in her lifetime she was to make her family and her race proud.

2 Little Rock

"The Negro Paradise"

In the late nineteenth century, Little Rock was a bustling, but lovely, town. Located on the Arkansas River, it had a medium-sized population of about 38,000, 70 percent white and 30 percent black. Sometimes known as the "City of Roses," Little Rock was surrounded by flowers including white dogwood and magnolia blossoms, and everywhere one could detect a hint in the air of the fresh scent of burning pine wood. By 1900, the city could boast of thirteen miles of paved streets, a seven-story skyscraper, a modest public library (for whites only), seventy-five churches, eight cemeteries, several theaters, and a thriving business section.[1] Among the businesses were 29 blacksmith shops, 38 dry-goods firms, 27 hotels, 2 ice houses, 43 restaurants, 170 grocers, and the Egyptian Anti-Dyspeptic Meal Co., a health food store—surely one of the nation's first.[2]

Just beyond the confines of the city, the landscape was completely rural. Farms, where cotton and sugar cane were grown, were numerous. Crucial to the cotton industry, the country's fourth largest inland market, were six new railroad lines which fed into the city. Chickens and other livestock, vegetable gardens, and fruit trees were found in the yards of most homes.[3] Young boys could earn a living by collecting all the cows, taking them out to pasture, and returning them to their owners at sundown. On the outskirts of Little Rock, seven miles from the city, in a place named "Sweet Home" by black Methodists, one could still find horse-driven sugar cane mills.

Although Little Rock had its police force, it was still close enough to frontier days to employ typically old-fashioned methods of deterring would-be criminals. Once at the local funeral parlor, two dead bandits were put on display in the window to reveal vividly their gunshot wounds. Composer William Grant Still, who moved there from his native Woodville, Mississippi, as a child, remembered,

"One was a big white bandit who had tried to rob a little white railway clerk of his diamond. In the struggle, the mail clerk's .45 caliber gun went off when it was thrust up against the robber's chest. The big hole it made was left visible by the embalmers so that we could see it plainly when the body was displayed in the funeral parlor's window. The other was a Negro bandit, whose body was also intended for display."[4] It was not a sight one would easily forget.

Because of its importance as a market and shipping point for agricultural products, Little Rock rapidly developed an efficient transportation system. Although many roads were still dirt, the city could boast of thirteen miles of paved streets. Riding stables offered horses for rent, but by 1891 the newest mode of transportation was the streetcar (electric trolley).

Little Rock had its seamy side, too. For only a medium-sized town, the city had 62 saloons, its own brewery, and enough gambling dives to satisfy anyone interested. In 1891, a reporter described one "resort" located just across the Arkansas River in North Little Rock this way:

> It consists of a store building composed of a bar and lunch counter in the front room, a billiard hall and a dance hall in the rear, in which at one end is a raised platform or stage, where the most obscene and revolting orgies are enacted. In the same lot are several cabins occupied by the lowest type of women who have given up their lives to prostitution. Here white and black mingle together, and it is here that toughs and criminals of all classes make their rendezvous.[5]

Negroes comprised fully one-third of Little Rock's population. In the little more than thirty years since the Civil War, Negroes had worked hard to buy land, earn a living, and educate their children. Most of the city's blacks lived in poverty in 1896; they had limited education and few advanced skills.[6] While Little Rock had its sections of fine homes, it had its rustic cabins as well. Many of the poor lived in "Lick Skillet" or "Hard Scrabble," housing settlements erected after the Civil War that were modeled after plantation quarters. These homes were simply built; the very small living accommodations were placed in long rows, with passageways between the rows.[7] In the years after emancipation, many small entrepreneurial enterprises were developed; thus, a stratum of the black middle class was formed. Little Rock also had a small, but significant, upper class, to which the Smith family belonged. It was comprised of the "old" families, those who were born in slavery in Little Rock, and the "new" families, those skilled and often well-educated blacks who moved to Little Rock just prior to and during Reconstruction. These two groups, attaining their wealth in a variety of ways, combined to form the nucleus of black Little Rock's political, economic, and sophisticated social base.

Little Rock developed a self-sufficient Negro community that provided for every aspect of its needs. Domestics, skilled artisans, and the Negro professionals, while not in the same social class, all contributed to the city's economic prosperity. An 1898 survey shows blacks owned 8 wood and coal yards, 10 blacksmith shops, a cigar and tobacco stand, 2 hotels, 9 restaurants, 2 jewelry stores, 3 tailor shops, a drugstore, and a mortuary. Negroes established their own institutions, including a home for the elderly and a cemetery. In 1903, Mifflin W. Gibbs opened the Capital City Savings Bank. In two years the bank's assets grew from $10,000 to $100,000.[8] The survey also noted that there were 15 cobblers, 15 dressmakers, 2 upholsterers, and 2 confectioners; among the professionals were 55 teachers and educators, 38 ministers, 6 lawyers, 5 physicians, and 1 dentist—Dr. Smith.[9]

Black newspapers promoted and supported the activities and goals of the community. By 1900, the state had 30 black newspapers, although only a handful existed at any one time. In Little Rock, these included the *Arkansas Dispatch*, *Sun*, *Baptist Vanguard*, and *National Democrat*. The press encouraged self-help activities, advocated cultural pride, and published many stories on black leaders who could provide role models and show what could be accomplished by the race.[10]

Forming the backbone of the Negro community were the city's 24 Negro churches. There were three African Methodist Episcopal Zion (AME Zion), five African Methodist Episcopal (AME), two Colored Methodist Episcopal (CME), one Episcopal, one Congregational, one Presbyterian, ten Baptist, and the Church of God, a holiness church.

The church the Smiths attended was no less an indicator of their upper-class status within the black community. Both the Smith and the Still-Shepperdson families were active in Allison Presbyterian church, a relatively small congregation that Dr. Smith had helped to found. They, and other upper-class blacks, were attracted to the sophisticated worship experience, which included non-emotionally delivered sermons, and these well-educated members preferred music more closely associated to the European tradition. Florence Beatrice remained a Presbyterian all of her life, although she actively participated in the musical activities of other denominations. She developed and nurtured a love of church music throughout her career, becoming a prolific composer of vocal, choral, and instrumental music for church use.

By the late 1880s, black Arkansans had produced a socially, politically, and economically successful society, and they enjoyed an abundance of opportunities unparalleled in the South. For a time after Reconstruction, blacks were actively involved in the state legislature and shared other political offices with whites. This "power sharing" arrangement was in effect for nearly two decades.[11]

Until 1894, blacks held numerous county offices and seats in the state legislature.[12] During the Reconstruction years, Dr. Smith and many other prominent Negroes in Little Rock were active in politics at the state and local level. Blacks regularly held legislative posts under the Republican Party. Mifflin W. Gibbs, elected judge in 1873, was appointed United States consul to Madagascar in 1877. Calvin Sanders, a farmer and the owner of a block of ten houses and a farm of 160 acres, was a city alderman for two years. Dr. Smith was an elector of the state for the election of President James A. Garfield in 1880. In 1884, he was appointed by the state as one of the commissioners at the World's Fair Exposition in New Orleans.

On the local level, Dr. Smith was one of the most active politically within the Negro community, and he used his social position and wealth to continuously advance the causes of the community. The Colored State Fair, founded by Dr. Smith and held annually in Pine Bluff beginning in 1881, illustrates this point. Held on land owned by Wiley Jones, the fair attracted hundreds of people, both black and white. Farmers exhibited their goods, and here was an opportunity for black poets, musicians, and artisans to perform and display their crafts. Prizes were offered to blacks who competed in many categories from agriculture to the arts.[13] The fair was supported by stockholders, all prominent Little Rock Negroes, who were said to hold more than a half-million dollars in property.

By the 1880s, the success of the middle class was such that Arkansas became known as "the Negro Paradise."[14] It had become a haven for educated blacks, many of whom were the first generation born out of slavery, and skilled workers who were eager to move to the state for its political and economic opportunities. Those Arkansas-born blacks who left the state for their education returned to teach or develop their businesses.

Little Rock was growing by leaps and bounds and, for a time, it opened its arms to upwardly mobile blacks. The Negro middle class of Little Rock constituted a small but significant population. They owned considerable property in the city and they were very active in the social and political affairs of the community.[15] Mr. Asa L. Richmond became one of the wealthiest "colored gentlemen" of Little Rock after buying his freedom. A carpenter by trade, he owned 33 houses, netting him an income of $200 a month in addition to his business. Living more modestly was Solomon Winfrey. Born a slave in 1833 in Tennessee, Winfrey became one of the city's most respected Negro residents. Winfrey was brought to Little Rock in 1850 by the daughter of his master. After the war he earned a living as a brickmason and plasterer and later became one of the most successful contractors in the city. An active member of the First Congregational Church and in the Republican party, he owned four houses, which afforded him and his family a comfortable standard of living. Winfrey's daughter married John E. Bush, one of the most esteemed members of the black community. Bush, born a slave in Tennessee, was brought to Little Rock by his mother during the war. As founder of the Mosaic Templars, an important black fraternal organization known nationally, he earned a considerable fortune. Throughout the Reconstruction period, Bush was active in the Republican party.

There were several other prominent members of Little Rock's black community. Isaac Gillam Sr., also born a slave in Tennessee, settled in Little Rock and earned his living as a blacksmith, property owner, and dealer in horses. In the early 1870s, Gillam was elected city councilman and in 1879 he was elected state representative on the Greenback party ticket. His children, all well-educated, including a son who attended Yale University, were teachers in Little Rock's public and private schools and colleges.[16] Jefferson Gatherford and Marietta Kidd Ish also settled in Little Rock in the early 1870s. Both teachers, they were also very active socially. Their son, Jefferson Ish Jr., also graduated from Yale and returned to Arkansas to teach. He became involved later with the insurance division of the Mosaic Templars. Another son, William Stanley Ish, a graduate of the Harvard Medical School, practiced medicine in Little Rock for many years.[17]

Other affluent blacks included Albert Desha, justice of the peace and a landowner, and George E. Jones, a grocer, realtor, and undertaker. Jones built a three-story brick office building and owned sixty rental houses in Little Rock. Active in the Knights of Pythias and in the Allison Presbyterian Church, he was worth $50,000 at the time of his death in 1902.

One of Little Rock's most prominent citizens was Mifflin W. Gibbs, a native of Philadelphia. A free black, Gibbs made his fortune as a merchant during the California gold rush. He settled in Little Rock in 1870 and shortly after, in 1873, was elected judge, becoming the first black municipal judge in the United States. Thereafter, Gibbs was active in the Republican Party and received several federal appointments. Later, Gibbs became a U.S. Ambassador. Judge Gibbs's daughter, Harriet Gibbs Marshall, was the first black woman to graduate from the Oberlin Conservatory (1889). After graduation, Harriet Gibbs went to Washington, D.C., where she established and directed the Washington Conservatory of Music.

During the 1870s and early 1880s, Little Rock was considered to be a relatively enlightened community where the black middle class, at least to a limited extent, interacted with the white community. Many of these blacks belonged to professional associations with whites and conducted business with them. The city's relative racial tolerance meant that black professionals could enjoy a sizable white clientele, thereby significantly increasing their profit potential. In 1899, Charles Stewart, a Chicago Negro reporter, observed that urbanization in the South helped to facilitate changing attitudes of whites toward blacks. He noted,

> While in Little Rock I have visited the offices . . . of successful Negro lawyers, and have seen white men go in and consult with them. Negro doctors have white patients. Negro merchants have white customers and the like. Could these evi-

dences be considered taking away the manhood of a race? When I say that the negro has a better time in the south than in the north I am accused of catering to southern sentiment and prejudice, but the man who deals in facts and who visits this country must agree with me.[18]

These narrowly proscribed associations gave confidence to Little Rock's black youth, who grew up believing in racial equality. William Grant Still explained, "My association with people of both racial groups gave me the ability to conduct myself as a person among people instead of as an inferior among superiors."[19] This is not to say that blacks had no worries. To the contrary, beatings of blacks by white people, even by policemen, were not uncommon.

Dr. James Smith was one of the most esteemed members of Little Rock. He had professional associations with whites and he conducted business with them. His refined manners, cultural sophistication, and appealing (from a white person's point of view) outward appearance, all contributed to attracting and keeping his white patients; at least until the "Jim Crow" laws were instituted from the 1890s. In fact, Dr. Smith was Little Rock's leading dentist for both black and white patients for over twenty years and could even number one of the state's governors among his patients. Of the eleven dentists in town listed in the 1897–1898 city directory, Smith was the only black, and his business thrived. Already by 1889, he was so successful that his biography could be included among the eighteen "Prominent Colored Citizens of Central Arkansas" in the *Biographical and Historical Memoirs of Central Arkansas* (1889).

Although a humble man, Dr. Smith willingly served as a role model for the black community. Dr. D. B. Gaines, a Negro physician, commented on Smith's mannerisms and professionalism and used him as an example of what the "race" could accomplish. He wrote, "He is thoroughly prepared and courteous. He destroys the old and foolish saying that if a man is a Negro he is not respected by the wealthier class of citizens. In him is clearly demonstrated that if you have what the wealthy or any other class of citizens want and do what they want done you will be respected by them and have their patronage. Dr. Smith is a true example of manhood and a most gratifying exponent of racial possibilities."[20]

Dr. Smith had a reputation for being fair. Showing no favoritism toward his wealthier patients or to his white patients, Smith set standards by which everyone had to abide. First and foremost all had to wait their turn in his office. One patient reported that during her visit one day, she witnessed the governor waiting patiently for his appointment while Dr. Smith attended a "scrub woman!" Whether this story is fact or fiction, Dr. Smith was certainly a man of the people.

In 1881, three years after they married, the Smiths moved with their two children, Charles and Florence Gertrude, from Sixth St. to a larger home at 707

Broadway. The Smith's two-story residence was located in an interracial neighborhood. Little Rock was primarily segregated but rigid residential patterns were not yet established. The Smith family lived comfortably in their elegant, but quietly and modestly furnished home, adorned with a few of Dr. Smith's paintings and other works of art. One of his paintings, a southern cotton field scene, no doubt inspired by Little Rock's sprawling cotton fields, won a prize and was exhibited in 1893 at the Columbian Exposition in Chicago.[21]

The Smiths were involved in many community affairs and they socialized with black families who had similar interests. Mr. Charles Shepperson, a postal clerk; his wife, Carrie (Still) Shepperson, a teacher; and her son, William Grant Still were good friends of the family. Of the Smiths, Still said, "they belonged to our social set—which consisted of people who were interested in intellectual matters."[22]

Stimulating activities were organized by the middle class to enrich the social, political, and intellectual life of the black community. They danced and played cards but they also sponsored a number of cultural events. A variety of prominent Negro artists, who toured throughout the South performing and lecturing in black churches and community centers, were invited regularly to Little Rock. Richard B. Harrison—who later became famous as "De Lawd" in "The Green Pastures," a Broadway drama first produced in the 1930s—read from Shakespeare plays. Many years later, Harrison would be present at the first performance of Florence Price's E Minor Symphony. Carrie Still Shepperson was particularly active in promoting the country's leading Negro artists, including Clarence Cameron White, the noted composer and violinist, and E. Azalia Hackley, a singer and herself an important promoter of Negro artists. Carrie Shepperson also organized the Lotus Club, a literary group first organized for women that met regularly to discuss current events and debate political issues.[23] The community also sponsored a lecture series, and there was an Institute of Science that held regularly scheduled debates on such topics as "Is conscience a correct moral guide?"[24] Also, the Bay View Reading Club, a branch of the national organization, had a membership of twelve teachers, each of whom brought one book each month to be read by the whole group. Dr. Smith also led a literary club for some of the prominent men in the community.

Given that suitable black hotels in Little Rock were few, prominent blacks and those of middle-class status often stayed with the Smiths or the Sheppersons while they were doing business or visiting the city. Through Dr. Smith's professional reputation and social activism, it was not unusual for Florence Beatrice to find some of the nation's leading black musicians, civil rights leaders, and other professionals staying at the Smith home. In 1889, when she was two years old, the noted black abolitionist Frederick Douglass stayed at the Smith home while he was in town to give a public lecture on "self-made men" at the Capital Theater on Markham St.

The hall was crowded with blacks and whites eager to hear the distinguished orator; the gallery was packed exclusively with Negroes and the floor was filled with whites. On the podium with Mr. Douglass were representatives of both races. To the right of the speaker were the black dignitaries, Judge Mifflin W. Gibbs, Councilman Green W. Thompson, Prof. J. Talbot Bailey, and Dr. Smith; and to Douglass's left were prominent whites including Pulaski County Judge W. F. Hill and former Little Rock mayor John Gould Fletcher.

The day following the lecture Douglass granted an interview with a white reporter from the *Arkansas Gazette* at the Smith home. The reporter was seemingly more awestruck by the Smith home than by the distinguished guest. He began his report with a description of Smith as "a colored man, but with so complete a polish in manners, dress, language, and appearance that he may be truly called a negro in name only." In describing the Smith home, the reporter was "most agreeably impressed with the air of refinement and taste exhibited in every feature of his home. The furniture was elegant in kind and very tastefully arranged, and on the center table in the sitting room was noticed among other books, 'Poetry of Flowers,' 'Gems of Song.' and of a professional nature 'Dental Cosmos.'" Although the reporter probably did not intend to be so tactless, it is evident that personal wealth and cultural sophistication were equated with white social values.

During the interview, the reporter asked Douglass about his impressions of Arkansas. In his reply, Douglass commented that he had been treated well, with one exception. That is, for the first time ever, Douglass reported, he was refused admission to a public dining room. Two days later an outraged white person from Pine Bluff fired back at Mr. Douglass for the public airing of his mistreatment in Little Rock and for Douglass's apparent memory lapse. In an *Arkansas Gazette* article, "Correcting Fred Douglass: Arkansas not the first to Refuse Him Admission to a Public Dining Room," the Arkansan wrote,

> It is strange indeed that Mr. Douglass does not remember one memorable incident in his experience to which I was myself an eye-witness. It was, I think, in 1852 that a very large number of delegates to the free soil national convention at Pittsburg, Pa., sat down at the table of the railroad station at Alliance, in the good old republican State of Ohio, where Mr. Douglass was politely requested by the proprietor to take his dinner at a separate table provided for colored persons, and on his refusal to do so was summarily ejected from the room.... Poor old Arkansas has quite enough to bear up under, without being thus erroneously distinguished as the only country [*sic*] on earth that has treated Mr. Douglass discourteously.[25]

At the conclusion of Douglass's interview he was pressed further to discuss his impressions about race relations in Arkansas. Douglass commented:

> It gives me great pleasure to find that the race, as a whole, enjoys a large degree of contentment at the relations existing between it and your own race. I find that the colored man is a citizen in feelings as well as in law, and he talks [of] Little Rock and Arkansas with a great degree of enthusiasm, and expresses a profound faith in the future greatness of your city and state. It is a condition of affairs that I trust may continue and strengthen.[26]

But this was not to be.

* * *

As a young child, Florence Beatrice witnessed a marked change in the political climate in Little Rock. The process of disfranchisement began in earnest in the early 1890s, as blacks were systematically barred from the vote through illiteracy laws and poll taxes.[27] Whites were aggressive in their methods of removing Negroes from holding office, and they began the process of instituting Jim Crow segregation laws that would ultimately threaten to disfranchise blacks forever. The first resolution by the House of Representatives, introduced in 1891, was the Tillman Separate Coach Bill, which would require separate seating on trains for black and white passengers. The resolution, as introduced by Senator J. N. Tillman, proposed strict guidelines for its implementation. It stated that all persons "in whom there is a visible and distinct admixture of African blood" were to be judged Negro. Railroad officers would be charged $25 for not obeying; passengers who violated the law could be fined $10–$200. The rationale for the bill argued that whites found Negroes objectionable, even unclean. The editor of the *Fort Smith Times* wrote:

> The people of Arkansas have borne with this Negro nuisance on railroads a long time, hoping that the Negroes would learn how to be decent, and while a great many of them do behave themselves, others are intolerable. In this portion of the state the people have no conception of the degree of offensiveness borne by respectable people at the hands of drunken, insolent blacks in the black district of the State. A Saturday night train out from Little Rock to Pine Bluff is hardly safe, to say nothing of the fact that not one in eighty uses Pear's soap or any other kind.[28]

Outraged by the egregious insult explicit in the Tillman Bill, Dr. Smith and other blacks were equally aggressive in their opposition. At a meeting of over 600 blacks at the First Baptist Church on January 19, 1891, a special committee of Little Rock's race leaders including Dr. Smith; John Bush, cofounder of the Mosaic Templars; George Perkins, attorney and former city councilman; W. H. Scott, landowner and also former city councilman; and Rev. Y. B. Sims, pastor of the black First Congregational Church, drafted resolutions opposing the Tillman Separate Coach Act. These resolutions denounced the separate coach proposal as caste legislation, warning that under no circumstances should attempts be made to determine a person's race by appearances only and that such an action would invite rudeness and could lead to embarrassing errors. The committee predicted that some white people, including railroad conductors, might even abuse their privileges. The committee made their own suggestion:

> An act to promote the comfort of passengers on railway trains can be better obtained, with honor to the State and justice to all concerned, by compelling the railway companies to provide first-class and second-class accommodations, with charges accordingly, by which means the respectable travelling public would be relieved of contact with objectionable persons of whatever race or class.[29]

The committee's recommendation went unrecognized as blacks continued their fight to the state capitol. On January 27, Dr. Smith, Rev. Asberry Whitman, Rev. H. T. Johnson, and Joseph A. Booker drafted speeches and addressed the House of Representatives in a protest meeting with about 400 people in attendance.

Professor Booker was the first speaker. Speaking to deaf ears, he tried to refute the argument by whites that educated and prosperous Negroes were "offensive," and he pleaded with the legislature not to adopt the impending bill. Dr. Smith was the next speaker, and his passionate speech moved the entire audience. In addressing the claim by whites that certain Negroes were "immoral," Dr. Smith blamed whites at corner grocery stores for selling blacks "mean whisky full of dynamite." He argued also that the deportment of many educated blacks entitled them to first-class accommodations, particularly since the Negroes in Arkansas owned 8 million dollars in taxable wealth and were entitled to respect as taxpayers. Smith continued, "Ignorance is contagious. To force the better Negroes into contact with the more degraded would be to force the race backward." All four speakers mentioned that they had no doubt that the accommodations for black and white passengers would never be equal and they appealed for first- and second-class services for all races.[30]

The underlying motivation behind the Tillman Bill was not simply a sudden aversion to physical contact with blacks. Rather, whites rigidly rejected the social and political strides of middle-class blacks. They were so fearful of blacks that their intent was to enforce implicitly strict codes of sexual conduct; whites were vehemently opposed to miscegenation and intermarriage.[31] Blacks had to be stopped. In spite of the four impassioned speeches, the voice of the Negro went unheard and the legislation passed overwhelmingly.

The legislative process to disfranchise Negroes had now gained momentum. The 1891 election law stipulated that county judges and clerks would oversee the balloting at polls. Since these political appointments had been made by a racist governor, it was impossible for blacks to imagine an impartial election. Further, the law stated that only precinct judges could mark ballots for those who were illiterate. While only 13.4 percent of Arkansas' white males needed assistance at the polls, over half of the state's black males, 55.8 percent, were illiterate in 1890, insuring that the balloting could be skewed. Election Day, September 1892, was disastrous for Arkansas' black population. With no hope of fair election results, most blacks did not even bother to vote. By 1894, when Florence Beatrice was but seven years old, there was no black representation in either house of the Arkansas legislature, and only a few minor posts for blacks in local government remained.

With their political and social status changed forever, the black middle class was plunged into a state of personal confusion. Heretofore, they moved about the city comfortably, coming into occasional contact with white people, but not feeling threatened by them. With the institution of rigid segregation laws, this was all changed. Never abandoning hope, Dr. Smith embraced his heritage and continued to work for the advancement of the race. Specifically, he maintained his involvement in service-oriented activities, primarily advocating the importance of education for black children and helping to improve the public school system.

While Dr. Smith was becoming more and more politically active and further steeped in his racial heritage, Mrs. Smith fought the impending paradox in her life. She isolated herself from most blacks not of her social standing, preferring to socialize with members of her own class. Mrs. Smith was part of the black elite whose comfortable lifestyle allowed her a prominent place in Little Rock's black community. She believed that her financial status—that is, income received from her husband's dental practice; a considerable inheritance she received from her mother, Mary Gulliver, who died in Indianapolis on May 10, 1889;[32] and her own real estate transactions—would enable her to buy a respectable bourgeois black life. On the other hand, with the Jim Crow laws firmly in place, she was relegated to second-class citizenship, a position that was fast becoming a way of life for all Little Rock Negroes.

Fair-skinned enough to be mistaken for white, Mrs. Smith was not yet ready to "pass," but she resented the mandates and restrictions imposed upon her as a woman of color. She was among those mixed-blood Negroes that considered themselves racially superior to "pure" blood Negroes. Although she married within her social class, Mrs. Smith took advantage of her caste privilege as a light-skinned, middle-class Negro to achieve social status, but it could not totally obliterate the reality of her mixed racial heritage.

By the turn of the century Little Rock's attitude toward blacks had changed. Cultural sophistication was equated with white people, and to be Negro implied a plebeian perspective and lack of refinement—all in a world where cultural mores, political access, and economic wealth were controlled by white America. Understanding this dichotomy, Mrs. Smith wanted desperately to emulate whites, to an extent that sometimes alienated her friends and family. This attitude wreaked havoc on young Florence Beatrice.

Once, when Beatrice was a young girl, she was invited to participate in a wedding. Some years later, Beatrice's daughter explained, "My mother was a bridesmaid and her mother forced her to wear such an elaborate dress that she outshone the bride. This hurt my mother very much, but everyone understood and didn't blame her. The dress was embroidered very lavishly in seed pearls and it was impossible for the bride to be more expensively dressed."[33] How embarrassing for her! Through no fault of her own, Florence Beatrice outdressed the bride. As a matter of pretense and a misplaced display of wealth, her mother showed a remarkable lack of good judgment. Although Beatrice survived the event with the understanding and sympathetic support of those attending the wedding, she would never forget the incident. Conflicting attitudes toward class would come to play a significant role in her life.

For years, the attitudes of Mrs. Smith created tension between herself and her daughter. On the one hand, Mrs. Smith appears not to have shared her husband's commitment to moral and social advancement of the race; instead, she sent her daughter conflicting messages about what it meant to be a privileged Negro of prominent social standing. On the other hand, Mrs. Smith only wanted the best for Florence Beatrice. She encouraged her daughter's high aptitude for music, both in performance and her budding interest in composing. She also shielded her daughter, albeit in insufferable ways, from the escalating racial atrocities that threatened all people of color, men and women, throughout the South. In spite of the posturing, Mrs. Smith was probably still a role model for her daughter. She was an achiever—intelligent, determined, and goal-oriented, she got things done. Her mother's fortitude is, in part, the substance of which Florence Beatrice was made.

3 The Pursuit of Education

Elementary and High School

Through the 1890s, Dr. Smith's dental practice continued to grow and prosper. By 1895, he moved his office from his home and opened his own office at 701 Main St., the office he was to have until he retired fifteen years later.

Although Dr. Smith's work and political activities kept him busy, he still found time for his many hobbies, including painting, writing, and inventing. On June 25, 1889, the *Arkansas Gazette* noted the invention of Dr. Smith's peach seeder. This contrivance which could pit seeds at the rate of six bushels per hour was thought to be useful in Little Rock's canning industry. Dr. Smith was offered the handsome sum of $10,000 for his invention, manufactured by the Clark Novelty Company of Rochester, New York, which he promptly refused. A modest man, Dr. Smith was shy in exploiting his achievements publicly.[1] Always experimenting with gadgets, Dr. Smith also received a patent for a weatherboarding gauge by which carpenters could more easily weatherboard houses.

By 1899, Dr. and Mrs. Smith had been married twenty-three years. Charles, Beatrice's brother, was twenty-one and still living at home and Beatrice was twelve. Living with them was Virginia Seeta, a seventeen-year-old woman from Alabama who was probably attending one of Little Rock's black colleges. With her children now grown, Mrs. Smith decided she would return to work full time. She secured a job as secretary to the black-owned International Loan and Trust Co., located in the same building as her husband's dental office. And the next year, presumably with the money that she inherited from her mother, she became the proud owner of a restaurant, the Flora Cafe, located just down the street at 712 Main St.

Two-income families were not uncommon in black households during the 19th and early 20th centuries. Many women worked as teachers, and more commonly as domestics, helping their husbands to support the family. What is unusual here is the nature of Mrs. Smith's endeavors. As an entrepreneur she not only owned her own business but from as early as August 1888 until 1911 (one year after her husband died), Mrs. Smith was involved in real estate, buying and selling property under her own name. Her transactions enabled her to claim a measure of financial independence uncommon among women of her time.

Although fairly astute as a businesswoman, Mrs. Smith, headstrong and self-assured, sometimes erred in judgment. Shortly after the Smiths married, she acquired 500 acres of land. Against all advice, including her husband's, she later sold what turned out to be very valuable property. It became a busy section of town and worth a small fortune.[2]

The Smiths' joint incomes allowed them the opportunity in 1899 to move into a very fashionable neighborhood, where they purchased a large Victorian home at 2100 Broadway on an elegant tree-lined street. The house, carpeted throughout, had at least three bedrooms with walnut and oak furniture, a kitchen, a dining room with a china closet, a sewing room with two sewing machines (a Singer and a Wheeler and Wilson). The parlor was elegantly furnished with walnut furniture, marble tables, and an Ivers and Pond piano that Mrs. Smith, who was a well-trained pianist, used to entertain her family and friends, playing hymns and her favorite parlor music. As in their former home, the room was adorned with art, including some of Dr. Smith's paintings.[3] The family's income afforded them luxuries not commonly found in black homes at the turn of the century, including an extensive library. The room was comfortably furnished with a three-piece leather set, which made reading there most enjoyable. There was no public library for Negroes in Little Rock, so Beatrice, who had a passion for reading, spent much of her time in her father's favorite room. There she could read the works of Shakespeare and other great literary works that her father avidly collected. Beatrice also loved to read her father's medical books and journals. She even contemplated a career in medicine at one time, but the obstacles in pursuing a formal medical career were difficult for women and nearly insurmountable for black women. While still a young girl, Florence Beatrice could barely imagine a black female physician.[4]

Although Beatrice abandoned any hope of a medical career, she maintained an interest in medicine all her life. In 1948, she could share vicariously in the achievement of Edith Irby Jones of Hot Springs when she became the first black woman to be admitted to a southern all-white medical program at the University of Arkansas. Price wrote to Dr. H. Clay Chenault, supervisor of medical education and hospitals, commending the university for its bold actions. Chenault's comments quoted in the *Chicago Tribune* that most struck her was that Jones "will be a part of her class just like any other member."[5] On a sweltering Chicago summer's day, August 26, 1948, she copied those precious words into her diary. But in the 1890s this could have been only a dream.

It is ironic that Beatrice cast aside her interest in the medical field but ultimately had a formidable career as a composer. The field of serious musical composition was almost wholly dominated by men at the turn of the century. At the time she completed high school in 1902 only three American women composers had succeeded in having their large-scale classical works performed by major orchestras—Margaret Ruthven Lang, Helen Hopekirk, and Amy Cheney Beach—and it is very unlikely that Florence Beatrice had heard any of their orchestral music. Beatrice could not have known, but she would break racial and gender barriers for African American women composers.

It was through her mother that Florence Beatrice was exposed to music as a child and from whom she took her first piano lessons. Proud of her daughter and wanting to encourage her interest in music, Mrs. Smith presented Beatrice in a recital when she was just four years old. The occasion was a visit to the Smith home by the distinguished black concert pianist John Boone and his wife. Boone, known as Blind Boone, was enthusiastic about the young child's first public performance. In turn, Boone played for her and her parents. Perhaps he played some Beethoven, or Liszt, or dazzled the Smiths with the typical 19th-century virtuoso renditions of opera transcriptions and cyclone imitations for which he was so well known throughout the United States and Europe. Florence Beatrice and Blind Boone maintained a friendship for many years, and Boone performed for her again when she joined the faculty of Clark University in Atlanta in 1910.[6]

Although Beatrice showed an unmistakable gift for piano playing, she showed an equal interest in composing. She worked diligently at her craft, although it is not known if she studied composition formally. By the time she was eleven, Beatrice sold her first composition to a publisher.[7] Investigation has not revealed the piece; perhaps it was for a local publisher whose catalog no longer exists.

* * *

Beatrice attended Union School, a combined elementary and high school for black children.[8] William Grant Still, eight years her junior, also attended Union School. Though they were educated in a segregated school that did not have the same facilities as the white elementary schools, Price and Still were fortunate to have been taught by Mrs. Charlotte Andrews Stephens, one of the most remarkable teachers in Little Rock's history. In spite of the fact that Mrs. Stephens's salary was meager and her earnings were substantially lower than those of white teachers, she dedicated herself for seventy years to teaching Little Rock's black children.

Charlotte Stephens, Dr. Smith, and other community leaders were actively involved in efforts to support the education of black children—to establish schools and to improve the conditions under which black children were educated. They felt strongly that education was the means by which Negroes would become independent and responsible citizens. James D. Anderson, in *The Education of Blacks in the South, 1860–1935*, explained that "ex-slave communities pursued their education objectives by developing various strata, but the one they stressed the most was leadership training. They believed that the masses could not achieve political and economic independence or self-determination without first becoming organized, and organization was impossible without well-trained intellectuals—teachers, ministers, politicians, managers, administrators, and businessmen."[9]

There was much work to be done if black children were to be prepared to enter the workforce. At the time Price attended elementary school, the system of education for blacks in the South was still dismal. In 1900, almost half the Negro population in Arkansas was still illiterate.[10] That year 146,880 black students were registered for school, but only 90,437 attended. In contrast, 370,553 white students were enrolled and 249,105, more than two-thirds, attended.[11] The school year was significantly shorter for black students. On the average they went to school twenty days fewer than white students.[12]

The state appropriated far less money for each black child. On average, $2.13 was spent for each black child in 1900; more than twice that amount, $5.14, was allocated for each white child. The building values were equally reflective of the situation. In 1900, the value of black schools was $335,527, but the white schools were valued at nine times that amount, or $3,029,763. Black teachers, who dedicated their lives to teaching, were compensated at levels far below their white colleagues. For example, in 1916, white teachers in Arkansas were still paid almost three times as much as black teachers: the per-student state appropriation for paying white teachers was $12.95 while black teachers earned only $4.59 per pupil.

Little Rock's educational system was slightly better for black children than in many cities in the South. An informal system of education for blacks began in Little Rock when Rev. William Wallace Andrews, Charlotte Stephens's father, opened a private school in 1863.[13] Born a slave to Mary and Chester Ashley, a lawyer, Andrews was brought to Little Rock in 1821 at the age of four with his mother, who was Mrs. Ashley's maid. He described Little Rock then as a "pathless wildness" on the Arkansas River "about which the rest of the country was entirely ignorant." Even though it was essentially forbidden, he was taught to read and write by Mrs. Ashley, who "felt herself to be above both law and custom." He was also permitted access to the Ashley's vast library which was "supplied with reading matter of all sorts."

Andrews, who lived with cultured people, was provided with the tools of literacy. Surrounded by books, he proceeded to educate himself and then share his acquired knowledge with the other slaves in the Ashley manor. After Andrews married Caroline Williams, a slave on a nearby plantation, in 1848, he continued to provide education for other Negroes, including his wife who could neither read or write, "even at risk of punishment of himself and his pupils if the laws had been enforced against them." He explained to the group, "It will be safer if we kneel down. Nobody is going to interrupt a group of people who are praying." And with the slaves on their knees, facing their chairs, he began their lessons. The Ashleys furnished Andrews and his wife with a home where he provided religious instruction and training in reading and writing.

Finally in 1854, the year their daughter Charlotte was born, the Ashleys gave the black Methodists land on which to build a church. In 1863, when Little Rock was captured by Union troops, blacks seized the opportunity to incorporate a school within the church house. Wallace Andrews and an assistant organized the school, the first school for black children in Arkansas. After a few months, this modest school was relinquished to the Congregationalists of the American Missionary Society who were sent from the North to take over the school Andrews had started. They brought with them graded textbooks and slates upon which each child could write.

After the Civil War, blacks in Little Rock were quick to recognize the need for education. Education was one of the determining factors in establishing one's status in the black community and the best means to economic advancement. The federal government spent millions of dollars on education for Negroes, but blacks, whose passion for learning could no longer be denied, were impatient. With this recognition, they began to build their own schools and pay for their own teachers. An educational association was formed to raise money, pay teacher's salaries, and manage the private, segregated schools.

These self-help efforts and acts of determination were the foundation for building a public school system to educate Little Rock's black children. Through the combined efforts of the private support from Negro citizens, the Freedmen's Bureau, the government agency established to support education for Negroes, and the Society of Friends, Union School, the first public school for Negroes in Little Rock, was established in October 1867. The two-story school, which had two large rooms on each floor, was located in the Quakers' Negro school building on Sixth and State streets and was staffed at first with white teachers. In the spring of 1869, Charlotte Andrews, just fifteen, was hired to fill out the term of one of the white teachers. Thus she became the first Negro teacher in the Little Rock public school system. She was hired permanently the next year, along with three other Negro teachers.

Andrews's resolve to become a teacher resulted from the influence of her missionary teachers. Her love for teaching and passion for learning prompted her to take a leave after her first year of teaching. She had saved enough money for one year of college and went to attend Oberlin College, one of the few schools at the time to accept Negro students.[14] Charlotte Andrews became the first black woman from the state of Arkansas to go to college. She was partially enrolled in the Literary Course (studying Latin, Geometry, Ancient History, Evidence of Christianity, Biblical Antiquities, Elocution, and Rhetoric) and at the Conservatory of Music, though for just over two years. Although she returned to Little Rock periodically to earn money teaching at Union School, Oberlin was really beyond her means financially. Finally, in 1873, she abandoned any hopes of a college degree and returned to Little Rock permanently to teach in the city's black public schools. She married John Herbert Stephens, a carpenter, in 1877, and together they had six children (two of whom died in infancy).[15]

For twenty-six years, from 1869–1896, she taught grade school—all subjects and all classes. Stephens had her hands full teaching in her overcrowded classroom. At one time she had as many as ninety students in her classroom. Still, she was an excellent teacher and she was an overwhelmingly positive influence on her students. She was "always fair minded [and] she recognized the worth and dignity of the individual whether he was a little Negro beginner or a white supervisor." A white reporter once said, "Her diction is that of a person of highest culture and refinement, and one need only to converse with her for a few minutes to become aware of her keen, trained intellect and to realize that here is one of the outstanding women of the Negro race." Further, "she had this ability to cross over racial lines with her understanding and sympathies. . . . Always she taught her people to strive for better things."

Beatrice enjoyed school and she took her studies seriously. Her classes, adapted for the black children from a typical New England classical program for white children, included reading, spelling, writing, grammar, diction, history, geography, arithmetic, and music.[16] Beatrice advanced to high school where she continued to excel. She was one of two hundred students enrolled at Union School, which had expanded in 1876, nine years after the school opened, to include a junior and senior high.

The fact that Beatrice had a public high school to attend is significant. Most southern whites did not believe that higher education was necessary for black children, so states provided little or no funds for their instruction. The 1896 Supreme Court case, *Plessy vs. Ferguson*, allowed for racial segregation only if the facilities in public institutions were equal. But in the opinion of Supreme Court justice John Marshall Harlan equal facilities for both black and white students would hurt white children without advancing blacks. County school boards, in violation of the "separate, but equal" ruling of the *Plessy* case could justify then their discriminatory behavior toward black children with inadequate facilities and substantially less pay for Negro teachers than white teachers. It meant also that southern school boards did not have to offer public secondary education for black children while "proceeding with vigor" to increase the number of high schools available to white children.[17]

With ever-increasing enrollment and the need for more space, black school officials and community leaders urged the city to improve the Union School facilities. Finally, in 1902, the school was moved and its name changed to Capitol Hill, after its new location. Capitol Hill school was an old-fashioned framed red brick school building of moderate size. The school environment, surrounded by rocks and trees, was pleasant enough. It even had rough benches outside, built for the children to use during lunch hour.[18]

Although it was a new building, Capitol Hill school had limited resources. Of utmost concern to the community was the fact that the school had no library. Carrie Still Shepperson, William Grant Still's mother, was dismayed by the continued lack of support for black children. She set about to organize an alumni group to put on several benefit performances of Shakespeare plays, which netted the school several hundred dollars. With these funds, the Capitol Hill library was founded.

The high school was understaffed and underequipped with books but the teachers, many of whom were college graduates, did an excellent job of providing a solid education for the children.[19] Among the faculty was Carrie Shepperson who taught English in the High School Department. From her, the students learned Chaucer and Shakespeare.

Capitol Hill school emphasized a classical liberal or college preparatory curriculum. Accepting the philosophy of race leader W. E. B. Du Bois, community leaders felt that an academic program would provide a foundation for the "best intellectual traditions" and the best means to understanding their own "historical development and sociological uniqueness." Through this educational system, blacks would understand their "inherent rights to equality." At a time when industrial education was being promoted by Booker T. Washington, arguably the most influential black national leader, and others, as a more appropriate avenue for black children, black educators in Little Rock were adamant that classical objectives should be maintained.[20] Industrial education was offered as an elective for boys. Stressing self-determination, the students in the industrial courses learned practical skills with which they could buy land and earn a living.

The curriculum at Capitol Hill high school was demanding. Beatrice studied Greek and Latin. In addition, she studied three years of algebra, history, physics, and English. As electives, Beatrice chose cooking and sewing, courses that complemented her hobbies: painting china, knitting, and crocheting.

Florence Beatrice readied herself for college and a career as a music teacher and pianist. Although there is no extant evidence, it is likely that after her early training with her mother, Price studied piano with another local teacher, given her advanced technique by the time she entered college. Florence Beatrice was also an accomplished organist. Although Allison Presbyterian had only a piano, Price would have had access to the numerous organs in the city because of her parents' social and professional associations. Most likely, she took lessons from a white organist at one of the local churches.

Price graduated from high school at fourteen. Commencement day, 1902, was a great day for the young woman: she was chosen valedictorian of her class.[21] Little did she know on that day that her alma mater, in 1930 renamed Dunbar High School and Junior College, would honor her thirty years later as one of its most distinguished early graduates. Little did she know that the Negro community would want to greet her when she returned in a way befitting a celebrity. There was even talk of a parade. Her return home would, indeed, be a day of celebration.

4 The New England Conservatory of Music

Florence Beatrice stayed in Little Rock for one year after graduation from high school. She was accepted at the New England Conservatory of Music in Boston but would use this year to practice piano and organ and compose to ready herself for college. Perhaps because of her young age her parents thought it best to wait before sending her so far away from home. Florence Beatrice was a young, but independent girl of fifteen and she would soon be ready to leave the South in pursuit of educational opportunities.

Florence Beatrice's parents would have her attend only the very best and the New England Conservatory was the proper place for a girl of her social status. For them, the conservatory meant sending their daughter to a school where she would continue to refine her tastes in music and hone even more her social skills. In choosing a music school for Florence Beatrice, receptivity to Negro students had to be a consideration. The New England Conservatory had a long history of accepting Negro students, so it was thought that perhaps Florence Beatrice would be comfortable here. The Smiths probably had met and heard perform some of the notable black musicians who attended the Conservatory in the 1880s and 1890s. They included concert singer M. Sissieretta Jones ("Black Patti") (1880s), composer J. Rosamond Johnson (1890s), and pianist and writer Maud Cuney [Hare] (1890s). The Smiths surely knew of concert violinist Joseph Douglass, the first black violinist to make a national tour. He was enrolled in 1889 by his grandfather, abolitionist Frederick Douglass who also played the violin.[1]

In September 1903, Florence Beatrice arrived in Boston with her mother. The city was already a thriving and sophisticated musical town. From the early nineteenth century, Boston was the cultural center of New England. The Boston Academy of Music, founded under Lowell Mason; the Handel and Haydn

Society; and the Harvard Musical Association were well established. In addition, orchestral, chamber, and choral music concerts were regular fare. In 1862, music lectures were established at Harvard University and, in 1867, the Boston Conservatory and the New England Conservatory of Music were founded.

Boston's central musical institution was the Boston Symphony, founded in 1881, which had a concert series and public dress rehearsals. In 1900, the orchestra began playing in the newly constructed Symphony Hall, one of the finest auditoriums acoustically in the world. Located directly across the street from the New England Conservatory, Symphony Hall was also where visiting orchestras such as the London Symphony and the Theodore Thomas Orchestra (later named the Chicago Symphony) could be heard.

There were dozens of choral organizations in the city but the most notable was the Handel and Haydn Society, which featured oratorios and cantatas in their performances. Chamber music was also a staple of the community. The Kneisel Quartet (comprised of Boston Symphony members), the Boston Symphony Quartet, the Hoffman Quartet, and the Boston String Quartet were well established. There were also Sunday Chamber [Music] Concerts organized by Chickering & Sons, in Chickering Hall with a seating capacity of 800, located next door to the New England Conservatory. Chickering & Sons, along with Mason & Hamlin, were Boston's premiere piano makers, producing pianos that were used by the leading concert artists of the day.

Boston was known also for its long-standing support of American composers at a time when German romanticism was the most powerful influence in American art music. The city had long nurtured a tradition of serious musical composition, which included the works of the "Second New England School" of composers, notably John Knowles Paine, George Whitefield Chadwick, and Horatio Parker. These composers were trained in Germany, mastered the Austro-Germanic style of the romantic symphony and symphonic poem, chamber music, cantata, and opera, and returned to teach and direct the nation's most prominent music schools. Paine headed the music department of Harvard from 1867–1904 and became the first full professor of music there in 1875. Harvard thus became the nation's first college to offer music as part of its regular curriculum. Chadwick was affiliated with the faculty of the New England Conservatory for almost fifty years, heading the conservatory from 1897 until shortly before his death in 1931. And Parker headed the Yale School of Music from 1895–1918. Although they left behind a vast amount of literature that upheld the highest ideals in musical craftsmanship and pedagogy, these composers exerted their greatest influence as teachers and scholars.

Boston, too, had a publishing company that championed American composers. Although the Arthur P. Schmidt Publishing Co. had a large and diversified catalog, it was dedicated in its support of Chadwick, Arthur Foote, Edward

MacDowell, and Amy Cheney Beach, composers who were most notable among Americans in the late nineteenth century.

The city also believed in the importance of music education for children. As early as 1837, music was introduced in the Boston school system by Lowell Mason, church organist, composer, and cofounder of the Boston Academy of Music. Through Mason's efforts, Boston became the first free public school system in the country to offer music instruction.

The New England Conservatory of Music played an important role in the development of Boston's cultural life. Until the early decades of the twentieth century, American conservatories could not compete with their European counterparts. While America had adequate teachers of piano, violin, harmony, and singing, the musical standards, in general, were very low. However, by the turn of the century, Boston could emulate the challenging professional musical environment, which had long existed in Europe, in a way that few other American cities at the turn of the century could.

When the conservatory was first established it was affiliated with Boston University and offered an academic curriculum that paralleled a liberal arts program for music teachers. The Conservatory split with the University in 1891, and the music program at the Conservatory shifted from one of broad academic study to that of a highly specialized music program. Already a well-established composer, George Whitefield Chadwick was named director of the Conservatory in 1897, a leadership position equal to his stature as a composer.[2]

Prior to Chadwick's years as director, the Conservatory placed a heavy emphasis upon European musical training, similar to the Peabody Academy of Music, and the Oberlin Conservatory.[3] This meant class lessons in solfeggio, harmony, and language commonly found in European conservatories, especially Germany. German romanticism was a powerful influence in American art music from about 1865 to the turn of the century. During these years, German musicians continued to come to this country to teach, perform, and conduct America's newly formed orchestras. The symphonies, chamber music, and choral music of Handel, Mozart, Beethoven, and Mendelssohn constituted the core repertoire of performing music organizations and was the foundation of academic studies in the nation's conservatories and universities. For many, the German style and aesthetic represented the epitome of musical culture, and German teachers served as role models for aspiring young Americans.

Although the New England Conservatory was structured at first after European prototypes, Chadwick's ideals were wholly American. In contrast to both Peabody and Oberlin, which maintained their European traditions unabashedly, Chadwick sought to change the direction of the New England Conservatory. The faculty was more diverse, and advanced study in Europe was not a requirement for teaching there. In 1905, less than one-half of the 50 faculty members had advanced study in Europe.[4] There was good reason for this. By this time, the Conservatory could draw its faculty from the ranks of the Boston Symphony and the city's professional chamber and choral organizations, many of whom had their early training at the Conservatory. Further, Chadwick drew upon the employees of Chickering and Sons and Mason and Hamlin piano makers who taught organ and piano tuning and construction.

To be sure many of the faculty were resistant to the drastic changes in the direction of the Conservatory. Chadwick explained,

> These changes and innovations were not all accomplished at once or without some friction. The American teachers recognized the necessity of them and helped along as much as they could. The German teachers made no active opposition, but they had for so long run *little private conservatories* of their own with their pupils that it was hard for them to get the idea of a real school in whose interest every one must work.
>
> And as I assumed no arrogant airs, they perhaps thought I was "easy" and so began to tell me about how things were done in German schools. One day at lunch, when three or four of them were present, I told [Carl] Stasny directly that as I had been in two German schools since he had, I could perhaps tell *him* something about them. Which I proceeded to do. I also reminded him that Boston, Mass., was not Germany and that the Conservatory would remain an *American* school. After this I did not hear quite so much about "Chermanie."[5]

By 1903 when Chadwick wrote an article entitled "Musical Atmosphere and Student Life," in the *New England Conservatory Magazine*, he could strongly recommend American schools to train professional musicians. His philosophy was that American conservatories should cultivate a musical environment that would stimulate and challenge its students and consequently prepare professional musicians comparable to that of Europe.[6] During Chadwick's long tenure at the Conservatory, he dedicated himself to this goal. Further, Chadwick pointed to the progress that Americans were making in composition, citing Dudley Buck, John Paine, and J. D. Parker as examples. Although Chadwick advocated study in Europe to broaden one's horizons, he felt it was not required for those serious music students who attended the Conservatory and took advantage of all that it had to offer.

In order to accomplish his goals of establishing a nationally recognized musical institution, Chadwick had to change the mission of the Conservatory from that of essentially a singing school and boarding school for young women to one that would prepare professional musicians, men and women. Chadwick's first step was to move the conservatory, which had been located at the St. James Hotel in Franklin Square, to more professional surroundings suitable for teaching and performance needs. Completed in 1903, the new building, on Huntington Ave., was most conducive for developing talented students into professional artists. The new facility included Jordan Hall, a recital hall for concerts and opera performances, a music library, practice studios, and well-equipped classrooms. The New England Conservatory together with Symphony Hall, Northeastern University, the Museum of Fine Arts, the Gardner Museum, the Boston Opera House, and the Boston Public Library helped to define the cultural center of Boston.

Chadwick's emphasis on the highest standards in performance was evident in the teaching instruments that were installed for faculty and student use. There was a modern three-manual organ built by George S. Hutchings, a small three-manual Farrand & Votey organ in Henry Dunham's teaching studio, a three-manual (20-stop) E. M. Skinner organ and a two-manual (14-stop) E. W. Lane organ, both in teaching studios. The Conservatory also had ten small pipe organs for the students' practice, nine built by Lane and one by Skinner.[7] In addition to the upright practice pianos, there were a few grand pianofortes provided by the Hutchings and Sons and the Mason and Hamlin companies.

The music library at the Conservatory was one of the best in Boston, containing almost 5000 scores, books, and manuscripts. When Jordan Hall opened, it housed the scores for about 300 orchestral works, which Chadwick began to acquire actively the year before. The choral library was substantial as well. The nucleus was the entire library of the Boylston Club, a well-known mixed choral ensemble organized in 1873 under the direction of George L. Osgood. To it was added the complete library of the Boston Singers, an organization that succeeded the Boylston Club in 1893.[8]

Chadwick moved quickly to raise the academic standard of the Conservatory. He modified the curriculum from its earlier emphasis on singing and piano playing to one that stressed harmony, counterpoint, theory and analysis, and composition. In keeping with Chadwick's aim to establish a first-rate American music school, he developed his own harmony book, *Harmony: A Course of Study* (published in 1897), for class use. He explained, "I was ambitious to make the book a model of expression, most of the books on Harmony being more or less poor translations from the German."[9] The harmony book was generally well received by the faculty but, he added, "the old folks thought it was too 'advanced' and too difficult for the average student—which was perhaps true. It all depends on how much they want to learn!"[10] To complement the harmony classes, Chadwick also started classes in ear-training, dictation, and sight reading.

Given Chadwick's interests in conducting, establishing the school orchestra was of utmost importance. The orchestra was comprised mostly of students, but faculty members helped out the newly formed ensemble when some music, particularly twentieth-century scores, proved to be too difficult. He explained:

> But it was with the string department that the most radical changes were made. Mr. [Emil] Mahr had his pupils together for orchestral practice once a week. So

> did [Eugene] Gruenberg. Neither of them had anything to do with the other. Between them there were perhaps twelve or fourteen violins and violas and one or two violoncellos. So I informed both these gentlemen that the two classes were to be united under *my* direction and "advised" them to send their students to the class. It was rather slim at first, but after a little the students began to make application to join, whether Mahr or Gruenberg wanted them to or not. I moved the rehearsals into Sleeper Hall, coached Geo. S. Dunham [*sic*] on score reading, and, playing the wind parts on the organ, let the students into the rehearsal, and before long had the orchestra playing accompaniments to the easier concertos and arias. These I mostly borrowed from the *Harvard Musical Association*. Thus began the Conservatory orchestra, and it was one of the greatest factors in getting away from Franklin Square.[11]

The Conservatory instrumental program developed fairly quickly because many of the orchestral instruments were taught by members of the Boston Symphony. By March 1902, the orchestra could give its first concert as a "*complete* orchestra without the organ," that is, without organ students filling in the missing parts. Chadwick explained his goals for the program this way: "We cannot quite claim to have founded a real orchestral school, but at least we can from time to time educate orchestral players who can hold an honorable place in the best Symphony and Opera orchestras. . . . I felt, too that as soon as we could rehearse and give the concerts in a suitable place, it would be recognized by the public and give the Conservatory a prestige it had never before achieved."[12]

After the orchestra was established, Chadwick reorganized the fledgling vocal program so that it would equal the instrumental program in stature. Students were required to study French, German, Italian, piano, and harmony in courses distributed over four years.

Simultaneously, the opera school was formed in 1900 under the Italian conductor and vocal coach Oreste Bimboni, a conductor renowned in Europe, including work with the Vienna opera. Through the opera program Chadwick envisioned the Conservatory as a forum for the development of an American operatic theater not dependent upon European impresarios or performers for its existence. The first American opera workshop, the New England Conservatory Opera School, with coaches and other professionals drawn from the Boston Opera Co., offered the type of professional opera experience American singers lacked.[13]

Bimboni's first public program was a series of opera excerpts given on May 23, 1902. Chadwick explained, "Our first show was given at the Boston Theatre on May 23d, for which we hired some sixty players from the B.S.O. [Boston Symphony Orchestra]. Our orchestra was not yet ripe enough to be trusted under another conductor. Everything was topsy turvy at the N.E.C. for two weeks before the show. . . . Everything went smoothly except for the rather long waits [between pieces]. All Boston was there, and we probably got our expenses back (it was a free show) in advertising [for the Conservatory]."[14]

To complement the orchestra and opera concert series there were lectures for students, given by the conservatory faculty and outside speakers on organ construction, church music, and the history of musical instruments.

The New England Conservatory offered several degrees. Entrance requirements were flexible enough to admit hundreds of students annually, but only a few dozen really talented musicians completed the formal requirements necessary to receive the three-year diploma, the highest official certificate awarded by the Conservatory.

When Price began her studies in 1903, registration was approximately 2000, the greatest number of those students being young women.[15] For most women, conservatory training was similar to a finishing school. As the 1906 New England Conservatory yearbook, the *Neume*, explained, "it makes her independent and self-supporting, more intellectual and refined, an ornament in society, and a pleasure to family and friends."[16]

Some women utterly transcended this subsidiary role and pursued music professionally. During the 1890s, Boston cultivated an environment that began to take women composers and musicians seriously.[17] Women were actively involved in all aspects of the city's cultural life. Professional performing ensembles were numerous and well respected. The Eichberg Ladies Quartet, the Ladies Philharmonic Orchestra, and the Fadette Women's Orchestra, the first professional women's orchestra to gain national recognition, had regular concert seasons and attracted large audiences.

This was also the time when women composers made their mark in the composition of large-scale works. There were three outstanding women composers who, not coincidentally, had premieres of orchestral works in Boston by 1900. Margaret Ruthven Lang (1867–1972) was the first woman to have an orchestral work performed by a major American orchestra. Her *Dramatic Overture* was premiered by the Boston Symphony in 1893. Helen Hopekirk (1856–1945), a Scottish emigré concert pianist, first performed with the Boston Symphony in 1883, and she performed again with that orchestra in 1900 when they premiered her Piano Concerto in D Major. An earlier *Concertstück* had been played by the orchestra in 1894. Mrs. H. H. A. Beach (Amy Cheney Beach) was the first American woman composer to achieve international recognition. Her Mass in E-flat was first performed by the Boston Handel and Haydn Society in 1892 and her Gaelic Symphony in E minor, which has received widespread attention in recent years, was premiered by the Boston Symphony in 1896. Beach's Piano Concerto in C-sharp minor was performed by that orchestra in 1899.

Equally impressive are the musical contributions of African American women musicians in Boston during the late nineteenth century. In a recent study of black women musicians in Boston, Josephine Wright cites no fewer than eighty-one black women involved in classical music from ca. 1870–1900.[18] Thirty-three musicians worked as professional or semiprofessional performers including seventeen prima donna singers, five pianists, six organists, three pianist-organists, one virtuoso violinist, and one virtuoso multiinstrumentalist. Approximately twelve black women can be documented as music teachers during this period, although Wright suggests that this number may actually have been higher. Several black female authors are also included. One writer, Rachel Washington, a concert pianist, organist, and teacher of many of Boston's leading Black musicians, published a theory book, *Musical Truth* (Boston, 1884).

Wright also identifies eight black women composers active during the same period. The music of three of these women, Carrie Melvin Lucas, her sister Louisa Melvin Delos Mars, and Miriam Benjamin were published as well. Carrie Lucas's ballad, "You Know," published in 1887, was popularized by her husband, Sam Lucas, the well-known minstrel entertainer. Louisa Mars composed five full-length operettas, and between 1889 and 1896 three of them, now lost, were published. Miriam Benjamin composed two marches that are of historical interest. Her march, "The Boston Elite Two Step," was performed by the United States Marine Band under John Philip Sousa ca. 1891–1892 and was later published in 1895. Her second march, "The American Bugle Call," was used as the campaign song for presidential candidates Theodore Roosevelt and Charles Fairbanks in the election of 1904.

At least twelve of the women cited in Wright's study attended the New England Conservatory of Music. Three of these women became nationally known. Concert singer Nellie E. Brown-Mitchell matriculated during the 1870s. She founded her own concert company and toured with it in the late 1880s to early 1890s prior to settling in Boston to teach in the late 1890s. Concert pianist Maud Cuney (later Cuney-Hare) attended the Conservatory in 1894 and later concertized throughout the United States as accompanist for baritone Harry T. Burleigh. Cuney-Hare's *Negro Musicians and Their Music* is a seminal study of the history of black music. Soprano M. Sissieretta Jones, "The Black Patti," studied at the Conservatory during the 1880s and later achieved international recognition as a concert artist.

Boston and the New England Conservatory, with its well-established teachers and the modern facilities, provided much inspiration for Florence Beatrice. With every intention to master her studies, she was ready to meet the challenge set forth by the prestigious music school. The time was right for a young, aspiring woman composer and performer to excel in music professionally and she intended to take advantage of every opportunity the Conservatory had to offer. The impetus to succeed was already in her soul, aided by her parents and by the rich cultural environment in which her family was a part.

Florence was an ambitious student, fully dedicated to her studies at the Conservatory. She enrolled in a double-degree program—the soloist's program in

Curriculum—Florence Beatrice Smith
New England Conservatory of Music, 1903–1906

1904 (1903–1904)	
1st Semester	2nd Semester
Piano—Edwin Klahre	Piano—Edwin Klahre
Harmony—Benjamin Cutter	Harmony—Benjamin Cutter
Organ—Henry M. Dunham	Organ—Henry M. Dunham
[Music] History Lecture	Music History Lecture (pass)
Concert Deportment—Gertrude I. McQuesten	
1905 (1904–1905)	
1st Semester	2nd Semester
Piano—Edwin Klahre	Piano—Dr. J. Albert Jeffrey
Harmony—Benjamin Cutter	Analysis—Benjamin Cutter
Organ—Henry M. Dunham	Organ—Henry M. Dunham
Theory—Louis C. Elson	Theory—Louis C. Elson
Concert Deportment—Clayton D. Gilbert	Concert Deportment—Clayton D. Gilbert
Normal Lecture—F. Addison Porter and Francis A. Henay	
Hand Culture—Francis A. Henay	
1906 (1905–1906)	
1st Semester	2nd Semester
Piano—Dr. J. Albert Jeffrey	Piano—Dr. J. Albert Jeffrey
Organ—Henry M. Dunham	Organ—Henry M. Dunham
Counterpoint and Composition—Frederick Converse	Counterpoint and Composition—Wallace Goodrich
Ensemble—Joseph Adamowski	Piano and Organ Tuning—Oliver C. Faust
Choir Training—Wallace Goodrich	Choir Training—Wallace Goodrich
Piano Sight Reading—Charles F. Dennée	Piano Sight Reading—Charles F. Dennée

organ and the teacher's program in piano through the Normal Department. The original Conservatory grade card has been lost, but the registrar's office conserves a handwritten, almost indecipherable 3-by-5 index card, actually a shorthand version of her courses from which her curriculum can be determined.[19]

The New England Conservatory had much to offer organ students. It was recognized nationally for its facilities and its highly regarded faculty. Of particular interest to organists was the Conservatory's well-stocked library; at this period many American conservatories did not have the works that we have come to think of as standard works available to any student. Also, the large churches of Boston and the vicinity constantly offered students an opportunity to hear the best church music and organ performances by the Conservatory faculty and visiting artists, both in church services and in recital.

The soloist's program in organ, Price's primary course of study, attracted only the brightest and most talented organists. The program was designed to train church organists and choir directors and, for advanced pupils, to prepare them for concert performance. Church positions requiring well-trained organists were becoming more plentiful, and talented, creative organists could always find good jobs. For the three years that Florence matriculated at the Conservatory, she studied organ privately with Henry M. Dunham, concert organist and chairman of the organ department.

The requirements for graduation in the organ soloist program were rigorous. Price took several courses in theory, including ear training (solfeggio) and dictation, harmony and analysis, and counterpoint. She also had to attend lecture courses in English literature, music history, orchestral instruments, organ construction, and history of organ literature. There was also a separate course in "Ritual Music" (liturgical playing) in the Protestant Episcopal Church, which Price apparently did not take. Concert deportment was also part of the curriculum.

In addition, there were performance-oriented courses including choir training and accompaniment, service playing, and improvisation. She received instruction in orchestral score reading and practice in reducing for organ at sight full scores of choral works with orchestral accompaniment, an optional course offered only to advanced students. This was both a difficult and an essential part of any organist's training at the time. Typically, church organists accompanied the choir in performances of oratorios or cantatas when an orchestra was not available or was unaffordable. And until 1902, the organ students played with the student orchestra by filling in the missing wind parts of the fledgling and newly developed ensemble.

It is interesting to note that all of the organ students studied tuning, the practical business of keeping an organ in tune. The philosophy was that there should be no gender discrimination in any course of study at the Conservatory and that all students should be able to maintain a pipe organ as well as play it, a task unthinkable to most organists today. F. W. Hall, principal of the tuning department explained:

> The object of this is to prepare the organist to remedy any ordinary defects to which the organ is subject in an intelligent and workmanlike manner . . . [so the student] goes to any part of the world well prepared not only to play his organ but as well to keep it in perfect repair. . . . The fact that this school opens another opportunity for self-help for women and for their successful competition with men we will not now discuss, as that feature at once commends itself to public favor.[20]

The organ department had a placement service for its advanced students, securing church jobs for most of them. For a short time, it appears that Price played for the Unitarian Church in Natick, Massachusetts, just south of Boston. This was a prestigious job at a small (65 pews), "fashionable and historical church located on the spot where Honeywell [*sic*] preached to the praying Indians of the New England Colonies."[21] This church, rebuilt by a Mr. Hunnewell who had given the money to repair the church and its organ after the disastrous fire of 1874 destroyed all the churches in Natick, had a small two-manual seven-rank pipe organ.[22] Price put her organ training to good use throughout her career. It is not known whether Price maintained a church job when she returned to Little Rock or when she moved to Chicago, but she did play organ recitals regularly (which often included her own compositions). She composed sacred music for church use, including incidental music for preludes and offertories, choral, and solo vocal music.

The Normal program, the second degree program in which Price was enrolled, was designed to provide practical training for music teachers through study in music education. It required students to teach two years in the normal department preparatory school for children between ages nine to fifteen.[23] Florence taught music to these children twice a week. She met with a supervisor and attended general class sessions weekly where the student teachers had an opportunity to teach, criticize, and discuss each other's work. The Normal program included also lectures on hand culture to discuss the physiology of the hand and arm, and the relationship of the brain's function to the central nervous system to its impact on keyboard performance. Further, she was required to attend lectures on the necessary qualifications of a successful teacher, the principles of psychology, the formation of habits, the development of taste, and the relation of psychology to music.

Although Price's studies at the conservatory were concentrated in teaching and organ performance, she was becoming more serious than ever about her interest in composing. While a student at the conservatory, Price wrote her first symphony and a string trio, both based on Negro folk music. Neither of these scores has survived. Although Florence Beatrice was enrolled in composition classes with Wallace Goodrich and Frederick Converse, two very solid teachers and composers, she had an opportunity to study composition with George Whitefield Chadwick. She showed Chadwick, known to be a very accessible teacher, her symphony, and to her delight the eminent composer offered her a scholarship to study with him in his private studio.[24] Although Chadwick's position as director of the Conservatory precluded him from teaching many students, he accepted a few of the most gifted students, giving them two-hour lessons and teaching many of them without pay.[25]

Price's interest in studying with Chadwick may have been twofold. As a student, she certainly had much to gain from working with such a well-respected teacher. But she may have been drawn to Chadwick for another reason. In Chadwick, Price found a sympathetic teacher and perhaps even inspiration. Although Chadwick never acknowledged any real interest in African American folk music, he was often cited by contemporary music critics as a pioneer in efforts to free American musical expression from the Germanic style. His compositions, some of which suggested Negro folk melodies and rhythms, may have been a model for her. (In 1922, William Grant Still studied with Chadwick briefly.)

This was a time in American music history when composers began to express an interest in nationalism—the conscious effort by composers to betray their American roots in music. Although many of the efforts by American composers at the turn of the century were valiant, few of these compositions are memorable. When Antonin Dvorák came to the United States in 1895 and heard the rich traditions of African American and native American folk music, he urged American composers to make use of this unique source material. Years before Dvorák's exhortation on American musical nationalism, Chadwick's own compositions were providing models of the influence of African American folk music in American composition. For example, the scherzo second movement in his Symphony No. 2, published in 1886, sets a syncopated primary theme with a pentatonic melody that is somewhat characteristic of African American plantation melodies. Louis Elson, writing in 1915, noted that Chadwick's work predated Dvorák's arrival in this country and was "the first real effort of an American composer to utilize the only folk song which our country possesses—the music of the South, the themes of the plantation. This occurs in the scherzo, the second movement"[26] (see example 1).

During this time, Price, as a composer, may have struggled with the conflicts inherent in her upbringing. She went to the Conservatory as a piano and organ student, preparing primarily to be a teacher—a profession that everyone, including herself, expected of her. But she had a need to compose and she was talented enough to do so. Living in Boston and studying with Chadwick opened up a whole new world for her. Boston fostered, indeed nurtured, women composers, and Chadwick accepted women in his studio and treated them seriously. In Price, he saw promise as a composer. In many ways, Chadwick reinforced her identity as an African American and conveyed to her, through his own compositions, positive attitudes toward black music. At the same time, Price found composing to be liberating, an avenue through which she could express

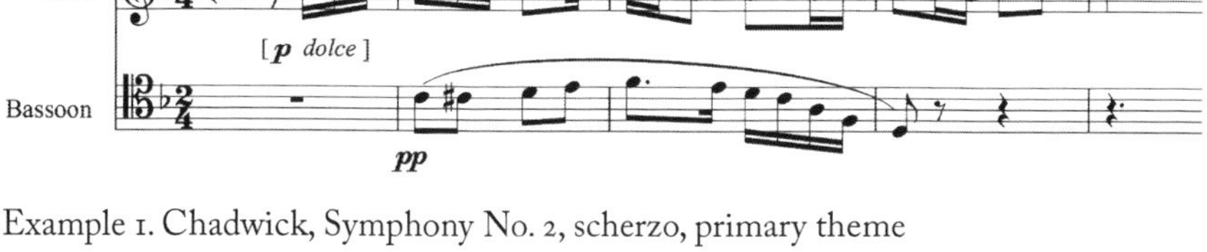

Example 1. Chadwick, Symphony No. 2, scherzo, primary theme

herself honestly. For her, it was both an intellectual and emotional expression. One of the ironies that was to play itself out throughout her career, in even her earliest compositions, was her use of plantation melodies and melodies that were written in the manner of African American folk music. For so long this music was shunned by the black upper and middle class, but Price embraced it and passionately incorporated this music into many of her compositions.

* * *

During Price's years at the Conservatory, she had numerous opportunities to perform. Of utmost importance to Chadwick was the establishment of a concert series where advanced students and faculty could perform for each other. Ten public subscription concerts were given each year by the Conservatory chorus, opera department, orchestra, and members of the faculty. An additional four public concerts, including the annual commencement concert, were given by advanced students. In order to give students ample opportunity to perform, a weekly afternoon concert, not open to the public, was given by students. By 1904–1905, Florence Beatrice's second year of study, the concert series was in full swing. There were about 85 concerts given that year; the following year, there were 68 concerts given from September to June. In addition, students had many opportunities to hear the eminent artists and ensembles of the day, including Fritz Kreisler, Harold Bauer, David Bispham, the Kneisel Quartet and the Hoffman Quartet, the Handel and Haydn Chorus, and the Boston Symphony. The Symphony often performed works by Chadwick, who sometimes conducted the ensemble as well.

Only the best students were given an opportunity to perform recitals at the conservatory. Programs indicate that Florence Beatrice was chosen to represent her class on numerous occasions. Chadwick attended every student recital, so there was extra incentive to play well.[27] In her second year of study Florence Beatrice played Robert Schumann's Variations for piano, op. 5, on the pupil's recital (November 26, 1904). Later that academic year, she played François Theodore Dubois' (1837–1924) *Fiat Lux* for organ on the same series (June 9, 1905). But the highlight of the 1904–1905 academic year was a special program (November 15, 1904) on which she performed Felix-Alexandre Guilmant's (1837–1911) Sonata in D Minor in the presence of the composer. All were thrilled with pride when Guilmant came "forward at the conclusion of the number and publicly congratulated her upon the execution and interpretation of the difficult number."[28] Guilmant, on his third and final American concert tour, concluded a series of performances, which began in St. Louis, in an all-Guilmant recital at Boston's Symphony Hall (November 24).[29]

Also in attendance at this performance was Clarence Cameron White. White, considered one of the leading black concert violinists of the time, toured widely throughout the United States and Europe during the first two decades of the twentieth century. It is not known whether White met Price in Little Rock or in Boston, but a 1935 *Chicago Defender* article mentions that White was seated in the audience with a "host" of Price's friends.

In her third year, Price was again active as a recitalist, often featured in the evening recital series of advanced students. On January 5, 1906, she closed the program of piano, organ, and violin music by seven members of her class by performing the first movement of Gustav Merkel's (1827–1885) Second Sonata in G Minor, op. 42, for organ. Two months later (March 23, 1906), she again closed the Recital of Advanced Students by performing Nicolas-Jacques Lemmens (1823–1881) "Adagio and March" from *Sonate Pontificale* for organ.

June 1906 was a busy month for the graduating student. Price performed a movement of a work by Carl Reinecke (1824–1910), for piano, in an afternoon pupil's recital June 1. Her organ playing must have been exceptional by now, for she performed again that month, closing the commencement concert program. She performed her teacher's, Henry M. Dunham's, Sonata in G Minor on the great organ in Jordan Hall. This performance was no doubt the culmination of her performance studies at the Conservatory. In a graduating class of almost 50 performers, she was one of nine students asked to perform.

Price performed all of the organ programs at the Conservatory on the very large three-manual organ in Jordan Hall. This required a solid technique and a thorough mastery of organ registration. Built in 1903, the electro-pneumatic organ was built by the Hutchings-Votey Organ Co. with a state-of-the-art stop list drawn up by faculty members Chadwick, Goodrich, and Dunham. Their intention was to design a "model" concert instrument which could be used to perform with orchestra and accompany a chorus as well.[30]

Of the 2000 students who were admitted to the conservatory with Florence Beatrice in 1903, only 58 students received degrees during the class commencement ceremonies in June 1906: 31 in piano, 7 in organ, 7 in voice, 4 in violin, and 9 in tuning. Of those receiving degrees, about one-third were men, 5 pianists, 3 organists, 2 violinists, 1 student in voice, and all the students in tuning. Although the normal course usually took four years to complete by itself, Florence Beatrice really excelled at the conservatory and completed *both* degree programs—Teachers Diploma in piano and Soloists Diploma in organ—in only three years. The Soloists Diploma was the highest attainable certificate awarded by the Conservatory[31] and it was an exceedingly difficult program to complete. That year, Florence Beatrice was the only student to receive two degrees.

* * *

It is not clear where Price resided while attending the Conservatory. The school maintained separate residences for their male and female students. The women's dormitory was located on Hemenway St. Arrangements were made for the men to live in boarding houses in the area for a fee of $6.00 a week for room and board. Apparently Price did not reside in the women's dormitory but maintained an apartment in Boston.

Why did Florence Beatrice live in an apartment on her own, even if the Smiths could afford it? (It cost approximately $250 a year for tuition at the Conservatory plus room and board.) One explanation is that the Smiths may have been trying to protect their daughter from any possible act of discrimination in the dorm. While the New England Conservatory and Harvard University welcomed minority students in small numbers, both races accepted racial segregation and were quite willing to maintain separate social lives. Referring to his student days at Harvard, W. E. B. Du Bois said, "a colored person in Boston was more neighbor to a colored person in Chicago than to a white person across the street."[32] Du Bois' point was made vivid as he recounted the difficulty of Maud Cuney [Hare] in the New England Conservatory women's dormitory in the 1890s. After the conservatory tried to "Jim Crow" her, that is, segregate her from the other students in the dorm, the Negro students at Harvard and elsewhere came to her defense and won their case for equality.[33] Discrimination was a fact of life, even in New England. Many years later, Price's daughter offered this explanation of her grandmother's actions: "My grandmother didn't want my mother to be a Negro, so when she took her to Boston she rented an expensive apartment with a maid and forced my mother to say her birthplace was not Little Rock but Mexico."[34]

This statement, concerning Price's residence and the change of her race, is puzzling, to be sure, and there are far more questions than there are answers. When Florence entered the Conservatory her hometown was listed as 7th and Main St., Little Rock. Recitals given in her second year at the Conservatory confirm this address. In her third year, the recital programs and the graduating class picture lists Pueblo, Mexico, as her hometown. Why the change of address? Did Mrs. Smith change her daughter's address for its inherent social implications? Did Florence Beatrice "pass" for white in her last year at the conservatory? Was this the thinking of Florence Beatrice's mother whose own life as a black in Little Rock was nearly in shambles now? Florence Beatrice was very light-skinned, but perhaps her subtle Negro features could be explained away. In her graduating picture, Florence Beatrice appears to be the only Negro woman in her class.[35] (Price is in the second row, second person from the right. There appears to be one Negro male in the class).

The inquiry suggests yet another scenario. As is common in conservatories today, studio teachers, who meet regularly with students one-on-one, often become a student's mentor. Perhaps Price's organ teacher, Henry Dunham, or her composition teacher, George Chadwick, who was particularly sensitive to black students, discussed with her the dismal chance she would have building a career as a pianist, organist, and composer as a Negro musician. Passing for "Spanish," to allow for her light-complexioned olive skin, not an uncommon occurrence during this time, would give her a much better chance of having a professional career.

Mulattoes passing for white in order to survive is not uncommon in African American history and the examples of mulattos "changing" their racial affiliation to "white" are plentiful. In his later years, Du Bois recalled his interest, while attending Harvard, in a young woman who had the "insuperable handicap of looking white." The woman "passed" and was admitted to Vassar College, which then refused admission to Negro students.[36] William Grant Still remembered a friend of his mother's, "a well-to-do lady," who "just got tired of being colored." One day the woman moved herself and her family to a white suburb of Little Rock.[37]

Southerners were preoccupied with race definitions and, given the marked change in the political and social climate, which now existed in Arkansas, perhaps Mrs. Smith thought it advantageous for her daughter to "pass," at least temporarily, while she was so far away from the protection of her family. From 1890 through the first decade of the century, laws disenfranchising blacks were passed throughout the South and "Jim Crow" laws made color caste legal. Lynching, segregation, and racial inequities became part of one's consciousness despite efforts to shield oneself from the institution of racism.

Whatever the case, at this point in her life, Florence Beatrice, just sixteen or seventeen years old, was obedient and did what her parents and teachers suggested. Giving Pueblo, Mexico, as her hometown, she "passed" for one year.

There are no verifiable reasons for the conscious decision to list Price as a temporary resident of Mexico in order for her to pass as Spanish but the inquiry is relevant to the study of Price's music. Confronted with a conflict of racial identity, one that may have been initiated and given validity exclusively by Mrs. Smith, it is clear that after graduation from the New England Conservatory, Price made a choice about her racial allegiance. Informed by her training at the Conservatory and through her experiences growing up in the South, Price's music bears witness to the confirmation of her racial identity as an African American. Many Negroes, like Price, were proud of their ancestry and rejected any occasion to deny their black heritage. Florence Beatrice Smith Price would never "pass" again.

5 Return to Little Rock

Why Florence Smith returned to Little Rock after graduation from the New England Conservatory is not clear. The political situation there was even more frightening now. Negroes had been stripped of all their political and personal rights. Aggressively contributing to the downward spiral in race relations was Governor Jeff Davis who served that office from 1902 to 1907. The movement to disenfranchise blacks was completed in 1906, the year Florence Beatrice returned from Boston, with the institution of white primaries throughout the state ordered by Governor Davis. Davis's advocacy of white supremacy provided stimulus for the pervasive evil that segregated blacks and whites and excluded blacks from any avenue of political power.

Yet, Florence Beatrice recognized that there was little or no chance that a Negro could teach at a predominantly white school in the North. Equally difficult was establishing a career as a black instrumentalist or composer in those days, particularly for women. White concert managers often would not book black instrumentalists because audiences were not ready to accept black performers playing the concert repertoire (music primarily written by European composers) and there was little concert music by black composers save for some piano literature and music for violin and piano. There were a few exceptions. Pianist Blind Boone was successful because, in concert, he presented himself as a curiosity.

Price probably returned home for another reason as well. She may have felt a sense of responsibility. Following in the footsteps of many native Arkansans who went north for their education, including her teacher Charlotte Andrews Stephens, she returned home to be of service to Little Rock's black community. Her mission: to be among those who dedicated their lives to teaching the masses of illiterate Negroes living in the South. Blacks were attending schools in large numbers now. There was good reason to do so: A good education meant economic prosperity and a higher social status in the community. Only through education could there be true freedom and racial equality.

Because of her formal education, Price, a teacher, would be among the most respected people in the community. Doctors, lawyers, dentists, and clergy were also included among this select group. As Willard Gatewood explains, "Because attendance or graduation from college by blacks, not to mention the acquisition of advanced degrees, was so rare, those who did have college diplomas enjoyed special distinction and were expected to assume leadership roles."[1]

In 1906, the same year in which Negroes became completely disfranchised in Little Rock, Dr. Smith, Price's father, completed and published his novel *Maudelle: A novel founded on facts gathered from living witnesses.*[2] Dr. Smith could not yet be vindicated politically and socially in the courts but he could vent his feelings of anger and frustration in a story of miscegenation and unrelenting discrimination. By strongly advocating the quest for education, he expresses his pride in the Negro race and his hope for the future at a time when "Cotton was King, and Slavery Queen of the South."[3] In the preface he explains, "Let no one imagine the author domiciled in a brown stone front mansion in a fashionable neighborhood of some large city in the North, East or West, and weaving an imaginative story; but on the other hand, let him fix in his mind one who has had thirty years' actual experience in the South."

Maudelle is a powerful and passionate story told through the eyes of "living witnesses." The story takes place in antebellum Kentucky and tells the true story of a Senator George Morroe who takes a Negro slave, Mary, as his common-law wife (their names have been changed to preserve their identity). The union produces a daughter, Maudelle, a mulatto or "a yellow nigger." After the Senator marries Mary on his deathbed, his wife and daughter stand to inherit a vast estate. However, Mary is killed by vicious attackers, and thus, Maudelle spends much of her life in legal pursuit of her property and in search of safety. Armed with advice given to her by her father before his death, Maudelle, who is held in bondage at one point in the novel and is later released, works during her lifetime for the rights of the disenfranchised.

The book is written as a powerful attack on the system of slavery and its brutal injustices and it also provides an exposé on the harsh realities of life for both "pure" Negroes and mulattos. From a white person's vantage point, Dr. Smith's book vividly makes the point that there was little distinction between them. Maudelle, an educated "yellow nigger," is chastised because she dares to "sit up straight and look you in the face and talk smart, and really expect you to treat her with as much consideration as if she were white."[4] Speaking to the senator, the outraged white community feared that "one educated nigger could plunge the state of Kentucky into insurrection and murder us all."[5]

Written as an objective but historically based narrative, the book further serves as a powerful forum for disseminating information regarding Negro culture to the white reader, for whom the book no doubt is intended. Within the context of Maudelle's story, Smith interjects dramatic commentaries on the social, political, and religious milieu of antebellum and postbellum society. Speaking indirectly, he provides insight from a black vantage point, on the psychologically complex relationship of master and slave, attitudes of field slaves to domestic slaves, attitudes of Negroes to whites, attitudes of whites to mulattos, and attitudes of Negroes and whites toward miscegenation. At times, the assertions are sermons that morally chastise whites; at other times, these bold statements are "psychological whippings," meant to claim aggressively the Negro's right to participate fully and equally in society.

Through the story of *Maudelle*, which ends in the Reconstruction period, Dr. Smith continued to advocate strongly for black education in the early years of the twentieth century. He wrote,

> After travelling through all the Southern states and noting every phase of the condition of the negro and the tone and temperament of the whites, she [Maudelle] saw but one hope for the negro, but one hope for a self-sustainment in the struggle of life, and that hope was education; not simply an education that ends with a knowledge of a few textbooks, but an education which develops the whole man.
>
> "The head, heart and hands," said she, "must enter into the work for a successful life." And without this the majority of negroes will never advance a step from the gloomy background where slavery left him.[6]

The tragic mulatto story or moralist drama has a long tradition in African American literature. One of the earliest novels on this subject was written by William Wells Brown, himself a slave mulatto. In *Clotel: Or the President's Daughter*, published in 1853, Brown expressed the ambiguous plight of mulattos in both black and white worlds. Isabella, a black slave, is a victim of a white male's sexual advances and she has a daughter, Clotel, who is despised by blacks for her light skin color. After Clotel grows up, she escapes to Europe and marries an African, an act that moves both mulattoes and blacks to embrace her. Ultimately, she is reconciled with her white father, who accepts her black husband and begins to overcome his racism. In writing *Clotel*, Brown sought to overcome his own pain as a mulatto slave. Living on a plantation in Missouri, he witnessed his mother being sent away to the New Orleans slave market for attempting to run away with him to Canada. Brown experienced also the pain of being separated from his sister, who, as a young child, was sold to the deep South.

Moral uplift of the race through education continued to be a common theme for black writers through the turn of the century. This subject found its way into musical sources as well. The most well-known example is Scott Joplin's opera, *Treemonisha*, completed in 1905. The opera is set in 1884. Treemonisha, the opera's eighteen-year-old heroine, is the only educated person living on an Arkansas plantation. She succeeds in outmaneuvering the local conjurors who constantly deceive the illiterate and superstitious community. Ultimately, Treemonisha, a symbol of an educator, is heralded as their leader. An interesting parallel is that Florence Beatrice, from the same state, was nineteen when she started upon her career as a teacher and a leader.

Florence Beatrice probably felt compelled to give back to her community in no small measure. By returning to Little Rock, she would fulfill her father's hopes and dreams and that of the black community by participating in the education of the black youth of Arkansas.

Teaching in Little Rock's Negro community had changed little since Florence left three years earlier. Black teachers, whose dedication was widely known, still received unequal pay for equal work. In 1909–1910, the years that Price taught in Arkansas, black teachers were paid $30.36 per month while white teachers were paid $40.52 per month.[7]

Although the task of educating Little Rock's black children was challenging, it was not hopeless. Black community leaders—such as Dr. Smith; Charlotte Andrews Stephens, Florence Beatrice's elementary school teacher; and Scipio Africanus Jones, Little Rock's most prominent black attorney, who would become a law partner of Thomas J. Price, Florence Price's future husband—worked zealously to provide support for Little Rock's Negro students. The cohesion of the black community was demonstrated in 1907 when the school board began receiving political pressure from the city to move Capitol Hill School, the high school Florence Beatrice attended, from the white section of town to a new location in a less desirable part of town. The black community rallied together to block the decision. The situation was ultimately defused when Jones sold some of his property to the community so a new school could be built. A suitable spot was found on West Eighteenth Street and the property (about a block) was purchased from Jones for about $7400. The new school, the M. W. Gibbs High School, was named for Little Rock's prominent Negro judge. Now in a larger building, the classes were expanded to include grades eight through twelve.[8]

By 1900, Arkansas' several black colleges, many of which were church-related, had begun to supply the growing demand for black teachers. (Heretofore, many black schools had a predominance of white teachers, most of whom were from the North). As one Little Rock black administrator explained, "There is a growing desire on the part of the colored people to have their schools supplied with teachers from their own race. With this desire we are in hearty accord, and we hope the day is not far distant when a sufficient number of well-educated efficient colored teachers can be found."[9]

The academic programs at these colleges were designed to provide primary education for children and to train teachers and ministers. Given the paucity of schools for black children, it was often the responsibility of the Negro colleges to provide instruction at all levels—elementary, secondary, and college. In addition to offering the standard liberal arts or academic curriculum, vocational and home economics courses were offered as well.

When Florence Beatrice, now 19 years old, began her teaching career in Arkansas' black colleges, her first appointment was at the Cotton Plant–Arkadelphia Academy in Cotton Plant, Arkansas.[10] Supported by the white Presbyterian church, the small coeducational school for Negroes had a liberal arts, secondary school curriculum. It was here that she met Neumon Leighton, a white musician, who became a lifelong friend and a promoter of her music. Leighton, who was interested in black music, lectured frequently on the subject. Price met him at a lecture and, as their friendship grew, he discussed her music at length, often introducing her to his audiences at the close of his talks.[11]

After less than one year at Cotton Plant, Florence Beatrice began teaching at Shorter College in Argenta (North Little Rock), an appointment she held from 1907 until 1910. Shorter College, begun in 1886 as Bethel University, originally founded and supported by the African Methodist Episcopal Church, was one of Little Rock's three four-year, church-related colleges for black students. The others were Philander Smith, founded in 1877 by the Freedmen's Aid Society of the African Methodist Episcopal Church, and Arkansas Baptist College, founded in 1884.

Many of the students attending Shorter College were poor and paid only a fraction of the cost necessary to attend the school.[12] Most of the cost, approximately $11.00 a month, was paid by the A.M.E. church. The cost per pupil was as follows:

Tuition	$1.00
Washing, light, fuel	$1.50
Board	$6.00
Instrumental Music	$2.50

There was an additional incidental fee of $.25 a term for each student, and the women were expected to do their own washing.

Like many other black colleges, Shorter College had several departments distributed among three main divisions—elementary, secondary, and college. The 1906–7 catalog shows these departments: college, normal (teaching) academic, theological, English, primary, music, sewing, and printing. That year the college employed ten teachers. Of the few hundred students who attended the college, the majority were enrolled in the elementary program, a lesser number in the secondary program, and the college division, which emphasized theological studies, only enrolled a few.[13]

The college department stressed courses such as the Bible, history, algebra, Latin, geometry, spelling, and science of government. The normal course, where teachers were trained, was parallel to a secondary or high school program. The courses in this program included English literature, Latin, chemistry, various education courses, ethics, and arithmetic. The scientific course led to the Bachelor of Science degree. Those students took courses in the Bible, rhetoric, Caesar [Latin], French, German, trigonometry, algebra, and conversation and composition. By 1912, the college offered courses in law, domestic science, and nursing.

Shorter College was in every sense a Christian school. The religious life of the students was as important as their academic studies. Morning prayers were held in the Chapel each day, and the Bible was used as a textbook in each division of the school throughout the student's entire course of study. As part of her job, Florence Beatrice probably played for chapel services each day and for the worship service on Sunday.

Discipline was the order of the day. Uniforms—women wore navy blue serge suits with Oxford caps and the young men wore navy blue military jackets and trousers with matching caps—were mandatory for Sunday services, public exercises of the school, and for whenever students went off campus. Everyone was expected to purchase their own uniform (for a cost not to exceed ten dollars), but the dressmaking department stood ready to duplicate the outfits in a cheaper material, if necessary.[14]

During her tenure at Shorter College, Price headed the music department. Although no records remain, based upon school documents, she probably taught music education and instrumental music at all levels, from the elementary to the college level. In addition to playing chapel services each day, she no doubt played organ and piano concerts for the student body and faculty to enrich the cultural life of the college.

* * *

While Florence Beatrice was teaching at Shorter College she lived at home with her parents. In 1909, after over thirty years of practicing dentistry in Little Rock, Dr. Smith retired. Mrs. Smith seems to have left work by then, too, for she is no longer listed in the city directory as the secretary for the International Life and Trust Co., a job that kept her active for many years.

In August of that year, Dr. Smith made out his will. He left his son, Charles W. H., and his daughter, Florence Beatrice, the same amount, $5.00. To his wife, Dr. Smith left all of his remaining property and insurance policies. On April 17, 1910, after three weeks of illness, Dr. Smith died at the age of 67.[15] The rather long obituary for the distinguished man lists his many accomplishments, including his pioneering dental work in Chicago and Little Rock (he was the first black dentist to practice in both cities), and his reknown as an artist, inventor, and author. A history buff and an authority on the Civil War, Dr. Smith was working on a second novel, *Black Mammies of the South*, at the time of his death.

Dr. Smith was given a rather large funeral by his wife, who spared no expense in burying her husband. There were plenty of flowers, and she ordered an extra five dozen chairs and a couch for the church. After the service, his hearse was pulled by five horses; he was laid to rest in a fraternal cemetery on Willow Ave.[16]

Curiously, the obituary and all of the probate records list Mrs. Smith and Florence Beatrice as his only survivors; no mention is made of his son, Charles. The probate records list Dr. Smith's last residence as "unknown" although the local newspapers establish his home at 3420 High St. Apparently, Dr. and Mrs. Smith moved from their large home on Broadway to a smaller residence in their retirement years.

For the year that it took to settle all of their business, Mrs. Smith lived at 1315 Gaines St. She went about the business of settling her husband's estate fairly quickly. Dr. Smith's probate records reveal an interesting financial situation for him and his wife. It appears that at the time of Smith's death he was deeply in debt, owing creditor after creditor. The papers also show that he had little cash (which explains why he left his children so little money), and he owned almost nothing except his dental equipment and his beloved books.

With little personal property of his to dispose of, there were few complications. The biggest hassle seems to have been the numerous claims against the estate. One debt for $122.25 owed to Dr. William LaPorte was paid by selling what little personal property Dr. Smith did have. His bookcase, books, including the *Encyclopedia Britannica* and dental books, and dental equipment valued at about $50.00 were all sold to Dr. LaPorte for $135.00 cash. Of the approximately $1000.00 of remaining claims, only about $50.00 was allowed by his wife to be paid. Other claims, including $8.00 owed to his patient Fannie Dale, the balance due to her on a set of lower teeth, and $95.07 owed to Dr. M. W. Patric, a Rochester, New York, machinist, for materials sold to Dr. Smith to make a pea sheller, were disallowed and apparently never paid. Two other claims, which appear to be money borrowed by Dr. Smith (for $700.00 and $152.20) for personal reasons were laid aside by Mrs. Smith for further investigation.

With her son gone, her daughter gainfully employed at Shorter College, and the continuing racial atrocities in Little Rock, Mrs. Smith decided to leave the South and return to her hometown, Indianapolis. Florence Irene Smith could take no more of Little Rock. She could take no more of being Negro, and worse, a southern Negro. Yes, Florence Irene Smith, knowing she could pass for white, decided she would do just that. She would destroy all evidence of her Negro life with her Negro husband in Little Rock, return to Indianapolis, and pass for white forever. Many years later, her granddaughter explained, "My grandmother destroyed many pictures and valuable data because she didn't want to be connected with her life in Little Rock after my grandfather died. Her family was white. She decided to go to the other side."[17]

Once Dr. Smith's few personal belongings were discarded, Florence Irene went about selling all of her own personal items and the considerable Little Rock property that she had acquired. First, in February 1911, she sold back to George Heard for $4000 a house that she bought from him exactly one year earlier for the same amount. The next month she gave away to the Southern Trust Co. several lots of land for $1.00. All that was left now were the contents of her once elegant home. With the legal help of Thomas J. Price, she sold off everything to Benjamin Jefferson for $250.00. All of the furniture, carpeting, the piano, cooking utensils, dishes—everything was sold! She wanted to leave absolutely no trace of her existence in Little Rock. With her entire household sold on March 15, 1911, Florence Irene Smith left Little Rock for good—and she never looked back.

There is no extant evidence regarding Price's feelings during this time. Surely, she felt a tremendous loss in the death of her father, a role model from childhood. Dr. Smith was her spiritual, moral, and familial anchor (mentor) and his death must have affected her dramatically.

She lost her mother, too, physically and spiritually. Although Price probably understood her mother's need to leave Little Rock and "pass," there must have been an emotional conflict within Price herself. Did she feel relieved that she no longer had to contend with her mother's racial ambiguities or was she resentful that her mother did not have the courage and moral fortitude to remain in Little Rock as a black person? We do not have the answers to these questions, but the resulting decision left Florence Beatrice alone, without a home and without a family.

In many ways, this must have been a time of soul-searching for her. No longer would she be in the shadow of her parents. All of her family ties were gone, even her brother, who was presumably already passing in the white world. These emotional experiences would give her strength. It was now time to discover her own identity. Who was Florence Beatrice Smith and what did she want to do with her life? The answers to these questions would evolve, through her music, over the next twenty years.

6 Clark University and Marriage

Probably needing to put Little Rock behind her for a while, Florence Beatrice, at age 23, decided to leave her hometown in September 1910, five months after her father died. She accepted a prestigious teaching position as Head of the Music Department at Clark University in Atlanta.[1] Florence Beatrice was a single woman striking out on her own. Her mother was fiercely independent; now, she would be also. For a time, she would satisfy the urge within herself to pursue a high-powered career.

Although Florence Beatrice was eager to meet the challenge that awaited her, getting to Atlanta by train would be arduous. One of the most insidious acts of race discrimination was the treatment of blacks on the railroad. Dr. Smith's prediction of unequal treatment of blacks on public transportation systems after the institution of Jim Crow laws was an understatement. The hostile environment created by white ticket agents at the train station was nothing less than appalling. After waiting for what probably seemed like an eternity (the white passengers were waited on first), blacks were met by salespeople with rudeness and condescension. They often cheated black customers, confused the illiterate, or charged them higher prices for their tickets.

Getting comfortable in the noisy, small, dirty, and smelly accommodations for the long trip to Atlanta was impossible. A professional woman of Florence's social standing must have barely tolerated the degrading conditions. W. E. B. Du Bois, in his autobiography, provides a vivid description of this human abasement. He writes:

> The "Jim-crow" car is up next to the baggage car and engine. The train stops out beyond the covering in the rain or sun or dust. Usually there is no step to help one climb on, and often the car is a smoker cut in two and you must pass through

the white smokers and then they pass through your part with swagger and noise and stares. Your apartment is a half or a quarter or an eighth of the oldest car in service on the road. Unless it happens to be a through express, the old plush is caked with dirt, the floor is gummy and the windows dirty.

The white train crew from the baggage car uses the "Jim-crow" to lounge in and perform their toilet. The conductor appropriates two seats for himself and his papers and yells gruffly for your tickets before the train has scarcely started. It is best not to ask him for information even in the gentlest tones. His information is for whites chiefly. . . . Toilet rooms are often filthy. If you have to change cars be wary of junctions which are usually without accommodation and filled with quarrelsome whites who hate a "darky dressed up."[2]

Du Bois was preparing to leave Atlanta just about the time Florence Beatrice arrived there. He taught at Atlanta University and for thirteen years (1897–1910) was involved in a series of sociological studies that "formed a current encyclopedia on American Negro problems."[3] The legal proscriptions for blacks in Atlanta in 1910 were not unlike those in Little Rock. Blacks could not vote since the establishment of the "white primary." There was limited access to all public facilities—restaurants, parks, museums; "open to the public" and "white only" were almost synonymous. Du Bois explained:

I stayed on the campus as much as possible. My contact with the surrounding white city was limited to some necessary shopping. I did not vote since the "white primary," which was the real election, was closed to me. I did not enter parks or museums. I assumed that when the public was invited to any place or function, either the white people were meant, or, if not, attendance of Negroes meant segregated parts or times. Once I remonstrated with a colored teacher of literature for attending the "Jim-crow" section of a theater in the top balcony. She answered: "Where else can I see Shakespeare? I cannot afford to go to New York."[4]

Once Price arrived in Atlanta, she surely welcomed the safe haven of Clark University's campus. Clark welcomed Florence Beatrice with open arms. At a time when most black colleges had more white teachers than black teachers, Clark considered itself privileged to have such a well-educated Negro woman on its faculty.[5]

When she arrived at Clark, she found the academic situation to be very similar to that at Shorter College. The aim of the University was threefold—"to lift the cultural level of the [Negro] masses," to motivate the students to the highest possible personal achievement, and to perform community service.[6] The school offered courses at all levels. The Grammar School Course enrolled the largest number of students. The Normal course, established to train teachers, was the equivalent of a four-year high school program. The College Preparatory Course, also a four-year program, was a liberal arts program designed to prepare students for college work. The full College Course enrolled the fewest students and led to the Bachelor of Arts degree.[7] Students interested in the ministry were trained at the Theological School, which later became Gammon Theological Seminary.

In addition, there was an Industrial Department and agricultural training. The agricultural program was one of the most important departments of the University. Corn, cotton, cabbage, okra, sweet potatoes, and white potatoes were cultivated by the students on 120 acres of land, and cows, hogs, and poultry were bred on the 300 acres of wooded pastures.[8] The development of successful farming to improve the economic strength of the community was important at a time when much of the Negro population in the South lived in rural areas. In addition to supplying food for the dining hall, training students as agricultural workers, and aiding farmers in the state, farming provided work for the students to pay for the expenses of school. In 1909, the students earned eight cents per hour. The emphasis on self-help was also an important part of the philosophy of the Industrial Department, which included carpentry, blacksmithing, printing, housekeeping, sewing, and dressmaking. In 1911–1912, Clark University enrolled 479 students, an increase of 72 students from the previous academic year. Of that number, 40 students took music classes.[9]

In addition to providing a sound academic and industrial program for the students, the faculty and administrators of the University felt strongly about their cultural life. Many of the students attending Clark came from rural areas where their home and community life was very simple. A program of rhetoric, which was held once a week in the chapel, was established to provide an opportunity for students to hear and recite the works of classic authors, poets, and playwrights.[10]

The music department was an integral part of the rhetorical program. As head of the music department, Price's appointment as composer, artist-in-residence, and music teacher was critical to the cultural life of the University. Under her direction, the students performed the great piano works of Beethoven, Mozart, Chopin, and Brahms, and vocal performances of ballads and parlor music and operatic arias were common. She regularly gave organ and piano recitals and she brought nationally recognized artists to the campus to give concerts. Through these artists the students learned not only to appreciate the European concert repertoire, but they also gained an appreciation for music by members of their own race.[11]

Students at Clark University were hearing a wide variety of music by the most prominent Negro artists of the day. Performances included those by concert singers Emma Azalia Hackley (1867–1922), Anita Patti Brown (ca. 1870–ca. 1950), and Florence Cole Talbert (1890–1961), who performed throughout the nation and in Europe); instrumentalists such as Joseph Douglass (1871–1935) and Clarence Cameron White (1880–1960), who were the two leading black concert violinists; Carl Diton (1886–1962), the first Negro pianist to make a transcontinental tour; and Hazel Harrison (1883–1969), an enviable concert pianist, who was known internationally. The students at Clark University heard the finest music, including arrangements of spirituals and instrumental music by Negro composers. The performers, particularly the instrumentalists, locked out of most concert halls because of their race, benefited, too, because it provided them with an opportunity to perform.

The students lived vicariously through these artists who continued to survive and thrive in spite of the difficulties they faced. Later in their careers, many of these performers became teachers and served as mentors for young instrumentalists and singers, often providing scholarships to aspiring musicians. Most important, they instilled pride in their Negro audiences by insisting that the roots of Negro music would not be forgotten. The students at Clark University embraced the music of Negro composers with enthusiasm. Like their sister institutions, the school choir traveled extensively, publicizing the school and popularizing Negro spirituals. Through the music program, under Florence Smith's direction, the students developed their talents, and their cultural awareness was extended from the campus into the community.

Price became friends with many musicians in Atlanta during her tenure at Clark. One musician, Kemper Harreld (1885–1971), an established educator, accomplished pianist, and concert violinist, was brought to Atlanta in 1911 by Atlanta Baptist College (now Morehouse College) President John Hope to establish the music department. At the college, Harreld established the orchestra and string quartets, and led the Glee Club to become a nationally respected ensemble. Price and Harreld maintained their friendship long after she left Atlanta. She occasionally saw him when his choir performed in Chicago, and they appear to have corresponded with each other through the 1940s.

* * *

While Florence Beatrice was teaching at Clark and furthering her professional career in Atlanta, she was thinking about a young, handsome attorney, Thomas Jewell Price, whom she met while she was still teaching at Shorter College. Already a distinguished lawyer in Washington, D.C., Price had arrived in Little Rock in 1908.[12] It is no coincidence that Price and the Smith family became friends. Dr. Smith's reputation was well known (his accomplishments were reported in the black newspapers nationwide), and their home was always open to new residents of Little Rock's professional community. Also, given Mrs. Smith's business dealings, procuring a good lawyer was of utmost importance to her. It was Thomas Price who helped her sell her household goods in March 1911 before she left for Indianapolis.

Price was born in New Haven, Connecticut, April 2, 1884, to Eugene B. and Caroline Roberts Price.[13] After graduating from Hillhouse High School (1902),

Price left Connecticut, for Howard University in Washington, D.C., where he received his law degree in 1906. While attending Howard, Price began clerking for the distinguished black judge Robert H. Terrell (1904–1907).

The son of Harrison Terrell, Judge Robert Terrell was from one of the leading black families in Washington.[14] Appointed to the municipal judgeship by Theodore Roosevelt, he held a number of positions in the federal government. In 1891, Robert Terrell married Mary Church, who was to become equally well-known and respected. Mary Terrell was one of the foremost spokespeople for black women's rights, organizing the National Colored Women's League in 1892 and, in 1901, becoming the first president of the National Association of Colored Women's Clubs of America.

Robert and Mary Terrell's circle of friends included the most prominent blacks in Washington and many well-known, and influential, white persons. Thomas Price took advantage of the opportunity to socialize with Washington's "aristocrats of color." The group included only those who had graduated from the best colleges and who were culturally sophisticated, that is, they "cultivated a taste for good music" and had "a deep interest in the questions of the day," including discussions of race. In describing Washington's black elite, poet Paul Laurence Dunbar, who lived next door to the Terrells, put it this way: "'The social life of the Negro' was more sophisticated than in any other city in the country, and could no longer be 'laughed at or caricatured under the name of *colored sassiety*.' Further, he cautioned the outsider to observe the strict class lines explaining that one would no more gain admission to the 'black 400' without 'a perfect knowledge of his standing in his own community than would Mrs. Bradley Martin's butler to an Astor ball.'"[15]

Price's hard work and the connections he made through Terrell paid off. After passing the bar exam, he earned a special certification to try cases in the U.S. Supreme Court and in the U.S. Circuit Court of Appeals in the 7th and 8th districts of Washington, D.C. In 1908, he moved to Little Rock to join the law firm of Scipio Africanus Jones, the city's most prominent black lawyer. From 1908–1921, Price and Jones were partners, establishing one of the most powerful and lucrative law firms in the city. Their office was located downtown at 402 W. Markham.

Born a slave on the farm of Dr. Sanford Reamey at Tulip, Arkansas, during the Civil War (ca. 1863), Scipio Africanus Jones had moved to Little Rock around 1881 to attend the Philander Smith College and study teacher education at Shorter College. Since there was no law school available to a black student, Jones studied law in his spare time as an apprentice in a white law firm. Thirty years after Jones passed the Arkansas bar exam, he argued and successfully won, with the help of his partner, Thomas Price, one of Arkansas' best known cases: the Elaine Race Riot case of 1919. In this case, which was typical of the rising racial tension in Arkansas and throughout the South, the prosecutors had charged only a group of blacks with murder in the aftermath of a riot in which both blacks and whites were killed. Jones successfully argued the case through the Arkansas courts to the Supreme Court in 1923. Remarkably, the court ruled in favor of Jones's clients. Jones continued to emerge as a state leader in Arkansas politics in many unsuccessful efforts to repeal Jim Crow Laws and unseat the "Lily Whites" who were excluding blacks from all positions of power in the state.[16]

Price and Jones were involved in real estate as well. From 1908 to 1911 Price was a stockholder in Jones's Arkansas Realty and Investment Company, and together with his law practice, he earned a comfortable standard of living. By 1921, Thomas Price opened his own law office at 906 Broadway, right next door to 904 Broadway, the office of his colleague, Scipio Africanus Jones. Price remained at this office until he left Little Rock in 1928.

During the summer of 1912, Florence Beatrice returned to Little Rock to marry this successful young lawyer. They were married by a justice of the peace, September 9, 1912.[17] For a year, the couple lived at 1904 Cross St.; in September 1913, they moved to a lovely home at 2417 Cross. The house was located near Dunbar High School in a middle-class, predominantly black neighborhood. Price's neighbors were also professionals, many of whom taught at the high school.

After they married, Thomas and Florence Price probably never considered settling anywhere other than Little Rock. Despite the collapse of Reconstruction, the institution of Jim Crow laws and the rise of violence toward blacks, Little Rock was considered a good place to be for upwardly mobile blacks. Little Rock's middle-class blacks had changed little since its emergence in the late 19th century. Education, wealth, and respectability remained the foremost criteria for membership in the "aristocrats of color." As in Reconstruction days, their cultural life centered around literary and musical activities, the black institutions of higher learning, and the church.[18]

The heart of the city was Ninth Street. It was here that the offices of most blacks—physicians, lawyers, businessmen, could be found. Blacks ventured to Ninth St. to find everything from "medical services and spiritual nourishment to Saturday night entertainment." Ninth St. was referred to as "the Line," because it was here that black and white Little Rock were separated.[19] Mrs. Judith Finn, one of Price's former students, remembers the street this way:

> [It was] a busy, busy street on every corner. People who were shopping on Main Street, especially men, and people who came from the Rock Island Station in the East End would walk to Main Street and stay awhile. Then they would continue around the corner, Ninth and Main on down to . . . Ninth and Arch. And they would congregate there in groups and they would always have a lot of fun. . . . It was a nice and exciting place on Sundays. After church everybody was going to the drug store getting ice cream, sitting down. As I say, that's where you intermingled and met other children.

> One of the centers of activities along the Ninth St. corridor was the Mosaic Templars building. Many professional offices were located in the building, including many of the city's black doctors, and there was an auditorium where dances were held. In the 1930s all of the famed big jazz bands came to play there including Cab Calloway and Louis Armstrong.[20]

By all accounts, Florence Price and her husband were active in Little Rock's black community. In addition to teaching, Price was president and director of the Little Rock Club of Musicians, an organization that sponsored musical programs for the community.

Thomas Price was a much sought-after lawyer. In 1914, he was elected to serve as an alternate delegate to the Pulaski County Negro Republican Convention, one of the two segregated conventions (one black and one white) held that year in Little Rock.[21] He was also legal advisor to several black organizations and fraternal groups, including the Supreme Royal Circle of Friends of the World (from 1917), Knights of Pythias (1924–1928), Arkansas Supreme Liberty Life Insurance Co. (1924–1928), and the Arkansas Standard Life Insurance Co. (1918–1928). Perhaps one of Price's most important positions was as attorney to the Mosaic Templars, an international benevolent organization for Negroes. It was founded in Little Rock by John E. Bush, and its headquarters was based there. Price was also a District Grand Secretary for the Odd Fellows and a Grand Chancellor for the Knights of Pythias.

The Prices started a family soon after they were married. Their firstborn child was a son, Thomas Jr., whom Florence Beatrice always called Tommy. Price was proud of her son and she immediately set her feelings to pen in a poignant art song, "To My Little Son," for voice and piano. The lyrics, by Julia Johnson Davis, vividly capture a mother's love for her son and the bond that exists between them:

> In your face I sometimes see
> Shadowings of the man to be
> And eager—dream of what my son shall be,
> Dream of what my son will be in twenty years and one
> When you are to manhood grown
> And all your manhood ways are known,
> Then shall I, wistful try to trace
> The child you once were in your face

Price uses romantic harmonies to set the two-verse ballad in which she indulges in word painting as the mother gazes into her young child's face dreaming of his future. In the opening measures, Price uses arpeggiated seventh chords at deceptive cadences to create an impressionistic, dreamlike flavor. In the second stanza, a short chromatic passage captures a nostalgic moment in "Then shall

I, wistful try to trace" before leading the listener back to the gentle moment of the beginning of the poem.

Unfortunately, Price never had a chance to experience the sentiments expressed in this poem. She suffered one of her greatest personal tragedies early on in her marriage when her son died while an infant. Although there is no date on this manuscript, "To My Little Son" is probably one of Price's first surviving art songs. (See example 2.)

Example 2. To My Little Son, mm. 1–12

The Prices had two other children. Their daughter, Florence Louise, was born July 6, 1917, and a second daughter, Edith Cassandra, was born March 29, 1921.[22] After the children were born, Perry Quinney (later Johnston) moved in with the Price family and took care of the girls. Quinney was attending Arkansas Baptist College, not far from the Price home, and she needed a place to live. Having a caretaker to help with her children gave Price some time to teach, compose, and be active in outside musical activities. It was not long before Perry Quinney and Price became the best of friends—a friendship that was to last a lifetime.

When she married, Price abandoned her college teaching career and, like many women, she stayed home to raise her children. In her spare time, she taught private lessons in her home, both piano and violin. Quickly, Price became one of black Little Rock's most sought-after music teachers. She had a reputation for giving her students a very solid background in piano technique and theory. She was a very firm piano teacher but well-liked. Each of her students was given two half-hour lessons each week in which he or she performed the piano literature and also did exercises in musical transposition (that is writing down a tune in many different keys) in a music writing tablet. They were also expected to keep a notebook to jot down other pertinent information.[23]

Rather than relying solely on the piano method books of others, Price wrote her own "studies" at beginning, intermediate, and advanced levels, each emphasizing a different aspect of piano technique. Many of these pieces have fanciful titles that appeal to the imagination of children; none of the pieces at the elementary level was published. These simple works, numerous in number, include, for example, "Brownies on the Seashore," a study in three sharps (the most advanced key signature in the series) and "Brung, the Bear," which stresses the five-finger hand position and the use of the thumb on the black keys. "The Froggie and the Rabbit" is a study in rhythm, and "Golden Corn Tassles" is an exercise in contrasts between legato and staccato. Other pieces introduce six-eight rhythm, shift of hand position, intervals, or strengthening fingers (the fourth finger of the right hand, for example).

One noteworthy example at the advanced elementary level is "The Old Boatman." This short work is a particularly good example of Price's lyrical writing in which she captures an old man reflecting on his life at sea. Typical of Price's writing, even for children, is that she creates the image of not just any boatman, but a southern boatman. The melody here, stated first by the right hand then by the left, is characteristically pentatonic, betraying its roots in African American folk traditions. The added "blue" notes (for example, the lowered seventh in m. 6) contribute to the nostalgic feeling of the black seaman (see example 3).

Many of Price's intermediate-level pieces feature characteristic African American dance rhythms. "Levee Dance" (Theodore Presser, 1937) and "Ticklin' Toes" from *Three Little Negro Dances* (Theodore Presser, 1933) are typical. Most

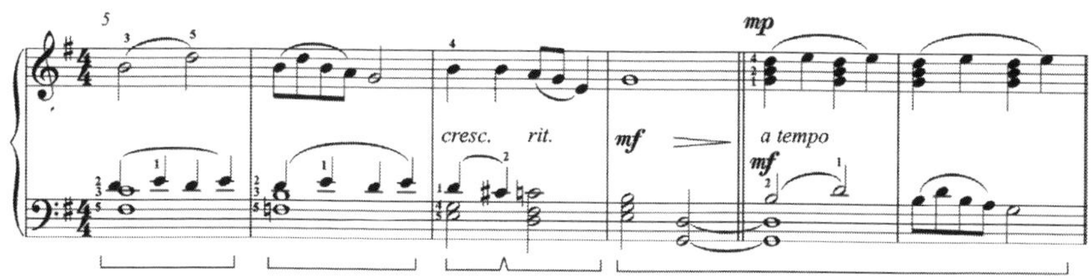

Example 3. The Old Boatman, mm. 5–10

unusual about many of these pieces is Price's use of 4/8 rhythm. This occurs most frequently when the composer is interested in highlighting rhythmic intricacies, usually the juba-dance rhythms with its highly syncopated right hand and steady um-pah pattern in the left hand. Price is interested in authenticity here. By using a 4/8 meter rather than the more common 2/4 meter (particularly for beginning students), she is better able to maintain the stateliness and elegance of the cakewalk (or juba dance) and other characteristic antebellum black folk dances. Further, and most important, the offbeat phrasing in 4/8 contributes to the pronouncement of the rhythmic energy (see example 4).

Price's popular "At the Cotton Gin" (G. Schirmer, 1928), a work for a late intermediate player, requires the pianist to negotiate both straight rhythms and syncopated patterns, a wider range of the keyboard (about 4–1/2 octaves), key changes (A-flat major to E major and back), and harmonically altered triads.

For the advanced student, there are many unpublished piano works, including "Moon behind a Cloud," "Flame," and "Placid Lake." These works have much in common with Price's large-scale works such as "Dances in the Canebrakes" and the Piano Sonata in E Minor, but they are much shorter (two to five pages typically). Large chords, varied rhythms alternating triplets and sixteenths in succession, grace-note arpeggios, many tempo and dynamic changes, rhythmic figures shared between the hands, and extended chromatic chordal passages are all common features.

Among Price's many students, Solar Carethers became a successful school teacher. Price was a major influence on Carethers and they would become close friends. Another of her students, Lucius Sterling Todd, became a professional pianist, arranger, and orchestra leader. He formed the famed Rose City

Example 4. "Ticklin' Toes" from Three Negro Dances, m. 1–4

Orchestra, which played in Little Rock from 1913 to 1919. The orchestra went on to play throughout the country and established itself at the Savoy Hotel in Chicago.[24]

Price continued to work on her composing and soon began to receive outside monetary support to encourage her work. Throughout the 1920s, foundations began to support black composers and performers with awards and fellowships. The Rockefeller and Rosenwald Fellowships were primarily offered to performers. In 1925, Casper Holstein, a black businessman from New York, began to offer prize money to composers through the black periodical *Opportunity*. Other important fellowships that were established included the Harmon Foundation Awards for composition and performance and the Rodman Wanamaker Musical Composition Contest, established in 1927, offering prizes in several categories: songs, choral works, symphonic works, and solo instrumental pieces.[25]

Price entered several of her small-scale piano compositions into these competitions. Using the southern landscape as her inspiration, Price composed *In the Land O' Cotton* for piano, which tied for second prize with Edmund Jenkins's Cello Sonata in A Minor in *Opportunity* magazine's Holstein prize in May 1926.[26] Judges for these competitions included performers, educators, and composers of international stature. For this contest, Frank Damrosch, founder of the Institute of Musical Art (later Juilliard School of Music), and R. Nathaniel Dett, the noted Negro pianist, composer, arranger, and educator were among the judges.

In 1927, Price was again awarded second prize in the same contest for *Memories of Dixieland* for piano.[27] The *Opportunity* article citing the award noted that both of her parents were deceased and that her daughters, Florence and Edith, now ages 10 and 6, respectively, took after their mother and were actively involved in music. In the same year, her husband entered her piano piece, *At the Cotton Gin, a Southern Sketch*, in a contest, without her knowledge, and Price won not only cash but its publication by G. Schirmer.[28]

Price continued to pursue composition and began to contact publishers. In 1926, she corresponded with The Arthur P. Schmidt Co. in Boston, on her husband's law office letterhead, about publishing her newest composition, "Impromptu" for piano.[29] The first letter from Price, dated June 25, 1926, is a simple note attached to her submission of the score. The second letter dated September 17, 1926, reads:

> Gentlemen;- About eight weeks ago a musical composition for piano entitled "Impromptu" was mailed to you for examination with return postage enclosed. As I have received no word from you, I am wondering if the manuscript has been inadvertently overlooked or perhaps its examination delayed.
>
> Yours every truly, (Mrs.) Florence B. Price

The Schmidt Co. responded on September 20, 1926. They acknowledged receipt of her manuscript and told her that the editor would consider it upon his return from Europe. On September 24, 1926, Price eagerly replied that she would await the editor's response to her work.

The reason for Price's persistent contact with Schmidt is clear. Schmidt was the first publisher to specialize in art music of American musicians, issuing teaching pieces for instrumentalists, art music for the well-trained amateur and professionals, and church music. And most important, as women composers struggled to gain recognition, Schmidt's catalogue, which included 12 percent women composers between 1876–1958, was not overlooked.[30] Although there were many reasons to hope that Schmidt would publish some of her music, she was disappointed ultimately. In a letter dated November 6, 1926, Schmidt declined to publish "Impromptu." The letter from Schmidt to Price is not extant; however, they marked her letter of June 25 with the notation "I 11–6–26," their shorthand for "sent form-letter #1 [the rejection letter] November 6, 1926."[31]

Serious about improving her craft as a composer, Price spent the summers of 1926 and 1927 in Chicago studying composition, harmony, and orchestration at the Chicago Musical College.[32] She, like hundreds of black musicians from the South, enrolled in one of Chicago's many music schools for summer study. The Chicago Musical College, for the most ambitious and talented, meant professional contacts and associations that could further the success of one's career.

The Chicago Musical College had an internationally known faculty. Price studied composition with Carl Busch and Wesley La Violette and harmony and orchestration with La Violette. She also did some additional work in composition with Arthur Olaf Anderson. And, perhaps contemplating the possible financial necessity of a career in public school music, she took a course in Public School Music Methods. Arnold Volpe, the distinguished Russian-born conductor, violinist, and composer, had just been hired by the faculty to teach counterpoint and composition, and Price was probably introduced to his music as well.

It is evident from her frequent trips to Chicago that Price anticipated leaving Little Rock as early as 1926. Apparently, financial difficulties were beginning at home. Price probably did not make much money as a piano teacher, and it appears that by the late 1920s her husband's law firm was also not doing well. Her student Mrs. Finn reports,

> I saw Mr. Price in the home before he went to work in the mornings. He was a lawyer and . . . I was thinking also how softly she would speak to him about leaving home and going down to see about his work. 'Cause I had been in other peoples homes when their husbands and wives would [be] talking together [and] it was much harsher. But she said so sweetly what she said to him. And she was stern

with that. She meant for him to get out there and find something to do. Lawyers weren't making money then.[33]

To make matters worse, the racial tension in Little Rock was becoming ever more intolerable through the late 1920s. Racism even dampened the professional aspirations of Florence Beatrice. When Price applied to the Arkansas Music Teachers Association, in spite of her impeccable academic and teaching credentials, she was denied admission because of her color.[34]

Through the 1920s, Little Rock became ever more dismal and frightening. Like all southern states, Negroes continued to be disenfranchised, oppressive codes of conduct replaced the familiar slave codes, segregation became law, and racial violence was on the increase.

The Negro newspapers repeatedly carried stories of racial atrocities. In 1927, Mrs. Fannie Watts, owner of 80 acres of land, was forced to leave the state because she refused to sign over her property to whites.[35] Young black men were particularly vulnerable. The *Cleveland Gazette* reported a typical situation on September 10 of that year. "The innocent, Winston Pounds Jr., age 23, who was employed on the woman's farm, was lynched by a Kluxer mob, last week Thursday night, near here after a report had been circulated that the woman (white) had been frightened by a prowler who entered her bedroom window and whom the woman said looked like a 'Negro.'"[36]

Lynching persisted even in middle-class neighborhoods of prominent blacks such as the one that the Price family lived in. One of the most heinous incidents was the lynching in front of the prominent Bethel A.M.E. church in 1927 of a black man, John Carter, soaked in gasoline and burned in public as a means of not only punishing Carter but also of controlling the black community. Blacks were outraged by the incident and the black press was very outspoken in its objections. The *Cleveland Gazette* used this headline for the May 14 article detailing the situation: "Mob Lawlessness: That Lynch-Murder and Burning at the Stake in Arkansas, Last Week, Inexcusable in a Civilized Country—Fear." The article explains:

> It is sickening to read of such an incident as occurred in Little Rock on Wednesday. You cannot reconcile the idea of lynching a Negro and then burning his gasoline-soaked body in public with the principles and standards that are supposed to prevail in this country. Admitting that he assaulted a white woman and that this is one of the most offensive crimes conceivable, the lawless manner of his execution is still more offensive. It is to be hoped that the grand jury which indicted him, and which warned [the] people of Little Rock that it was prepared to investigate and punish mob violence will do its duty. Lawlessness on the part of white people never was and never will be an effective remedy for lawlessness on the part of colored people.[37]

The article then goes on to say that Mayor Moyer and Acting Mayor Alderman Bilheimer, who could have prevented or ultimately stopped the lynching, chose not to order police interference while Carter was being burned, explaining that the [white] "mob was in no humor for argument."

Without the assurance of police protection, the black community had nowhere to turn. It was, appropriately, both angry and fearful. Mrs. Finn described the community feelings this way:

> It was like a very scary day and everybody was in the house. . . . And everything was quiet and seem like a gloomy afternoon. I can always remember that. Whenever it seem like trouble; our parents kept us inside. But I did hear about the man hanging up there on the corner which cause many a prominent citizen to pack up and leave. . . . They got together and it seem that all of them left.[38]

The Prices had good reason, like so many other Arkansas blacks, to fear for their lives. In late 1927, a young white child was allegedly killed by a black man. The white community was out for blood with a vengeance—black blood. Whites wanted to retaliate by killing a "comparable" black child, that is, they wanted to murder the child of a prominent black Little Rock family. The apparent victim was to be Florence Price's youngest daughter, Florence Louise. Given that the Price family was one of the most influential black families in Little Rock (and Price's parents before her), they were an easy target. With no hope that the police would intervene and give them protection, Florence Price and her two daughters fled to Chicago for safety; they were followed a few months later by her husband.[39]

For black citizens, Little Rock had become a shadow of its former self and the Price family could tolerate no more. By moving to Chicago from the South, the Price family followed the path of hundreds of Negroes from the turn of the century through the three decades after World War I. For most Negroes, the impetus behind this mass migration was basically economic. Chicago was considered by many to be a land of opportunity and Negroes wanted to escape from a section of the country where freedom and equal opportunity were denied them. Chicago surely had more to offer the Price family. And Price did, indeed, prosper in Chicago. Her career aspirations would be fulfilled, for it was here that she would establish herself nationally as a concert pianist and organist, teacher, and composer.

11

The "Dean" of Negro Composers of the Midwest

7 VeeJay and the Black Metropolis

In the first years of the twentieth century, large numbers of blacks moved from the South to the nation's northern cities, forced out by the changing system of southern agriculture and the brutality of southern racial prejudice. Chicago gained from the great migration of Negroes who came to the city from 1914–1918 to fill the war industries' labor needs.

Chicago, like Harlem, was seen as the land of opportunity where the hopes and dreams of Negroes could be fulfilled and where their achievements would be recognized by the world. And, as Chicago became more cosmopolitan with its influx of creative, self-assured, and sophisticated Negroes, the city became more appealing to others who wanted to venture north. 1924 to 1929 were prosperous years in the Negro community. By 1930, the Great Black Migration had produced a broad base of over 75,000 Negro workers, creating the so-called Black Belt. From it rose a professional and business class that was stable and prosperous.[1]

When Price and her family arrived in Chicago by 1928, they found a vibrant and culturally rich African American community. Negroes were thriving in all of the arts—literature, poetry, dance, theater, the visual arts, and especially music. By now Chicagoans were cultivating every genre of black music and the city prided itself on its diverse musical heritage. Vaudeville, jazz, blues, gospel, and concert music could be heard everywhere—in churches, concert halls, black-owned theaters, and the stage.

The Pekin Theater, the first black-owned theater in the country, was one of the centers of musical activity in the city during its short-lived existence (1905–1916). Robert T. Motts, the proprietor and manager, "realized a life long ambition to give the members of his race a strictly high class place of amusement, where they may go and be entertained by the leaders in the profession of their race."[2]

Motts brought a variety of the finest in black entertainment to Chicago to perform at his theater. Under the musical direction of jazz pianist and composer Joe Jordan, the programs at the Pekin theater changed weekly ranging from vaudeville and musical theater to classical music. With Flournoy Miller and Aubrey Lyles who were later to write the script of *Shuffle Along*, Jordan wrote the theater's first musical, *The Man from Bam* (1906), which featured Miller and Lyles in the leading roles. Audiences heard the diva Sissieretta Jones ("Black Patti"), the famed vaudeville team of George Walker and Bert Williams, and songwriters Bob Cole and J. Rosamond Johnson. One especially well-attended concert on 4 December 1906 featured the music of the Anglo-African composer Samuel Coleridge-Taylor who was making his second American conducting tour. For this concert, the performers included Coleridge-Taylor, Harry Burleigh, Will H. Tyers, Will Marion Cook, and Joe Jordan with the Pekin Orchestra.

By the 1920s, Chicago had become the center of the jazz world. Black jazz musicians first began arriving in the city in 1893, attracted by the World Columbian Exposition. It was here that Scott Joplin, W. C. Handy, Arthur Marshall, and Louis Chauvin had an opportunity to hear each other play that hot new music—ragtime. The metamorphosis from ragtime to jazz was made soon after with the arrival in the city of Jelly Roll Morton. In 1905 Morton collaborated with Joplin and Porter King on the celebrated "King Porter Stomp," now a jazz standard. The tune became well-known when it was recorded in 1924 by Joe "King" Oliver, who moved to Chicago from New Orleans in 1918. Oliver's acclaimed Creole Jazz Band, boasting some of the best musicians from New Orleans, including Baby Dodds and Louis Armstrong, was considered to be the most important exponent of New Orleans–style jazz, attracting hundreds to the Lincoln Gardens to hear them play.

Chicago was jumping with jazz clubs and black entertainment venues by the late 1920s, all located around State Street between 31st and 35th Streets.[3] "The Stroll," as the area was known to the black community, featured an abundance of theaters, cabarets, and dance halls.[4] By the time the Prices arrived in the city, the Grand Theater, a vaudeville house seating 1000, had become notable for hosting some of the biggest names in jazz and blues, including Bessie Smith, Ethel Waters, and Cab Calloway. The Vendome Theater, across the street from the Grand, employed Erskine Tate's fifteen-piece Symphony Orchestra from 1918–1928 which played for dances and stage shows. In 1925, Louis Armstrong, having returned to Chicago after playing with Fletcher Henderson in New York, joined Tate's band as star soloist. Nearby, at the Dreamland Cafe, pianist Lil Hardin Armstrong led a band from 1925–1926, which included her husband, Louis.

By early 1928, the jazz scene had shifted to 47th and South Parkway with over ten black jazz bands and orchestras. The elegant Savoy Ballroom, which could accommodate 4000 dancers, opened in November 1927, featuring Charles Elgar's eighteen-piece orchestra and Clarence Black's fourteen-piece band with strings. In 1928, the 3500-seat Regal Theater, featuring talking pictures and stage shows, opened next door to the Savoy with two large bands—Fess Williams and Dave Peyton. That same year, the Grand Terrace Cafe became home to the Earl Hines Orchestra, one of Chicago's hottest jazz bands.

Chicago also became the blues capital of the urban North, home to itinerant Mississippi Delta bluesmen. They came in search of work in the city's steel mills, stockyards, and packing plants, hoping for recording opportunities with such companies as Paramount, Okeh, Columbia, and Vocalion. Tampa Red, Big Maceo, Big Bill Broonzy, Sonny Boy Williamson, and "Georgia Tom" Dorsey all came north and "citified the country blues."[5] It was in the 1920s and 1930s that blues piano, or boogie-woogie, was developed into an art form, performed in the Black Belt's rent parties by Jimmy Yancey, Meade Lux Lewis, Albert Ammons, Pine Top Smith, and others.

In the 1920s and '30s, Chicago—the birthplace of gospel—saw the composition and publication of its first gospel songs, known as "Dorsey songs," named for the former bluesman and later gospel pianist and songwriter. Thomas A. Dorsey, the Father of Gospel Music, settled in Chicago in 1916 where he began his long career writing over 1000 songs and publishing well over half of them. In 1932, after Dorsey's wife and child died, he penned his most well-known song, "Precious Lord Take My Hand." By the early 1930s, Chicago had become the citadel of the genre. In 1932, Dorsey and Sallie Martin established the National Convention of Gospel Choirs and Choruses, which first met in the Pilgrim Baptist Church. The new music had gained momentum from the 1920s to the extent that, by the time of its first convention, the 3000-seat church was filled to capacity. Gospel music had appeared in black communities at the right time. The Depression hit poor people especially hard and the optimistic, hope-filled lyrics of gospel eased the pain and lessened the burdens.

Much overlooked in writings on the music of Chicago from this period is the rich and vibrant world of concert music, which the black community began to cultivate from as early as the late 1800s.[6] The first "All Colored Composers Concerts" were organized in 1913 by Mr. William Henry Hackney to expose the community to a variety of music and literature written and performed by Negro artists. The aim of the programs was "to exploit the creative talents of the Negro, so that when the music of the country, known as American music, has reached a high plane of development, the Negro can show that he has had a part in its making, and his startling originality will be made more manifest."[7]

The Second Annual All-Colored Composers Concert held at Orchestral Hall April 1, 1915, was characteristically eclectic. It featured the popular vocal music of J. Rosamond Johnson, Will Marion Cook, and Samuel Coleridge-Taylor, and art songs and spiritual selections of Harry T. Burleigh and Coleridge-Taylor. These songs were performed by the Umbrian Glee Club, and solos were rendered by tenor Hackney and soprano Maude J. Roberts. Among the composers represented that evening was Nora Lena James. Both Roberts (later George) and James (later Holt) would become influential music critics writing for the *Chicago Defender* and other black newspapers. The featured performer that evening was concert pianist Helen Eugenia Hagen who performed her own Piano Concerto in C Minor in a two-piano version with T. Theodore Taylor. She also performed Coleridge-Taylor's *Transcriptions of Negro Melodies*, op. 59, which included his popular "Bamboula" (African Dance).[8]

Some of Hackney's programs varied to include literary readings and dramatic recitations. In one program on May 28, 1916, Mr. Hackney presented R. Nathaniel Dett, then head of the music department at Hampton Institute, in a recital of his own compositions. Mrs. DeWitt Smith, a Chicago native, then read twelve of Paul Laurence Dunbar's poems "in a manner that held her audience spellbound." On the same program, Hackney sang several art songs and spirituals by Harry T. Burleigh.[9]

Of the variety of classical music offered, choral music performances drew large audiences. The Chicago Umbrian Glee Club, under the direction of organist Walter R. Gossette, was founded in 1895 by Edward Morris at Bethel A.M.E. Church. This male choir was one of the city's prominent concert choirs. They, too, sang a wide variety of music, including spiritual arrangements by Harry T. Burleigh and William Dawson, and classical selections by J. S. Bach, Handel, and Mozart.

The Mundy Choristers, under the direction of James A. Mundy, was organized in August 1929. Mundy began with fifteen members, and at the height of its existence during the early 1930s, the choir grew to about 75 members. Noted for its versatility, the choir sang spirituals, work songs, popular music, and classical music, including selections from opera. They did radio broadcasts and became the official chorus of the 1933–1934 World's Fair Century of Progress Exhibition.

Churches in the city were at the center of much of the black community's musical activity. At least once a month on Sunday afternoons, the Metropolitan Community Center Church, Olivet Baptist Church, Grace Presbyterian, and Bethel A.M.E. Church held musicals where fine talent could be heard. The choir of the Metropolitan Community Center Church, under the direction of Professor J. Wesley Jones, gave special programs on the fourth Sunday evening of each month and, under the sponsorship of the Cadillac Company, they broadcast many of their programs.

The choir of the Olivet Baptist Church, under the direction of composer and organist William Henry Smith, had a membership of 150 persons. This choir, which could sing in several foreign languages including Yiddish, Russian, Italian, Latin, and French, held musicales every third Sunday evening. The group made several radio appearances over WGN and WJJD and toured throughout the Chicago area.

The afternoon programs at many of these churches were quite varied. They regularly featured art songs, arrangements of spirituals, instrumental and chamber music, and church music by black composers. Opera and oratorio arias were standard fare as well. On occasion, members performed entire opera scenes (Verdi was the favored composer), even dressing up in costume and acting out the excerpts for special programs. Samuel Coleridge-Taylor's *Hiawatha's Wedding Feast*, in full performance or in excerpt, was performed on numerous occasions, always receiving an ovation.

None of the musicians for these programs were paid; these musicales became an important part of the training process for black musicians whose performance opportunities were limited. Black churches became the salvation for black performers and composers anxious to hear their own creative work. Simultaneously, it gave black audiences a chance to hear art music.

Shortly after her arrival in Chicago, Price affiliated with Grace Presbyterian Church, founded in 1888 and located at 3600 Vincennes Avenue. The membership of the church in 1936 was 450, a modest size compared with other black denominations in the city. A deeply spiritual person, Price had attended church all of her life and she was glad to have found a church home. When she joined Grace, Price was very familiar with the social proscriptions of this congregation. In Chicago's black churches, a caste system that separated dark-skinned blacks from light-skinned blacks was implicit. Grace was a church that attracted only fair-skinned blacks who were middle-class and well-educated professionals. It could count some influential and wealthy people among its congregation, including Dr. George Cleveland Hall, a noted physician; Judge Albert B. George, the first black judge of the municipal court; and Robert S. Abbot, editor and owner of the *Chicago Defender*. The members were staid in their manners, and they prided themselves on their sophisticated and unemotional participation in the worship service. William Everett Samuels, a lifelong member of Grace Presbyterian, explains:

> It was sophisticated—you know, Presbyterians are a sophisticated sort of people. . . . You go there and listen to a sermon and you never hear an amen or no shouting, or no grunting or groaning[.] [Y]ou just hear an intelligent sermon, and if you like it, alright, and if you don't, alright, and that was it. . . . We used to have service in the morning, but the Sunday School was in the afternoon. . . . I had a little orchestra and we used to play the church hymns for them. . . . It was an all

colored church. Most of the people that went there were yellow. It was prejudiced really. St. Thomas Episcopal and Grace Presbyterian, they were sophisticated. You had to be yellow to be welcome.[10]

The musical offerings at Grace were in marked contrast to many of Chicago's black churches where one could expect to hear the newest gospel tunes by Chicago-based composers Dorsey, Roberta Martin, or Sallie Martin (no relation), among others. T. Theodore Taylor, with whom Price became good friends, played classical organ literature on the large pipe organ each week. In addition to fine music on Sunday morning, it was not unusual for the afternoon programs to begin with a major Bach Prelude and Fugue before the choir rendered a large-scale choral work or selections from several choral masterpieces, including oratorios and operas. Handel, Mendelssohn, Gounod, Brahms, and Wagner were favorite composers. They performed contemporary music, too, including organ and choral music by Price.[11] It would be some time before gospel music, with its secularly influenced rhythms, improvisational structure (requiring embellishment of the melody, harmony, and text) and performance in which the congregation participates in call-and-response fashion, would be accepted into the formal worship services of this, and other, middle-class churches.

Among the most popular events in the city were its choral competitions and music festivals.[12] Some of these events were held in Orchestra Hall where the large auditorium was often filled to capacity with congregants who were eager to hear competing choirs. One of the largest music festivals was held on Easter Sunday 1932 (March 27) and sponsored by the *Chicago Defender* Bud Billiken Club at the Metropolitan Community Church. The highlights of the program included orchestral selections by the Robert Harmony Syncopators, the Metropolitan church choir, and Billiken's 300-voice children's choir. Reportedly, there were thousands in the audience with many more people waiting outside to get in.[13]

Orchestra Hall was also the scene of a great many performances of black college and professional choirs. Hampton, Fisk, Tuskegee, Howard, and the Hall Johnson Choirs, who frequently appeared in the city, all sang there. Highly acclaimed soloists performed there too, including concert violinist Clarence Cameron White and concert pianist Hazel Harrison who were both, for a time, on the faculty of Chicago's National Conservatory of Music.

Chicagoans were equally interested in the musical education of their children. With the black migration, the black community was determined to properly educate its own. Part of the impetus behind this push for education came about between 1904 and 1910 with three visits to this country of Coleridge-Taylor. Recognized as one of England's most accomplished young conductors and composers, Coleridge-Taylor was conductor of the Handel Society in West London (1904–1912) and professor of music at the Trinity College of Music in London (1903–1912). His cantata, *Hiawatha's Wedding Feast* (1898), performed in this country as early as 1900, was in the repertoire of most black church and concert choirs.

Coleridge-Taylor's choral festival appearances and public recitals in the United States had a revolutionary effect on both white musical prejudice and black musical aspiration. For blacks, the results were immediate. Stimulated by his visits, music societies and clubs were formed and named after him to encourage young musicians and to provide them with opportunities for study and performance.

The insistence upon formal study and the demand for trained teachers, conductors, and composers led to the establishment of music schools and conservatories for black Chicagoans. The Coleridge-Taylor Music School, organized by Professor S. I. Lee, opened its doors in 1913, and by 1916 it was actively operating at 36th Place and South State Street, with some of the most prominent Negro teachers in Chicago on its faculty. They included violinist and baritone Theophilus P. Bryant, organist Walter Gossette, and pianist Estella Bonds, whose daughter, Margaret, was to become a nationally acclaimed pianist and composer. Hazel Thompson Davis, a protégé of Aida Overton Walker, the great Negro singer and dancer who was widely known in theater circles from the 1890s to 1910, taught stage dancing. From 1925 to 1928, the school was housed in the old residence of the opera singer Ernestine Schumann-Heink.[14]

In 1922, the National Conservatory of Music was founded by Pauline Lee, a graduate of Northwestern University. The conservatory was first housed in the Schumann-Heink residence, but it was moved to a location on Michigan Ave. The prestigious faculty included some of the most accomplished Negro musicians in the country. In addition to Clarence Cameron White and Hazel, were composer and choral, band, and symphony conductor N. Clark Smith and concert singer Florence Cole.[15]

The Normal Vocal Institute was founded in 1912 by E. Azalia Hackley at 3019 Calumet Ave. Although short-lived because of lack of funds, for four years teachers at the Institute taught hundreds of children the rudiments of singing and proper use of the voice. In order to raise funds for the school, Hackley traveled throughout the country giving recitals and teaching Negro children deep breathing and vocal exercises. In just over one year, she reached nearly 64,000 children.[16]

In 1919, Chicago hosted the National Convention of Musicians, from which was formed the National Association of Negro Musicians (NANM), an organization founded to promote black classical music and to support African American composers and performers of concert music. Branches sprung up immediately throughout the country. The first branch to form was the Chicago Music Association, which held its meetings every first and third Tuesday evening at the Wabash Avenue YMCA.

In its early years, the Chicago Music Association gave scholarships to young, deserving musicians. In 1922 when Miss Marian Anderson was in the city to appear as a soloist with the Umbrian Glee Club, she received the first scholarship to be awarded by the Association. Anderson was first heard in Chicago in 1919 as a high school student, and the Association sponsored her attendance that year at the first national NANM convention.

In 1922, a second Chicago branch of NANM formed, named for composer R. Nathaniel Dett. The R. Nathaniel Dett Club of Music and Allied Arts, which met bimonthly at the National Conservatory of Music, had a membership of about one hundred and included mostly younger and not yet well-established black musicians and composers. Opera singer La Julia Rhea and concert organist Orrin Clayton Suthern II were members of the Dett Club who would establish themselves nationally.

Arguably, the two Chicago branches of NANM were the most important classical music organizations for the black community from the 1920s–1940s. They continually sponsored musical programs that featured internationally known musicians in recital. They held lecture-performances for the benefit of both the black and white community, and Chicagoans were among the most visible participants at the national meetings. Members gave lectures throughout the city, and they promoted the work of African American composers in numerous concerts. In addition, Nora Holt, one of the cofounders of the Chicago Music Association, wrote a music column for the *Chicago Defender* from 1917–1923, an important black newspaper with both local and national editions; during 1919–1921, she published *Music and Poetry*, which chronicled black musical activity in the city. Succeeding Holt as music critic for the *Defender* was Maude Roberts George, who was elected president of the Chicago Music Association and of the national organization in 1932. Both Holt and George recorded the activities of NANM in the *Defender*, keeping black America apprised nationally of the organization's activities.

Price became one of the most active members of the R. Nathaniel Dett Club; she joined the club April 2, 1928, shortly after her arrival in the city. Although she was an official member of the Dett Club, holding various offices including chair of the composition committee, she was equally active in and became more visible through her activities in the Chicago Music Association. It was through this branch of NANM that Price met the most distinguished members of the black community, including Maude Roberts George, Estella Bonds, and concert singer Anita Patti Brown. Price was present at nearly every meeting of the Chicago Music Association. She gave talks on "current events," accompanied members of the club in performance on the piano or organ, demonstrated and lectured on rare keyboard instruments at local museums, composed music for members of the club, performed her own organ and piano compositions, and represented the branch at national meetings of NANM. Indeed, during the 1930s, rarely a week went by without some mention in the *Chicago Defender* of Price's activities.

* * *

The Price family settled at 3835 Calumet St. in the heart of the Black Belt. Florence Price and her husband became active professionally and socially and took advantage immediately of everything the city had to offer. In addition to her activities with NANM, Price set up a private piano studio in her home, and, with her children now a little older, she spent much of her time composing. The late 1920s and early 1930s were among the most productive years of Florence Price's career.

Price discovered she had a gift for writing teaching pieces for children—primarily for piano, but also some for organ and for violin with piano accompaniment. Creating a niche for herself in this genre, she found these compositions to be a profitable endeavor. She easily secured publishers, including G. Schirmer, McKinley, Theodore Presser, Gamble Hinged Music, Carl Fischer, and Clayton F. Summy.

In 1928, McKinley began to issue some of her teaching pieces. Price established a long-term relationship with McKinley; they published over twenty-five of her compositions for children throughout her career. *Playful Rondo* (1928), *By Candlelight* (1930), *Mellow Twilight* (1930), all for violin and piano: *Five Easy Compositions* and *The Zephyr (Mexican folk song)*, both for piano solo; and arrangements of *Annie Laurie* and *Silent Night* (all in 1929) were among the first to be published. G. Schirmer also began publishing her music in 1928. *At the Cotton Gin, A Southern Sketch*, a moderately difficult composition for piano that was written in Little Rock and submitted into a composition contest by her husband without her knowledge, was published first in Schirmer's Grade IV method book. It was this composition that won Price a cash prize and a publishing contract with Schirmer that was to last many years.

In December 1929, Price once again pursued the Arthur P. Schmidt Co. in Boston about publishing nine of her teaching pieces for piano: *Joy in June*, *On Top of a Tree*, *A Wee Bit of Erin*, *The Bridle Path*, *Pensive Mood*, *Dark Pool*, *Undecided*, *Dainty Feet*, and *Tecumseh*. All of the compositions were tentatively accepted, but ultimately, none of them were published. *Tecumseh* was published later by Carl Fischer in 1935.

Price's teaching pieces were issued in various ways. Some of them were grouped together under one title but sold separately. For example, Fischer issued two series of pieces under the title *Pieces We Like to Play*, one published in 1935 (including "Sachem's Pipe" and "Tecumseh,") the other in 1936 (including "The Butterfly," "The Gnat and the Bee," and "The Goblin and the Mosquito").

Among her most popular pieces in this category was the set *Three [Little] Negro Dances*. The *Dances*, based on characteristic Negro folk dances with their um-pah chordal left-hand accompaniment and lively syncopated melodies, include "Rabbit Foot," "Ticklin' Toes," and "Hoe Cake." All three dances were published individually by Presser in 1933. The *Dances* proved to be so popular that Presser reissued them together, in 1949, in their Grade III teaching method book. Presser published also a band arrangement of the *Dances* in 1939, omitting "Little" from the title. Arranged by Erik W. G. Leidzen, the *Dances* remained in the repertoire of American bands, including the U.S. Marine Band, for years.

In addition to teaching pieces and classical pieces for various ensembles, she wrote popular music, sometimes under the pen name "VeeJay." Some of these songs were arranged for radio commercials; others were sung in the theater, and at musicals throughout the city. Many set texts by Chicagoans: a group of love songs by Sal Janeway Carroll including "Love Dreams," "In Back o' the Clouds," "Let's Build a Little Love Nest," and "What's the Use?" (all composed in 1930); settings by Grace Linley published by the Linley Music House including "The Island of My Dreams" and "You Didn't Know This Baby" (both 1928); settings by Frank Blaha including "Just a Dream That Never Came True" and "Won't You Please Play Santa Claus?" (both 1928); and a setting by Joseph R. Gregory, "A Smiling Face; Fox Trot" (1928).

Many of the popular songs follow the Tin Pan Alley song format. That is, the verse describes a sentimental or tragic situation and is followed by a chorus that expresses reaction to the situation and provides the songs' melodic hook. "You're in my heart to stay" (c. 1948) with words by LeRoy DeGregory is typical (see example 5). The verse begins on the tonic and simply outlines a descending C major scale before it cadences on the expected dominant. The text is simple enough, too: "All my love and all my heart you took with a kiss. Tho we are many miles apart, Always remember this." The chorus follows with an equally unpretentious melody and accompaniment, which never diverges much from tonic to dominant save for an added flat six and flat seven in two measures. These pitch digressions add to the sentimentality of the song and would have been expected unconsciously, even anticipated, by listeners.

Price became a composer of choice for many of Chicago's classical performers. Much of her music was performed during the Sunday musicals at the black churches, and she was among a select group of black composers whose music was in the repertory of white soloists and ensembles as well.

Her best-known song from this period, "Moon Bridge," arranged for solo voice and piano, was also arranged for women's chorus (SSA). Both arrangements

Example 5. You're in My Heart to Stay, mm. 1–18

were published by Gamble Hinged Music in 1930, and there is evidence that both arrangements were performed on numerous occasions in the 1930s. The text was written by Mary Rolofson Bamble, wife of the publisher. Among the ensembles to perform "Moon Bridge" was the Chicago branch of the Treble Clef Glee Club, which Price conducted. The Treble Clef Club was a national body, established by a "select group of black women" in Washington, D.C., in 1897 for the purpose of studying and performing classical music.[17]

The piece is in a straightforward ABA form. The graceful melody in the A section is supported by an F major arpeggiated accompaniment, describing a "bridge of golden [moon]beams, where the fairies came to play" (see example 6). The composer briefly introduces a series of secondary dominants with added sevenths and ninths, arpeggiated as grace notes, a gesture typical of Price's art

Example 6. Moon Bridge, mm. 1–12

songs. At the close of the A section, simple chromaticism, leading from and returning to an E-flat7 chord, serves as a dominant substitution at the cadence. Price uses word painting in the B section to describe textually and musically the moonlight veiled by mist. The last line of the B section describes the disappearance of the bridge "under the sea" and with it the moonbeams, which even the fairies could not save. Here, D major is tonicized as the voice is absorbed by the big chords in the piano accompaniment. The concluding A section in which the moonbeams reappear, now dancing on "dewy grass" until the morning, closes triumphantly in F major, where the composition began.

Price's arrangements of spirituals were also frequently performed. Since it was and continues to be customary for singers and black choirs to conclude their concerts with a group of spirituals, there were many opportunities for this literature to be performed. Price arranged many well-known spirituals including "Go Down, Moses," "Peter, Go Ring Dem Bells," and "You Won't Find a Man like Jesus." She also arranged other, less familiar spirituals, such as "Death's Gwineter Lay His Cold, Icy Hand on Me" and "Lord, I Can't Stay Away."

Most of Price's spiritual arrangements are very straightforward. She modeled her arrangements on those of African American composer and concert singer Harry T. Burleigh. Burleigh's arrangements of spirituals for voice and piano, starting with his *Deep River* published in 1916 and continuing in a rich series of arrangements published in the years from 1917 on, established the tradition of the concert spiritual. Like Burleigh, Price is careful to set the texts in bold relief. The accompaniment is never so elaborate, either harmonically or texturally as to obscure the simplicity of the original tune and the directness of the text. The balance between the vocal line and the piano are carefully preserved.

Two of Price's relatively unknown spiritual arrangements in this style are "I Am Bound for the Kingdom" and "I'm Workin' on My Buildin'," published together by Handy Bros. in 1949 under the title *Two Traditional Negro Spirituals*. These tunes were sung to Price by Malinda Carter, a former slave who was owned by Squire Carter of Rutherford County, Tennessee. Price met Mrs. Carter through her granddaughter, Fannie Carter Woods, a Chicago resident and concert singer who premiered many of Price's songs.

Both of these settings are unusually short (perhaps the reason for issuing them together in publication) and both use the standard ABA (refrain-verse-refrain) structure. "I Am Bound for the Kingdom," recorded by Marian Anderson for Victor Records, begins with a threefold repetition of the title phrase and it concludes with the tag "Glory in My Soul" (see example 7). The verse of the spiritual reads:

> If you get there before I do, / Glory in my soul, /
> Look out for me I'm a-comin' too—/ Glory in my soul.

The reader will readily recognize a similarity to one of the many verses of "Swing Low, Sweet Chariot," one of the most familiar of all slave songs. The verse reads:

> If you get there before I do, / Comin' for to carry me home, Tell all my friends I'm comin' too. / Comin' for to carry me home.

The tunes of the two spirituals are remarkably similar as well (except for the addition of the expressive flat seventh repeated in "I Am Bound," leading this writer to believe that "I Am Bound for the Kingdom" is, in fact, an amalgam of the two spirituals). Certainly, the verse in "I Am Bound" is a recognizable adaptation of the verse of "Swing Low."

Example 7. I Am Bound for the Kingdom, mm. 1–10

Although "Swing Low" is much more graphic in its imagery, both spirituals can be understood in the same contexts. As is the case in many spirituals, the text is best understood as a double entendre. "I Am Bound for the Kingdom" can be interpreted to mean that the slave poet/singer is looking forward to the escape of the soul, to a better life in the hereafter. Simultaneously, the text can be read literally; the individual could be referring to escape of the physical self in this life through the surreptitious Underground Railroad.

The publication's companion piece, "I'm Workin' on My Buildin'" is quite different in character (see example 8). The refrain begins with the oscillating minor third that characterizes many of the more plaintive spirituals, for example, "City Called Heaven" ("I am a poor pilgrim of sorrow") and "Sometimes I Feel like a Motherless Child." The verse, on the other hand, is fairly declamatory. This spiritual appears to have had numerous verses, each singer adapting the text to fit his/her individual situation and needs. Mrs. Carter, who may have been a bit more pious than some of her fellow slaves, chose this text:

> If I was a mourner (verse 2 reads "sinner") / I'd tell you what I'd do, / I'd give my heart to Jesus / and work on my buildin' too.

But a less God-fearing individual expressed his or her repentance this way:

> If I was a gambler / I tell you what I would do, / I'd throw away my gamblin' dice / an' work on the buildin' too.[18]

Example 8. I'm Workin' on My Buildin', mm. 1–17

Price's most frequently performed spiritual arrangement, "My Soul's Been Anchored in de Lord," is a notable exception to the simplicity of these songs (see example 9). Arranged for concert singer Marian Anderson and made famous by her, the accompaniment is equal in importance to the melody. The expansive piano part, featuring large block chords that span the keyboard and punctuate the text, is reminiscent of the role of the orchestra in romantic opera. "My Soul's Been Anchored" was written in 1937 and published by Gamble Hinged Music the same year. Price also arranged the spiritual for solo voice and orchestra and for SATB chorus and piano. The solo arrangement has been recorded by Miss Anderson, Ellabelle Davis, and Leontyne Price.

Not everyone appreciated Price's arrangement of "My Soul's Been Anchored," particularly its interpretation by opera singers. Novelist and music critic Carl Van Vechten voiced his disparagement by calling Price's score and Leontyne Price's rendition of it "unbearable" and "in very bad taste." Generally speaking,

Example 9. My Soul's Been Anchored in de Lord, mm. 45–56

he said, "it is utterly impossible for white people to comprehend the Negro's point of view in spirituals or other things Negro; and so the final word on the spiritual had to be spoken by Negroes." He added, "Even so, some of the worst arrangements of spirituals were done by Negroes."[19] Although Van Vechten may have discredited the work, "My Soul's Been Anchored" was a commercial success, remaining in print longer than any other of her publications. (It finally went out of print in the 1970s.)

In the late 1920s and early 1930s, Price's compositional output is startlingly eclectic. That is, she composed for a wide variety of venues, in the manner of a musician seeking to make a living by writing music while simultaneously pushing the envelope as a composer of classical music. On the classical front, she was one of the most visible members of NANM, a mainstay of artistic idealism, on both the local and national levels. She held a variety of offices and her music was championed and performed regularly by esteemed artists, including organist Orrin Clayton Suthern II and pianist/composer Margaret Bonds, all of whom were associated with the organization. It was through NANM that Price met concert singer Marian Anderson, who had about fifty of Price's songs in her collection and who performed the composer's songs worldwide. Among her publishers in this realm are Lorenz, Galaxy, G. Schirmer, Presser, Handy Bros, and Edward B. Marks.

Her compositional output in the popular music realm is large, producing music for an entirely different set of publishers, including Linley Music House. Other than in her writing for voice, she was most prolific in producing pedagogical works, ostensibly to support herself and her family, much of which was published by McKinley, Clayton F. Summy, Carl Fisher, and others.

To take this one step further, Price explored all of the professional avenues available to her as a composer and performer when she moved to Chicago in 1927. Her highest aspiration was certainly to achieve success in the concert hall. Nevertheless, she navigated and thrived in these other realms as well. One of the reasons may be that she was an improviser of some repute, which gave her an advantage in writing in popular music idioms. While other composers of the period (George Gershwin, William Grant Still, and James P. Johnson, for example)—all composer/performers conversant in improvised oral traditions as well as the written tradition—are known for their achievements in traversing the terrain between classical and popular music, as a female composer, Price's overall body of work stands as unique.

8 "My Soul's Been Anchored in de Lord"

In addition to taking care of her family, teaching, composing, and her outside musical activities, Florence Price found time to further her musical studies. Through the efforts of Charles Haake, a member of the faculty of the American Conservatory of Music, she won a scholarship to study orchestration at the conservatory in 1929.[1] Haake and his wife, Gail, were the editors of the Oxford Piano [Methods] course in which some of her music would later be published. Price and the Haakes became longtime friends, and it was through them that Price met many of the accomplished white performers and composers in town. A real Renaissance woman, both in the ideological and in the artistic sense, Price continued to take graduate courses in the 1930s. She studied at the Chicago Teachers College and at the University of Chicago, pursuing her interests in the liberal arts and in foreign languages.[2]

For all of the semblance of happiness—a burgeoning career, extracurricular activities including her involvement with the National Association of Negro Musicians, taking additional classes, and the appearance of a stable home—Price's family life was actually in shambles. With the 1929 stock market crash, America plummeted into the Great Depression. Jobs were hard to come by, even for lawyers. It appears that Thomas Price went for long stretches without working, and the financial strain of a home with no primary wage-earner pushed Thomas and Florence to their limits. It was not long before the Price family plunged into dire financial straits. Marion Ross, daughter of Price's good friend Perry Quinney Johnston who lived with the Prices in Little Rock and took care of the girls, remembers this:

> I just remember that when she first went to Chicago she did have quite a struggle getting started. She was married to an attorney and apparently that marriage did

> not last. I don't know at what point. Rather, they were married when she went to Chicago or rather that dissolved before they went. I do know that there were some really hard times financially for her.[3]

Desperate, Price became innovative in her efforts to earn quick cash. Apparently a very creative organist, she became adept at accompanying silent films on the organ in movie theaters, a skill she may have acquired in Boston.[4] Most of these theaters were located in "The Stroll," also known as the "Broadway of the Black Belt." Featuring fifteen vaudeville and movie houses, each of these venues hired pianists and organists to play for the stage productions and silent films.[5] Some of this music was improvised but most of it was scored. Occasionally she provided filler by playing "ditties" which she composed, or she sight-read music that was already composed for a particular film.

This versatility was not unusual for many of Chicago's black classical and jazz musicians who were adaptable enough to play popular music for the theater. Playing in a variety of styles was the key to survival, especially during the Depression. One jazz musician, William Everett Samuels, remembers the situation this way:

> The Black musicians who played classical music hung on. They survived the thirties. They were working in the theaters. They could always play, people like Dave Payton [*sic*] and Erskine Tate, Jimmy Bell, Walter Dyett. They were all playing. They were all playing that classical music because they had to play it in the theaters all the time. You see, all that stuff was scored [playing along with the silent movies] and they had to read the music. Much of it was classical. Blacks came out to hear it and see the movies. That's right. It wasn't that they liked the classics. It was not necessarily middle-class Blacks that come to see the movies—it was all kinds. It was everybody. If you went to see the picture, you would have to hear the music. . . . Some go to see the pictures; some go to hear the music going with it. They just took it all in the package. You got a dose of culture.[6]

Price was one of the few women organists working along The Stroll. It appears that she was completely accepted by her male colleagues; all that was required for any musician was good "chops," that is, an unequivocal ability to sight-read and know one's instrument well. Although Price may not have wanted to work in this capacity, in the short term it was a decent way to earn a living and she was good at this work, both in her role as composer/improvisor and performer.

Without a steady job and completely frustrated, Thomas's relationship with Florence changed. His frustration and anger ultimately led to violence. On September 17, 1929, after one of their many arguments, he struck her with his fist, slapped her face, and knocked her down. Two months later, on November 15, he beat her again, striking her in the face with his fists. This time he threatened to kill her. Yet again, on February 19, 1930, Thomas was totally out of control.

He threw his wife to the floor where he choked and beat her. He threatened to kill her and this time he meant it. Pulling out his gun, he started to chase her but Florence ran from their home to the safety of a friend.

By now, there was a pattern to Thomas's behavior. It began in Little Rock. Florence had a successful music studio, Thomas was in and out of jobs. Although Florence tried to keep her family together for as long as she could through years of physical and verbal abuse, she could not take it any more. Thomas would have to leave. On March 10, 1920, he moved to 535 E. 34th St. On August 26th, after five months of separation, Thomas was served a summons to appear in divorce court on September 1. At the divorce proceedings, Florence testified that she was a "kind, affectionate, chaste, and dutiful" wife, and that "notwithstanding her love and affection" for her husband, he was "guilty of repeated cruelty towards her." She had a witness, who was in their home on two of the occasions, testify to several of the battery charges. Thomas Price, present at the hearing, did not testify in his own behalf.

Of utmost concern to Florence were her two daughters, Edith, nine, and Florence, fourteen. She asked presiding Judge John J. Sullivan for sole custody of her children. She also asked the judge to award her $25 per week from her husband's earnings (according to Florence, Thomas was earning $300 per month at the time of the hearing). She mentions in the deposition (given prior to the hearing) that she had no means to support herself and her children and that she was dependent upon the "charity" of friends and her parents. (She mentions both her mother and father, which is odd given that her father died in 1910). She also petitioned the court for all of the house furnishings, which she had bought herself.

On January 19, 1931, Judge John Sullivan granted Florence B. Price a divorce from Thomas J. Price. The grounds: "extreme and repeated cruelty." Florence was granted everything she asked for: sole custody of her girls, $25 per week in alimony and child support, and an additional $100 in court fees. No mention is made of the furniture but presumably she was granted that, too.[7]

Florence Price was now free—free from the mental, emotional, and physical abuse that she had endured for so long. Why did she stay in this dreadful marriage for as long as she had when it was clear that her marriage was falling apart before she left Little Rock? In spite of the abuse, the reasons are not difficult to discern. Like most abused women of her time, she felt trapped. She did not earn enough money to support herself and her daughters, so she endured. She survived to take care of her young daughters. At the worst time, she absorbed herself in her art and she relished the love and support of her friends. Above all, she prayed for a way out.

The thought that Florence was finally free was at least as frightening as it was hopeful. Could she make it on her own? Not yet. Sometime after she moved to Chicago, Florence met Pusey Dell Arnett, a successful man who worked for the Atlas Insurance Co. Only one month after her divorce from Thomas Price, Florence, now 42, married Pusey Arnett, age 55, thirteen years her senior.[8] After their marriage ceremony on Valentine's Day, 1931, Florence Price (she kept her former married name and occasionally used Price-Arnett) and her daughters moved in to Arnett's home at 4404 Vicennes Ave. Did Florence Price love Pusey Dell Arnett? If the court transcripts claiming that Florence Price still loved her husband are true, then probably not. She undoubtedly married him for the security. Perhaps they were good friends and both in need of companionship. Marrying Pusey Dell Arnett offered Florence Price a way out and she took it. She would have a safe home, the care, concern, and support of Arnett, and no financial worries. No one would hurt her again.

* * *

In January 1931, the very month in which her bitter divorce was final, Price began work on her first symphony, in E Minor, her most important and largest work to date. It was this symphony that was to occupy much of her time for the next two years. She even welcomed a painful accident which gave her time to compose. In a letter to a friend she wrote, "I found it possible to snatch a few precious days in the month of January in which to write undisturbed. But, oh dear me, when shall I ever be so fortunate again as to break a foot."[9]

In February 1932, she saw this announcement in the black newspapers and journals:

> ANNOUNCEMENT FOR THE RODMAN WANAMAKER COMPETITION
>
> The Rodman Wanamaker competition which gave five awards for Negro music in July, 1931, has been renewed for another competition to end July 14, 1932. There will be two classes: Class I, songs without [*sic*] words; Class II, piano compositions. The $500 prize for a symphonic work or concert suite, which was offered in 1931, has been extended to 1932.[10]

Another announcement appeared a few months later:

> Annual Wanamaker Music Contest (first contest, 1926) is announced in Philadelphia under the auspices of the Robert Curtis Ogden Association & the National Association for Negro Musicians. Prizes for: a) songs with words, b) piano compositions, c) symphonies, total $1000. Prize-giver, Captain John Wanamaker Jr.

Sponsored by the Robert Curtis Ogden Association and the National Association of Negro Musicians, in memory of Rodman Wanamaker, the Wanamaker Contest was established in 1927 to offer prizes to African American composers. Like the Rockefeller and Rosenwald Fellowships, composition prizes offered through *Opportunity* magazine, and the Harmon Foundation Awards, the Wanamaker contest was prestigious and provided long-overdue recognition for African American composers.

What an incentive! One thousand dollars was an enormous sum of money and Price was eager to compete for it. In midsummer 1932, with the Symphony in E Minor completed, she entered the symphony, along with three other compositions in the Wanamaker competition. Her tone poem *Ethiopia's Shadow in America* was also entered in the symphonic category, and she entered two piano compositions in the Class II category, the Sonata in E Minor and her *Fantasie No. 4*. Price was already familiar with the Wanamaker contest, for her piano work, *Cotton Dance*, had won honorable mention in the 1931 competition. (Margaret Bonds won Honorable Mention in the same contest for her piano work, *A Dance in Brown*). With that vote of confidence, she was ready to try again.

Through the month of September, black Chicagoans waited "with baited [*sic*] breath" to hear the results of the competition.[11] The winners would be announced at the fourth Sunday of the month program at the Metropolitan Community Church. The day finally arrived. The church was filled to capacity that afternoon and enthusiasm was especially high during the special music festival, given the anticipation of the award announcements. Reservations were made from white groups from the north side of Chicago (North Shore), and many teachers from the Loop schools were in attendance. The high-profile competition even attracted the attention of noted composers, including Charles Wakefield Cadman who was visiting Chicago from Los Angeles. He shared with the group news of his latest opera.[12]

The program rendered by the church choir under the direction of J. Wesley Jones, executive secretary of NANM and organizer of the afternoon festival, was of its usual high standard. Spirituals were sung, with Corinne Payton, Johnella Williams, and Magnolia Lewis as soloists. The Treble Clef Glee Club, under the direction of Price, was well received, and there were additional solos by Gorham Black and Mrs. Ruth Hardison. Mrs. Lillian LeMon of Indianapolis, president of NANM, was then introduced, greeting the audience on behalf of the national body.

At the close of the program Major Harry Scroggins of Philadelphia, representing Capt. John Wanamaker Jr., was presented by Mrs. Maude Roberts George, a member of the NANM board of directors. "Greatly impressed with the large group of outstanding musicians in Chicago and the great activity among them," Major Scroggins greeted the audience on behalf of Capt. Wanamaker; Franklin N. Brewer, manager of the Wanamaker store; friends of the Robert Curtis Ogden Association; Miss Mary E. Vogt, organist and music director of the store; and the judges. Scroggins, in telling the history of the Wanamaker award, said:

> This is the fifth contest for composers of the Negro race and was originated by the late Rodman Wanamaker. Since his death, March 9, 1922, his son, Capt. John Wanamaker Jr., in memory of his distinguished father, whose deep interest in the Race and its native gift of music prompted the series of awards, has continued these contests. After listening to the program of the National Association of Negro Musicians, Inc., in the Wanamaker store July 30, 1926, the association members were guests of the Robert Curtis Wanamaker store. These contests are conducted by and the prizes offered through the Robert Curtis Ogden Association of the Wanamaker store of Philadelphia.

The judges for this contest, constituted a group of distinguished composers, musical directors, and critics, including Frank Black, composer and music arranger; Edward B. Cullen, music instructor and band director; George P. Spangler, special assistant of instrumental music in Philadelphia public schools; William T. Timmings, composer and organist; and Arthus A. Rosander, director of bands for the Wanamaker store. Notable African American composers J. Rosamond Johnson and Melville Charlton (also an organist) rounded out the group.

And then the big moment arrived. The $500 first prize was announced in the symphonic work or concert suite category for band, orchestra, or chorus: Miss Florence B. Price won for the Symphony in E Minor! The honorable mention was shared by J. Harold Brown of Indianapolis and Price for her *Ethiopia's Shadow in America*. Then the piano composition first prize was announced. The $250 first prize was awarded to Florence B. Price for her Sonata in E Minor! Honorable mention again was shared by Hugo Bornn of New York City and Price for her *Fantasie* No. 4. This work is probably the *Fantasie Negre* No. 4 in B Minor, 1932, which was laid aside, revised, and premiered in 1937.[13] The song class was the third award of the evening. The $250 first prize went to Margaret Allison Bonds, Price's friend and former student, now a senior at Northwestern University, for her song "The Sea Ghost," an art song she had submitted for course work there.

Price's luck was beginning to change. She was newly married, she had won $750 of the $1000 offered by the Wanamaker Co. and her student had won the remaining $250. And, she won honorable mention for the other two compositions she submitted. The recognition that would come from the national competition would no doubt be a real boost to her career.

9 Black Satin Clothes at the Fair

One week after the Wanamaker awards were announced, the week of October 15, 1932, black Chicagoans had a lot of musical activity and national news to talk about. Appearing at the State-Lake theater was Adelaide Hall. Star of several highly acclaimed New York musical productions, including *Runnin' Wild* (1923) and *Blackbirds of 1928*, and soloist with Duke Ellington's band at the Cotton Club, her performances were a big hit in town. News of the third production of the play *Porgy* by Dorothy and DuBose Heyward, being cast in New York for a cross-country tour, was the talk in theater circles. The political discussion centered around Gov. Franklin D. Roosevelt, who was in the midst of presidential campaigning (which he won by a landslide one month later). African Americans paid particular attention to the Scottsboro case, in which nine black youths in Alabama were convicted by an all-white jury of raping two white women on a freight train near Scottsboro, Alabama, in 1931. Their fate was now before the Supreme Court. (One month later the youths were sentenced to long jail terms.) And on a celebratory note, two Negro pilots, Thomas C. Allen (age 25) and J. Herman Banning (age 32) completed the first transcontinental trip ever made by "Race fliers" on Sunday morning, October 8, at 10:40 a.m. They left California, Wednesday, September 21, with only $25.00 in their pockets and arrived on the East Coast two and one-half weeks later, exhausted but exuberant.

Chicagoans were still talking about the Wanamaker awards and they were thrilled that two of their own had won. Only days after the announcements were made, the Chicago Music Association got busy planning a gala celebration in honor of Price and Bonds at their regular Tuesday meeting. Estella Bonds chaired the special program, which included community singing led by George Guliatt, a selection by an *a cappella* woman's quartet known as the

Harmonious Four, directed by William Henry Smith, a selection by baritone John Green, and a talk on current topics by Price. In the weeks following the prize announcements, Price and Bonds were "showered with letters and expressions of congratulations." It was noted by the press that Price was a bit shy, even "retiring," and winning the Wanamaker prizes was a major achievement that would now bring her music to the fore.

These prizes did indeed bring Price national attention. In 1932, Frederick Stock, conductor of the Chicago Symphony Orchestra who was appointed Music Advisor to the Century of Progress Exposition, Chicago's 1933 World's Fair, took notice.[1] Of the numerous scores he perused for performance, he was particularly impressed with Price's Symphony in E Minor. He would premiere the work in the orchestra's initial series of concerts at the Exposition in June.

Price had indeed come a long way professionally in such a short time. She relished the thought that the conductor of one of America's finest orchestras would give her first major work a hearing before a national audience. That Frederick Stock took a personal interest in Price was characteristic of the conductor, who had been programming American music and supporting American composers since he became conductor of the Chicago Symphony in 1905. As Dena Epstein has written, "Yet perhaps Stock's most significant contribution, one that has been all but forgotten, was his lifelong service to American composers. He encouraged them, performed their music often and repeatedly, held public rehearsals to permit additional performances, and praised them in countless interviews."[2]

Stock's enthusiasm for America and American music was radical for his time. As early as 1914, Stock (b. Prussia, 1872–d. Chicago 1942) began conducting orchestra rehearsals in English with his primarily German musicians, and by the 1917–1918, season he announced that each program would include at least one work by an American composer.[3] Although Stock was criticized for his decision to program "too many novelties . . . especially works of American and Chicago writers," he was not deterred from his commitment to American composers. In designing the music series for the Fair, he announced that he was interested in "Chicago talent first and American talent second, and [that] . . . European representation will be drastically limited."[4]

The months before the performance of her symphony were hectic for Price. Although she had yet to complete a final copy of the symphony, she fulfilled her professional obligations during the remainder of 1932. In October, she gave talks on "current events" for two meetings of the Chicago Music Association. On Thursday, November 3, she gave a talk on black composers and she accompanied soprano Gladys Nelson, also a member of the Chicago Music Association, in a program for the Twentieth Century Club, a white organization. In December the Chicago Music Association visited the rare instrument collection at the

Harding museum, where Price talked about historic organs and performance practice, and she and Estella Bonds demonstrated the eighteenth- and nineteenth-century pianos while the group sang. The club was also fascinated by listening to Blanche Walton play a piano that was once owned by Franz Liszt.[5]

December 1932 was to mark another milestone for Price. Her *Fantasie Negre* in E Minor for piano (apparently not the same work that won the Wanamaker Honorable Mention) had attracted the attention of Mme. Lumilla Speranzeya, a Russian ballet teacher of the Chicago Art Theater, who choreographed a ballet for the work. The dancers were a group working with black choreographer Katherine Dunham, who was interested in forming a permanent dance troupe. Several members were connected also with the Cube-Masque Little Theater at the University of Chicago. The ballet was premiered to much acclaim at the elegant Stevens Hotel Beaux Arts Ball accompanied by pianist Margaret Bonds who had worked for months with the group.[6]

The *Fantasie Negre* in E Minor, a setting of the spiritual "Sinner, Please Don't Let This Harvest Pass," is one of Price's most expansive and most difficult works for piano. Price's skills, not only as a composer but as a pianist, are most evident here. The *Fantasie* is a one-movement tripartite work unfolding as a set of variations on the theme in the first and third parts. Typical of much of Price's piano music during this period, the *Fantasie* is in the Romantic style. An *andante* sixteen-bar introduction of broken chords in various rhythms, essentially a prolongation of the dominant, serves principally to provide a harmonic framework for what is to come. The A section, marked *tempo moderato*, consists of four variations of the spiritual with a long introduction between variation one and two (sixteen measures) and an even longer coda (twenty-two measures; see example 10).

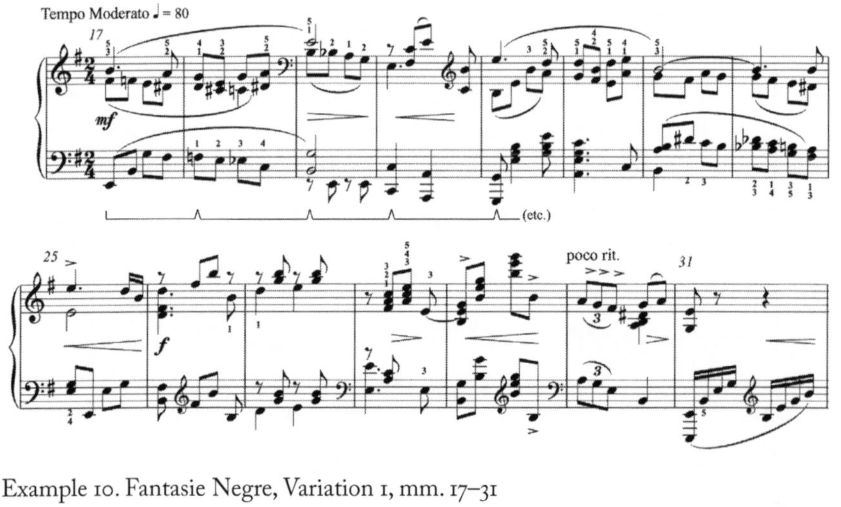

Example 10. Fantasie Negre, Variation 1, mm. 17–31

In the variations, the melody is tossed between the hands but it is never disguised. There are also several changes in texture. In variations one, two, and four, the melody is accompanied by a contrapuntal line that becomes increasingly more chromatic. In variation 3, Price's fondness for chromatic accompaniment provides a highly energized foil for the chordal melody in the left hand.

The *andante cantabile* B section, in G major, is short and offers repose from the constant motion of the previous section. This section—twelve measures of simple melody and underlying accompaniment (with a nine-measure tag)—is perfectly symmetrical in its phrasing. It thus contrasts quite dramatically with the syncopated chords, harmonic and rhythmic complexities, and wide-ranging dynamic levels of the close of the preceding section.

The second set of variations (A') is in the tradition of nineteenth-century virtuoso piano music. The spiritual melody is wholly transformed here and is subjected to octave and rhythmic displacement and chordal treatment with harmonic alterations (see example 11).

The left hand is particularly challenging, with lines moving from one end of the keyboard to the other, in varying rhythms and at a relatively fast tempo. In the last variation, the left hand must play octave arpeggios, all the while maintaining the legato line required as accompaniment to the melody. After a

Example 11. *Fantasie Negre*, Variation 2, mm. 141–153

most interesting execution of the spiritual melody in several guises, the *Fantasie Negre* concludes with a rather simple articulation of syncopated E minor chords and arpeggios.

That Bonds was chosen to accompany the dance troupe in the *Fantasie Negre* ballet is not surprising. During the 1930s, Bonds became well-known for her interpretations of Price's music, which she performed on numerous occasions. Bonds played Price's piano compositions at the local NANM meetings of the Chicago Music Association and she also performed at the national meetings of the organization.

Margaret Bonds was indeed a gifted pianist. She received her first piano lessons from her mother and, from the age of five, she was under the tutelage of Martha B. Anderson. When she was about eight years old, Margaret became the pupil of T. Theodore Taylor of the Coleridge-Taylor School of Music, where her mother was on the faculty.

Bonds was active as a performer and was an officer in the youth department of the Chicago Music Association. On numerous occasions, she was asked to represent the branch at the annual National Association of Negro Musicians conventions. In return, the organization gave Bonds scholarship money to help her pursue her studies. As a youngster, Bonds also won several contests and scholarships at the Chicago Musical College. Bonds went on to study piano at Northwestern University. In her junior year (1932), she gave a recital at the University that was attended by many members of the Chicago Music Association, including Price. On her program, Bonds played works by Scarlatti, Bach, Debussy, Milhaud, and Dohnanyi.[7]

Although Bonds was a very accomplished pianist she was equally interested in composing. But, because of her young age, Bonds received little support to pursue composition, an area of music still dominated by men in the 1930s. In Price, Bonds found an immediate role model. It was Price, sympathetic and interested in the gifted student, who accepted her as a composition student and encouraged her endeavors.[8]

Bonds's musical study was also taken very seriously by singer and actress Abbie Mitchell, with whom she spent a great deal of time. Mitchell shared with her classical vocal literature as well as art songs and spiritual arrangements by African American composers. Bonds greatly admired Mitchell, who taught the young girl "the importance of the marriage between words and music."[9]

Bonds also had an opportunity to study composition for a short time with composer William L. Dawson, who arrived in Chicago in the summer of 1926 just before Price.[10] Dawson took courses in harmony and orchestration at the Chicago Musical College and the American Conservatory of Music (MM, 1927), both schools where Price also studied. There is no evidence that Dawson and Price spent any social time together in Chicago, but the two composers

-worked together at the national NANM conventions, where they often provided leadership in the myriad of workshops that were offered.

It was in Chicago that Dawson began work on his *Negro Folk Symphony*, premiered by the Philadelphia Orchestra in 1934. Dawson, along with Price and William Grant Still, would become America's first African American symphonists and the race would lift them up as role models, proud of their accomplishments.[11]

In Dawson, Bonds found a teacher who had mastered European forms and techniques, arranged spirituals, and played jazz. Bonds's predilection for jazz-flavored harmonies in her compositions may well have been inspired by her work with Dawson. Dawson left Chicago in 1931 to direct the Tuskegee Institute School of Music, where he was to establish an international reputation as a composer and director of the Tuskegee choir.

Bonds's and Price's relationship grew, and they were often featured on programs together, including the Sunday afternoon musicals and special music events. One such occasion in which they played was the annual Julius Rosenwald Memorial Concert, Sunday, February 12, 1933. Rosenwald, a wealthy benefactor who established a Fellowship for African American performers, was held in high esteem by the black musical community. Based in Chicago, the Rosenwald Fund fellowships were among the most distinguished awards given to African Americans between 1928–1948. Awards, offering support in the early stages of their careers, were made in medicine, law, journalism, education, the social sciences, and the fine arts. Over the years, awards were given to Marian Anderson, Ralph Bunche, Charles Drew, Langston Hughes, Ralph Ellison, Jacob Lawrence, W. E. B. Du Bois, and William Grant Still. For this concert, which drew a large crowd, Price performed the third movement of her organ sonata and Bonds was the piano soloist.[12]

The following month, Sunday, March 19, Bonds and Price played Price's two-piano arrangement of the spiritual *Sinner Please Don't Let This Harvest Pass* at the Berean Baptist Church. This is almost certainly the *Fantasie Negre* in its two-piano arrangement. (Price also arranged it for orchestra.) The afternoon program featured two sopranos, Lessie Brooks and Rosa Page, and several choral numbers under the direction of Isaac T. Yarborough. But "the audience was stirred to prolonged applause" when the Price piece was played.[13]

The Berean musicale was in honor of Marian Anderson, who was in town to perform over NBC radio. Miss Anderson was a frequent visitor to Chicago, and she and Price became very well acquainted over the years. Anderson's library contained over fifty of Price's art songs and arrangements of spirituals, many of which were written for and dedicated to her.

During the 1930s, Price and her music were well received in white musical circles. She was in constant demand to perform on the organ or the piano, present her compositions, or lecture on various topics. She received many requests during February, which then had an "Interracial Week." For instance, in February 1933, she played some of her piano music for the Celia Parker Wooley committee of the Chicago Woman's Club, an organization in which she would later become the first black member.[14]

The degree to which the white establishment respected Price as a composer was evident in an opportunity she had to work for WGN radio when her friend Louis White, soloist with the WGN radio symphony orchestra, asked her to orchestrate music for his broadcast performances. Price met Louis and his wife, Helen, also a singer, through the R. Nathaniel Dett Club. White was first hired by WGN in 1930 to sing on Sunday mornings, accompanied by the piano trio known as the Tone Casters, and also by Allen Grant, the staff pianist. In 1932, White, now well-known to radio listeners, was asked by the station to expand his slot to a half-hour weekly program. He understood that he would be paid very little for his performances but, given that it was all too rare for black musicians to sing with an orchestra, he welcomed the opportunity. White chose his own music each week, which usually included an opera aria, an aria from an oratorio, an art song, and contemporary compositions.

Of particular interest is that the radio station never announced to its primarily white listeners that the popular baritone was black. Although not in agreement with the station's mandate, White accepted it, understanding that the acknowledgment that he was Negro would alienate many in the audience who did not want to hear a black man sing classical literature. Since he desperately needed the income to support his family, White suppressed his inclination to reveal his race for the four years that he was under contract by the station. For the same reason that White remained invisible, Price was anonymous to the station's listeners. Although she was becoming steadily known to both black and white musicians, she was never acknowledged by the station over the air for her work. Black jazz and concert violinist Walter Dyett (on the faculty at the Coleridge-Taylor School of Music and Wendell Phillips High School), who also orchestrated music for White's performances, remained in the background as well.[15]

At the point when White was particularly discouraged, he considered every alternative available to him to earn a living in these hard times. His friend, concert singer and actress Abbie Mitchell, made a reasonable suggestion. Light-skinned White could "pass," for he would surely find a job more easily as a white person than a black one. White never considered the option, however, because if he took on this new persona he would have to leave behind all traces of his former life, including his darker-skinned wife and daughter.

Fed up with the blatant racism, White left WGN in 1934 for what he hoped would be better opportunities in New York. The situation in New York was almost as difficult, but shortly after his arrival in the city he was hired by George

Gershwin to understudy Todd Duncan's "Porgy" in the first production of *Porgy and Bess* in 1935. While based in New York, White and his wife performed in Lew Leslie's London edition of the "Blackbirds of 1930" and with Duke Ellington's band at the Cotton Club from 1937–1938. In the late 1930s, the Whites returned to Chicago. The "Singing Whites," as Louis and Helen White were affectionately called by black Chicagoans, premiered many of Price's art songs and arrangements of spirituals throughout her career, and they were counted among her very good friends and supporters.

During the early months of 1933, while Price worked as a freelance arranger at WGN radio, she continued to work on her symphony, composed small-scale pieces, performed, and lectured. One of her more enjoyable activities during this time was directing her Treble Clef Choir, which performed as part of a large music festival March 12, at Orchestra Hall. The featured choir was the 200-voice Metropolitan Community Church choir, under the direction of J. Wesley Jones, who sang spirituals, contemporary music by black composers, and excerpts from oratorios and opera. Ranging through the whole of the black music tradition, Price's choir sang several selections including her own "Banjo Song," Ethelbert Nevin's very popular "Mighty Lak' a Rose," Will Marion Cook's spiritual arrangement "You Must Have That True Religion," and Thomas Dorsey's gospel tune "I Am Singing in My Soul."[16]

There was much to do in the remaining few months before the June Chicago Symphony concert. Although she gave a talk at the Tuesday, March 28, meeting of the Chicago Music Association, she basically withdrew from all activities in order to copy out the parts of her symphony.[17] Rushed to meet her deadline, Price enlisted the help of friends, including Margaret Bonds, to help her complete the music copying on time. Margaret Bonds explained, "During the cold winter nights in Chicago, we used to sit around a large table in our kitchen—manuscript paper strewn around, Florence and I extracting parts for some contest deadline. We were a God-loving people, and, when we were pushed for time, every brown-skinned musician in Chicago who could write a note, would 'jump-to' and help Florence meet her deadline."[18]

In April, Price was present at the debut of the Florence B. Price A Cappella Chorus, organized and directed by Grace W. Thompkins, secretary of the Chicago Music Association. On that occasion, several soloists rendered selections, the choir sang, and Maude Roberts George, president of the Association, installed the officers of the choir. Price, who had celebrated a birthday the week before, said that "it was the happiest one she had ever had" and she "acknowledged in a very beautiful way the honor which had been bestowed upon her in the naming of their group" [after her.][19]

The time was busy for Margaret Bonds, too. In addition to helping Price copy the parts of her symphony, she was preparing the solo part of John Alden

Carpenter's *Concertino* for piano and orchestra for a performance with the Chicago Symphony on the same evening in which Price's symphony would be played. In May 1933, just prior to her graduation from Northwestern University with a Bachelor of Music degree, she performed her senior recital, attended by a large group from the Chicago Music Association. She played a challenging program including music by Franck, Debussy, Villa-Lobos, and as preparation for the June concert, she played the solo part of Carpenter's *Concertino* in a two-piano arrangement. Maude Roberts George, now editor of the music column in the *Chicago Defender*, wrote enthusiastically about Bonds's performance. She said, "Miss Bonds is a brilliant pianist, and [has] splendid technique and plays not only with intelligence but with real musical feeling. A charming stage presence is coupled with genuine love of her art, which thrills her audience as she seems to completely lose herself in the interpretation of her music. Her program throughout was played with an accuracy which brought her many personal compliments from the teachers and musicians present."[20]

Anticipation heightened when it was announced that the special guest soloist for the June 15 concert would be world-renowned tenor Roland Hayes. The *Chicago Defender* reported that Hayes's appearance "immediately found anxious music lovers all over the city purchasing tickets upon the opening day of the ticket sale." It was noted that this would be the first time that Chicagoans would hear Mr. Hayes sing with full orchestra. Chicago Fiskites planned to turn out in large numbers, too, to hear one of their own. (Hayes had studied music at Fisk University and he had been soloist with the famed Fisk Jubilee Singers).

The "interracial committees" of the city not only helped to promote the concert but were very busy organizing post-concert parties. A special reception for Hayes would be hosted by Price and Margaret Bonds, to which many of the NANM members, who were actively selling tickets for the concert, were invited. One special guest at the Price/Bonds reception was the actor Richard B. Harrison, "De Lawd" of the Broadway play *The Green Pastures*, who had read Shakespeare to black Little Rock in the 1880s.

Few other black musicians could have generated this much excitement for a concert—particularly for black audiences. Hayes was a role model and an inspiration for the community. A pioneer in breaking down racial barriers, Hayes was the first black male to win international recognition as a concert singer, though his road to success was arduous.[21] Because no white manager would do so, Hayes began to arrange his own coast-to-coast concert tours, drawing standing-room-only audiences. White promoters claimed that "It will never happen here. The public won't accept a Negro on the concert stage . . . that's American tradition." It was not long before Hayes proved them wrong.

As was common for black concert and opera singers, Hayes won recognition in Europe first. He made his first European trip in 1920, making his debut in Aeolian Hall in London. One year later, he gave a command performance before King George V and Queen Mary. Not all Europeans were receptive to Hayes. In 1924 before his performance in Berlin, the newspaper carried a story about "the calamity of a black man coming into Germany and defiling the great names of music and poetry, a man who at best can only remind us of the cotton fields of Georgia." That evening Hayes walked onto the stage amidst a volume of hisses and boos. But after the tenor sang Schubert's "Du bist die Ruh," one of the German people's favorite art songs, the audience which had been hushed during the performance, gave him a thunderous applause. November 16, 1923, Hayes made history again when he sang with the Boston Symphony, probably the first time a black concert singer appeared with a major American orchestra. Among the pieces that he sang on that occasion were two of the songs he sang for the Chicago audience: Berlioz's aria "Le repos de la sainte famille" from *L'Enfance du Christ* and his arrangement of the spiritual "Bye and Bye."

Throughout his career, Hayes served as a mentor for young singers and provided scholarships to aspiring musicians. Most importantly, Hayes stood as a symbol of racial pride. Here was a black American musician who "faced his own destiny and stopped apologizing for his music."[22] Correspondence between Price and Hayes reveals that the two became friends after the 1933 concert. Hayes would visit Price in Chicago when time in his busy schedule permitted. In April 1935, for example, after his appearance with the Duluth Symphony, Hayes spent a few days relaxing at her home before his next engagement.

The night of the concert, Chicagoans filled the Auditorium Theatre to capacity. It was hoped that this concert would be held in a new facility on the fairgrounds, but the Depression had made this economically unfeasible. Unfortunately, the plans that were underway for a new concert hall had to be laid aside. The Friends of Music who sponsored the Century of Progress Exposition series chose the Auditorium as the alternative venue. All of the symphony programs for the fair, including this one, were free. This program was broadcast live over NBC radio.

At the conclusion of her symphony, Price, elegantly dressed in a long white gown, was recalled to the stage again and again to acknowledge the long and enthusiastic applause. Her symphony won critical acclaim, and it marked the first large scale work by a black woman composer to be played by a major American orchestra. Bonds, too, made history that evening, becoming the first black instrumentalist to appear with the Chicago Symphony.[23]

With the June 1933 Chicago Symphony Orchestra concert, the "Negro in Music" was celebrated both as performer and composer in grand style. This concert was recognized as a historic event by music lovers from all over Chicago, both black and white, who came to hear the program. Mr. and Mrs. John Alden Carpenter, who were seated in four center boxes on the lower tier, had brought with them special guests: George Gershwin, who had played a concert at the Auditorium Theatre just the night before, and diplomat Adlai Stevenson, his wife, and sister, who were in town from Washington, D.C., to visit the fair. One social critic for the *Chicago Daily Tribune* even found it appropriate to headline an article, "Black Satin Clothes Seen at Symphony: Many Box Parties at Fair Concert," detailing the attendance and the attire of Chicago's elite and their enthusiastic response to the evening. The article reads, in part, "A large and appreciative audience in the old Auditorium last night cheered Chicago's Symphony orchestra. The hundreds of music lovers enjoyed the Symphony in E Minor and John Alden Carpenter's 'Concertino. . . .' Not since the eighties [1880s] has there been such a response to [a] summer night musical program."[24] Florence Price, composer, had arrived, at last.

10 Spirituals to Symphonies

A Century of Progress

The Century of Progress concert was featured in articles by both the black and white press, though the historic concert held special meaning for Chicago's black community. Robert Abbot, editor for the *Chicago Defender*, captured the emotional response of the audience to the evening this way:

> No one could have sat through that program sponsored by the Chicago Friends of Music at the Auditorium theater last week and not have felt, with a sense of deep satisfaction, that the Race is making progress in music. First there was a feeling of awe as the Chicago Symphony orchestra, an aggregation of master musicians of the white race, and directed by Dr. Frederick Stock internationally known conductor, swung into the beautiful, harmonious strains of a composition by a Race woman. And when, after the number was completed, the large auditorium, filled to the brim with music lovers of all races, rang out in applause both for the composer and the orchestral rendition, it seemed that the evening could hold no greater thrills.[1]

It is curious that the editor of the *Chicago Defender* fails to mention Price by name preferring to accentuate the cultural significance of the experience. Of course, the *Defender's* black readers knew to whom Abbott was referring; he was invoking a kind of common familiarity that bonds the black community. That this concert marked the first time that a major orchestra had performed a work by a black woman composer was not mentioned.

Nahum Daniel Brascher, editor-in-chief of the Associated Negro Press, wrote a piece for the *Chicago Defender* in which he praised the progress of "race musicians." Headlined "Roland Hayes Concert Shows Progress of Race in Music," he wrote, "The occasion was the very last word in music achievement. For us the last word is the first opportunity. It was the first opportunity for such a setting; it was successful absolutely on merit, and it is the beginning of a new era for us in the world of music."[2] Brascher goes on to recount the success of black classical musicians from Coleridge-Taylor to William Dawson who was then completing the score of the *Negro Folk Symphony*, which would be played by the Philadelphia Orchestra the following year.

Brascher's article was his own testimony of how far the Negro had come musically. He recounts a lengthy list of the race's musical achievers, many of whom he knew personally ("Years of contact in the newspaper world has given me a cordial acquaintance with most of our outstanding musical people"), and he includes James Reese Europe, Will Marion Cook, Roland Hayes, Paul Robeson, and others. It is interesting that even after the successful and historic performance of Price's symphony, Brascher fails to include Price among his list of the musical achievers. Her name is simply included as part of the evening's program.

When Brascher and Abbott wrote their "reviews," they were not really concerned, after all, about the musical content of the concert. They were interested in its social and cultural significance—that is, the advancement of the race through a very powerful medium: classical music and the orchestra. The attitudes of Brascher and Abbott must be framed, also, in the context of the philosophical goals of the black middle class. The performance and compositions of classical music by blacks was equated with social status and uplift of the race, what Willard Gatewood has termed "the genteel performance."[3] Musicologist Lawrence Schenbeck put it this way: "The cultivation of European classical music had proved to be an ideal vehicle for practicing genteel behaviors: at once, it marked out the practitioner[*sic*], whether performer or listener, as a member of an elite group, and by example it instructed the less fortunate in proper values and behavior. When such instruction was carried on via the social pages of the newspapers, its power was enhanced even as the distance between the elite and the masses was maintained and, in fact, emphasized."[4]

The visual impact of this concert was of import, too. A classical concert of black soloists and black composers amid the backdrop of the all-powerful (and exclusionary) white orchestra with a white conductor constituted black achievement and advancement on many levels. This point was probably not lost on anyone, least of all Price who grew up in the segregated world of Little Rock. Abbott knew that Brascher would contextualize this concert in a way few could. Brascher's article becomes even more significant because it was read by blacks nationwide.

Maud Roberts George wrote her music review but it appeared only in the local (Chicago) edition of the paper.[5] Her article is critically disappointing as it rehashed, for some odd reason, a music review written by Edward Moore for the *Chicago Tribune*. George's article features Roland Hayes's performance to which she devotes most of the critique. The remaining few paragraphs are devoted to Price's symphony and to Bonds's performance of Carpenter's *Concertino*. Nowhere in George's article does she mention the Coleridge-Taylor works.

It was the white press, in 1933, which, in many ways, validated Price's musical skills, given that they were relatively uninterested in social decorum or historical significance. For these critics, Price's symphony was the highlight of the concert program, even as Roland Hayes and Margaret Bonds's performances were enthusiastically received. Lengthy reviews were carried in all of the local newspapers the following day. Glenn Dillard Gunn of the *Chicago Herald & Examiner* commented that "Mrs. Price's symphony proved to be highly interesting to her audience. Its orchestration is handled in orthodox fashion and it 'sounds.'" The music critic for the *Winnetka Talk* praised her symphony and mentioned that "it is believed that an outstanding composer has been discovered."[6]

Both the critics of the *Music News* and the *Chicago Evening American* were particularly interested in the underlying African American musical characteristics inherent in her score. The critic from the *Music News* wrote, "Mrs. Price's work displayed a distinct flair for composition, and like the good workman and musician that she is, she made use of thematic material and racial characteristics. I found the choral [choral-like] treatment of the second movement highly exhilarating." Herman Devries of the *Chicago Evening American* was equally impressed. He wrote,

> Florence Price's Symphony in E minor wins warm applause from sophisticated audience. Mrs. Price's symphony won the Wanamaker contest, and though we did not hear the other contestants, we can readily understand her success. The symphony is ably, intelligently constructed and conceived. There's abundance of typical coloring and atmosphere, and if I were to express a preference for any specific division of the score we would say that the third and fourth movements are more nearly a perfect portrait of Mrs. Price's evident intention to be herself and to reflect herself in terms of modern orchestral language and resource. She is not an imitator, but let us say a follower of the best traditions of our day, if our day can be said to possess traditions.[7]

The longest and most interesting review was written by Eugene Stinson of the *Chicago Daily News*. He highlights both Hayes and Price in his column "Music Views":

> There is one artist who appeals to all Americans as representative of the Negro race's remarkable capacity in art, and he is Roland Hayes. This distinguished tenor sang last night with the Chicago Symphony orchestra in the Century of Progress series given at the Auditorium under the auspices of the Chicago Friends of Music, Inc. It is possible to prefer another type of voice to Mr. Hayes's and even another

type of singing. But granted Mr. Hayes's voice—which I find beautiful—and granted his repertory which must be considered of the highest grade—there is no vocalist before the public who displays a more consummate mastery of the means at his disposal or a more subtle and delicate taste as interpreter. His attainments are excellent without regard to his heritage, but his singing is doubly beautiful because in meeting the highest artistic standards it sacrifices nothing of the essential characteristic of the Negro spirit in art.

Indeed, if we consider the Negro's history in the "Century of Progress" now being celebrated, there is no one with whom to compare Mr. Hayes except a few men of his own race but [of an] entirely different calling. It must have been stimulating to two other Negro artists to have a share in the program to which last night he added so much dignity and beauty.

These were a composer and pianist both Chicagoans. A symphony by Florence Price had its first performance on this occasion. It is a faultless work cast in something less than modernist mode and even reminiscent at times of other composers who have dealt with America in tone. But for all its dependence upon the idiom of others, it is a work that speaks its own message with restraint and yet with passion. Miss Price's symphony is worthy of a place in the repertory.

Margaret Bonds, a brilliant and dependable pianist, gave an admirable performance of John Alden Carpenter's "Concertino[,]" a compact and effective work, [and] one of the earliest jazz studies of this interesting foreshadower of so many modernist tendencies.[8]

* * *

What is the context in which to evaluate this program featuring Roland Hayes singing the music of Berlioz, Coleridge-Taylor, and two spirituals? And why did Stock include two works by Coleridge-Taylor on the concert? Why was Price's symphony the subject of so much press? We should consider the musical and historical context in which Price's symphony was written and performed before proceeding with an analysis of it. Further, it will be informative to consider the statements by both Eugene Stinson and Herman Devries who found Price's symphony conservative and even "reminiscent at times of other composers." Stinson found Carpenter's "jazz-based" *Concertino* a modern composition compared with Price's work.

Price's composition was actually the second in a trilogy of symphonies written by African American composers in the early 1930s. In 1931, William Grant Still's *Afro-American Symphony* was premiered by the Rochester Philharmonic under Howard Hanson. In 1934, the year after Price's Symphony in E minor was performed, William Dawson's *Negro Folk Symphony* was presented by the Philadelphia Symphony under the direction of Leopold Stokowski. Black Americans were proud and in awe of these composers. In 1935, the African American writer and composer Shirley Graham boasted of their accomplishments: "Spirituals to

Symphonies in less than fifty years! How could they even attempt it? . . . And one of them is a woman!" she exclaimed in an article in which she recounts the development of African American art music from the triumphs of the Fisk Jubilee Singers and their concert spiritual arrangements in 1871 to the critical acclaim of Still's, Price's, and Dawson's symphonies.[9]

Implicit here is the recognition that during the early years of the twentieth century, African American composers focused primarily on smaller forms of composition—art songs, solo piano music, music for violin and piano, and choral works. By the 1920s and 1930s, these composers were ready to meet with the challenge of large-scale forms, an endeavor that had proved difficult before, as the unsuccessfully produced operas of Harry Lawrence Freeman and Scott Joplin attest.[10] Scott Joplin (1868–1917) wrote two operas: *A Guest of Honor*, 1903, now lost, and *Treemonisha*, completed in 1905. With no hope of finding a producer, Joplin staged *Treemonisha* himself in 1915 without scenery, costumes, or orchestra. The performance was a failure. While the inspiration, creativity, and technical mastery to write orchestral music was there, the practical conditions were not. There was little feasibility with regard to performance possibilities and given that publication was an equally unlikely goal, it was financially impractical.

This was, in fact, a time when performances of symphonic music by American composers, in general, was a novelty. John Mueller in *The American Symphony Orchestra* points out that from 1925–1950, the names of 280 American composers appeared on the regular subscription program of the ten oldest major symphony orchestras. Of these, 50 percent of the composers had been played by only one orchestra, while only 6 percent had been heard in each of the ten orchestras. He concluded that most performances of American music during this period were purely tokenism. Fully one-third of Mueller's list of composers was foreign-born. No women composers were represented and only one African American composer, William Grant Still, is listed.[11]

On the other hand, Chicago and Boston were the most supportive of American composers. In fact, almost 40 percent of the American music performed by the Chicago Symphony from 1925–1950 was contributed by local composers. In part, this was due to the fact that Chicago, an important musical center, attracted a number of composers to it.

What was the impetus behind the creation of the first symphonies by African American composers? Part of the inspiration was the American works of the Bohemian composer Antonin Dvořák. Dvořák visited this country from 1902–1895, and during his sojourn he issued a challenge to American composers to develop a national school of composition. Dvořák's article, "Music in America" in *Harper's Magazine* (February 15, 1895), in which the composer states his views, has been quoted often. He wrote:

> A while ago I suggested that inspiration for a truly national music might be derived from the Negro melodies or Indian chants. I was led to take this view partly by the fact that the so-called plantation songs are indeed the most striking and appealing melodies that have yet been found on this side of the water, but largely by the observation that this seems to be recognized, though often unconsciously, by most Americans.
>
> It is a proper question to ask, what songs, then, belong to the American, and appeal more strongly to him than any others? What melody could stop him on the street if he were in a strange land and make the home feeling well up within him, no matter how hardened he might be or how wretchedly the tune were played? Their number, to be sure, seems to be limited. The most potent as well as the most beautiful among them, according to my estimation are certain of the so-called plantation melodies and slave songs, all of which are distinguished by unusual and subtle harmonies.[12]

Dvořák was led to broaden his views about what constituted a "national" American music, stating, "it matters little whether the inspiration for the coming folk songs of America is derived from the Negro melodies, the songs of the creoles, the red man's chant, or the plaintive ditties of the homesick German or Norwegian" and that "the germs for the best music lie hidden among all the races that are commingled in this great country." He continued to acknowledge his profound interest in black folk music sung to him by his student Harry T. Burleigh.[13]

Dvořák's most influential work for American composers was his Symphony No. 9, "From the New World," premiered by the New York Philharmonic in Carnegie Hall, December 15, 1893. Harry Burleigh worked closely with the composer preparing the score for the performance. "I copied many of the orchestra parts of the 'New World' Symphony from his original partitur, getting it ready for its first performance by the Philharmonic," he recalled.[14] When Burleigh was asked about his own influence on the symphony, he stated, "[Although] the workmanship and treatment of the themes [of the symphony] was and is Bohemian . . . there is no doubt at all that Dvořák was deeply impressed by the old Negro 'spirituals' and also by [Stephen] Foster's songs. It was my privilege to sing repeatedly some of the old plantation songs for him in his house, and one in particular, 'Swing Low, Sweet Chariot,' greatly pleased him, and part of this old spiritual will be found in the second theme of the first movement of the symphony."[15]

To be sure, Dvořák's pronouncements regarding African American folk music were controversial, and discussions regarding the use of this material in composition ensued for years. Composers, at first, could not imagine celebrating the music of a once enslaved race. James Creelman, editor of the European Edition of the *New York Herald*, wrote a lengthy article on June 21, 1894, titled "Dvořák's

Negro Symphony," in the *Pall Mall Budget*, a London newspaper, describing the genesis of Dvořák's symphony and its critical reception. Creelman writes:

> How well I remember the rainy day in New York when the Bohemian composer told me, between whiffs of cigar smoke, that a new school of music in the Western World might be founded on the so-called Negro melodies! His splendid peasant-face was radiant with prophecy as he talked about the American composers of the future weaving the humble folk-songs of southern plantations into glorified forms. Within two weeks I had set forth this picture before the public in a series of articles, and a storm arose. From east and west, from north and south, from France, Germany, Russia, and Italy came protests and denunciations. What! Build symphonies, oratorios, and operas upon the songs of a debased and enslaved race? It was madness[,] sacrilege. Besides, there was no such thing as national music: art could not be localized and a hundred other formulas quite as false and narrow.
>
> Well, when Dvořák realized what he had done, he locked himself in a room and turned the lights out. For an hour he remained alone. No one knows what he did, but I strongly suspect that he folded his arms, set his teeth and stared at the darkness. It is a way he has when the world is too much for him. The next day Dvořák wrote an article reiterating his theory. He declared that the Negro melodies expressed every shade of feeling or thought—merry, frolicsome, tender, passionate, bold, solemn, majestic . . . But Dvořák stood his ground. He had gone to America in search of new territory, and having found it, he was not to be frightened away.
>
> At last the strain of the controversy became too great, and in sheer desperation the great Bohemian announced that he would write a symphony suggested from beginning to end by Negro melodies. . . .
>
> A great audience gathered to hear the first performance of the symphony in New York last winter, and I had the satisfaction of sitting beside Dvořák in his box, and hearing the roar of applause that swept through the hall at the close of the concert. . . . The critics mobbed the composer's box, each struggling to be the first to congratulate him. And when it was over and he reached the street, Dvořák took his hat off and mopped the perspiration from his brow. "It is well," he said in his simple way. "He who will can, he who can must."[16]

This symphony, like no other, impelled American composers to look seriously at both Native American and African American folk materials for their source of creativity. Dvořák was able to capture the pathos of many black spirituals so vividly that many people believe that the soul-stirring faux-spiritual melody of the Largo second movement is authentic. This movement became famous when William Arms Fisher, one of Dvořák's students at the conservatory, added the text "Goin' Home" to the tune.

For Still, Price, and Dawson, another inspiration was certainly the music of Samuel Coleridge-Taylor. A nationalist composer who looked to both his native Britain and to his black heritage as sources of inspiration for his compositions, Coleridge-Taylor was the most important composer of African descent at the turn of the century. Coleridge-Taylor was keenly interested in African American folk music, the result of contacts he had with black Americans early in his career. In 1897, he met the celebrated poet Paul Laurence Dunbar who had come to England to read some of his poems. The two men gave a series of joint programs, which included musical settings of seven Dunbar poems. Two years later, in 1899, the composer heard the Fisk Jubilee Singers in concert, which inspired several works including the well-known *Twenty-Four Negro Melodies, Transcribed for the Piano* (1905) and *Symphonic Variations on an African Air* (1906, based on the spiritual "I'm Troubled in Mind").

Coleridge-Taylor is best known for his trilogy of cantatas based on Longfellow's texts: *Hiawatha's Wedding Feast* (1898; "Onaway! Awake Beloved," the tenor aria, was well-known), *The Death of Minnehaha* (1899), and *Hiawatha's Departure* (1900). He also composed other choral music, an opera, a symphony, chamber music and art songs. His popular *Bamboula*, which concluded the Chicago Symphony concert, was originally written for piano and is based on spirited African dance rhythms. Coleridge-Taylor's "Danse Negre," the final movement of his *African Suite* (1898) (originally for piano quintet but later orchestrated by the composer), was inspired by the poetry of Paul Laurence Dunbar and may well have been a direct influence for Price's *Fantasie Negre*, for piano, also based on characteristic black folk dance rhythms.

Although Coleridge-Taylor died at the young age of 37, his influence as a composer and conductor was widespread. During his three visits to the United States between 1904 and 1910, Coleridge-Taylor made many friends and acquaintances, including some of the most distinguished musicians of the day. Among them were black songwriters James Weldon Johnson, J. Rosamond Johnson, Bob Cole, and concert violinist Clarence Cameron White. Other professional associations included George Whitefield Chadwick, Horatio Parker, and singer Alma Gluck. Coleridge-Taylor's passion for excellence also led him to the African American leader and educator Booker T. Washington, in whom he found a kindred spirit. On one of his visits, Coleridge-Taylor was even invited to the White House by Theodore Roosevelt. The esteem with which American and European composers and conductors held Samuel Coleridge-Taylor warranted a generous inclusion of his music on this special occasion celebrating the accomplishments of musicians of African descent.

Thus, two internationally respected composers—and not coincidentally, both European—validated for both black and white American composers the beauty of African American folk music and led the way for its use in large-scale instrumental forms. For the first time, Americans could envision the artistic viability of black music in the concert hall. It contrasted sharply with the stereotype that most Americans came to know of black music through the stage in the form of minstrel shows. The inherent subtleties of the spiritual, in rhythmic, harmonic, and melodic design, offered a myriad of possibilities to those who first arranged them in instrumental forms. The music of Coleridge-Taylor and Dvořák's epoch-making "New World Symphony" were testimony of the universal appeal of the songs of black people.

Ironically, these slave songs had flowed through the heart of the South from the 1830s, but recognition of the moving simplicity and profound but characteristic originality of the spirituals was to come later. They were neglected by slave owners and even by second- and third-generation African Americans, who, anxious to nullify their slave heritage, disdained them. It was not until the 1870s, after choral arrangements sung by the Fisk Jubilee Singers and other black college choirs received widespread recognition in this country and abroad, that the creative potential for the use of the spiritual was perceived.

In 1903, W. E. B. Du Bois wrote an unforgettable essay, "The Sorrow Songs," the last chapter of *The Souls of Black Folk*. Here he gave the spirituals a serious reinterpretation as an expression of innate triumph.

> Little of beauty has America given the world save the rude grandeur God himself stamped on her bosom; the human spirit in this new world has expressed itself in vigor and ingenuity rather than in beauty. And so by fateful chance the Negro folk song—the rhythmic cry of the slave—stands today not simply as the sole American music, but as the most beautiful expression of human experience, born this side of the seas. It has been neglected, it has been, and is, half despised, and above all it has been persistently mistaken and misunderstood; but notwithstanding, it still remains as the singular spiritual heritage of the nation and the greatest gift of the Negro people.[17]

Few composers considered the use of Native American and African American folk music until after Antonin Dvořák's time in this country. There were traces of nationalism in the music of American composers early in the nineteenth century, most notably in the music of William Henry Fry (1813–1864), Anthony Philip Heinrich (1781–1861), and Louis Moreau Gottschalk (1829–1869), who wrote a popular piano piece *La Bamboula* (Op. 2) subtitled "Danse des Negrès," composed in 1844–1845, but the influence of German art music held a firm place in American music composition until late in the century.

As I stated in an earlier chapter, George Whitefield Chadwick's Symphony No. 2 is often cited as a pioneering work in its musical expression of America, however unconscious that expression might have been. Edward MacDowell (1861–1908), perhaps the best known American composer of the nineteenth century, was not an advocate of nationalism, but in practice he was sympathetic to Dvořák's convictions. MacDowell's *Indian Suite for Orchestra*, published in 1897, represents one of the most successful endeavors of the period to incorporate American folk music, specifically Native American themes, into large-scale composition.

During the early years of the twentieth century the nationalist movement began in earnest. One of the most articulate champions of American composers and their cause was Arthur Farwell (1872–1952). In 1901, he founded the Wa-Wan Press for the primary purpose of promoting "by publication and public hearings, the most progressive, characteristic, and serious works of American composers, known or unknown."[18] As a publisher, Farwell gave priority to compositions that incorporated Negro songs, Indian melodies, cowboy songs, and America's newest indigenous music—ragtime. Of particular interest is that even the most prominent African American composers were not represented in Farwell's ten-year venture.

American composers were truly inspired by the success of Dvořák's "American" compositions—the "New World Symphony," the "American" Quartet, Op. 96, and the "American" Quintet, Op. 97—and by new opportunities to have their music published and performed. American composers flooded the concert halls with compositions incorporating black folk themes and Indian melodies. Henry Gilbert used Negro themes extensively in orchestral works—the *Comedy Overture on Negro Themes* was written in 1905, *Negro Rhapsody* for orchestra was published in 1912, and *The Dance in Place Congo* was written as a symphonic poem in 1906–1908 and revised as a ballet in 1916. Daniel Gregory Mason wrote a string quartet on Negro themes in 1918–1919 (published in 1930). John Powell, Harold Morris, Williams Arms Fisher, Henry Schoenfield, and Louis Gruenberg also wrote orchestral works that stressed the use of black folk music.

Briefly popular, the efforts of these composers have all but disappeared today. In their attempts to capture an American spirit, compositions with incongruous materials were created by grafting Native American or Negro folk elements onto late-nineteenth-century German structures. The early nationalists, earnest in their endeavors, lacked the cultural identification necessary to make the source material sound convincing out of its original context.

In an exposé, "Towards an American Music," composer Daniel Gregory Mason made a confession that summarizes the agonizing and continuous soul-searching of the American post-romantics in the early years of the twentieth century. His statement also makes clear how much this material was misunderstood and how condescending some composers were toward the use of ethnic materials. Speaking not only for himself, but for an entire generation of composers, his statements warrant quotation in full:

> How far was our leaning on folk-songs an unconscious means of escape from our shame in our own nakedness in confrontation with the rich raiment of European music? . . . For my own part, I confess that my joy in the use of beautiful simple tunes like "Deep River" in my first experiment in this direction, the *Quartet on Negro Themes*, was partly due to their giving me a chance to indulge my own naiveté without a sense of inferiority. The childlike quality of the tunes answered something

childlike in me. They would not have given the same release to a more complex or intellectual temperament. Yet gradually I came to see that there was wisdom as well as wit in Arthtus Whiting's question to my brother already recorded, after the first performance of the Quartet: "Is there any Negro blood in your family?" It pointed to a lack of complete correspondence between the temperament of the composer and the material of the composition. The material was scarcely complex enough for me, or I was scarcely simple enough for it—put it either way you choose. One result was that I coupled these highly primitive tunes with more complex elements of style assimilated from elsewhere, with which they discorded.

This discordance in style, which it took me some years to recognize and admit to myself, my friend [Edward Burlingame] Hill was keen enough to detect at once. "Despite many attractions and even beautiful episodes," he wrote me," I feel that there is little stylistic adjustment to the themes. Instead of having the treatment grow naturally out of the latter it seems as if . . . you forced them into harmonic and contrapuntal combinations which . . . do violence to their original character." How true this was I realized very slowly. Ten years later, completely revising the quartet, I came with almost a physical jolt upon "Deep River," most essentially simple of tunes, harmonized with the luxurious sliding "ninth chords" of sybaritic Debussy, and realized that I had committed a musical miscegenation that would have horrified [American composer] John Powell.[19] Debussy among Negroes!—only the sardonic wit of a Whiting could do justice to such a solecism.[20]

Aaron Copland aptly expressed the ideal that these composers strived for but which few were able to realize:

> The use of such materials ought never to be a mechanical process. They can be successfully handled only by a composer who is able to identify himself with, and reexpress in his own terms, the underlying emotional connotation of the material. . . . It is the reflection of those qualities in a stylistically appropriate setting, imaginative and unconventional and not mere quotation, that gives the use of folk tunes reality and importance.[21]

There was much experimentation in the quest for, as Copland put it, "a music that would speak of universal things in a vernacular of American speech rhythms."[22] While the generation of American composers who matured at the turn of the century looked to Native American music and African American spirituals as a source of creative inspiration, a younger generation coming into maturity during the 1930s, turned to "modern" music, that is, jazz. One of the few "older" composers in this group was Chicago-based John Alden Carpenter whose jazz-inspired works, including the ballets *Krazy Kat* (1q921) and *Skyscrapers*, commissioned by Sergei Diaghilev for the Ballet Russes (1926), were highly successful. It is from the vantage point of American musical nationalism, both from a conservative stance (Price) and in its modern guise (Carpenter) that the Chicago Symphony concert for the 1933 World's Fair Exposition was conceived.

11 The Symphony in E Minor

First and second generation African American composers closely identified with African American folk material and they eagerly appropriated it in small- and large-scale forms. Indigenous dance and other folk music, both sacred and secular, provided the foundation for the music of most of the black composers born before 1900. These composers, almost all nationalists, consciously turned to the folk music of African Americans as a basis for composition. Their mission was to prove to the world the inherent worth and musical richness of this material. These composers were willingly tied to their historical past through the use of folk music while simultaneously expressing themselves as individuals. In the 1930s, much of this music was considered conservative, but to these composers cultural expression outweighed any alliance with modern techniques. As these composers discovered, nationalism and modernism do not always readily coexist. In a poignant essay, "African-American Music: The Hidden Tradition," composer Hale Smith explains, "The telling of one's own story has long been a tradition of African American life. It is a tradition that extends centuries back into our collective histories. By telling our own story we speak, ideally, to and for us all. By being individuals, we have a chance of becoming universal. The true jazz musician recognizes this by preferring individuality to virtuosity, and it is a point understood by all genuine artists. The black composer of formal music also has considered technique as being subordinate to expression and has nearly always written with a live audience in mind."[1]

Harry T. Burleigh was the first black composer to gain national recognition. Of his more than 300 compositions, best known are the *Six Plantation Melodies for Violin and Piano* (1901), *From the Southland* for piano (1914), and *Southland Sketches* for violin and piano (1916). Burleigh's greatest legacy are his solo arrangements of spirituals for voice and piano, which have now become part of the standard repertoire in American song. Other composers, including

John Rosamond with his brother James Weldon Johnson, Clarence Cameron White, R. Nathaniel Dett, and John Wesley Work II, all published collections of spirituals or used spiritual melodies in their concert works during the first decades of the twentieth century.

The first symphonies by African Americans to be performed by major American orchestras—William Grant Still's *Afro-American Symphony* (1931), Florence Price's Symphony in E Minor (1933), and William Dawson's *Negro Folk Symphony* (1934)—fall within the context of American musical nationalism.[2] Still's *Afro-American Symphony*, composed in 1930, was written as part of a symphonic trilogy based on a composite musical portrait of the African American. When the work was completed, the composer added program notes and appended descriptive verses from poems by Paul Laurence Dunbar to each movement. The themes in Still's celebrated and often performed work are original, but the melodic contour and flavor are wholly African American. The primary theme of the sonata form first movement, for example, is a twelve-bar blues, and the secondary theme of that movement is in the style of a spiritual. The third movement, a syncopated dance, is notable for its inclusion of the tenor banjo, the first known use of this instrument in an orchestral work. Dawson's three-movement symphony differs from Still's work in that it is highly programmatic; the understanding of the symphony depends, in part, upon the recognition of the spirituals that form the basis of the work. Dawson scored his symphony for a romantic-era orchestra, but it includes an African clave and Adawura.

These compositions also represent the musical culmination of a black cultural awakening, referred to as the Harlem Renaissance or New Negro Movement, which emerged in metropolitan cities throughout the country in the 1920s and continued to the early 1930s. Nationalism was the backdrop from which the New Negro adapted old artistic forms into self-consciously racial idioms. This race consciousness united black intellectuals with common attitudes, ideals, and a sense of purpose.

The Negro Renaissance spawned a surge of literary, artistic, and musical creativity by America's African American artists. The affirmation of the values of the black cultural heritage had a decisive impact on William Grant Still, Florence Price, and William Dawson, who had as their primary goal the elevation of the Negro folk idiom, that is, spirituals, blues, and characteristic dance music, to symphonic form. This goal was accomplished through the fusion of elements from the neo-Romantic nationalist movement in the United States with elements from their own African American cultural heritage. In Still's *Afro-American Symphony* Price's Symphony in E Minor, and Dawson's *Negro Folk Symphony*, the Afro-American nationalist elements are integral to the style. The deceptively simple musical structure of these symphonies is inherently bound to the folk tradition in which they are rooted.

Dvořák's Symphony No. 9 and the spiritual inspiration of Samuel Coleridge-Taylor had a most decisive impact on Price. Although her score is relatively unknown, Price's work contributes significantly to the American nationalist movement and to the musical legacy of the Harlem Renaissance.[3] Price had become familiar with the use of vernacular elements in serious composition through her studies with George Chadwick at the New England Conservatory, but an examination of Price's symphony reveals that she thoroughly studied Dvořák's score. In its overall content, formal organization, orchestration, and spirit, she seems to have taken the Bohemian composer's directive quite personally.

Both Dvořák's and Price's symphonies are in the key of E Minor and both works have subtitles that suggest the inspiration for their primary source material. Originally subtitled the "Negro Symphony," Price's work assimilates characteristic Afro-American folk idioms into classical structures. Price abandoned a title that would have suggested a programmatic work and, perhaps, would have limited the perception of the symphony's scope. The subtitle has been almost obliterated from the score. Price apparently changed her mind prior to the first performance; none of the reviews refer to its programmatic name.

Price's score specifies a standard romantic-era orchestra, but she has augmented the percussion section to include several "special effects" instruments: cathedral chimes, small and large African drums, wind whistle, and orchestral bells.[4]

The first movement of the Symphony in E Minor is structured in sonata form. It begins with a six-measure introduction in E minor with the bassoons carrying a simple melody accompanied by strings. The bassoon melody then becomes a countersubject to the principal theme of the exposition, announced by solo oboe and clarinet. Significantly, the principal theme and its countermelody are built on a pentatonic scale, the most frequently used scale in Afro-American folk songs. The simple harmonization of the theme—i, iv, v, i—grows out of the suggested harmony of the theme itself. Note that the harmonization is entirely in the minor mode (see example 12).

The secondary theme, in G major, is played first by a solo French horn accompanied by sustained strings (see example 13). The treatment of the theme is markedly Dvořákian in its flavor and even resembles the melodic contour and orchestration of its counterpart. Written in the same key, Dvořák's melody is played by a solo flute and accompanied by strings.

In the development section, harmonic and motivic alteration of the themes is explored, but, in contrast to the exposition, the texture is primarily contrapuntal. At times, the themes are restated simultaneously. Also included in the development are inversions of the secondary theme and the primary theme. A modified recapitulation follows the development.

The second movement of the symphony also emulates Dvořák. Dvořák's famous Largo melody is framed by an introduction played by clarinets, bassoons, and brass. The composer has based his melody on a pentatonic scale on

Example 12. Symphony in E minor, movement 1, primary theme, mm. 7–10

Example 13. Symphony in E minor, movement 1, secondary theme, mm. 71–75

A-flat—A-flat, B-flat, C, E-flat, F (the second part of the melody introduces the lowered 7th in A-flat major—G-flat). The overall structure of Dvořák's Largo melody is ABA.

The second movement of Price's symphony is a hymn in E major. One is struck immediately by the similarity to Dvořák's interesting orchestration. Price's twenty-eight-measure hymn is played first by a brass choir (four horns in F, two trumpets in A, three trombones, and tuba). Price's interest in church music and the idiosyncrasies of organ sound probably also inspired this instrumentation. Organists often will draw a brass chorus on the organ as an alternative to foundation stops in hymn playing. The use of 16', 8', and 4' reeds produce a colorful and powerful, but not necessarily overbearing, sound.

In ABA form, the melody (played by the first trumpet) is built on a pentatonic scale on E (E, F#, G#, B, C#) (see example 14). Harmonically, the complexity of the hymn is a marked departure from folk music. One can observe that this arrangement, while melodically inspired by the spiritual, is solidly rooted in instrumental writing. The four-part chorus features rich sonorities which make use of raised sevenths, ninths, and appoggiaturas. The flutes and clarinets provide short interjections between phrases (these interludes provide a call-and-response format with the hymn melody), while African drums and timpani provide a continual underlying pulse. This parallels the verse-and-refrain form common in many Afro-American spirituals and other sacred music.

Of further interest in comparing the two movements is the way in which solo instruments are featured in both Dvořák's and Price's scores. For the famous Largo melody, Dvořák uses an English horn solo over a homophonic string accompaniment. Price's movement includes clarinet and English horn solos in fragments of the hymn melody over sustained strings.

Always committed to African American musical principals, Price turns directly to her roots for the third movement, thus departing significantly from

This score has been transposed. Price calls for horns in F and trumpets in A.

Example 14. Symphony in E minor, movement 2, mm. 1–5

Dvořák's European-derived scherzo. Entitled "Juba Dance," this movement is based on the syncopated rhythms of the antebellum folk dance, "pattin' juba." The dance involves a pattern of foot-tapping, hand-clapping, and thigh-slapping in intricate rhythmic patterns. Typically, slave fiddlers and banjo players would accompany the dancers' percussive body movements. There were several variations to the dance. According to the narrative of Lewis Paine in *Six Years in a Georgia Prison*, "This is done by placing one foot a little in advance of the other, raising the ball of the foot from the ground, and striking it in regular time, while, in connection, the hands are struck slightly together, and then upon the thighs. In this way they make the most curious noise, yet in such perfect order, it furnishes music to dance by."[5] Solomon Northup in his autobiography *Twelve Years a Slave* published in 1853, describes another variation of the dance: "[It was] accompanied with one of those unmeaning songs, composed rather for its adaptation to certain tune or measure, than for the purpose of expressing any distinct idea. The patting is performed by striking the hands on the knees, then striking the hands together, then striking the right shoulder with one hand, the left with the other—all the while keeping time with the feet and singing."[6]

For Price, the rhythmic element in Afro-American music was eminently important. Referring to her Symphony No. 3, which also uses the juba as the basis for a movement, she wrote, "In all of my works which have been done in the sonata form with Negroid idiom, I have incorporated a juba as one of the several movements because it seems to me to be no more impossible to conceive of Negroid music devoid of the spiritualistic theme on the one hand than strongly syncopated rhythms of the juba on the other."[7]

Price was the first composer to base a movement of a symphonic work on the rhythms of the juba, although the most famous and popular instrumental version of the juba is the fifth movement of R. Nathaniel Dett's *In the Bottoms* piano suite published in 1913, which Price surely would have known.[8] In addition to its use in the first and third symphonies, the syncopated rhythms of this dance are also used in the third movement of the *Piano Concerto in One Movement* (1934) and the third dance from the *Suite of Dances* (1939) (see example 15). Several works for piano, including "Ticklin' Toes" from the third dance from *Three Little Negro Dances* (1933) and "Silk Hat and Walking Cane" from *Dances in the Canebrakes* (1953), are also based on the antebellum folk dance.

Through minstrelsy the juba dance, or rather its later manifestation, the cakewalk, became popular in Europe in the 1880s and 1890s. It was not long before European art music composers were writing music based on the same rhythms. Claude Debussy was one of the first composers to make use of this new music that developed into ragtime. Debussy's "Golliwog's Cakewalk" from the *Children's Corner* piano suite (1905) foreshadowed the fascination of European composers with America's syncopated music of black folk origin.

Example 15. Dance No. 3 from *Suite of Dances*, mm. 1–8

Price sets the juba dance movement of the E-minor symphony in rondo form. In the A section, the violins present a sprightly, syncopated eight-measure rhythmic motive, simulating an antebellum fiddler. Against it, an "um-pah" bass is provided by a tonic-dominant pizzicato ostinato in the remaining strings and percussion (see example 16). The figures that form the basis of the dance are African-derived, entering the juba dance by way of black banjo and fiddle music with its percussive accompaniment of hand-clapping and foot-tapping.

Example 16. Symphony in E minor, movement 3, Juba Dance, mm. 1–5

The last movement of the symphony, marked "Finale," is the most straightforward. A Presto movement in E minor, in duple meter, its melodic and harmonic content is based on a four-measure triplet figure that ascends and descends around an E natural-minor scale (see example 17). Flutes, oboes, and violins render the unison line, and the remainder of the orchestra accompanies with sparse chords. The general form of the fourth movement loosely resembles a rondo.

In writing about the Still, Price, and Dawson symphonies of the early 1930s in an article discussing Dvořák's influence on American composers, the prominent literary critic Alain Locke, an ardent spokesman of the Harlem Renaissance, noted, "But with the successful presentation of symphonies based on folk themes from each of these young composers [Still and Dawson] in the last year, the hope for symphonic music in Negro idiom has risen notably. In 1935, ten years after his enthusiastic championing of the serious possibilities of jazz, Leopold Stokowski was able to present with his great Philadelphia Orchestra William Dawson's *Negro Folk Symphony*; certainly one of America's major contributions thus far to symphonic literature."[9] For Locke, the symphonies of Still and Dawson, based on recognizable folk themes and idioms, no doubt seemed the proper model for works by black composers.

The absence of overt identifiable ethnic characteristics in Florence Price's Symphony in E minor, such as quotations of black folk themes or the use of a blues progression, caused Locke to criticize her symphony in the essay cited earlier. He treated the discussion of her symphony as though it had no racial references, asserting, "In the straight classical idiom and form, Mrs. Price's work vindicates the Negro composer's right, at choice, to go up Parnassus by the broad high road of classicism rather than the narrower, more hazardous, but often more rewarding path of racialism. At the pinnacle, the paths converge, and the attainment becomes, in the last analysis, neither racial nor national, but universal music."[10]

Example 17. Symphony in E minor, movement 4, mm. 1–7

Before examining Locke's criticism of Price's work, one must be clear about those particular characteristics of Afro-American music that distinguish it from other types of music. Call-and-response organizational procedures, dominance of a percussive approach to music, and offbeat phrasing of melodic accents have been documented as typical musical characteristics in African American music. A predilection for a percussive polyrhythmic manner of playing and the inclusion of environmental factors as integral parts of the music event, such as hand-clapping and foot-patting, are also common characteristics.

Example 17. (*continued*)

Alain Locke's approach to black music was based on the degree to which certain black musical characteristics were present in a given composition. While this approach is valuable, it limits the scope of the black music tradition. If one examines Price's symphony from the qualitative perspective, rather than from Locke's quantitative approach, it becomes evident that Price's music is reflective of her cultural heritage.

As a close examination of Price's Symphony in E Minor has revealed, by no means did she exclude racial elements. Price's symphony, like Still's, does not depend upon the quotation of folk songs for its distinctive ethnicity. R. Nathaniel Dett has explained: "As it is quite possible to describe the traits, habits, and customs of a people without using the vernacular, so it is similarly possible to musically portray racial peculiarities without the use of national tunes or folk-songs."[11]

An analysis of Price's Symphony in E Minor reveals the presence, to a significant degree, of many of these and other underlying conceptual approaches to Afro-American music. For example, Price demonstrably transforms the polyrhythmic manner of approaching rhythm and the inclusion of environmental factors into musical entities in the juba-dance third movement. The steady accompaniment of the melody is a direct manifestation of physical body-movements that were the essence of "patting juba."

In recent articles, Olly Wilson has pointed out that the sound ideal in African American music is a heterogenous one. A tendency to maintain an independence of voices by means of timbral differentiation, or stratification, is common. Nowhere in Price's symphony is this clearer than in the second movement where the tonal colors of the brass choir and woodwind ensemble are juxtaposed with large and small African drums, cathedral chimes, and orchestral bells. Call-and-response patterns, also exhibited in this movement, between the brass choir and the woodwind ensemble, are another example of stratification.

Cultural characteristics are also borne out implicitly in the themes of the first movement. The first melody is based on a pentatonic scale, one of the most frequently used scales in Afro-American music. The preference for duple meter with syncopated rhythms and altered tones (lowered third and seventh, the so-called "blue notes") are also specific features of Afro-American music that characterize the melodies of this movement.

These traits in themselves may not be exclusive to black music, but in combination they are fundamental to the African American music tradition. Price's approach to composition derives essentially from African American music, and the predominance of these core characteristics is the best evidence for this.

Locke's criticism of Price's symphony must be examined also from another perspective. Despite the appearance of equal participation of women in the Harlem Renaissance, in music, literature, the plastic and visual arts, patterns of exclusion were notable, especially by men in influential positions.

Although Locke's role in the Harlem Renaissance was controversial, he was an ardent spokesperson whose ideas gave "definitive shape" to the New Negro movement. Locke, however, personally and professionally favored men. His contempt for women in the classroom and disparagement of their intellect, which were carried over into his arts critiques, are well documented.[12] Although Price had a supportive professional environment in Chicago that included both men and women, one must wonder if Locke's widely read, perhaps deliberate misrepresentation of her symphony impressed her. Price never defended her work against Locke's criticisms. Perhaps she felt vindicated by all of the critical acclaim she received.

An impartial examination of Price's symphony reveals that she does not abandon her African American heritage. Rather, the symphony inherently incorporates many aspects of the black music tradition within a Euro-American medium—orchestral music. In a more subtle way than either Still's *Afro-American Symphony* or Dawson's *Negro Folk Symphony*, Price's compositional approach does make manifest the Afro-American heritage in music. As Samuel Floyd has stated, "When it [the music of black American composers] successively communicates essentials of the Afro-American experience, in spite of its European basis, it becomes something more than either European or Afro-American. It becomes, to some extent, at least, black music."[13] Following the first performance of the symphony, Edward Moore of the *Chicago Tribune* wrote, "Mrs. Price . . . displayed high talent both in what she did and what she omitted, each one of which is a test for a composer. She has based her work on racial folk song idioms, choosing some first-rate melodies and harmonizing them fully and yet with the essential simplicity that they demand. She would seem to be well acquainted with the use of orchestral instrumental color. With these merits she has another and perhaps greater one. She knows how to be concise, how to avoid overloading and elaboration. The performance made a well-deserved success."[14]

Racial pride was quintessential to the Harlem Renaissance and the black nationalist movement in music. It was this attitude of black pride and consciousness that permeated much of Florence Price's music of the 1930s and the Harlem Renaissance, and the New Negro Movement was the background against which she developed as a composer.

The New Negro Movement understood the potential of Afro-Americans and strove to reinforce their dignity. Rooted in the hope for the future of black people, African Americans no longer apologized for their musical heritage but rather celebrated their cultural uniqueness. For Price, the Negro idiom in music became a source of inspiration in serious composition. One hears this music not as propaganda but as an important legacy of the New Negro's contribution to America's writings.

The Old State House, Little Rock, Arkansas.

Florence Beatrice Smith, n.d. Photo believed to have been taken around 1906. It was given to Kemper Harreld (1885–1971), who was head of the music department at Atlanta Baptist College (presently Morehouse College) from 1911–1953. Harreld founded the Morehouse College Glee Club and was its first director.

Thomas J. Price, n.d.

Florence Price's daughters: Florence Louise (in plaid) and Edith Cassandra.

Riverwood home, n.d.

Several of the composers involved in the August 25, 1934, "O Sing a New Song" Negro Pageant at the Century of Progress Exhibition. Front row, left to right: William Grant Still, H. Lawrence Freeman, W. C. Handy, J. Rosamond Johnson, Will Vodery. Back row, third from left: Charles Cooke. Back row, fifth from left: Noble Sissle. Image of William Grant Still used by permission, all rights reserved to William Grant Still Music.

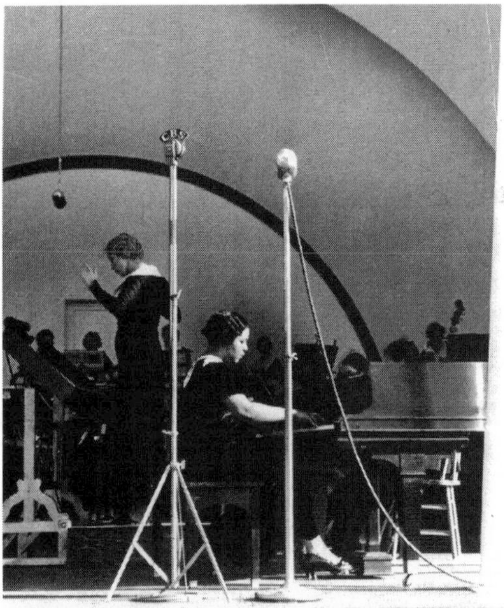

Margaret Bonds as guest soloist with the Woman's Symphony Orchestra of Chicago, 1934. Ebba Sundsstrom, conducting. Performance of Florence Price's *Concerto in One Movement*.

Florence Louise, 1940.

Edith Cassandra, n.d.

Florence Louise (left), Marion Quinney Ross (middle), unidentified person (right), 1946. Ms. Ross is the daughter of Florence Price's close friend Perry Quinney.

Edith Cassandra, n.d.

Florence Louise [Robinson], n.d.

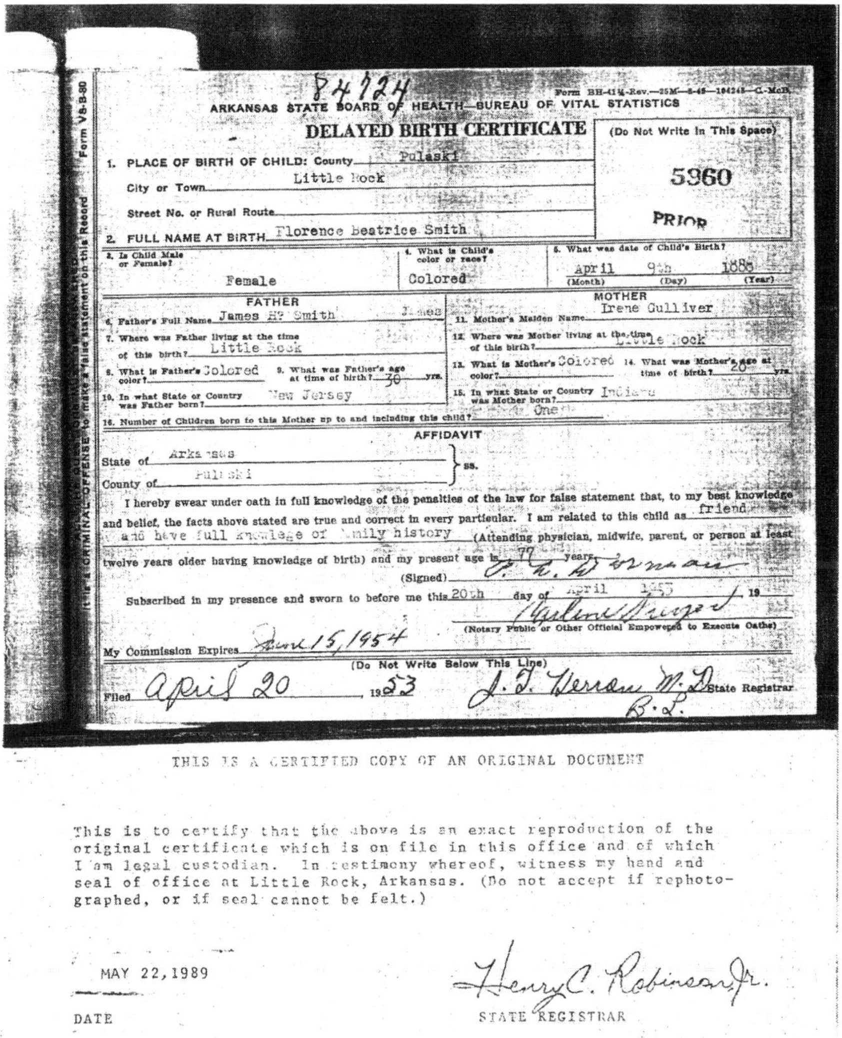

84724

Form BH-41½-Rev.—25M—8-45—104245—C.-McB.

ARKANSAS STATE BOARD OF HEALTH—BUREAU OF VITAL STATISTICS

Form VS-B-80

It is a CRIMINAL OFFENSE to make a false statement on this Record

DELAYED BIRTH CERTIFICATE

(Do Not Write In This Space) 5360 PRIOR

1. PLACE OF BIRTH OF CHILD: County Pulaski
City or Town Little Rock
Street No. or Rural Route
2. FULL NAME AT BIRTH Florence Beatrice Smith
3. Is Child Male or Female? Female
4. What is Child's color or race? Colored
5. What was date of Child's Birth? April (Month) 9th (Day) 1886 (Year)

FATHER
6. Father's Full Name James H? Smith James
7. Where was Father living at the time of this birth? Little Rock
8. What is Father's color? Colored
9. What was Father's age at time of birth? 30 yrs.
10. In what State or Country was Father born? New Jersey

MOTHER
11. Mother's Maiden Name Irene Gulliver
12. Where was Mother living at the time of this birth? Little Rock
13. What is Mother's color? Colored
14. What was Mother's age at time of birth? 20 yrs.
15. In what State or Country was Mother born? Indiana
16. Number of Children born to this Mother up to and including this child? One

AFFIDAVIT

State of Arkansas
County of Pulaski } ss.

I hereby swear under oath in full knowledge of the penalties of the law for false statement that, to my best knowledge and belief, the facts above stated are true and correct in every particular. I am related to this child as friend and have full knowlege of family history (Attending physician, midwife, parent, or person at least twelve years older having knowledge of birth) and my present age is 77 years.

(Signed) [signature]

Subscribed in my presence and sworn to before me this 20th day of April 1953 19

[signature]
(Notary Public or Other Official Empowered to Execute Oaths)

My Commission Expires June 15, 1954

(Do Not Write Below This Line)

Filed April 20 1953 J. T. Herron M.D. State Registrar B.L.

THIS IS A CERTIFIED COPY OF AN ORIGINAL DOCUMENT

This is to certify that the above is an exact reproduction of the original certificate which is on file in this office and of which I am legal custodian. In testimony whereof, witness my hand and seal of office at Little Rock, Arkansas. (Do not accept if rephotographed, or if seal cannot be felt.)

MAY 22, 1989
DATE

Henry C. Robinson Jr.
STATE REGISTRAR

Florence Beatrice Smith, Delayed Birth Certificate, April 20, 1953.

Lawrence Robinson, Florence Louise's son, 1965.

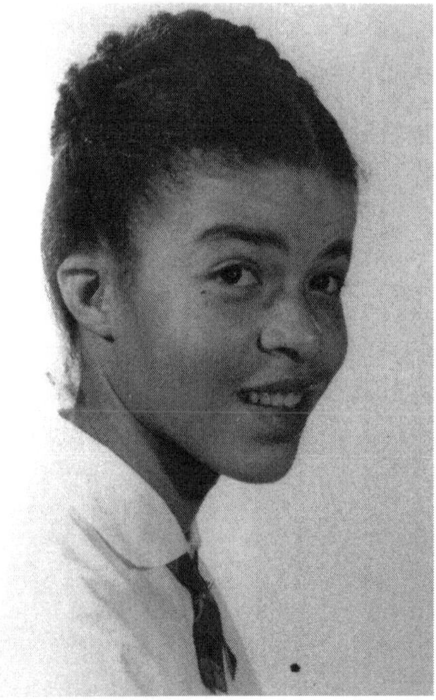

Vicky [Taylor Hammond], Edith's daughter, 1956, age 12.

Lawrence and Timothy Robinson in front of the Florence B. Price Elementary School, Chicago, 1964.

Florence Beatrice Smith, 1940.

Florence Beatrice Smith, 1940.

12 O Sing a New Song

The remainder of 1933 was a dizzying flurry of activity for Florence Price as she steadily gained recognition as a composer. Just two weeks after her symphony was performed by the Chicago Symphony she was invited to play two of her piano compositions at Kimball Hall, July 1, 1933, in a program of original compositions organized by members of the American Conservatory faculty. Among those participating were two of Chicago's distinguished composers, Arthur Olaf Anderson with whom Price had studied, and organist Leo Sowerby, a prolific composer of church music, with whom Price had developed a cordial professional relationship.[1] Price played the first movement of her award-winning Piano Sonata in E Minor and "Little Cabin Lullaby" from her newly composed *Dances in the Canebrakes* for piano.[2]

This concert marked the beginning of numerous performances of the Piano Sonata and the *Dances.* For those pianists who wanted to perform large-scale piano works by a black composer, Price's compositions were a welcome addition to the repertoire. The three-movement sonata, which is rather conservative harmonically and structurally, is an expansive work in the romantic tradition. The first movement adheres closely to classic formal design—a sonata form movement with a slow introduction. The first theme, in E minor, is a confident and uplifting spiritual-like theme (see example 18). A short transition leads to a threefold statement of a lyrical second theme in C major (see example 19). Both themes are aptly treated in the development and recapitulations, sometimes accompanied by straightforward harmonies and sometimes with more nebulous modulating sequences.

The tender *andante* second movement is in rondo form. Once again, Price has written a lyrical spiritual-like theme, treated with characteristic syncopated rhythms and simple harmony (see example 20). Price's love of romantic music is

Example 18. Piano Sonata in E minor, movement 1, theme 1, mm.13–21

Example 19. Piano Sonata in E minor, movement 1, theme 2, mm. 53–61

particularly evident here; the two secondary themes are reminiscent of Chopin and Schumann, respectively (see example 21).

The sonata ends with a virtuosic *scherzo-allegro*. The final movement is divided into two sections. The main theme of the first section is a descending E minor scale that gives way to a lyrical cantabile theme (see example 22). The second section is based on syncopated dance rhythms, which Price found particularly expressive of her African American roots. This leads to some brilliant passage work in which the motives are taken through several modulations and meter changes.

Dances in the Canebrakes, "based on authentic Negro rhythms," became a favorite of pianists and is one of Price's best-known works. The work was

Example 20. Piano Sonata in E minor, movement 2, primary theme, mm. 1–10

Example 21. Piano Sonata in E minor, movement 2, first episode, mm. 21–24

Example 22. Piano Sonata in E Minor, movement 3, mm. 318–328

published in 1953 by Affiliated Musicians/Mills Music as a three-movement suite, each movement with a fanciful title.[3] All three dances follow a ternary format but each is quite different in character. "Nimble Feet," the most lively of the published dances, is characterized by a dotted-rhythm melody in the bass that is taken over by the right hand on its repeat. "Tropical Noon," the second of the three dances, is an introspective movement. The titles of these movements changed over time; based on the mood of this dance, this movement may have been originally the "Little Cabin Lullaby" performed in 1933 for the American Conservatory audience.

"Silk Hat and Walking Cane" aspires to capture the essence of the cakewalk, a favorite antebellum dance. The descriptive title refers to the fine attire slaves wore during the merriment as they pranced around in high-step, each couple hoping to win the coveted prize cake. First introduced to white audiences through minstrel shows, the cakewalk became the rage of Europe by the turn of the century. The music that accompanied the dance was characterized by its syncopated melody, played by a violin or harmonic, for example, and accompanied by the steady beat of foot-tapping and hand-clapping. Originally in E-flat and later transposed to F major, "Silk Hat and Walking Cane" aptly captures the grace and spirit of the original dance (see example 23).

Throughout 1933 and 1934, Price remained visible at the Century of Progress Exhibition. The National Council of Women sponsored a series of composer-artist programs given each Tuesday and Thursday throughout the fair in which Price, one of the few black artists invited to perform, was a regular guest. On Thursday, July 13, 1933 she gave a 30-minute lecture to the large audience and played a group of her own piano compositions. Soprano Cleo Wade, a member of the Chicago Music Association, who also performed, was accompanied by Price.

The momentum of recognition for Price continued through the summer of 1933. On July 30, Price was accorded one of the highest honors for an Illinois composer. She was invited to present an entire program of her compositions at the Illinois Host House at the Exhibition. The program included art songs,

Example 23. "Silk Hat and Walking Cane," mm. 1–4

part-songs, piano music, and music for violin and piano. For the program, which attracted many of Chicago's most respected composers, Price was assisted by violinist Walter Dyett and her Treble Clef [Glee] Club. Composer Carrie Jacobs-Bond, probably America's most successful female songwriter of the time (she is known for "I Love You Truly"), whose music was often programmed alongside Price's, was one of the invited guests to this special program.

In the midst of the Century of Progress activity, the annual convention of the NAACP met in Chicago that July, and the organization looked to the Chicago Music Association to provide music for the week's events. Although the members of the Association were feeling a bit hassled and overwhelmed by having so many demands placed upon their time and talents by both the NAACP and the Fair activities, many of these musicians took the rush of events in stride. Since the NAACP had agreed to provide transportation to and from its meetings, the Association members did the best they could to accommodate the civil rights organization. Among the soloists to appear were Fannie Carter Woods, for whom Price arranged several of her spiritual settings, and Margaret Bonds. The Olivet Baptist Choir, Smith Concert Singers, the Umbrian Glee Club, and Price's Treble Clef Club were among the featured choirs.

One of the striking features of the Fair was its pageants or plays with pre-composed unrelated music. These pageants were venues that featured many of Chicago's talented artists, including African Americans. In mid-August, one of these pageants was presented by the International Congress of Women at the Stevens Hotel in a program of African American music. The International Congress included only a few black members in its organization, but they were supportive of black women's struggle for equal rights. The program, written by Sally Steward, then president of the National Association for Colored Women and a vice president of the International Congress, honored three of Chicago's prominent black artists: concert soprano Anita Patti Brown, concert pianist Hazel Harrison, and Florence Price as both concert pianist and composer.

The pageant interspersed spirituals with art songs and instrumental music. The numbers that were singled out for being particularly well performed included the spirituals "Steal Away" and R. Nathaniel Dett's choral version of "Somebody's Knocking at Your Door." The Imperial Opera Co., under the direction of Gertrude Smith Jackson, sang William Dawson's art song "Out in the Fields," and in her role as one of the "daughters" in the pageant, Margaret Bonds performed Price's *Fantasy Negro* for piano. Maude Roberts George, who reported the event in the *Chicago Defender*, remarked that officers and foreign delegates of the Congress were present for the program and that "300 extra chairs were brought in to accommodate the vast audience."[4]

With so much activity during the spring and summer of 1933, Price took a much-needed vacation from mid-August to mid-September. She even missed the National Association of Negro Musicians annual convention in Indianapolis, an event she almost always attended. Although the Chicago Music Association received many requests to meet the now well-known composer, Price left the city for her summer home, called Riverwood, in Kankakee, Illinois. An older home with a large front porch where Price spent many hours looking out at the woods before her, Riverwood was her escape from the madness of the city. Her daughters loved it there, too, although after they were grown she often went there alone. Sometimes Perry Quinney, Price's longtime friend and confidant from Little Rock, would come to visit. They reminisced about the Little Rock of old and about plans to visit and travel together in the future. The respite from the city did Price good, for that September the *Chicago Defender* reported that the "restful atmosphere has greatly improved her" and that Price was even able to get some work done while she was away.[5]

When Price returned from vacation, she immersed herself in her work once again, continuing to perform and give lectures. In late September, she gave a talk in appreciation of the Ferrell Symphony Orchestra, an orchestra of black musicians founded in 1921 by Dr. Harrison H. Ferrell, a violinist and conductor of some repute. She also performed that same week for the R. Nathaniel Dett Club.

With the activities of the Fair continuing in full swing, Price's Treble Clef Club was busier than ever. They appeared regularly at the Exhibition at the invitation of James A. Mundy, director of the Mundy choristers, who organized programs of African American folk music and guest artists three times a week. In late October, the Mundy choristers and the Quinn Chapel Choir made their regular appearances at the Floating Theater. That week, their program coincided with the activities of the Illinois Federation of Music Clubs, and, at the Federation's request, a special performance of black music was organized. As the only black member of the Illinois Federation of Music Clubs, Price was probably the liaison between the almost all-white group and the black choirs. Once again black music was featured at the Fair. For this occasion, the Billingsly Men of Song under the direction of Herman Billingsly, Price's Treble Clef Club accompanied by Estella Bonds, and special guests, the Tennessee State College Choir, performed to the delight of the predominately white audience, who showed a genuine appreciation for the musical offerings of the black choirs.[6] Before leaving Chicago, Tennessee State's choir was invited to the home of Robert S. Abbott, editor of the *Chicago Defender*, where Price participated as hostess to the young choir.

Early 1934, with no signs of activity letting up, Price composed a new choral work, *New Moon*, for the Florence B. Price A Cappella Chorus, directed by Grace W. Tompkins. The choir was organized in January 1933 and, although an amateur group, it steadily received praise for their programs, often performing to capacity audiences throughout the city.

Although Price had been enormously busy with outside music activities for months, she was already working on her next large-scale work, a piano concerto. The earliest references to the concerto are from October 1933, when Price's friend and patron Helen Armstrong Andrews, who would be the dedicatee of the Concerto, wrote to the composer about the work.[7] A diary entry dated Tuesday, December 5, 1933, informs us that efforts continued on the concerto through 1933.[8] The entry reads:

> Met Dr. Frederick Stock on Michigan Ave. He stopped, shook hands and chatted. Asked what I was working on. Told him I was working on a piano concerto. "Good," he said. "Why not have the young woman (Margaret Bonds) who played so well (referring to [John Alden] Carpenter's *Concertino* on same night my symphony was played) learn it so it can be played." I reminded him of his advice to me to hear all the rehearsals I could and asked him if there was a chance of getting in to any of his. He said he would speak to Mr. Voeghi. [*sic*, Henry E. Voegeli, manager of the Chicago Symphony Orchestra]

Two days later her request was approved.

> went up to Chi. Symph. Orch. Office. Saw Mr. Voegeli, business mgr. Asked him if Mr. Stock had spoken to him about me getting in to rehearsals. Said he had not seen Mr. Stock since Mon. He seemed surprised that Mr. Stock should think of having me passed in. However, he sent a man down with me who unlocked a door apparently used by those connected with the office upstairs. I had the fine chance of listening to the pianist Schnabel in rehearsal.[9]

These diary entries show, once again, how supportive Stock was of Price and how interested he was in her career. Stock maintained his interest in the concerto for some time. In a letter to Price, February 6, 1934, Eric DeLamarter, assistant conductor of the symphony, wrote: "If you will bring your concerto down to Orchestra Hall any morning next week, I will see that Mr. Stock has a look at it."[10]

Some people thought it advantageous for Price to play the solo part of the concerto herself. Mrs. Andrews wrote: "Thank you for the honor you are to do me and which pleases me very much. I am glad that you have written something of this kind and can appear before the public and play the solo part. It will make you known and of course it will help to advertise you. I think it is wonderful for a woman to be able to write music as you do and again I must tell you how proud I am of you and interested in your success."[11] Indeed, the composer was at the piano at the first performance in Orchestra Hall on June 24, 1934. The occasion was the sixty-seventh commencement exercises of the Chicago Musical College, where Price was taking graduate courses in composition and orchestration.[12] The composer-pianist, representing her class in composition, was featured on a program that included movements of Beethoven's Piano Concerto in C Minor, portions of Weber's *Der Freischütz*, and Edward Lalo's *Symphonie Espagnole*.

At this premiere, the concerto "scored a big success," as a review in the *Chicago Musical Leader* attests. A lengthy article in the *Chicago Tribune* headlined the performance of the concerto in its review: "PLAYS COMPOSITION AT COMMENCEMENT. . . . As the concluding number on the lengthy program, Mrs. Price played her Concerto in D Minor for piano and orchestra, accompanied by the symphony orchestra of the college. Equal in length to some symphonies, the concerto, aside from its technical perfections, disclosed a thematic substance rich in syncopated and spiritual colors."[13]

Price played her concerto again in the two-piano arrangement two months later on August 30, at the national convention of the National Association of Negro Musicians in Pittsburgh, with Margaret Bonds playing the orchestra reduction. In addition to Price's concerto, the program included several selections by concert violinist Louis Vaughn Jones accompanied by composer and pianist Camille Nickerson. Jones, head of the string department at Howard University, had concertized through Europe during the 1920s and was a favorite performer at the NANM conventions. For the Pittsburgh audience, Jones performed violin works by Kreisler and Heifetz and he included spirituals arranged by Coleridge-Taylor ("Deep River") and by himself ("Calvary"). Concert soprano Lillian Evanti also performed that evening. She sang Verdi arias and concluded her portion of the program with Harry T. Burleigh's spiritual "Lord, I Want to Be a Christian," dedicated to her by the composer. Miss Evanti was accompanied by William Duncan Allen, a pianist who later earned international recognition as accompanist to baritone Todd Duncan.

Reviewed by both the *Pittsburgh Sun Telegraph* and the *Pittsburgh Press*, Price's concerto received critical acclaim. Of particular note are the reviewer's impressions of Price's evolving musical style—a style that now revealed a voice all her own. J. Fred Lissfelt of the *Sun Telegraph* wrote, "Florence Price's contribution in the form of a piano concert was by far the most important feature of the concert for here we see what the Negro has taken from his own idiom and with good technique is beginning to develop alone. There is real American music and Mrs. Price is speaking a language she knows." After describing the formal structure of the concerto, Ralph Lewando of the *Pittsburgh Press* added, "Coherent musical ideas prevail throughout, and the thematic material is logically developed."[14]

In fact, Price's *Concerto in One Movement* had been performed just prior to the NANM convention. The performance given on August 25, was a feature at the largest of the Century of Progress Exhibition's Negro pageants, "O Sing A New Song," an extravaganza "presented by the Negroes of America at Soldier Field."

The three-act pageant was conceived as a retrospective of the transformation of the African to the African American—from the life as a free people through the dark days of enslavement (Act I ends with a scene called "Ghost Ship: The Voyage") and, after Emancipation, to the emergence of a spirit-filled people, determined and hopeful. The pageant was, in particular, a celebration of black music, dance, and drama in its continuum of African origins through the 1920s.

Composer Noble Sissle, the overall director and producer of the production, stated in rather romantic language:

> The Negro will be his own historian in song and drama at the coming pageant. There will run through his story the cadence of his climbing feet, both in the weird beating of the African tom-tom and in its modern elaboration, the monotonous minor of the blues. But above that cadence will rise like the sound of lifting wings the exaltation of the spirituals.
>
> The Negro has come down the centuries to this hour in pathos and patience, in tragedy and tears, but always with a rainbow cast about his shoulders. He has lived by his dreams. Today he reads the future of his race in the fruitful lives of men who have distinguished themselves as educators, as scientists, as writers, as painters, and greatly as composers of music. Dreams are coming true.[15]

This pageant could boast of the participation of many of the most prominent black composers and performers in America. The pageant began with a lengthy Prologue comprised of orchestral music in which four composer/performers conducted the orchestra in his or her own work. N. Clark Smith, a winner of the 1930 Wanamaker composition competition, conducted the ensemble in the first two movements of his *Negro Choral Symphony* for orchestra and chorus. Next on the program was Harry T. Burleigh who offered an "Ode to Ethiopia." This work is almost assuredly the composer's *Ethiopia Saluting the Colors*, originally an art song written for solo voice and piano (1915) and later orchestrated. It is doubtful that Burleigh both sang and conducted his own piece; it is more likely that N. Clark Smith, already on the podium and a seasoned conductor, led the orchestra in this dramatic song. Burleigh's setting both salutes the colors of the Ethiopian flag—yellow, red, and green—and gives a dramatic interpretation of Walt Whitman's narrative describing a black slave woman, "Ethiopia," being watched by a Union soldier as she curtsies while observing Sherman's army regiment pass in review.

Third on the program was Price's *Piano Concerto in One Movement*, which she may have conducted herself, as the program suggests.[16] For this performance, Margaret Bonds played the solo part. Abbie Mitchell concluded the Prologue with an unidentified song. The opening recitation of the pageant, entitled "Chronicle One," was given then by Richard B. Harrison who narrated the entire pageant.

Composers Harry Lawrence Freeman, N. Clark Smith, Will Vodery, and Will Marion Cook provided original music for the dramatization of Act I, *Africa*. The setting is an African village where men and women work and pay homage to the gods through dance and song, and where children play. Each of the ten sections has a descriptive title: The Man from the Jungle, Tom-Toms (Freeman), Iron Workers (Smith), Muttering Thunder (Smith), Bamboula Fire Dance (Smith), Bangangi (Smith), The Lion Hunt (Freeman), The Two Moods—Sadness and Happiness (Vodery). The climax of *Africa*, entitled "Kings Kraal" (Freeman), is the horrifying capture of the village King and his subjects by Portuguese slave traders. The act closes with Cook's "Ghost Ship: The Voyage," symbolizing the crossing of the Atlantic in slave ships. Katherine Dunham, who was now well known for her pioneering interpretations of African and African American folk dance, was the lead choreographer for this portion of the pageant.

Act II, Plantation Life, recounts the birth of the spiritual in the dark days of slavery. Orator and abolitionist Frederick Douglass makes an appearance during the course of the episode, as does Abraham Lincoln (both played by local actors), who frees the slaves at the conclusion of the act. Expressing the spiritual fervor of Emancipation, the Chronicler/Narrator reads:

> Their necks bent down with chains, their souls
> Translating into song the inward hope,
> They moved to the old beat of the strong heart.
> And then, amid the clamor of the guns, a voice
> Proclaiming Freedom, and the chains fell off
> And a light flooded over them—free—free!
> And they stood upright, singing, in the sun.

Booker T. Washington (played by local actor Herman Lawrence) opened Act III, *America*, with a soliloquy on education. At the turn of the century, Washington was the most influential race leader, and as head of Institute he symbolized the importance of the advancement of the race through self-determination. From there, Act III is a celebration of the African American's contribution to American music and dance in all of its manifestations. There was minstrel music provided by the Eighth Regiment Band, the American Legion Band, and the Wendell Philips [High School] Boy's Band, with singing by the Federal and Umbrian Glee clubs. The Fisk Jubilee Singers who brought the world the Negro spiritual were depicted by the Cotton Pickers Quartette, the Metropolitan Community Church Choir, and the Mundy Singers.

The second half of Act III illustrated twentieth-century vernacular forms by a star-studded group of musicians. The famed Bert Williams and George Walker vaudeville team was represented by members of the Umbrian Glee Club conducted by Will Marion Cook. A rendition of Scott Joplin's "Maple Leaf Rag" was interpreted by jazz pianist Earl Hines whose band was in the midst of a residency at the Grand Terrace Ballroom in Chicago.[17] Pianist J. Rosamond Johnson played reminiscences of the popular songs he had written as part of the songwriting team of Bob Cole and the Johnson Brothers. Much of America, both black and white, knew the hits from their successful operettas—*The Shoo-Fly Regiment* (1906) and *The Red Moon* (1908) with all-black casts, and *Sleeping Beauty and the Beast* (1901) and *Humpty Dumpty* (1904), which were white musicals.

Black dance was well represented at the pageant, too. Tap dance great Bill Robinson did a rendition of "The Step Dance." White dancer Irene Castle performed some of the dances she made popular with her husband, Vernon. All of white America danced the turkey trot, the fox-trot (both invented by James Reese Europe), the one-step, and the Castle Walk to music composed by black composer and bandleader James Reese Europe.[18] The pageant audience continued to clap their hands and tap their feet to the upbeat music of Eubie Blake and Noble Sissle's *Shuffle Along* (1921). Sissle led his band and a group of singers from the Grand Terrace Ballroom in a medley of hits from the successful Broadway show. Who could sit still while the band played "Shuffle Along," "Love Will Find a Way," "In Honeysuckle Time," and "I'm Just Wild about Harry"?

And what would American music be without the blues? The pageant concluded with the "story of the St. Louis Blues," conducted by the composer himself, W. C. Handy, and sung by Abbie Mitchell. In the spirit of the communal black church or an African celebration, the audience participated in the singing of the "National Negro Hymn," *Lift Every Voice and Sing*, written by James Weldon and J. Rosamond Johnson, at the close of the program. They also sang "O Sing a New Song," written especially for the occasion by Will Vodery and Noble Sissle. In the midst of the Depression, the optimistic, almost banal text must have been particularly uplifting to so many in the mostly black audience.

> Be glad you're living—Songs of thanksgiving
> Keep worry off your mind
> So let us sing the story
> Make heaven ring with glory
> You'll find your troubles
> Will float like bubbles
> Let's Sing a New Song

There was little during the course of the Century of Progress Exhibition that would rival this pageant in size and importance for black people. The African American was chronicled as a people of fortitude from slavery to Freedom and they paid homage to their African roots. Some of the most influential black artists in America participated in the event, sharing their African American creative gifts with the world. As the primary organizer and promoter of the event, it was important to Noble Sissle that all of black music be documented. Although during the course of the story, classical music is virtually omitted, the musical Prologue is given over entirely to large-scale concert music by black composers. That Price was invited to conduct her Concerto in this star-studded venue for so large an audience is testimony to the high esteem with which she was regarded as a composer by the early 1930s.

13 The *Piano Concerto in One Movement*

Price's concerto received widespread attention a few months later when it was performed on October 12, 1934, by the Woman's Symphony Orchestra of Chicago under the direction of Ebba Sundstrom at the famous Ford Symphony Gardens at the Century of Progress Exhibition.[1] Margaret Bonds, who had played the concerto twice before, was the soloist.

The Woman's Symphony was a well-respected ensemble in the city, and they were invited to perform at the Fair on numerous occasions. They played the dedication concert of the Ford Symphony Gardens on June 7, 1934, for an audience of over 2000. Boasting a state-of-the-art performance shell, the "Gardens" was a new orchestra hall on the grounds of the Fair built by Henry Ford. During the 1920s and 1930s, about thirty women's symphony orchestras were organized to provide professional opportunities for women to perform the symphonic repertoire.[2] The Woman's Symphony Orchestra of Chicago, with 100 women players by the 1933–1934 season, became probably the best known of these orchestras because of its regular concert season and radio broadcasts.

One of the orchestra's primary goals was "to present to the public compositions of American women composers, especially Chicago women composers, and also to engage Chicago artists as soloists."[3] The lack of serious opportunities for the orchestral music of American composers and women composers was an ever-present issue. Here was a very respected institution devoted to eradicating both obstacles. Composer Eleanor Everest Freer in an acerbic article, "Discrimination against American Music," in the *Musical Leader* spoke out publicly against this double discrimination. She wrote:

> Why—when public performance of an American woman's composition, on programs of a strictly classic type, meets with the same acclaim as the imported work,

> why does there still exist discrimination (among the powers that be) against this native music? In France, Chaminade enjoys equal success with all French composers of equal ability. Are we less just towards ou[r] women? It would seem so; in which case, why encourage women to enter this field? I have found that the greatest barrier against success for the American composer has been the slogan of half a century: "If we want good music, we'll import it"—a policy adhered to by too many publishers, teachers, and artists, and in consequence, too large a public. It is death to the advancement of American Musical Art.[4]

With such staunch support by the Woman's Symphony Orchestra of Chicago, the performance of Price's *Concerto in One Movement* marked the beginning of a long and fruitful association between the orchestra and the composer.

The October 12 program, devoted to women composers, was divided into an afternoon program and an evening program. Both of these concerts were broadcast on WBBM-CBS radio. Before the concerts, Carrie Jacobs-Bond, who delivered an address on "Women in Music," and Mrs. H. H. A. Beach (Amy Beach), arguably America's most distinguished woman composer, whose *Gaelic Symphony* was being performed on the evening program, were honored at a luncheon.

Of the eight compositions on the afternoon program, which included Cecile Chaminade's *Concertstueck* and Eleanor Everest Freer's ballet "Fantasie" from *The Legend of Spain* (orchestrated by George Dasch), it was the Price concerto that received special attention. Music critic Glenn Dillard Gunn, writing for the *Chicago Herald and Examiner*, began his review with a few condescending remarks about women: "As is the habit of the ladies, the event was somewhat overwhelmed by the social amenities. Carrie Jacobs-Bond delivered an address on 'Women in Music' which ended as a deft tribute to Henry Ford's generosity." When Gunn turned his attention to the music, his attitude changed. He continued, "Mrs. Bonds remarks were interesting, but the quality of the music presented by Ebba Sundstrom's players was, on the whole, still more interesting. FLORENCE PRICE'S CONCERTO BRILLIANT":

> A nationalist in my attitude toward the art, it is pleasant for me to record the brilliant success of Florence Price's piano concerto as presented by Margaret Bonds and the orchestra. This work was first heard in one of the Chicago Symphony concerts in the Auditorium theater during the first year of the fair and, as duly reported on that occasion, it represents the most successful effort to date to lift the native folk-song idiom of the Negro to artistic levels.
>
> It is full of fine melodies deriving from this source directly or by imitation. The quasi-symphonic treatment of these ideas shows abundant resource, both harmonic and orchestral. Finally the piano part is expertly set upon the keyboard and was brilliantly played by Margaret Bonds.[5]

The Woman's Symphony was an important institution in bringing Price's music to the fore. Her music won critical acclaim and, most important, widespread recognition.[6] Carrie Jacobs-Bond, whom Price had met the year before when she was invited to hear some of Price's music at the Illinois Host House, came behind the curtain at the conclusion of the program. Tilting her head back, Jacobs-Bond remarked, "Ah, that was beautiful."[7]

* * *

Price's concerto is extant in two complete manuscripts. One manuscript is an arrangement of the concerto for solo piano and orchestral reduction; another is an arrangement for two pianos, the arrangement most often used from the mid–1930s-1940s. Using the extant parts and the orchestral reduction, it is possible to reconstruct the orchestral forces in the Concerto. They are typical of the Romantic-era orchestra: 2 flutes, 2 oboes, 2 clarinets, 2 bassoons, 4 horns, 2 trumpets, 2 trombones, strings, and percussion.[8]

Though the concerto, in D Minor, is titled a "Concerto in One Movement," its three sections correspond to the three movements of a standard concerto. As in many of her large-scale works, the concerto embraces aspects of the romantic tradition, but it also embodies many melodic, rhythmic, and harmonic aspects of African American music. The first section, in a modified sonata-allegro form, unfolds a spiritual-like theme; the second section is in the familiar call-and-response form of many African American folk melodies; the third section, a modified rondo, is based on the rhythm of the juba dance.

The first section of Price's concerto does not conform to the classical model of first-movement concerto form in which the principal themes are introduced in a double exposition, first by the orchestra, then by the solo. In Price's concerto, after the orchestra briefly announces thematic fragments of the primary theme in the opening nine measures, a piano cadenza ensues, deferring the expected orchestral exposition (see example 24).

Price's introduction is reminiscent of the introduction in Brahms's Piano Concerto No. 2 in B-flat, Op. 83 (1882). Brahms's concerto omits the standard

Example 24. *Piano Concerto in One Movement*, Introduction, mm. 1–3

orchestral exposition in favor of an introductory horn solo whose thematic material is completed by the piano. After two statements of sharing material in this manner, there is a piano cadenza followed by the expected orchestra tutti. An earlier model where the orchestral exposition is modified by the introduction of a piano cadenza is, of course, Beethoven's Piano Concerto No. 5 ("Emperor").

Price's concerto differs significantly from both of these examples, however. At the conclusion of the cadenza, when we expect a tutti statement of the main theme in the tonic, the orchestra tempts the listener further with fragments of the primary theme, accompanied at times by the piano, but does not state it fully, preferring to digress harmonically and melodically.

After a lengthy 92 measures of introductory material, the primary theme is finally disclosed. Developed from small thematic cells given in the introduction, it unfolds over fifty-three measures (mm. 93–146) as a large-scale musical organism that will assert itself melodically and harmonically through the whole movement. Its essence is a sixteen-measure plaintive melody; the primary theme betrays its roots in the African American spiritual (see example 25). The theme is Price's own although the chorus resembles the spiritual "Po' Mourner's Got a Home at Las'" (see example 26).

In contrast to the slowly evolving spiritual melody, the martial secondary theme in B-flat major is very short (m. 162). (see example 27). This rhythmically vital theme suggests—no doubt unintentionally—the opening of the second subject from the first movement of Beethoven's Fifth Symphony.

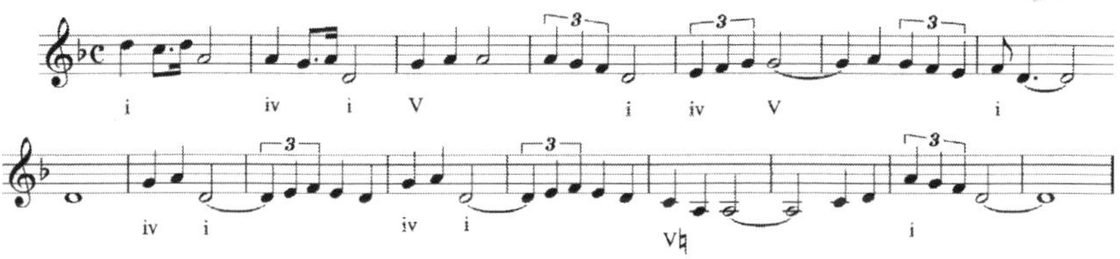

Example 25. *Piano Concerto in One Movement*, primary theme, mm. 93–146 (condensed)

Example 26. "Po' Mourner's Got a Home at Las'," mm. 3–7

Example 27. *Piano Concerto in One Movement*, second theme in B-flat, mm. 162–163

The development of the opening section is the part of the concerto that is most revealing of Price's use of rhythm and harmony. It begins in the tonic, with the opening of the principal and secondary themes in counterpoint. The D minor tonal center quickly gives way to a harmonically and textually rich passage impressionistic in flavor (see example 28).

Harmonically, the development section never strays far from the tonic, although augmented sixth chords and chromatically altered chords of dominant function are introduced. Melodically, the spiritual theme virtually disappears in this section. At the close of the development the harmony leads to a deceptive cadence on the Neapolitan, which substitutes for the six-four chord that traditionally introduces the soloist's cadenza.

Price's concerto dispenses with a cadenza, but the close of the development provides an opportunity for some virtuosic playing by the soloist. Polyrhythmic figures, cascading seventh chords with added sixths, and arpeggios ascending with their leading tones are brilliantly interwoven by the solo into the orchestral fabric and provide the climax that one would expect at the close of the recapitulation or coda (see example 29).

The development closes with an extended cadential passage (a prolongation of the dominant) which leads directly to the transition to the *Adagio* second section of the concerto. There is no formal recapitulation; the piano, marked *accelerando* and accompanied by full orchestra, briefly reiterates the opening motive of the tonic to conclude the first section of the work.

There are several plausible reasons for the omission of the expected recapitulation. First, an unusually long time is spent setting up the primary theme in which the introduction is a kind of development in itself. Second, the brief secondary theme in B-flat major is never really developed either melodically or

Example 28. *Piano Concerto in One Movement*, mm. 180–184

rhythmically; it is therefore not necessary to recapitulate it in the tonic. Third, the single-minded drive for harmonic unity—this section is almost solidly in D minor—limits the harmonic tension/resolution inherent in the usual tonal relationship between the exposition and the recapitulation. Most important, the essence of the first section of the concerto is the spiritual itself, a theme that Price composed. The form of this movement grows out of the gradual unfolding of the primary theme itself. A second full-scale unfolding or a condensed version of the theme would be anticlimactic.

Example 29. *Piano Concerto in One Movement*, end of development, mm. 209–219

The form of the second division, in D major, is similar to the most common poetic structure found in African American folk music—call-and-response—in which a solo line alternates with a refrain. This form is manifested as follows throughout the section: a recurring oboe solo takes on the role of the leader, the call or verse, and the solo piano that of the response or refrain (see example 30a). The leader's "call" is characteristically improvisatory, as, most often, the singer would invent words as he sang. Similarly, the musical solo, here the oboe solo, explores rhythmic and melodic alterations of its line and possibilities of reharmonization. Consider the variations of the oboe solo in example 30b.

Example 30a. *Piano Concerto in One Movement*, mm. 230–236 ("response")

Example 30b. *Piano Concerto in One Movement*, ("call")

The lyrical refrain, played most often by the piano accompanied by the strings, sets the mood for the whole of the adagio section. Unlike the verse, the refrain typically returns in its original form.

The interweaving of the melodic solo verse (and its countermelodies) with the chordal refrain results in an interesting texture that contrasts polyphony and homophony. The resulting musical structure in call-and-response form provides an opportunity for both the piano (refrain) and solo oboe to share important material equally. Ultimately, the two entities coalesce to close this section of the concerto as contemplatively as it began.

The third division of the concerto, marked *allegretto*, abandons the lyrical melodies of the preceding divisions for the rhythms of the antebellum black folk dance, "pattin' juba." By now, the syncopated rhythms of the juba dance have become a staple in Price's compositions. Although the third section of Price's concerto is not entitled *juba*, it is clearly a variation of the popular dance. The rhythm is manifested as follows: either the piano or the orchestra is responsible for maintaining the steady rhythm in duple meter while the other provides the syncopated melody (see examples 31a and 31b). Set in a modified rondo form, the format begins typically A-B-A-C, but following the second episode (C), there is an extensive development of principle theme. Although we anticipate the return of the "A" theme at the conclusion of the section, the primary theme is never recapitulated.

Example 31a. *Piano Concerto in One Movement*, section 3, mm. 340–345

Example 31b. *Piano Concerto in One Movement*, section 3, mm. 356–361 ("cakewalk rhythms")

Although the rhythms of the juba provide the foundation of both the third section of the Concerto and the "Juba" movement of the Symphony in E Minor, the dance in the concerto stands out as a real tour de force for the composer. In the symphony, the formal organization is a fairly straightforward rondo. But in the concerto, the form is manipulated to accommodate a more expansive dialogue between the solo piano and the orchestra, in which the themes are taken through a whirlwind of harmonies. By maintaining the character of the antebellum folk themes, however, from the simple syncopations of the opening measures through the use of polyrhythms and additive rhythms in the closing measures, this section of the concerto never loses touch with its roots. The rhapsodic final section provides a most exuberant close to the concerto.

The structure of Price's concerto is unusual, almost entirely abandoning classical concerto procedures. If there is a model for Price's one-movement work, it is not clear.

The idea of linking movements in a piano concerto with dramatic transitions was not new. Mendelssohn's Piano Concerto in G Minor, first performed in 1835, and Clara Schumann's Piano Concerto in A Minor, which she premiered with Mendelssohn conducting the Leipzig Gewandhaus Orchestra in November 1835, for example, are three movement works without breaks between the sections.

Although Mendelssohn's concerto is externally nontraditional, internally, his concerto conforms to conventional structures. Schumann's and Price's concerti are far more adventurous in that they allow the thematic content to determine the formal structure. Omitting traditional cadenzas, both composers prefer to develop melodic, rhythmic, and harmonic ideas in which technical prowess becomes an integral part of the overall compositional fabric, rather than an appendage to it.

What is most unusual about Price's score, of course, is the omission of the recapitulation in the first section of the concerto. Schumann's concerto is notable for this as well. The development section of Schumann's work leads directly to a coda, which serves as a transition to the second movement.[9] The complete theme of the opening movement never returns and the tonic (A minor) returns only in the final movement.

While there are some similarities between Price's and Schumann's concerti, it is unlikely that Schumann's score is a model for Price, since her concerto was not introduced to American audiences until the mid–twentieth century. Also, it is clear that formal structures in Price's concerto often deviate from established rules of musical form in deference to influences that are implicitly African American. Even more than in the Symphony in E Minor, Price's music betrays her philosophy as a nationalist composer—as an African American. But while the symphony is almost a musical tribute to Antonin Dvořák, the concerto is wholly her own.

* * *

The performances of the concerto with the Woman's Symphony Orchestra of Chicago and at the pageant, like the performance of the Symphony in E Minor with the Chicago Symphony the previous year, gave Price considerable exposure. People by the thousands came to the fairgrounds to hear music—both popular and classical. As the Official Guide Book of the Fair boasted, "The musical world within the Fair is undoubtedly the largest collective effort of mankind in the realm of rhythm and tone. . . . From the hillbilly songs of the National Barn Dance, with a capacity audience visualizing their radio favorites, we may change to the Floating Theater and find an ensemble of strings and voices bringing the music of opera. The Mundy Chorus of 150 and the DuSaible Singers of 500 [both black choirs], celebrated for Negro spirituals, present concerts several times a week. . . . And orchestras—the Chicago Symphony, the Woman's

Symphony of Chicago . . . and the various ensembles for accompaniment and broadcast provide an ever-changing program."[10]

By summer 1934, the Fair was attracting huge numbers from all parts of the Midwest and the East brought in by the Baltimore, Ohio, Chicago, Milwaukee, St. Paul, New York Central, and Pennsylvania trainlines. Saturday, August 18, just one week before Price's concerto was performed at the pageant, the Fair boasted a record attendance of 169,179 visitors, many of whom came to attend the *Chicago Tribune*'s musical festival and then went to the Fair to spend the rest of the evening.[11] Further, many of Fair events were being covered by the major newspapers, including the *Chicago Tribune* and *Daily News*. And for African Americans, the *Chicago Defender* often gave detailed information about the musical performances in both its local and national editions.

Through these newspaper accounts, Price continued to receive wide recognition. She was acknowledged as a talented composer by internationally acclaimed artists who were involved in the Fair directly or visiting it. Price was featured, for example, in a lengthy article in the *San Antonio Register* after opera singer Lillian Evanti heard the performance of the concerto with the Woman's Symphony in October and was asked about her impressions of the concert. Evanti's comments appear in an article, "Woman Composer Shows Great Talent: Wins Acclaim in Field Rarely Invaded by Women—Work Performed by Chicago Symphony Orchestra" in which the singer praises Price for her accomplishments.

During the early to mid-1930s, Price was very prolific. In two years, 1931–1933, she wrote or completed several orchestral works, piano works, and numerous songs, and won composition prizes. She was performing both piano and organ, lecturing, and teaching. Most importantly, her music was being heard regularly; even the orchestral works were being performed. Black artists, who often performed her music, were her extended family and they supported her efforts. White musicians gave her many opportunities, too; her ability to cross racial boundaries worked to her advantage. These were good years for Florence Price professionally but personally the tide was about to change yet again.

14 Performing Again

By the mid-1930s, Price's career was going strong, but personally these years were turbulent ones. Evidence shows that by 1934 Florence Price and Pusey Dell Arnett were separated and that she had moved out of her second husband's home.[1] Since Price and Arnett did not divorce, there are no records that reveal the cause of the separation.[2] For a while, Price, with her daughters in tow, moved from home to home. In fact, friends of Price report that she took her daughters everywhere with her—to her NANM meetings, concert performances, and church. In the few short years that Price was married to Arnett, her colleagues with whom I spoke never mentioned a second husband nor is he ever mentioned in the *Chicago Defender*, which detailed Price's activities during this period.

Price's oldest daughter, Florence Louise, had graduated early from Wendell Philipps High School, at age fifteen, in February 1932. She was an honor student, maintaining an "A" average through her course of study.[3] Interestingly, the graduation, which was reported in the *Chicago Defender*, mentions that Florence and Thomas Price were "prominent members" of the black community.

After leaving Arnett, Price was financially desperate. Immediately she turned to her friends for help. Temporarily, she and her daughters lived at 3806 Calumet Ave. at the home of T. Theodore Taylor, the pianist/organist of her church. She moved again to the home of Estelle Bonds. Bonds owned her own home in a middle-class, mixed neighborhood. The large three-story, ten-room house on Wabash Ave. and 66th included a living room, dining room, and kitchen downstairs and bedrooms on both the second and third floors. Margaret Bonds explained, "At one point Miss Price was in such bad financial shape that my mother moved her into our house with her two children in order to relieve her mind of material consideration."[4] Mrs. Bonds was a generous woman and was known to help anyone who fell upon hard times. While Price was living there,

Louis and Helen White and their daughter lived there, too. Mrs. White said that Bonds had an "open house" and she just "took people in." While Price and the White family paid no rent, they did contribute toward the food expenses.[5]

Although living with Bonds was not an ideal situation because of the number of people living there, there were some advantages for Price. Estella Bonds was one of the pillars of the black community, and artists, musicians, poets, writers, and dancers, all conspiring to support each other, frequented her home. Bonds's home was often the venue for informal concerts by Chicagoans or black artists passing through town. Others came to just share in the fellowship. Margaret Bonds said, "From my mother, I had actual physical contact with all living composers of African descent." She added, "My mother had a collector's nose for anything that was artistic, and, a true woman of God, she lived the Sermon on the Mount. Her loaves and fish fed a multitude of pianists, singers, violinists and composers, and those who were not in need of material food came for spiritual food. Under her wings many of a musician trusted."[6] This was a wonderful opportunity for Price to meet distinguished black artists, including sculptor Richmond Barthé, and poets Countee Cullen and Langston Hughes. It was at this time that Price became especially close to Margaret and began to support the young pianist in her interest in musical composition.

At some point in 1934, Price was able to move into an apartment of her own at 4611 S. Wabash, where she and her children lived until 1937. They moved to 647 E. 50th Place where they lived until 1941. Although her new home on E. 50th was bigger, the neighborhood left much to be desired. Community services were not at all what they should have been. Poor postal service, which Price found exasperating, was but one indicator of the deteriorating community.[7]

Price and her daughters also had to be concerned for their safety. With so many blacks unemployed, Chicago's South Side had become a dangerous place to live. Writer Arna Bontemps, who moved to Chicago in the fall of 1935 to attend graduate school at the University of Chicago lived on the same street, less than one block from Price at 703 E. 50th. Bontemps, who was certainly no stranger to crime, having lived in New York City for many years, described the city's skyrocketing crime rate this way: "The openness of it so startled us that we could scarcely believe what we saw. In a few months my feeling ran from revulsion to despair. . . . We had to fly home each evening before darkness fell and honest people abandoned the streets to predators. Garbage was dumped in alleys around us. Police protection was regarded as a farce. Corruption was everywhere." Bontemps went on to explain that his home had been broken into twice and that once while he and his wife were asleep, they awoke to find a prowler in their bedroom.[8]

Once Price moved into her place on Wabash Ave., she again began to accept invitations to perform. Although she preferred to spend her time composing, she did play recitals upon occasion, usually associated with the National Association of Negro Musicians programs or the church musicales.

Late in 1934, she received a letter from her former student Solar Carethers with a special request, which she contemplated in earnest. Would she consider returning to Little Rock, her hometown, to play a benefit piano recital at Dunbar High School? If she accepted, the concert, sponsored by the Philander Smith College Alumni Association, would be held Tuesday, February 19, 1935.

When Price left Little Rock for Chicago she showed no interest in returning to the institutionalized racism of the South. There was really no need—she had no family there and the violence and racial animosity continued unabated. On the other hand, the concert would give her a reason to visit longtime friends, some of whom she hadn't seen in many years. There was another reason to consider the invitation. Dunbar High School had special meaning for her. Located near her former home on Cross St., it was the successor to Union School, Price's alma mater.

The history of the transformation of Little Rock's black high school is an interesting one. In 1902, the year Price graduated from high school, Union School was moved to Capitol Hill and renamed accordingly. In 1907, the year after Price returned to Little Rock, the high school was moved once again, to 18th and Ringo Streets, where it became the M. W. Gibbs High School (actually it hosted grades eight through twelve), named for the black city judge. Gibbs remained the black high school until 1930.

The academic standards at Gibbs were very high and no one really thought of the segregated school as being in any way inferior, in spite of fact that in 1930 Gibbs High facility was "near condemnation." The teachers were dedicated and the curriculum was sound, preparing those who aspired toward college. Throughout its almost thirty-year history, Gibbs High School, and the Union School before it, maintained a college-preparatory, liberal arts emphasis.

In 1928, when it was apparent that Gibbs High was no longer structurally fit as a place of learning, the board of education authorized a new building but without funding. That same year the Rosenwald Fund, the principal source of financial support for black public education in the late 1920s–1930s, chose Little Rock for its pilot program in public secondary education. Although blacks in the city were initially overjoyed that their children might get a new school, there was a problem. The Rosenwald trustees challenged the notion of a classical education for Little Rock's black youths. They stated quite explicitly that college-bound courses for black children were a waste of time.[9] The school system would have to change its curriculum to align itself with vocational offerings leading to menial jobs, as opposed to professional ones.

R. C. Hall, the superintendent of schools, wanted the Rosenwald funding any way he could get it, but when the city's black residents objected vigorously to the proposed change in educational philosophy, Hall backed down and sided with the community. The philanthropists persevered anyway, citing their own study of Little Rock, which showed that of the city's 25 percent black population, most were employed in common labor—men as cooks, gardeners, barbers, truck drivers, and railroad workers, and the women as seamstresses, cooks, and laundry women. In spite of the black community's continued objections, the newly erected school was named the Negro School for Industrial Arts when it opened in 1929. This did not last long: by the time the school was officially dedicated on April 14, 1930, the curriculum had been modified to include both a classical/college-bound track and an industrial/vocational program, and its name had been changed to Paul Laurence Dunbar High School.[10]

In spite of some reservations, Price returned to Little Rock in 1935 to play the recital. By doing so, she would give back to the Little Rock community that had nurtured her. She was all too aware of the racial barriers that made the lives of black children ever more challenging.

While not explicit in any of the advertisements for the program, this concert was most assuredly a benefit for the Dunbar school. Although the new school had a modern auditorium with a seating capacity of 1600, a cafeteria, a library, 40 classrooms, and 7 industrial shops, in no way could it compete in its facilities with the white Little Rock High School, nor was it intended to. "Separate but equal" was the law of the land, but while black schools were certainly separate, they as certainly were not equal. Little Rock High, built in 1927, cost $1.5 million; Dunbar was built at a cost of just $400,000 in 1928. Little Rock High was a larger building with a library of 11,000 volumes in 1927, while Dunbar's library had 5000 in 1930.

The alumni of Little Rock's black high school were proud of Price, for here black people could witness the success of one of their own. Miss Solar Carethers, Price's former student and an alumna of Philander Smith College, organized the event. And, an event it was. The *Arkansas Democrat* carried two notices. The first one, February 17, 1935, read:

> Florence B. Price who twice won the Wanamaker music prize in 1931 and 1932, will be presented in a piano recital at the Dunbar High School auditorium at 8 Tuesday evening. She is the only woman member of her race who has composed and written a symphony. Her prize winning "Symphony in E Minor" was played during the Century of Progress Exhibition in Chicago, by the Chicago Symphony Orchestra. She is a member of the Chicago Woman's Organist Association. Special reserved seats have been arranged for white persons. Price of admission will be 25 cents for adults and 15 for students and 50 cents for reserved seats. In her recital Tuesday evening, she will play only her own compositions.[11]

The *Arkansas Gazette*, February 19, carried the following notice of the affair under the headline, "Negro Composer to be Heard: The Philander Smith Alumni

Association, Negro, will present Florence B. Price, pianist, and composer, in a benefit concert at 8:15 tonight at Dunbar High School. The program will include a prize winning piano 'Sonata' by the artist who has won several prizes for her work, including the Wanamaker prize of $750.00 in 1931. Seats will be reserved for white persons."

The return to her hometown was triumphant. Enthusiastic friends and members of the Philander Smith alumni wanted to greet Price at the train station with a brass band. Other, more conservative members of the group thought that such an outward expression of pride and emotion would be out of keeping with Price's reserved manner and with the dignity of her achievements.[12] So the group had to be content with the customary publicity befitting any "celebrity." The streetcars carried advertisements, show-cards were placed in store windows, restaurants, cafes, and in all of the colleges and schools, and the local newspapers, both black and white, covered the story.[13]

Price was excited to return to Little Rock to visit old friends. A friend of hers in Chicago even made a few special outfits for the trip.[14] Her best friend, Perry Quinney Johnston, would be there. Former students Edith Flake and Judith Finn would be there, too. Surely she would also see Charlotte Andrews Stephens, her former teacher. (Stephens would retire in 1939 after seventy years of teaching in Little Rock's public school system.)

By all accounts, the concert was a success. The *Arkansas Survey-Journal* reported, "Mrs. Florence B. Price, noted musician of Chicago, thrilled a magnificent audience of eager listeners at the Auditorium, Tuesday night, February 19, where she appeared in recital. All of Little Rock turned out to hear, and sat spellbound throughout the entire performance."[15] Not just Little Rock was there that evening; people came from miles around to hear her play. Solar Carethers remembered that there were people in the audience from Pine Bluff to the south of Little Rock, Hot Springs to the west, and a group of white students came from a college in Searcy, to the north.

It need not be pointed out to the reader the irony in the fact that Price, a black pianist playing at a black school, sponsored by a black organization, appeared before an audience in which the white members received preferential treatment (reserved seating), a legally sanctioned protocol in the South now. No matter, Price's return home was a success: she played well, she helped raise funds to support the Dunbar school—much as Carrie Still Shepperson, William Grant Still's mother, and other caring black members of the community had done for the Union and Capitol Hill schools when she was a child. Her community was proud of her and they showered her with affection to let her know it.

When Price returned to Chicago, she shifted her performance energy from the piano to the organ. The following month (March 1935) she became a member of the Chicago Club of Women Organists (CCWO), an organization that was formed in 1928.[16] The members of the CCWO were not only church organists but many of the women had been active theater organists and had accompanied radio broadcasts as well.[17] One wonders why it took seven years after the formation of the organization for Price to join it, given her previous work as a theater organist and composer for radio and her experience as a church organist. Was race a militating factor? The Chicago Club was all white (Price became the first person of color invited to become a member), but Price had been integrating professional organizations since her arrival in the city. One wonders if the organization had not extended an invitation for her to join them before now or whether Price just did not have the time to become involved. No matter—once she joined she became an active member. She often performed on their concerts and her music was also programmed by them.

The CCWO programmed both Price's vocal and organ music. Her octet, *The Wind and the Sea*, was performed by eight singers at the April 5, 1937, concert at the Kimball Organ Salon. A setting of Paul Laurence Dunbar's poem, this octet was written for the R. Nathaniel Dett Ensemble, who premiered the work in July 1935. Her ever-popular arrangement of the spiritual "My Soul's Been Anchored in de Lord," written in 1936, was sung at a program at St. Luke's Chapel (later renamed Grace Episcopal Church) in 1938. As is typical of most local chapter meetings, members are given opportunities to hear practical vocal, choral, and organ music appropriate for church services, weddings, and funerals. At one such meeting, May 3, 1943, members heard Price's newest composition, "God Gives Me You," a song written for her daughter Edith's wedding.

The first time she performed for the group was November 19, 1936, at La Vere Memorial Temple in Evanston, Illinois. Price's diverse interests in composition are most evident in the works she chose to play on this concert. The formal training in organ she received at the New England Conservatory betrays itself in the large-scale Passacaglia and Fugue. She also offered the audience more familiar fare—"Dainty Lass," an original composition, which was probably written along the lines of an American folk tune, melodic and simply harmonized. She rarely played a program where her own heritage was not either implicitly or explicitly acknowledged; an arrangement of the spiritual "Steal Away" was the chosen offering of that afternoon.

In Price's oeuvre, there survive twenty documented works for organ in three categories. The first two categories—teaching pieces and church music—were characteristically practical. "Allegretto," "Retrospection" (originally titled "Elf on a Moonbeam"), and "The Hour Glass" are all examples of organ works for beginners. Her service music includes "Adoration," published in *The Organ Portfolio* (Dayton, Ohio: Lorenz, 1951); "In quiet mood" (published by Clayton F. Summy in 1951); and "Offertory" (published by Lorenz in 1951). These compositions for church services are relatively short, suitable for preludes, offertories, or communion.

The third category of organ music is the large-scale concert works. In addition to the Passacaglia, other works include the Sonata No. 1 for organ composed in 1927, and the Suite No. 1 for organ first performed by Price herself for the CCWO April 6, 1942, at Grace Episcopal Church on the sizable three-manual Estey organ.[18]

Of these works the Suite was, perhaps, played most often by Price and others. A moderately difficult work in four movements, it is squarely in the classical organ tradition. Movements one and two, which are both in C minor, are an improvisatory "Fantasy" and a four-voice "Fughetta," respectively. The *andante cantabile* third movement, "Air," was so popular that it was often performed as an independent composition. It is an interesting movement in that it is among a few of Price's works that reveal the direct influence of jazz (see example 32). A bluesy, improvisational movement with no real melody, it moves through a series of jazz-flavored harmonies (flat 5 and flat 7 feature prominently) that convey a mood of repose.

Price's Suite is a challenging work and it attests to her technical accomplishments as an organist. In the "Fantasy" the organist must execute a thirty-second note scale passage leading to block chords in the opening measures (repeated in the B section and in the concluding A section), a passage reminiscent of some of Max Reger's organ works. (The opening of Reger's "Introduction and Passacaglia" in D minor is an example.) Elsewhere the organist must play chromatically altered chords against melodically disconnected pedals (see mm. 9–10 in example 33). The organist does get some reprieve, though, in that, atypical of most "Fantasies," which are through-composed by virtue of their improvisational nature, this "Fantasy," in a modified ABA form, has some repetition.

The last movement of the Suite, "Toccata," is equally demanding. It is a rondo movement, which features a sprightly syncopated melody in G major (see example 34). During the episodes of the rondo, sixteenth-note arpeggios alternating on three-manuals and sixteenth-note chords divided between the hands are characteristic. These passages, inspired by late Baroque organ literature, recall passages of the Bach's famous Toccata and Fugue in D Minor, for

Example 32. "Air," Suite for Organ, mm. 1–6

Example 33. "Fantasy," Suite for Organ, mm. 1–10

example. The lengthy coda harkens to late-nineteenth-century writing with its bravura five-note chords in each hand punctuated by octave pedals and chromatic manual scale passages over pedal-points that lead to a dramatic chordal close.

With the exception of the service music, none of the organ works—the teaching pieces or concert works—were published. Who, then, performed this music?

Example 34. "Toccata," Suite for Organ, mm. 90–101

There is no evidence that Price taught organ or that she had a church job while she lived in Chicago, but she could count some prominent organists among her close circle of friends, and it is well documented that she performed the concert works herself. Besides the Chicago Club of Women Organists, several members of both branches of NANM were organists. T. Theodore Taylor, director of music at Grace Presbyterian Church was a very fine organist, as was Estella Bonds. Price may have written some of the easy and moderate organ works for their students and it is very likely that these organists, among others, used her service music for church and performed the concert works at the Sunday afternoon musicals. Since Grace Presbyterian, where Price was a member, had one of the finest organs in the city, there is little doubt that Price practiced on this organ when time permitted and she probably used it to compose her concert works.

The Chicago Club of Women Organists kept copious notes regarding their attendees. An October 6, 1935, notebook entry lists Thomas Price as a program guest. This is, to say the least, curious and it is difficult to imagine why Florence Price's ex-husband would have been a guest of hers at a CCWO meeting, after their acrimonious breakup. Although I have not been able to trace Thomas Price's career in Chicago, it appears he stayed in the city at least until the early 1940s. He moved from E. 34th St. to 424 E. Pershing St. and resided there until the early 1940s. Until the 1940s, records show he maintained an office at 104 E. 51st.[19] The *Musical Courier*, July 1953, reports that Thomas Price died in 1942, a date that the author has not been able to confirm.

15 Professional Recognition

Reconciling Gender, Class, and Race

Price composed several large-scale works during the mid-1930s, a remarkable achievement, given that there were times when she was nearly homeless and penniless. She was nothing if not creative, determined, fiercely independent, and strong. In addition to the Symphony in E Minor and the Piano Concerto, two other orchestral works were completed. One of these works, the Symphony No. 2 in G Minor, is lost save for a single page at the Moorland-Spingarn Research Center at Howard University. The other work, *Mississippi River (The River and the Songs of Those Dwelling upon Its Banks)*, is a one-movement orchestral suite based on Negro folk themes. There is no evidence that the symphony or the suite were performed.

Mississippi River was completed in 1934 and dedicated to her teacher, Arthur Olaf Anderson. The work requires the normal complement of strings, winds, and brass, along with augmented percussion. Here, Price adds an Indian drum and a marimba. *Mississippi River* is one of the few Price works in which literal quotations of folk music constitute the core of the work. There are no less than six full-fledged themes quoted here—four spirituals: "Nobody Knows the Trouble I've Seen," "Stand Still Jordan," "Deep River," and "Go Down Moses"; and two secular, upbeat themes: a tune Price calls "Lalotte" and "Steamboat Bill River Song."

Price's piano teaching pieces continued to be an important source of income for her. However, so insecure was she about "selling herself" as a composer that there were times when she felt that she needed another voice, often male, to speak on her behalf. Henry S. Sawyer, who worked for Theodore Presser, became her ally. Probably referring to the newly composed *Three Little Negro Dances* ("Rabbit Foot," "Ticklin' Toes," and "Hoe Cake") for piano, issued separately by Presser in 1933, Sawyer wrote to Price March 5, 1933, that he really didn't need to be an advocate for her. Her music was well crafted enough, he felt, to be accepted by the press on its own. He wrote:

> As you may have suspected, I was fully aware of what was going on in the publication department relative to your compositions, but I am glad to tell you that they won out on their own merit, and would probably have been accepted had I not been there. All I did was tell them something about you, and that I had great faith in your final ability to make good. When I knew that the three numbers were to be accepted, I was as pleased as though they had been my own.
>
> I don't believe I ever told you that about a year ago six violin and piano compositions of my own were accepted and published by Presser. I will send you copies the first time I think of it. They are very different from yours, being on ancient patterns as is consistent with my advanced age. [Sawyer was 69 at the time.][1]

Again in 1937 Price sought Sawyer's intervention with Presser. The following letter suggests that Price probably sent a number of her teaching pieces to the publisher; some of which were, perhaps, rejected. In a friendly, almost chatty letter of September 20, 1937, Sawyer wrote: "It is always a pleasure when I have a chance to see new MSS from your pen. I wish more of them could be accepted, but the committee looks at every MS from a commercial as well as musical angle. Many compositions from well-known writers are sent back when there is little chance of their becoming 'sellers.'"[2] Although Presser did not accept all of her compositions for publication, they issued several of her works through the late 1940s. Presser published *Three Sketches for Little Pianists*: "Bright Eyes," "Cabin Song," and "A Morning Sunbeam" (1937); *Levee Dance* (1937); and an arrangement of the spiritual "Nobody Knows the Trouble I've Seen" (1938).

In addition to Presser, Price continued to work with other publishers she secured early in her career. McKinley published several sets of pieces including "Clover Blossom" with "March of the Beetles," "Criss Cross" with "Rock-a-bye" (both 1947), and several more pieces with no publication date indicated. Carl Fischer continued to issue her music, publishing an entire set of *Pieces We Like to Play* in 1936.

Among her new publishers were Oxford and Clayton F. Summy. Price was particularly overjoyed when *The Cotton Dance*, which won honorable mention in the 1931 Wanamaker composition contest, and her spiritual arrangement *Were You There When They Crucified My Lord?* were published in the *Oxford Piano Course*, Book V, in 1942. This would mean wide exposure of her music to beginning- and intermediate-level piano students, in which she had a particular interest. She began working with Summy late in her career, beginning in 1951. They issued "The Goblin and the Mosquito," (a reissue of the Carl Fischer edition, 1936) and two popular pieces, "The Old Boatman" and "The Sea Swallow."

Price's income from the mid-1930s derived from a variety of sources, none of them particularly lucrative: teaching, publications of teaching pieces and a handful of piano music and songs, occasional lecturing, recitals (outside of church), and accompanying. She handled her business affairs as best she could (and the continued correspondence with publishers proved to be very time-consuming). When one glimpses at the volume of music that Price wrote during the 1930s in all genres, it is staggering to recognize how little of it was copyrighted. Music was performed often, but because her scores were not protected under the law, she received no residuals.

In 1934, Price asked composer John Alden Carpenter about the requirements for becoming a member of ASCAP. Price had maintained a cordial relationship with the Chicago resident since the June 1933 performance of their music by the Chicago Symphony. On November 16, 1934, Carpenter responded, "Last week in New York, I talked with one of the officials of the American Society of Composers, Authors and Publishers and was informed that the requirements for membership in the Society are the publication of six or more compositions either for piano and voice, or orchestra by a publisher who is a member of the Society. The Presser Company are members." Price received an application later that month and on December 18, 1934, Carpenter wrote to her that he would sponsor her membership. However, the enrollment process in ASCAP was not completed for another six years, until 1940![3]

In the meantime, years of performance royalties went uncollected. To some extent, Price was aware of all of this lost income. Soon after she became a member of ASCAP, she wrote to the Society asking about "proper procedures in signing contracts, collaborating with writers, etc." In July 27, 1940, she wrote, "For example, negotiations are now going forward with a publisher for the publication of a song [probably "Songs to the Dark Virgin," published by Schirmer in 1941]. It is not clear to me whether I should sign contracts as in the past or consider this act as having been delegated to ASCAP through my affiliation as a member. I would also like to know if it is now ethical for me to have singers continue to use unpublished manuscripts intended for submission to publishers, without in any manner contacting ASCAP."[4]

In the same year, on February 26, 1940, Price was accepted for membership in the National Association for American Composers and Conductors, an organization founded in 1933 "to arrange and encourage performances and works by American composers and to help develop understanding and friendly cooperation between composers and conductors."[5] An affiliation with the New York–based NAACC would present Price with opportunities for a critical hearing of her music in a broader arena. Only a few months later, she received a letter from Paul Berthoud of the NAACC with a request for her to send some of her chamber music for a Sunday evening concert series of contemporary

American music during the 1940–1941 season.[6] Programs have not been located to confirm whether or not any of her music was performed.

Price's daughter, Florence, who was still living with her mother, became actively involved in helping her mother to promote her career, something Price admitted having great difficulty doing for herself. March 4, 1940, she wrote to Claude Barnett, founder of the Associated Negro Press:

> Dear Mr. Barnett,
>
> Because mother is so reticent about mentioning her own achievements and because she feels that she is imposing on your good nature to give you such facts "so often" as she puts it, I decided I would take it upon myself to tell you that she has just been notified of her having been made a member of the National Association for Composers and Conductors. This organization is composed of America's most outstanding composers of classical music and conductors of the largest symphony orchestras.
>
> I feel sure that you, like others who know mother personally know that she is really too modest for her own good. Knowing that, I believe you will endorse my taking the initiative in getting this information into your hands.
>
> Yours truly,
> (signed) Florence Price[7]

Barnett was only too glad to oblige:

> March 9, 1940
> Miss Florence Price
> 647 E. 50th Place,
> Chicago, Illinois
> Dear Miss Price:
>
> Thank you for your letter of March 4. I am glad that you sent the article about your mother and we have taken great pleasure in reducing it to a story.
>
> Please tender our best regard to your mother.
>
> Sincerely yours,
> THE ASSOCIATED NEGRO PRESS
> Claude A. Barnett

The ANP was the oldest and largest of the black press services, with correspondence worldwide. Stories were compiled and disseminated throughout the country. A formidable organization, the ANP "helped to create a national black culture and [it] increased black awareness of trends and events in the nation at large."That Price would not have availed herself of Barnett's services is difficult to understand.

Price did take advantage of the opportunity to join several music clubs. In the 1930s, when segregated musical organizations were accepted a priori, Price is credited with breaking down racial barriers. In addition to integrating the Chicago

Club of Women Organists, she became the first woman of color invited to join the Illinois Federation of Music Clubs and the Musicians Club of Women.[8] That Price was black appeared not to be an issue for members of these organizations. Price became good friends with several members of the CCWO, including Eugenia Anderson, Berenice Skooglund, and Anamay Owen Wales. Mrs. Anderson, who played quite a bit of Price's organ and piano music, acknowledged that although everyone in the organization knew that Price was black she was treated like other members of the group. In fact, they even recognized that her education and playing skills were superior to those of many of the members. The Musicians Club of Women was equally responsive to Price and promoted much of her music. In one program, February 11, 1947, members performed the *Piano Concerto in One Movement* (two-piano version) and the art songs "Little Things" and "Hold Fast to Dreams." The Lyric Ensemble of the club performed the choral work *The New Moon*. On another program, February 8, 1949, her Suite for Brasses (2 trumpets, 2 horns, 2 trombones, tuba, and piano) was premiered.

The Illinois Federation of Music Clubs, with its international connections, was an important forum for the dissemination of Price's music. Members were performing it as late as 1974, more than twenty years after her death. Anamay Owen Wales, a member of the Chicago Club of Women Organists and president from 1970–1972, explained how she met Price through the interconnected circle of white musicians in Chicago. In 1974, while president of the Illinois Federation of Music Clubs, she wrote to historian Barbara Garvey Jackson, "Yes, the Illinois Federation of Music Clubs did promote many concerts for Florence. I have several pieces composed by Florence Price and we have a few in the Oxford Piano Course books. I was supervisor of class piano in Chicago Schools for 25 years, and worked closely with Gail Martin Haake and her husband Charles who were the editors of the Oxford Method. It was through them I met Florence Price. While attending the National Fed. of Music Clubs board meeting in Fargo in August [1974], we had a trip to the International Peace Gardens and heard the International Orchestra and Chorus who had just returned from a concert tour in Europe, perform. They played 2 numbers of Florence Price's that were not printed on the program. I had never heard them before and they were delightful."[9] Charles Haake was also on the faculty of the American Conservatory of Music and it was through him that Price won a scholarship in 1929 to study orchestration there.

Price was able to participate fully as a respected colleague in all-white organizations for a few reasons. She was a classically trained composer with a solid track record of impressive performances. She was very congenial, soft-spoken, and nonaggressive—attractive qualities that white America did not always associate with black Americans in the 1930s and 1940s. In other words, she was a nonthreatening, genteel black woman.

In what was a racially divided country, color-consciousness was all too pervasive. The very long and slow process to integrate African Americans fully into society had begun. With the inauguration of Franklin Delano Roosevelt in 1932, both black and white Americans paid close attention to the promise of civil rights policies that would change the face of the nation. It was late in his first administration, however, before Roosevelt actively associated himself with "Negro projects," but by 1935 the White House began to take a stand in favor of the principle of equal rights for all Americans, if but tentative and only in the interest of political expediency.[10] It was Eleanor Roosevelt who translated the New Deal's rhetoric into meaningful, committed action. She invited Negro and integrated groups of adults and children to the White House, she included blacks in her agendas, and, most important she influenced the president on important civil rights issues. It was Mrs. Roosevelt who paved the way for Marian Anderson's concert on the steps of the Lincoln Memorial before 75,000 people in 1939 when the diva was denied permission by the Daughters of the American Revolution to give a concert in Constitution Hall. In the years before and just after World War II, integration was not yet acceptable or comfortable for most Americans. That Price was invited to join the CCWO, the Illinois Federation of Music Clubs, and the Musicians Club of Women was, in part, a sign of the times.

In spite of the significant milestones in her life, Price still was not satisfied with herself as a composer. In a 1936 *Chicago Defender* interview, "Keep Ideals in Front of You, They Will Lead to Victory, says Mrs. Florence B. Price," the composer was asked if her success was not a source of great satisfaction, Price responded, "I feel deeply thankful for progress, but satisfaction—no, not satisfaction. I am never quite satisfied with what I write. I don't think creators ever are quite satisfied with their work. You see there is always an ideal toward which we strive, and ideals, as you know, are elusive. Being of spiritual essence they escape our human hands, but lead us on, and I trust upward, in a search that ends, I believe, only at the feet of God, the One Creator, and source of all inspiration."[11]

There is more to this seemingly unpretentious statement. It is true that Price was never egotistical about her work and she was never one to boast of her accomplishments, but this was only half of her reality. The consciousness that Price articulates here is, in many ways, about female socialization. Many women, particularly those from a middle-class upbringing such as Price's, lacked the confidence to promote themselves boldly.[12] Self-assurance and aggression, personality traits often associated with men, are a necessary means to success in most professions, particularly if one is outside the realm of an established network—that is, a system of access to people who are in positions of power—where contacts can be made readily.

While Price enjoyed a certain amount of respect as a composer nationally, most of the actual performances of her music, particularly the large-scale works, remained on the local level. However important Chicago as a center of musical activity might have been in the 1930s, it was, in fact, viewed by those on both coasts as essentially a provincial city.

In *Color, Sex & Poetry*, Hull points out how difficult it was for black women during the years of the Harlem Renaissance when contacts and support from within the circle of writers, artists, and musicians meant everything. She states, "Women received a good word or a small favor here and there. Yet the Renaissance, despite its veneer of equal opportunity, was a time when not only Harlem and the Negro, but men as usual were "in vogue." In a world that values and caters more to males, they enjoyed the lion's share of all the available goods and, in the field of literature, were more apt to be seriously encouraged as professional writers." Hull continued, "The issue here is not whether friends—male or female, homosexual or heterosexual—should help one another. However, when the persons are men with power and position who almost exclusively benefit their male friends, then women suffer."[13] Although Hull's statement refers to the literary circles of the Harlem Renaissance, women musicians faced similar circumstances.

Early in her career, Price recognized the conflict of her role as a woman and her role as a composer, and she was well aware of the polemics surrounding the female composer. In Judith Tick's article, "Passed Away Is the Piano Girl," in *Women Making Music*, the author outlines those traits of women composers, drawn from Goethe's concept of womanhood, which were defined through sexual stereotypes. Femininity in music was purported to be delicate, sensitive, graceful, refined, and more lyrical, while masculinity in music was defined as powerful, noble, and more intellectual. Songs and piano pieces constituted the core of a woman composer's oeuvre, while symphonies, opera, and chamber music remained the exclusive domain of men.[14] On the one hand, Price did not subscribe to the characterization of her music as in any way inherently feminine, but on the other hand, she admitted being shy and less aggressive than necessary to pursue and sustain a high-powered career as a composer. For some time, she suppressed her desires to be a successful nationally known composer of large-scale works, content to care for her family and reap widespread local acclaim as a composer of piano music, songs, and piano teaching pieces. Although her orchestral music was being performed by the Chicago Symphony, the Chicago Woman's Symphony, and several local symphonic bands, all highly respected musical institutions and numerous concert singers, Price's ultimate goal was recognition of her large-scale works—her symphonies, concerti, and symphonic overtures—by the old-guard East Coast musical establishment—the Boston Symphony, the New York Philharmonic, or the Philadelphia Orchestra. A performance of her works by one of these orchestras would ensure her place in the annals of music history. But this was not to happen in her lifetime.

Florence Price, like any woman composer of her generation, knew that the musical world viewed her work through a filter of stereotypes. She also knew that, in a concert life where the musical supply far outstripped demand, it was up to her to promote her music—especially the larger works, which would be performed only if those who controlled concert programming could be convinced that it was in their interest to perform them. Thus, beginning in 1935, Price wrote to Serge Koussevitzky, conductor of the Boston Symphony, to argue the case for her symphonies. Koussevitzky was well-known for his enthusiastic support of American composers; not only did he perform American works but he commissioned new ones as well.[15]

The first scores that Price sent Koussevitzky, August 8, 1935, carried with them only a brief note asking the maestro to please look at the Symphony in E Minor and the Piano Concerto "with a view of possible performance." There is no extant correspondence from Koussevitzky to determine what he thought of these two scores.

This request was followed several years later, September 18, 1941, with a very lengthy and detailed letter to the maestro describing her philosophy toward composition and detailing something of her background. She began by noting the recent performances of her works. The letter then reads:

> After graduating from The New England Conservatory I returned to my native South to teach. I have an accumulation of scores and manuscripts which during the past few years here in Chicago I have been bringing to light with the result—several performances. Having Colored blood in my veins, and having been born in the South, I believe I can say that I understand real Negro music as well if not better than the kind I studied in the East.[16] I have an Overture based on the Negro Spiritual "Sinner Please Dont [*sic*] Let This Harvest Pass" which was performed here with results most encouraging to me. Having read that you are particularly interested in American music I am hoping you will give something of mine a trial.

Price then goes on to describe her latest orchestral work, the Symphony No. 3, which was performed by the Michigan W.P.A. Symphony in November 1940.

Price persisted in pursuing Koussevitzky. Because music cost so much to reproduce in the 1940s, she rarely enclosed her scores with her correspondence; she would send Koussevitzky music if he would consent to look at it. By her third letter to him, July 5, 1943, Price immediately "cuts to the chase" and dispels, for Koussevitzky, what she perceives could be problematic issues for him. Note that as late as 1943 nationalism was still being debated.

She writes:

> My dear Dr. Koussevitzky,
>
> To begin with I have two handicaps—those of sex and race. I am a woman; and I have some Negro blood in my veins.
>
> Knowing the worst, then, would you be good enough to hold in check the possible inclination to regard a woman's composition as long on emotionalism but short on virility and thought content;—until you shall have examined some of my work?

As to the handicap of race, may I relieve you by saying that I neither expect nor ask any concession on that score. I should like to be judged on merit alone—the great trouble having been to get conductors, who know nothing of my work (I am practically unknown in the East, except perhaps as the composer of two songs, one or the other of which Marian Anderson includes on most of her programs) to even consent to examine a score.

I confess that I am woefully lacking in the hardihood of aggression; that writing this letter to you is the result of having successfully done battle with a hounding timidity. Having been born in the South and having spent most of my childhood there I believe I can truthfully say that I understand the real Negro music. In some of my work I make use of the idiom undiluted. Again, at other times it merely flavors my themes. And at still other times thoughts come in the garb of the other side of my mixed racial background. I have tried to for practical purposes to cultivate and preserve a facility of expression in both idioms, altho I have an unwavering and compelling faith that a national music very beautiful and very American can come from the melting pot just as the nation itself has done.

Will you examine one of my scores?

Yours very sincerely
[signed] (Mrs.) Florence B. Price

Price began to get frustrated in her attempts to persuade Koussevitzky to look at her music. The following letter, written on November 6, 1943, although sharing much of the content of the prior correspondence, carries a distinctly different tone and it was about as aggressive as she would ever get in trying to promote herself as a composer.

My dear Dr. Koussevitzky:

Unfortunately the work of a woman composer is preconceived by many to be light, frothy, lacking in depth, logic and virility. Add to that the incident of race—I have Colored blood in my veins—and you will understand some of the difficulties that confront one in such a position. My own detestable but seemingly unconquerable shyness has not served me to gain for me widespread hearing. The few times I have been able to overcome this handicap in the past and to manage to get a score examined I have met with most gratifying results, as you will note in the comments of critics quoted in my folder.

Now that duties connected with caring for parents and children have been lifted from my shoulders, I do so want to make tangible progress and to get examined and performed some of my accumulated scores.

In keeping with one last promise to myself that I shall no longer *hang back*, I am now being so bold as to address you. I ask no concessions because of race or sex, and am willing to abide by a decision based solely on [the] worth of my work.

Will you be kind enough to examine a score of mine?

Very truly yours
(signed) (Mrs.) Florence B. Price

Price did receive one shred of hope from this last letter when a reply from Koussevitzky's office, November 17, 1943, arrived explaining that if she sent a score to the conductor, he would look at it when his time permitted. In a heartfelt letter six months later, May 22, 1944, Price apologized profusely for not having sent any music to Koussevitzky sooner. She explained that after "making a fresh copy of the score [presumably the Symphony No. 3], an unexpected happening" sent her to the hospital for "many ensuing weeks." For his perusal, Price sent the Symphony No. 3 and an overture on a Negro spiritual (perhaps the one on "Sinner Please Don't Let This Harvest Pass").

Price's letters are masterpieces in economy, decorum, and, in her own way, authority. She tackles the issues of gender and race up front by mentioning and then dismissing them. She invites Koussevitzky to set aside prejudice and judge her work on its merits. She reveals her understanding of what she is up against in making this approach. And she ends her letters with deeply personal statements, touching on her own character and personal history, the place of "Negro music" in her work, and her firm belief ("unwavering and compelling faith") that she has been a participant in Koussevitzky's own quest to support American composers in their search for a national identity in music. Price's letters spanned nine years (1935–1944).

In her last letter to Koussevitzky, a follow-up letter to her May 22, 1944, letter, written in October of that year, Price inquired about her scores "hoping mightily" that he might like the overture, in particular. She received a speedy reply from his secretary at the end of that month (October 31, 1944). Although Koussevitzky looked at the Symphony score, no performances resulted from these efforts.[17]

There must have been many times when advancing her career seemed hopeless. She was a single mother trying to make ends meet. She struggled to find the time to compose and yet keep some semblance of her skills as a pianist and organist, and she tried desperately to overcome her self-destructive timidity in order to pursue her career more aggressively.

One day, when she was feeling particularly introspective she wrote "Resignation," a song set in the manner of a spiritual for which she wrote both the words and the music:

> My life is a pathway of sorrow—I've struggled and toiled in the sun.
> With hope that the dawn of tomorrow
> Would break on a work that is done.
> My Master has pointed the way
> He taught me in prayer to say:
> "Lord give us this day and our daily bread"
> I hunger; yet I shall be fed.

Example 35. "Resignation," mm. 6–9

My feet they are wounded and dragging
My body is tortured with pain—My heart it is shattered and flagging.
What matter, if Heaven I gain.
Of happiness once I have tasted:
But only an instant it paused.
Tho brief was the hour that I wasted,
Forever the woe that it caused.
I'm tired and want to go home—My mother and sister are there.
They're waiting for me to come—Where mansions are bright and fair.

Price poured her heart into the text of this poignant but simple spiritual song. The plaintive tune, in F minor, has only two phrases, which are slightly varied throughout the two verses. The first phrase rises and falls stepwise over the interval of a fifth (occasionally the line rises an octave but it falls back and settles on the fifth). The second phrase emphasizes an oscillating minor third (see example 35). Price's arrangement recalls Hall Johnson's well-known spiritual "City Called Heaven," published in 1930. Johnson set the text in a like manner: the phrase structure (emphasizing the oscillating minor third), key (also F minor), and context: "I am a po' pilgrim of sorrow, I'm tossed in dis wide worl' alone. No hope have I for tomorrow, I've started to make Heav'n my home."[18] There is one significant difference in the settings, of course. Johnson set a text by an anonymous slave poet, while Price wrote these words herself. Price's narrative is more personal, more fervent, more painful, more prayerful. The melodic repetition intended to allow for textual freedom, is never tiresome. Here the listener is allowed to witness Price's private search for self.

Price seemed to constantly struggle for inner peace even as she tried to reconcile issues of gender, race, and class in her career. She confronted these issues as aggressively as she could, as the letters to Koussevitzky attest. Empowered by the freedom to be herself, the resolution appears to be in the music. Price wrote in a style that betrayed her own voice as both a woman and as an African American.

16 The WPA Years

The 1929 stock market crash plunged the country into the Great Depression. Just as American composers seemed to be coming into their own, the economic austerity conspired with radio and sound films to put thousands of musicians out of work. To preserve their skills and avoid manual labor for which most musicians were unsuited, the government established the Federal Music Project in 1935 for unemployed musicians under the auspices of the Works Progress Administration (WPA), later renamed the Works Project Administration.

National in scope, the Federal Music Project (FMP)[1] had a multipurpose goal: "to provide employment for needy professional musicians, to involve them in socially useful projects, to preserve their skills by maintaining high standards of musicianship, and to offer the less privileged citizens throughout the nation opportunities to enjoy music."[2] At any one time during its existence, the relief program employed some 10,000-15,000 persons, including instrumentalists, vocalists, composers, teachers, librarians, copyists, arrangers, tuners, and music binders. Performing opportunities included every medium: orchestras, concert bands, chamber ensembles, dance bands, choruses, opera groups, and projects for teachers and composers. Serious efforts to collect and preserve American folk music were also part of the WPA. To qualify for the FMP, it was necessary to be enrolled on Welfare Relief or to be employed on another WPA project from which one could transfer. *The Keynote*, a Detroit Federation of Music publication, carried this call to area musicians in October 1939:

> W.P.A. Music Project Positions Open
>
> If you are now on Welfare Relief rolls or already on a W.P.A. project other than a music project, and are interested in becoming transferred to the Michigan Music Project of the W.P.A., please contact Mr. Herbert Straub, Project Supervisor.

> 100 W. Larned Street, room 409. There are positions open for the playing of any instrument, teaching, music copying and arranging, singing, accompanying, choir conductors or for leaders of all kinds.[3]

The impact of the WPA was potentially great. On the one hand, Americans heard an unprecedented number of compositions created at home and performed by American musicians. Through the WPA, music was brought to cities and small towns alike that had little or no opportunity to hear live orchestral or concert band music. Because the concerts were free, the WPA music programs were heard by millions. In May 1938, the National Director of the WPA Music Project, Dr. Nikolai Sokoloff, reported that there were WPA projects in 370 cities in 42 states, "and we have reached 92,000,000 people since the beginning of the project, by far the majority of whom have had no other contact with flesh-and-blood music." He added, "I was conducting a WPA orchestra in New York City and the musicians received great applause. From the podium, I told our musicians: You are the ones who are supposed to be on relief. In reality the audience before you through your music receives relief—relief from inferior music or a bored existence devoid of the art."[4] Prior to directing the WPA Music Project, Sokoloff conducted the Cleveland Orchestra, which he led from its founding in 1918 to 1933.

Although the Federal Music Project was an attempt to cope with unemployment, it also produced new forms of educational and cultural activities that placed emphasis on fostering American music and making music an integral part of the community. One such enterprise was the Composers' Forum-Laboratory, established in the fall of 1935 by Sokoloff. Through his endeavors, more than 6,000 American works were presented. The activity of the Composers' Forum was nationwide.[5] Various radio programs presented compositions first heard in the sessions; lectures, too, were offered and available to the listening public.

While the Composers' Forum-Laboratory offered performance opportunities for established composers, its most important single contribution was in providing opportunities for composers to hear their work and benefit from the critiques of their colleagues. At the opening session of the Composers' Forum-Laboratory in New York in October 1935, which presented a program of Roy Harris's music, it was stated: "Here music expressive of every shade of thought and feeling peculiar to this movement in history will have a hearing. We will consider every type of music written by competent musicians. The purpose of these Forums is to provide an opportunity for serious composers residing in America, both known and unknown, to hear their own compositions and to test audience-reaction." Over 150 composers in New York City, some conservative and some avant-garde, had their works premiered through this avenue, including Marion Bauer, Amy Beach, Marc Blitzstein, Aaron Copland, Carlos Chavez,

Ruth Crawford, David Diamond, Howard Hanson, Walter Piston, William Schuman, and Virgil Thomson.

These composers found that the benefits of having their music rehearsed, publicly performed by professional musicians, and discussed in an open-minded forum were incalculable. On June 23, 1936, in praising the results of the Composers' Forum-Laboratory for bringing forth and promoting American music, Samuel Chotzinoff wrote in the *New York Evening Post*: "So far the Federal Music Project of the WPA has done noble work for music in America. In fact, its labors in the cause of creative music are unique. Never before has there been so wholesale an exposure of a nation's creative sources." And Olin Downes, writing for the *New York Times*, January 10, 1937, observed, "This institution affords real laboratory work for American composers, in an eminently useful and practical way. There are sufficient musical forces available to provide any composer whose works are considered with such performers as his score requires. He can hear his song, a piano composition, works for chamber or large orchestra, or choral works. With these resources the Composers' Forum-Laboratory pursues its activities, which have had a decidedly stimulating effect in encouraging our young musicians to create and develop."

Some composers were disappointed by Forum opportunities, expecting far greater returns from the performing ensembles and the audiences alike. One dissident voice was that of Elliott Carter, who wrote of his impressions in *Modern Music*, December 1938.

> The WPA Composers' Forum-Laboratory in New York begins its fourth year with a brochure listing the one hundred and fifty-eight composers whose works it has played. Old and young, academic and "modern," ultra-dissonant and ultra-consonant, famous and obscure composers ranging from Mrs. H.H.A. Beach to David Diamond, from George Gershwin to the composition students of Eastman, Juilliard, Westminster, Bennington, Columbia, Sarah Lawrence and New York University. . . . There have been no recent rehearings of successful works. . . . Men who have been discovered in these concerts (I suppose there are some) are not played more in other places, nor have publishers rushed forward to print their works. The famous remain famous and the obscure men obscure. The concerts appear to have done nothing more than to give a small group of friends and others a chance to hear their works. But is this enough after three years' constant work? What I expected was that by now a group of people in the public would know what they wanted in American music and insist on hearing it from WPA organizations, and at other concerts.

To be sure, Americans were not always overly impressed with new and unfamiliar native works. The widespread apathy toward or disapproval of American music was firmly entrenched. What Americans wanted to hear remained the orchestral standards that were the staple of the repertoire of the major orchestras and chamber ensembles.

Most composers thought the benefits of the Composers' Forum far outweighed any shortcomings. One example is that of the then young composer William Schuman. As a result of hearing his First String Quartet and First Symphony rehearsed, performed, and discussed in October 1936, the works were laid aside for revision. After a period of further study, Schuman reemerged with his Symphony No. 2 (1937, first performed 1938) and his String Quartet No. 2 (1937). Both pieces were well received by the Composers' Forum.

Some of Price's most important and most creative works were written during the Works Progress Administration years. The WPA came about at a critical time for black artists. As the Harlem Renaissance languished (in part because there was no money to support artists), the WPA provided substitute support. In addition to aiding Price in her career, the careers of composers William Grant Still, Clarence Cameron White, Julian Work and his brother John Work III, Harry T. Burleigh, R. Nathaniel Dett, Carl Diton, W. C. Handy, and Eva Jessye were aided to some degree through the performances of their music by WPA ensembles. Ralph Ellison explained:

> For although a reaction to a national disaster [the Great Depression], they provided—as have most national disasters—the possibility for a broader Afro-American freedom. This is a shocking thing to say, but it is also a very *blues*, or tragicomic, thing to say, and a fairly accurate description of the manner in which, for Negroes, a gift of freedom arrived wrapped in the guise of disaster. . . . The WPA provided an important surge to Afro-American cultural activity. The result was not a "renaissance," but there was a resuscitation and transformation of that very vital artistic impulse that is abiding among Afro-Americans. . . . Afro-American cultural style is an abiding aspect of our culture, and the economic disaster which brought the WPA gave it an accelerated release and allowed many Negroes to achieve their identities as artists.[6]

The resident chamber ensemble for the Chicago Composers Forum-Laboratory was the Forum String Quartet, all members of the University of Illinois music faculty. (This is the quartet that premiered William Schuman's String Quartet No. 2 in New York in 1938.) Price took advantage of the professional ensemble to present some of her more challenging chamber music.

The occasion was a concert of her music together with the music of violinist/composer Clarence Cameron White held at the Federal Music Project Building June 15, 1937. White was a friend of Price's, having met her sometime before or just after she arrived in Boston. He even attended at least one of her recitals while she was at the New England Conservatory. White was no stranger to Chicago. During the 1920s, he taught violin for several summers at Pauline

James Lee's National Conservatory of Music. Although he moved to Boston in 1935, where he established a music studio, he frequented Chicago after that. One of the founding members of the National Association of Negro Musicians, he served as national president from 1922–1924. Through NANM, Price and White were in close contact with one another and they had occasion to work together professionally.

The Forum String Quartet performed White's quasi-programmatic Suite for String Quartet (1919); the remainder of the program belonged to Price. Her octet for piano quintet and vocal ensemble, *The Wind and the Sea* (1934), received its first major hearing on this date. Price played the piano part with the quartet. Written for the Dett Mixed Ensemble of the R. Nathaniel Dett Club, it had been given a less than satisfactory premiere two years earlier because of the work's difficulty. A recently composed Piano Quintet in E Minor (1936) with local pianist Marion Hall also was performed. Receiving its premiere performance on that evening was Price's *Fantasie Negre* No. 4 in B Minor (1932), also performed by pianist Marion Hall. (This is probably the same *Fantasie Negre* that won the honorable mention in the 1932 Wanamaker competition and later revised.) These pieces are among Price's most serious chamber works; unfortunately, none of the music programmed on this concert survives.

Outside of Chicago, Price became acquainted with musicians in the Michigan WPA and she benefited considerably by two of their ensembles. The Michigan Federal Music Project was among the largest of the WPA programs. It included eight instrumental music units in Detroit, furnishing steady work to 192 musicians. In 1938, the payroll gave $17,000 a month (over $200,000 a year) to Detroit musicians who would have otherwise been out of work. These ensembles included: the Detroit Civic Orchestra (renamed the Michigan W.P.A. Symphony); the Detroit Concert Band; a 19-piece Detroit Symphony Dance Band; two black dance orchestras, LeRoy Smith and His Orchestra, and the Wolverine Swingsters; a Tamburitza orchestra, and the Detroit Gypsy Orchestra, which performed principally in hospitals and institutes for the blind and deaf; and a quartet consisting of a pianist, violinist, cellist, and singer that was involved in music therapy experiments at a local hospital.[7]

A particular favorite of the 52-member Detroit WPA Concert Band was the band arrangement of Price's *Three Negro Dances*. Under the direction of Murdoch J. Macdonald, the band brought this work to thousands who heard it in auditoriums and parks for free.

Price received her widest exposure from the Michigan WPA Symphony Orchestra. Organized in early 1936, it was known as the Detroit Civic Orchestra; in 1939, it became an integral part of the Michigan Works Project Administration. Valter Poole made his first appearance with the orchestra during the

1937–1938 season and became the orchestra's regular conductor in 1938. Prior to his appointment with the orchestra, Poole was acting district supervisor of music in Detroit and a violist with the Detroit Symphony. He remained with the orchestra until its dissolution around 1942.

A formidable but unpretentious man, Poole had a particular disposition toward vernacular idioms. Inspired by his humble background, his serious interest in jazz, and by his close working relationship with African American musicians, he became an eclectic and adventurous concert programmer.

Born in "Pooleville" (now Ardmore), Oklahoma, in 1903, Poole learned the violin as a youth from listening to the musicians associated with all-black minstrel and tent shows that traveled from town to town. Poole explained:

> There was no music available in this little village and there would come little tent shows, you know, sometimes all-black shows. They were very popular at that time. My mother would go, you know, and they would enjoy it, and she said, "I wish my son would play." So the cowboys—we had cattle—the cowboys first made me a violin out of a cigar box and horses' tails. The hair was cut and that's what I had. And there was only one man that knew anything about the violin. He was the barber. There was a barber in the little town, Jinks Bethell his name. So he would come to my house and give me lessons without the knowledge of my father because to be a musician was a disgrace in that time. And my mother sold a dress and from the Sears Roebuck Company got a little violin.[8]

After graduating from the New England Conservatory of Music, Poole played trombone with various white jazz bands to earn money while he honed his conducting skills. Poole's jazz "chops" were good enough to be noticed by many black jazz band leaders, including Duke Ellington, Fletcher Henderson, Count Basie, and Louis Armstrong. After he became conductor of the WPA Symphony, Poole invited Duke Ellington's band to join with the orchestra in a special concert. It was a somewhat hair-raising experience for Poole but one that he remembered fondly:

> Of course he [Duke Ellington] came as a soloist, he and his band. I was the conductor and of course Duke, he was very popular. So every seat in the house was sold out and the band was put in front of me. It was down at the Ford Auditorium. And you know how a jazz band is made up. Everybody comes in and "Where's the score? Well, where is it?" They had to look in the bottom of the trunk to find it. . . . And then he would say, "Piano cadenza." Nothing would be written. We had only one rehearsal. They came in Thursday morning, you know, traveling by train, everybody.
>
> Then came the concert and we went along and conducted everything and by the way, the score [Poole's score] was not bound. So Duke would be playing this cadenza and I was getting nervous because I didn't know when the cadenza would be finished. You can't just do this.

> I was conducting the Detroit Symphony [Michigan W.P.A. Symphony] and [Ellington] as soloist with his band. You see, there were about fifteen or twenty men there from his band. One of the trombone players, I think one of them knew me from my trombone or heard of me from my trombone days. He was near me so I could speak to him and here was Duke playing. The house was full by this time. It was a trying moment. I was scared to death, frankly. I leaned over and I told him [the trombone player], "How long is this cadenza?" So he looked at me and he said, "I don't know." I said, "Well, haven't you played this piece?" Duke was still playing, you know, and he would play like this and he would look out and then he would go into something, you know. So I said, "You've played this before. Can't you give me some idea?" "Oh," he says, "if they like it, he plays longer." So I was afraid he would say, "Now, now" and I would be caught. So in desperation, without even thinking, I held up my stick like this and he then somehow or other sensed [it] and he made his arrangement going into the key and I came down [at exactly the right place.]

Poole programmed new works by American composers regularly, and he gave the Detroit premieres of pieces by numerous contemporary European composers. For example, one concert, December 4, 1940, featured the Detroit premiere of Dmitri Shostakovich's Symphony No. 5. The following concert, January 8, 1941, in an all-American program, new works by Michigan composers were introduced.

Throughout his career, Poole made special efforts in his concerts to advance the music of black composers and promote talented young black performers. On one concert he featured two young black soloists, Joseph Cole, baritone, and Clyde Winkfield, the "first race pianist" to be heard with the symphony. Winkfield was a native of Chicago and he had taught at the Allied Arts Academy founded by Margaret Bonds for talented black children in the mid-1930s. Both Cole and Winkfield had earned good press comments in their local concerts (they were well known in NANM circles), and their performance with Poole's orchestra proved to be a real boost to their careers. When asked about his support of black artists, Poole responded: "I have not favored. I have not favored a black person because he's black but because he's good. That's what I have judged on and that's what they have succeeded on because they're the same as anybody else."

It was this open attitude toward black musicians that prompted Valter Poole to feature Price and black soprano Celeste Cole in concert. The conductor premiered Price's Symphony No. 3 on the November 6, 1940, Michigan WPA Symphony Orchestra concert at the Detroit Institute of Arts. Also featured on the program was Price as soloist in her *Piano Concerto in One Movement*. The remainder of the program included Bach-Ormandy's "Wachet auf, ruft uns die Stimme," and selections rendered by the black soprano Celeste Cole, including

Verdi's "Ah fors e lui" from *La Traviata* and two spiritual arrangements, Hall Johnson's "City Called Heaven" and J. Rosamond Johnson's "Weary Traveller" [*sic*], both orchestrated by orchestra member Ursulescu.

Like the Symphony in E Minor and the Piano Concerto before it, Price's Symphony No. 3 earned an immediate success. J. D. Callaghan, writing for *The Detroit Free Press*, was particularly impressed by the symphony's underlying theme of regional Americanism. He wrote:

> *Symphony by Negro Writer Acclaimed at Institute Debut*
>
> First performance anywhere of Symphony No. 3, in C minor, of Florence B. Price, Negro composer, was given Wednesday night by the WPA Symphony Orchestra, directed by Valter Poole before an audience which comfortably filled the large Art Institute Auditorium.
>
> On the same program Mrs. Price played the solo parts of her Concerto in One Movement. Guest soloist of the evening was Miss Celeste Cole, Detroit Negro soprano.
>
> *Mrs. Price is convincing*
>
> Mrs. Price, both in the concerto and in the symphony, spoke in the musical idiom of her own people, and spoke with authority. There was inherent in both works all the emotional warmth of the American Negro, so that the evening became one of profound melodic satisfaction.
>
> In the symphony there was a slow second movement of majestic beauty, a third in which the rhythmic preference of the Negro found scope in a series of dance forms, and a finale which swept forward with great vigor. The third movement was named Juba by the composer, as a tribute to the African dances which were its inspiration.
>
> *Author wins credit*
>
> Beautiful and emotionally satisfying the whole work was, and there were moments in which true greatness seemed within the grasp of the writer. Other work in progress may well bring that greatness to actuality.
>
> Certainly Mrs. Price has achieved what few women of any race are capable of doing when she made her invasion of the symphonic field. The symphony is particularly appealing to Americans in that it is made up of the music which is native to us.

Finding the concerto unconvincing, the reviewer continued, "The concerto was less satisfying. It seemed that the composer allowed herself to be influenced too strongly by the masters of romanticism, and as a result the Negroid feeling of the work suffered by the infusion."[9] Two nights later, Poole conducted the orchestra in another performance of Price's symphony in a program that included Johann Strauss's *Tales from the Vienna Woods* and George Enesco's *First Rumanian Rhapsody.*

That the large Detroit Institute of Arts auditorium was filled almost to capacity is of interest. The premiere of Price's symphony had attracted considerable attention, even by the First Lady Eleanor Roosevelt who mentioned the work November 15, 1940, in her nationally syndicated column, "My Day." The WPA arts programs were among Eleanor Roosevelt's avocations, and she traveled around the country lending support where she could. Her article, subtitled "First Lady Describes Detroit Stay," details her short visit.

> I spent two of the pleasantest hours I have ever spent visiting Music Projects Tuesday morning in Detroit. Churches have given space for rehearsal to these WPA units, so it was in the basement of a church that we listened to a Gypsy band playing dance music, to which it was almost impossible to sit still.
>
> He was followed by another dance orchestra, and, finally, by a full symphony orchestra, the fourth best WPA orchestra in the country. They played two movements in a new symphony by Florence Price, one of the few women to write symphonic music. She is a colored woman and a native of Chicago, who has certainly made a contribution to our music. The orchestra rendered her symphony beautifully and then played a Bach choral which ended the concert, much to my regret.

Following the orchestra rehearsal, Mrs. Roosevelt visited a black church where she seemed to enjoy a rehearsal of the choir especially. The employment of the director of the group, "who was discovered digging ditches" prior to this, must have given particular satisfaction to the First Lady, who often lobbied her husband on behalf of the federally funded program.

A few days after Roosevelt's article, Price wrote a letter to the First Lady thanking her for her kind words. Mrs. Roosevelt, via her secretary, responded in kind:

> The White House
> Washington, D.C.
> Dear Mrs. Price,
>
> Mrs. Roosevelt asks me to thank you for your letter. She is glad if her mention of your symphony will prove helpful to you and sends you her best wishes.
>
> Malvina C. Thompson
> (Secretary to Mrs. Roosevelt)[10]

Valter Poole, himself, was actively involved in the publicity of this particular program. Given the premiere of Price's symphony in Detroit, a city with a large black population, it was important to Poole that the black community was well-represented in the audience. He explained his own recruiting efforts this way: "One of the things that I remember doing to publicize this concert was to go to the place where the black people all came to dance and to church. And I remember going in on a Saturday night. I was crazy at that time, you know, going in all alone and there being a big dance going on. I would go up to the orchestra, introduce myself, and have the drummer give a big, long roll, and then I would make a speech to all the people at the dance and tell them about this concert. It was a historical event."

Unfortunately, neither Poole's efforts nor Eleanor Roosevelt's visibility in Detroit prior to the performance drew the large numbers of blacks to the auditorium that they might have. What Poole failed to realize is that concert audiences in Detroit, particularly black audiences, were now polarized. And just because the concert featured black composers and performers, attendance by blacks as a sign of support was no longer to be assumed.

In some personal notes attached to a press release, Price wrote her own thoughts about the evening, which underscore this point. It is unclear to whom these remarks are addressed (the letter may have been to Price's friend, educator Kemper Harreld, who taught at Morehouse College in Atlanta until 1951 and Spelman College until 1952), but it can be inferred that Price was at a turning point in her life. She recognized that at least some of the early support that she had received by the black community was waning. She wrote:

> I was recalled to the stage again and again. Finally the women of the audience (White, I saw almost no colored faces at all) rose to their feet followed by the entire audience. I suppose that is something I should have publicized. However I am poor in pushing publicity when it comes to myself. I think most persistent efforts were put into trying to get you to publicize my music by using it in your concerts and to bring me to Atlanta in recital. This I tried without success over a period of about twenty years. I have finally learned that the successful ones among us are usually recognized by *us* only after the White man has put his stamp of approval on us.[11]

In the latter years of her life, Price began to express herself more strongly. The tone of this letter and the quite jaded comments are a by-product of Price having fought issues of inequality for years. For too long, she struggled for recognition—even from African Americans, at times. It was becoming more and more difficult to get her large-scale works performed and she was getting tired of it all. This letter is evidence of the apathy she felt toward the black community from time to time. It appears that although blacks were supportive of her more often than not, jealousy did rear its ugly head.

* * *

In Price's lifetime, ever so slowly, more and more opportunities for blacks in classical music began to open up and she used any well-deserved opportunities to her advantage to pursue her professional goals. Florence Price moved in both the black and white worlds of professional musicians, Du Bois' "double consciousness." She harbored no ill feelings toward anyone, in general, but there were some blacks who did not always understand or appreciate, and may have even resented, her success. Price's daughter, Florence Price Robinson, called it jealousy, but the situation was psychologically more complex.

That Price was occasionally the target of destructive envy is suggested in this letter from Price's daughter to archivist Mary Hudgins. There is no date on the letter, but from the context of the whole letter, it appears to have been written after 1963, about ten years after her mother died. Even then, some blacks continued to pass, if they could; others just struggled. Quoted below are two excerpts from an eight-page letter:

> One time there was an orchestra who was to broadcast mother's music. The NAACP went to the conductor and told him that mother didn't show [up] but she was [there]—and then had the nerve to call up mother afterward to say what she did. So I will never contribute a nickel to them with that and the other things that have happened to me and mine because of it. It just so happened that incident had gotten back to mother before the phone call and she was prepared to handle it as I never could handle it and say the correct thing. The word had come to mother via an associate editor of a music magazine. She used to always tell mother to use the word "American" [instead of "Negro"]. I could give you a list of Negro musicians [who "passed"] that would shock you—people who were opera singers, members of symphony orchestras (even women) that never let it be known. Of course I'd never do it.

And in the same letter, this story:

> One time my mother was in the hospital. She had had a coronary thrombosis attack. (She had always had a bad heart even as a child. In later years her condition was referred to as a "Blue Baby.") After she was well again some Negro musician said to her, "If it had been me I would have died. But you are the great Florence Price so you got extra care and service." Negro seemed jealous of her[,] whites always accepted her so much more readily.[12]

Price seemed to handle these negative situations in stride. Only rarely was she disillusioned by this small mindedness. Florence Price Robinson, her daughter, on the other hand, internalized these ill feelings. As a result, she almost completely distanced herself from the black community—the very backbone of her mother's early support.

17 The Chicago Renaissance

Soon after the performance of her Symphony No. 3 and the *Piano Concerto in One Movement* in Detroit, Price and her daughters packed up their things and moved again, in the spring of 1941, to a home in the Abraham Lincoln Center, 700 Oakwood Boulevard. The Center was like a settlement house located in a rather poor neighborhood. The upper floors of the building were residences, some of them apartments and others one-room dwellings. There was a community floor where meals were eaten together and lounges where the residents could socialize.

Lincoln Center was much more, though, than lodging for low-to-moderate–income people. It was like a community house for people with common interests. The Lincoln Center housed teachers, writers, artists, and others interested in culture and the arts. The residence was not open to the public; that is, when vacancies were available they were never advertised. As Eleanor Price (no relation), who taught music to the kindergarten children there, put it, "You had to be known to live there."[1]

The Center had several floors: the first floor had a large auditorium, a classroom, and smaller rooms for lectures and poetry readings given by Chicagoans and by visiting artists and writers from around the country. The second floor was primarily classrooms and offices. The third through the seventh floors were residences, although some floors had classroom space as well. Price and her daughter had a small apartment on the seventh floor and she had a music studio on the sixth floor.

Price was the only black teacher living at the Lincoln Center at the time. Most of the students were white and the neighborhood was primarily white. The perception of Price's personality from those who worked with her during this time is interesting. One said that "Price didn't cater to white people." In other words, she demanded respect and she got it. Another said that she was "stately, aloof, and always well dressed." Living in a world among whites, Price's façade was impenetrable.

As the most well-trained piano teacher at the center, Price had a huge studio. She taught both beginners and advanced students, numbering at one time close to one hundred. Because there were so many students taking piano lessons at the Center, the piano department had musical programs every month in order to give them an opportunity to play on a regular basis.

The auditorium of the Lincoln Center, which was open to the public, was a popular venue for classical concerts by black performers. The social space was comfortable enough to accommodate a mixed audience of white members of the community and blacks from around town. To facilitate the growing demand by artists to perform there, the Center established an interracial Allied Arts Committee. During the fall and winter concert seasons, the Committee organized Sunday music programs of interest to both black and white audiences. In the late 1930s and 1940s, this committee was chaired by Maude Roberts George, at one time the president of the National Association of Negro Musicians and music columnist for the *Chicago Defender*.

One of these concerts, on April 15, 1948, honored Price by featuring an evening of her music. Many of Chicago's distinguished musicians got together to recognize her and "to pay tribute to one of its own products, who has gained national fame as a woman composer."[2] Nora Holt, writing for the *New York Amsterdam News*, mentioned that just prior to the concert Price was in Los Angeles for a performance of her music. It is likely that the L.A. concert was sponsored by the very active Los Angeles chapter of the National Association of Negro Musicians. She had many friends in Los Angeles, including William Grant Still and his wife, Verna Arvey, with whom she probably spent some time. Price returned to Chicago just in time for the gala celebration. Two of the selections on the concert were old favorites, "The New Moon" and "The Moon Bridge," but there was also some music written especially for the occasion. The concert featured instrumental and vocal music:

Suite for Organ [ca. 1942]
Choral Selections for Women's Voices
Witch of the Meadow (Mary Rolofson Gamble) for SSA and piano [1947]
The New Moon (Anonymous) for SSAA and two pianos (four hands) [1930]
Four Songs for Bass-Baritone: "Easy Goin'," "Good Bye Jinks," "Summah Night," Dat's My Gal" (Paul Laurence Dunbar) [1935]
Three Miniature Portraits of Uncle Joe for piano, written to depict various stages of his life [at] 17, 25, and 70 [ca. 1947]
Songs for Soprano:
"The Moon Bridge" (Mary Rolofson Gamble) [1930]

"Little Things" (Joseph Stephens) [1947]
"Hold Fast to Dreams" (Langston Hughes) [1945]
Negro Folksongs in Counterpoint for String Quartet [ca. 1947]

Soloists for the concert were many of Price's friends: soprano Helen White, pianist Clyde Winkfield, baritone Shelby Nichols, pianist Jeanne Fletcher Mallette, organist Alyce Martin-Mein, the Lorelie Ladies Glee Club, and a string quartet under the direction of Dr. Raymond V. Girvin.

A few years before Price moved to the Lincoln Center it had become a magnet for writers and artists whose work was on the cutting edge; they could come and explore the new without retribution. The site was where the South Side Writers' Group met from 1936–1938, first under the leadership of writer Richard Wright and then with Margaret Walker.[3] This group was an important one. It consisted of about twenty black writers, all at the beginning stages of their careers, who met weekly at the Center to read aloud and discuss their works-in-progress. Most important, they explored the potential of their work for its broader theoretical implications of black art.

Richard Wright arrived in the Windy City from Mississippi in 1927, about the same time as Price, and it was not long before he joined the ranks of the unemployed. Like thousands of others, the Depression hit him hard; he was forced to live hand-to-mouth working on relief as a street-cleaner, ditch-digger, and hospital orderly. At the same time that he formed the South Side Writer's Group, Wright became employed on the Illinois Writer's Project. It became his salvation and provided him with the necessary security to work on his fiction.

The Illinois Writer's Project was arguably one of the most impressive units of the WPA. Writer Arna Bontemps, who arrived in Chicago in the fall of 1935 to attend graduate school at the University of Chicago, was introduced to the Writer's Project through his association with Wright in 1936. In 1939, Bontemps was formally hired to supervise the production of a local history called *The Negro in Illinois*. The list of writers employed by the Project were some of the most gifted in America. Besides Richard Wright and Margaret Walker, they included Katherine Dunham, a talented writer, although better known as a dancer and choreographer; novelist Willard Motley; and short story writer Frank Yerby. His white colleagues on the Project included Studs Terkel, who later hosted a radio program in the city, and young novelist Saul Bellow.

A subsidiary of the Illinois Writers' Project was called "The History of Negro Music and Musicians in Chicago" and, comprising over twenty boxes of material, it represents the most complete chronicle of black classical musicians found anywhere.[4] Several writers on the project had a hand in documenting this subject: it highlights the history of the city's black musical schools and teachers; it includes information on the Chicago Music Association (the parent branch of NANM); and it provides data about all of the city's black choirs (church—affiliated and secular), bands, orchestras, and musical organizations (various music clubs and the organized glee clubs). For each, there is information on the groups' founding, leadership, when, where, and how often the group met. Bontemps' organizational skills and the research and writing skills of his staff were exceptional.[5]

Scholars have argued that the authors of that project were part of a second flowering of black arts and letters known as the Chicago Renaissance, which flourished from 1935 to 1950. Richard Bone posits that a generation of black writers, almost all living in Chicago, came to maturity during that time and created works so central to black culture but yet so different in philosophical and political ideology from the generation before it, the so-called Harlem Renaissance or New Negro Movement, that we must reexamine black literature in a broader context.[6] This body of work, then, will emerge independently of its forebearers. When asked to compare the Harlem Renaissance with the Chicago Renaissance, Arna Bontemps, who lived in New York for seven years and was an active participant of the Harlem Renaissance, and who lived in Chicago and was equally active during its artistic heyday, writes: "Chicago was definitely the center of the second phase of Negro literary awakening. . . . Harlem got it[s] renaissance in the middle 'twenties, centering around the *Opportunity* [magazine] contests and the Fifth Avenue Awards Dinners. Ten years later, Chicago reenacted it on WPA without finger bowls but with increased power."[7] Bontemps considers the two movements equal in importance. The Chicago School, then, evolves as an extension, although ideologically distinct, from the Harlem Renaissance. The continuum of black arts and letters is thus much longer and is of greater significance than is considered by those who confine their attention to the Harlem Renaissance.

The central figure in this movement was Richard Wright, whose second novel, *Native Son* (1940), based on his experience in Chicago's ghettos, had a dramatic impact on black writing after it. His collection of short stories, *Uncle Tom's Children* (1938) was also written during this time. Arna Bontemps' novel *Black Thunder* (1936), Margaret Walker's volume of poetry *For My People* (1942) and Gwendolyn Brooks's collections *A Street in Bronzeville* (1945) and the Pulitzer Prize–winning *Annie Allen* (1949) can be included. Essential to the understanding of this movement is the work of sociologist Horace Cayton who, with St. Clair Drake, wrote *Black Metropolis* (1945) with an introduction by Richard Wright, a seminal study of black migration to Chicago.

Why did Chicago prove to be so fertile for this group of writers? By 1930, the South Side of Chicago constituted the second largest concentration of black folks in America, exceeded only by New York's Harlem. Most of them flooded the city from the South in search of work and opportunity. Then, too, the economic crisis of the Depression created commonalities among blacks and whites, where heretofore, they had lived and worked in segregated environments. Richard Wright summed up the forced integration this way: "I now detected a change in the attitudes of the whites I met; their privations were making them regard Negroes with new eyes, and for the first time I was invited to their homes."[8]

Such was the milieu in which these black writers lived and worked. The Great Migration, the Depression, and the adjustment to urban life provided these writers with vivid life experiences as subject matter for their art. Their political and sociological framework was integrationist, a view supported by the pioneering urban research of Robert Park and his student Horace Cayton. Cayton became director of the Parkway Community House in 1940, a social and recreational center for blacks located at 51st and South Parkway. His home was a gathering place for Chicago's young black intellectuals and for those artists visiting from out of town, including Langston Hughes who spent weeks at a time in Chicago during the 1930s and early 1940s.

Langston Hughes did not like Chicago much, once describing it as "certainly one of the chief abodes of the Devil in the Western Hemisphere."[9] The weather was either too hot or too cold, and it was dirty and an incubator for crime. On the other hand, Hughes very much enjoyed the hospitality of the black artistic and intellectual community. He became very good friends with Margaret Bonds, then a graduate student at Northwestern and who set many of his poems to music; Horace Cayton; Margaret Walker, also a student at Northwestern; and Richard Wright, an avowed leftist and one-time member of the Communist Party, a cause with which Hughes himself flirted.

There is little doubt that Florence Price became an acquaintance of Hughes as well. Their paths might have crossed at one of the social gatherings at Estella Bonds's home or at a concert or poetry reading at the Parkway Community House or at the Lincoln Center. At the very least, Price was in touch with Hughes regarding her musical settings of his poetry. In all, she set nine of his poems dating from 1935–1945.[10] In a letter to Arna Bontemps, November 8, 1941, not knowing that Price had recently moved, Hughes wrote:

> Dear Arna,
> Do you, by any chance, happen to know Miss Florence B. Price, 647 East 50th Place, just below you? It's she who set to music my *Songs to the Dark Virgin* that Schirmer's have just published.[11]

There is another situation that may have brought Hughes and Price into contact. In 1940, Arna Bontemps was named cultural director of the state-sponsored American Negro Exposition in Chicago, which was to be juxtaposed with the Diamond Jubilee of the Emancipation Proclamation. Bontemps persuaded Hughes to stay in Chicago for several months to write the book for *Jubilee: A*

Cavalcade of the Negro Theatre and for a revue called *Tropics after Dark*. Horace Cayton and St. Clair Drake comprised the research team, and Frank Marshall Davis was in charge of publicity. Margaret Bonds, who often collaborated with Price, was hired to score the music for *Tropics*; the music for *Cavalcade* was entrusted to W. C. Handy, Thomas A. Dorsey, and Duke Ellington. Neither show was produced as intended, however. The state grant money was confiscated by political crooks, and the unions (carpenters and musicians) conspired to sabotage Hughes's hard work, for which he was never paid.[12]

Price was in some ways bonded with many of these writers through the James Weldon Johnson Memorial Collection of Negro Arts and Letters, established at Yale University. In 1941, Carl Van Vechten, once a leading music critic in New York and novelist, donated the corpus of his Negro materials, much of it collected while researching his controversial book *Nigger Heaven* (Knopf, 1926). A commanding presence, Van Vechten, who was white, was seldom without the company of black artists. As Arnold Rampersad explains in *The Life of Langston Hughes*:

> Van Vechten had arranged for Paul Robeson's first Town Hall concert, listened to his most intimate confidences . . . and loaned him money. Van Vechten had renamed Hall Johnson's choir the "Harlem Jubilee," and commissioned a mural from Aaron Douglas. Dorothy Peterson, Zora Hurston, and Bruce Nugent were all devoted to him, as was W.C. Handy, the enterprising "father" of the blues, who was brought to Carl's home for cocktails by [Langston] Hughes. When *Handy's Blues: An Anthology* appeared that year [1926] (with sketches by Miguel Covarrubias), Handy credited Van Vechten with wielding "the pen that set tongues to wagging, ears listening and feet dancing to the blues."[13]

The James Weldon Johnson Memorial Collection of Negro Arts and Letters, named for the black poet, novelist, composer, diplomat, and civil rights leader—who died in 1938 and was one of Van Vechten's close friends—has come to be regarded as a major repository of literature and music manuscripts, recordings, correspondence, photographs, and memorabilia by black authors. Van Vechten hoped that by naming the collection for Johnson he would inspire others to contribute to this valuable repository. This proved to be the case. Among its treasures the collection contains forty-five scores of W. C. Handy, the manuscript orchestral score of William Grant Still's ballet, *Sahdji*, in which are found comments by Alain Locke and Bruce Nugent who collaborated on the scenario, and manuscripts, often with inscriptions, by Harry Burleigh, Margaret Bonds (who set many of Langston Hughes's texts), Hall Johnson, J. Rosamond Johnson, and popular songwriter Will Vodery. Price sent her autograph of the newly composed Symphony No. 3 to Van Vechten for inclusion in this important collection. Another work by Price in the collection is her setting of

Hughes's *Songs to the Dark Virgin*. Soon after she received the published score (G. Schirmer, 1941), she sent copies to the poet who, in turn, inscribed a copy for Van Vechten (dated 1941).

Price was not involved directly with Bontemps, Wright, or others on the WPA projects but her Symphony No. 3 in C Minor betrays the influence of their attitudes and writings on her work. By the mid-1930s, the ideals of the Harlem Renaissance no longer served her needs in large-scale works. The Depression hit black America especially hard; work was hard to come by. The idealism that had so engaged black artists, including Price, during the 1920s–early 1930s gave way to realism as they tried to survive.

18 The Symphony No. 3

Price thought about and worked on the Symphony No. 3 for a long period of time. In this work, she turned away from the compositional procedures she had used in the past, such as writing melodies and rhythms closely aligned with African American spirituals and black folk dance. In a letter dated to Frederick Schwass, an administrator of the Michigan WPA orchestra, dated October 22, 1940, she explained the genesis of the symphony:

> My dear Mr. Schwass:
>
> I have your letter of October 21. The Symphony No. 3 in C Minor was composed in the late summer of 1938, laid aside for a year and then revised. It is intended to be Negroid in character and expression. In it no attempt, however, has been made to project Negro music solely in the purely traditional manner. None of the themes are adaptations or derivations of folk songs.
>
> The intention behind the writing of this work was a not too deliberate attempt to picture a cross section of present-day Negro life and thought with its heritage of that which is past, paralleled or influenced by concepts of the present day.[1]

In her large-scale works, Price conceived of the orchestra as a vehicle for romantic sonority. Her first full-length symphonic works, the Symphony in E Minor and the Piano Concerto, use a medium-sized orchestra with woodwinds by twos. Later pieces, including the Second Symphony and the *Mississippi River Suite*, call for the normal complement of woodwinds in threes: piccolo, 3 flutes, 2 oboes, English horn, 2 B-flat clarinets (the Symphony in E Minor calls for clarinets and trumpets in A only), bass clarinet, and 2 bassoons. For Price's scores written after the *Piano Concerto in One Movement*, 4 horns, 3 B-flat trumpets, 3 trombones, tuba, harp, and strings are standard as well. The percussion writing becomes more colorful. In addition to timpani, the Symphony No. 3 requires orchestral bells, snare drum, bass drum, cymbals, triangle, and celeste in movement two. Movement 3 ("Juba") includes wood blocks, castanets, tambourine, xylophone, and sand blocks.

Symphony No. 3 distinguishes itself in significant ways from Price's earlier works. Although Price's predilection for melodic writing still abounds, the orchestral writing shows a mature grasp of orchestral technique. Gone are multiple doublings of the thematic material with chordal accompaniments and simple textures. Here, the melodies become an integral part of the whole fabric. As a result, the textures are richer and more diverse and include more contrapuntal writing than Price has utilized in earlier works. In addition to the larger orchestra, Price further explores her fondness for instrumental choirs in antiphony, particularly in the second movement. This represents an expansion of a much-discussed technique that Price favored in the first symphony.

The first movement, in sonata-allegro form, begins with an *andante* introduction in which descending chromatic chords in C minor (woodwinds and brass) set a morose tone that extends for the whole of its eighteen measures (see example 36). With a change in tempo to *allegro*, the primary theme is tossed between the lower and upper strings (see example 37). This theme (an eight-measure pentatonic theme on C) is spiritual-like, but the authenticity of the melody is obscured by its harmonic features (it includes both the raised and lowered seventh scale degrees). Interrupting the thematic discourse is a two-measure phrase in the flutes set as a whole-tone scale. The harmonic ambiguity in the opening measures of the exposition are unusual for Price.

Example 36. Symphony No. 3, movement 1, introduction, mm. 1–6

Example 37. Symphony No. 3, movement 1, primary theme, mm. 19–30

This new direction compositionally conveys a less conservative approach to the incorporation of black folk music in large-scale works.

The primary theme is ultimately absorbed into an extended bridge, which is interrupted by a false second theme, played by the strings, in G minor (see example 38). Here, the harmonic rhythm is slower and the tranquil melody is colored by the flatted fifth, raised sixth, and raised seventh scale degrees.

After the uncompromising intensity of what turns out to be a modulating passage, a lyrical second theme emerges in E-flat. Also a pentatonic melody, its beauty and richness contrast markedly with the primary theme. Price's interest in orchestral color is evident here. First announced by the trombone, the second theme weaves its way through the brass, which accompany it to an echo of the theme in a woodwind choir (see example 39).

The tonal ambiguity of the primary theme, its subsidiary themes, and the lengthy chromatic bridge that follows it provide ample material for a further working out in the short development section. (The second theme is not treated at all.) The recapitulation follows in the expected manner, omitting the "false" second theme. Price then launches into a 41-measure Beethovenian coda. Full of developmental procedures, this multisectional coda continues to explore the potential of the materials in reverse order from which they were presented. Beginning with the second theme, the themes are dramatically subjected to augmentation and diminution over four distinct changes in tempo and meter: *moderato assai*, 2/2; *tempo moderato*, 3/2; *andante*, 4/4; and *allegro*, 4/4. Invoking the same mysterious mood with which the movement began, the coda concludes with inversions of the Neapolitan over a tonic pedal in the brass and strings. Ethereally, the flutes

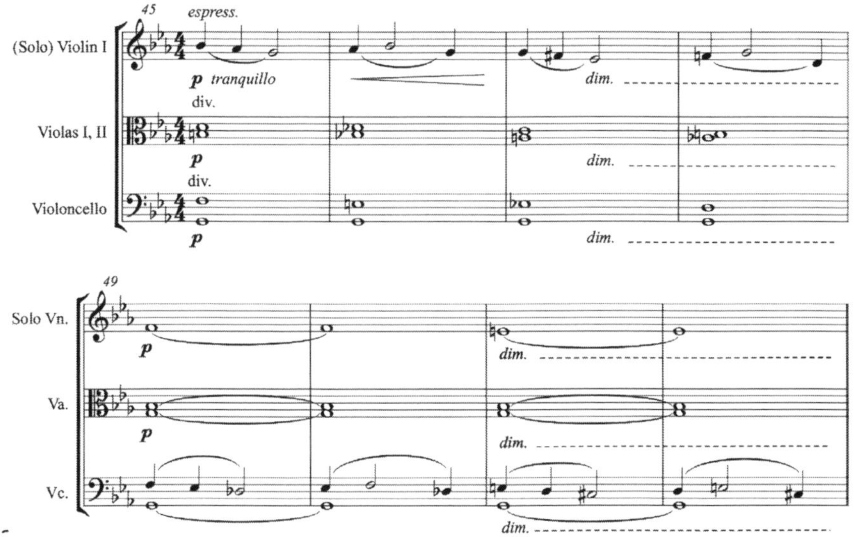

Example 38. Symphony No. 3, movement 1, false theme 2, mm. 45–52

Example 39. Symphony No. 3, movement 1, theme 2 (trombone solo), mm. 78–87

(and piccolo) answer with the whole-tone motive from the opening bars of the exposition. A *tutti sforzando* C minor chord closes out the movement.

Like the second movement of the Symphony in E Minor, the second movement of this symphony, marked *andante ma non troppo*, features antiphonal choirs of instruments in rich sonorities. This quasi-rondo movement is rich with beautiful melodies bathed in orchestral color. The influence of impressionism is particularly clear. The melodies are often accompanied by parallel chords, and phrases end without their expected resolutions.

The A section, in A-flat, presents two melodies. First, an oboe solo, accompanied by the lower woodwinds (English horn, clarinets, and bassoons), sings the eight-measure theme, which is spun out further by the string choir immediately following it (see example 40).

Example 40. Symphony No. 3, movement 2, A theme, A-flat major, mm. 1–8

Harmonically, this opening represents a departure for Price, who, in past large-scale works, would have established the tonic at the outset. Here, the A-flat tonic is delayed through the use of rich and colorful harmonies in the woodwind choir (IV with an added sixth, through vi to III).

Played by a solo bassoon, a haunting second theme emerges in F minor; more specifically, it is a pentatonic melody on F (see example 41). Again, choirs of instruments are explored; the theme is repeated by a woodwind choir, then tutti orchestra, before it dissipates through the brass choir and finally to the strings alone.

Section B begins in the unexpected and far-removed key of G major. A rather simple theme, seeming to suggest popular music, is rendered first by brass choir and celeste (see example 42).

But an abrupt digression to a dissonant polytonal passage based on a whole-tone scale in the strings dispels any notion that lightheartedness was the intention here. The chromatic motive is used effectively to modulate back to A-flat where the reorchestrated A section is repeated. The movement concludes with a plagal cadence suspended over the final eight bars of the movement. One

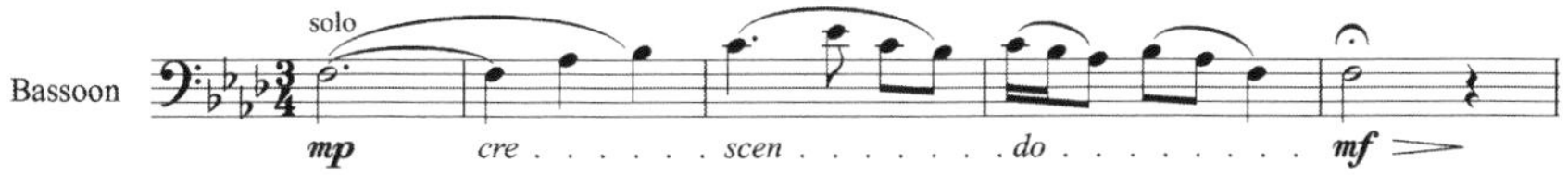

Example 41. Symphony No. 3, movement 2, theme 2, F minor

Example 42. Symphony No. 3, movement 2, B section, G major, mm. 61–65

might recall that the hymn of the second movement of the Symphony in E Minor evoked the spirituality of the church. The final ("Amen") cadence here is a conscious attempt to do likewise.

The rhythms of the antebellum dance "Juba" again form the basis of the third movement in rondo form (see example 43). But this "Juba" movement is significantly different from its orchestral predecessors. In both the Symphony in E Minor and the Concerto, the rhythmic foundation was clearly established at the outset: one group of instruments, usually the lower strings, maintained the steady rhythm while another group of instruments, for example, the upper strings, provided the syncopated melody that combined to characterize the rhythm of the dance. Here, any rhythmic ostinato is wholly absent. Rather, Price has added an array of percussion instruments—tambourine, sand block, wood block, castanets, snare and bass drums, cymbals, and xylophone—that are used to accentuate the rhythmic impulses underlying this dance movement in which the basic beat is implied.[2]

Polyrhythmic configurations are prevalent in the dance movements of the Symphony in E Minor and Piano Concerto, but nowhere in Price's orchestral music are the complexities of Afro-American rhythm more clearly demonstrated than in this movement. The implied metric organization of the first violin melody creates cross rhythms with the percussion, particularly in measures where the syncopation in the snare drum becomes more complex (see example 44). Characteristic

Example 43. Symphony No. 3, movement 3, juba dance

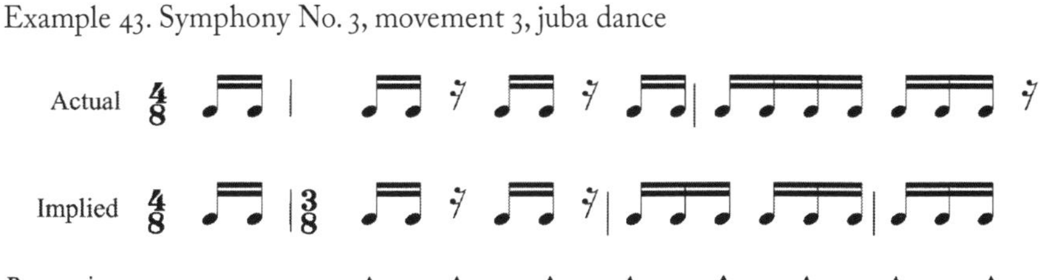

Example 44. Symphony No. 3, movement 3, rhythmic implications

of the African concept of musical time, equality is given to melody and rhythm. Varying degrees of metric clash between a melody and its accompaniment is a feature that is fundamental to African American dance music.

Another interesting feature of the opening measures is the irregular phrasing that complements the metric organization. The primary theme of the rondo is essentially nine measures subdivided into two four-bar phrases with a one-bar interruption: mm. 1–4 / m. 5 / mm. 6–9.

This movement diverges from its models harmonically also. In both the Symphony in E Minor and the Concerto, the simple harmony upon which the original "Juba" is based was a priori. In this movement, in E-flat, colorful chords pique the interest of the listener immediately:

harmony E-flat:	I	IV$\flat$7	vi7/E-flat	V6/4	V7/VII	I6/4
measure:	1	3		4	5	6

The unexpected shift in measure 5 to A7 (V7/VII) is a harmonic digression that one might hear in jazz, used here as a dominant substitution. In fact, the entire progression is close to a standard jazz progression: I-VI7-II7-V7-I. Although Price was not herself a jazz musician, hearing jazz music all around her in Chicago did have an unconscious impact on some of her compositions.

The rondo has two episodes. The first presents a tune in the flutes whose melodic contour is related to the A theme. The second episode is marked by tempo, key, and meter changes. A lyrical brass choir, *andantino*, with an underlying rhythmic accompaniment in the strings, provides a contrast in mood. An interesting instrumental combination in this episode is a solo flute and xylophone accompanied by sustained violins and pizzicato lower strings with trumpets. The xylophone, its progenitor in Africa, had a strong association with jazz by 1940. Throughout the episode, the listener will, at once, be reminded of Gershwin's popular music and the Latin-American habanera dance, which, long before 1940, had made its way into American popular music.

Similarly to the *finale* of the Symphony in E Minor, the last movement of the Third Symphony, in sonata form, is a scherzo in 6/8 (see example 45); but there are significant differences that mark the finale of the Symphony in C Minor as a more concise and well-crafted last movement than the earlier work. The primary themes of both finales are constituted from a triplet figure that outlines the tonic, but the added seventh in this movement gives the otherwise ordinary figure much-needed flavor. The differences in the textures of the two movements are also striking. The texture in the last movement of the first symphony essentially consists of the flute melody doubled by oboes (I, II) and violins while the remaining woodwinds, brass, and strings provide an accompaniment of block chords. The opening of this movement of the C Minor Symphony, similarly to other movements, features antiphonal choirs of instruments but now in canon (strings answered by woodwinds).

A modulation toward the secondary theme begins almost immediately. Modal mixture is a prominent feature of the secondary theme in G major/minor, first heard in the English horn doubled by the first trombone and accompanied by strings.

Example 45. Symphony No. 3, movement 4, primary theme, mm. 1–8

After a classic-style repeat of the exposition, the development ensues in G major/minor. Neither the primary nor the secondary theme is developed thematically. Rather, they are fragmented and repeated on different tonal centers, occasionally with chromatic alterations of the theme. At one point, the themes are combined: first theme in bassoons and cellos in C major / secondary theme in flutes and clarinets in G minor. Used in combination, repetition, modal ambiguity, and the inflected third and seventh scale steps are all characteristics of African American music.

The straightforward recapitulation concludes with the longest coda of any movement in the three symphonic works examined—70 measures. Essentially a prolongation of the dominant, it features sweeping crescendos from the lowest strings through full orchestra. And as if to tease listeners further, isolated instruments play fragments of the primary and secondary themes before "taking off" again through chromatic arpeggios, only to be temporarily interrupted by *tutti sforzando* chords. The movement concludes with a change in tempo and meter, to *andante* 4/4, which further accentuates the modal mixtures that have been a feature of this movement. In these measures, the woodwinds, brass, and lower strings oscillate between C major and C minor against a two-octave descending and ascending chromatic scale on C in the violins. The movement concludes with three emphatic C minor chords.

Price's last letter to Sergei Koussevitzky, September 18, 1941, provides a concluding thought on the substance of this major work. She wrote, "I have a symphony in which I tried to portray a cross section of Negro life and psychology as it is today, influenced by urban life north of the Mason and Dixon line. It is not 'program' music. I merely had in mind the life and music of the Negro of today and for that reason treated my themes in a manner difference from what I would have done if I had centered my attention upon the religious themes of antebellum days, or yet the ragtime and jazz that followed; rather a fusion of these, colored by present cultural influences."[3]

This letter reveals Price's recognition that she had moved in a different direction compositionally, one that while still steeped in the African American tradition, presents a modern approach—a synthesis, rather than a retrospective view, of African American life and culture. The necessity to write overtly black themes and underscore them with simple dance rhythms is gone. The Symphony No. 3 in C Minor reflects a maturity of style and a new attitude toward black musical materials.

19 Final Years

The Heart of a Woman

During the years of the Chicago Renaissance, it is clear that many blacks were feeling a sense of the city's artistic vibrancy. In a January 11, 1941, *Chicago Defender* article, "Chicago Retains Place as Center of Nation's Musical Activities," Grace W. Tompkins recounts the city's classical concerts by black musicians during the prior year. Concert singers Marian Anderson and Dorothy Maynor drew capacity audiences. Anderson sang two solo concerts and Maynor appeared with the Chicago Symphony. Paul Robeson distinguished himself in two concerts. He performed in Grant Park where he sang his famous *Ballad for Americans*, a cantata by John Latouche (words) and Earl Robinson (music), which he introduced over CBS radio in 1939. Robeson returned to Chicago a second time that year to give a solo recital at the Auditorium Theatre. Choirs specializing in the arrangement of spirituals including the Fisk Jubilee Singers, radio's famous Southernaires quartet and Wings Over Jordan also came to town. The Southernaires broadcast each week over NBC. It was their contemporary adaptations, that is, new texts sung to familiar melodies, which were especially popular. "Prayer of Love," for example, was based on "Swing Low, Sweet Chariot." Attracting both white and black audiences, Wings Over Jordan sang to a reportedly forty million listeners each Sunday morning on the CBS network.[1] A myriad of local soloists and instrumentalists provided further opportunity for Chicagoans to hear black classical artists each week. Tompkins also mentions the failed American Negro Exhibition in her article. Apparently, there was an opening concert of local soloists, but the several programs that were to follow were all canceled. In what amounts to a slight to New York City, Tompkins concludes by arguing that "Chicago is still the music center of the nation as far as Race musicians and musical activities are concerned. It is gratifying, in looking back, to note that we have in 1940 heard all of the best the country has to offer;

here in our own concert halls and church auditoriums." Noticeably absent from Tompkins's critique are the musicians who were involved in popular music, jazz, gospel, and blues, all styles of black music that were thriving in Chicago in 1940.

Still a formidable presence in the city, the National Association of Negro Musicians held its annual convention there in 1940. Among those particularly visible was W. C. Handy. Handy was one of a few musicians equally conversant in popular styles and classical music who appeared regularly on the classical music scene. His active participation in NANM and as a publisher bridged an artificial chasm between black classical musicians and those involved in popular styles of black music. At the conference, he gave an important talk on the effect that radio was having on the sale of musical scores and, specifically, on the impact of radio on black composers. Handy was in a good position to advise the group on this. Since he owned his own publishing company, his music and that of other black composers (popular songs, blues, and arrangements of spirituals) was becoming more widely available to the public. When Handy published his *Memphis Blues* in 1912 and the commercially successful *St. Louis Blues* two years later, he helped to standardize the twelve-bar blues form; the distribution of that music on record made a significant impact on the industry.

Other highlights of the 1940 NANM conference included an address to the attendees by special guest Marian MacDowell, widow of American composer Edward MacDowell. After a stirring homily on the richness of America's music, Mrs. MacDowell, now 83, gave a rendition of her husband's sentimental but enormously popular "To a Wild Rose" from the *Woodland Sketches* for piano. Indeed, one wonders what MacDowell would have thought about his wife's strong advocacy of American music. Acknowledged as the leading American composer of the late nineteenth century, MacDowell never considered himself a nationalist even though his widely acclaimed Suite No. 2 for orchestra, subtitled the *Indian Suite* (op. 48 begun in 1891 and premiered by the Boston Symphony Orchestra in 1896), appropriated Native American melodies as its thematic substance. MacDowell never aspired to write nationalistic music, and he had a particular distaste for concerts consisting only of American works. Increasingly, he refused to allow his music to be performed at events of all American music, insisting that music ought to be presented on its merits and not based on its composer's nationality.

Price was in select company when, at the conference, she, in the role of composer-performer-educator, led sessions on music education and performance techniques. Seminars were conducted also by composer Camille Nickerson, chair of the music department at Howard University; Kemper Harreld, chair of the department at Atlanta University; and William Dawson. The culmination of the NANM conference was a tribute to W. C. Handy and Price. Honored for their distinguished careers and for their lifelong commitment to black music, the two composers were almost overwhelmed by the adulation. Handy, at 67 years old, and Price, now 53, accepted the recognition of their colleagues and friends with heartfelt gratitude.

Price continued to write large-scale works during the 1940s and 1950s: in addition to the Symphony No. 3, she composed the Symphony in D Minor, which I assume to be her fourth symphony. The undated work is lost and there appear to have been no performances of it.

In May 1952, she also composed a second Violin Concerto, in D major, which was co-commissioned by the Illinois Federation of Music Clubs, the Chicago Club of Women Musicians, the Lake View Musical Society, and Mu Phi Epsilon. The work was premiered posthumously in 1953 by violinist Minnie Cedargreen Jernberg. The score that survives is for the soloist and piano (an orchestral reduction that has no indications of instrumentation). The one-movement work is sectional—each of the five sections in the first half is in a different key with accompanying mood and tempo changes. The soloist and the orchestra are full partners in the concerto, tossing the melodic material between them. The short, quiet *andante cantabile* middle section betrays Price's fondness for rhapsodic lyrical melodies in her large-scale works. The rousing fourth section requires the soloist to negotiate fast scale passages, arpeggios, and double stops. The second half of the work is a condensed reworking of the opening material.

Most of the music written during these years are chamber works, art songs, and arrangements of spirituals. The turn to smaller genres is easy to explain. During the Depression and in the war years, it was much more difficult for most composers without a commission or the support of the Federal Music Project of the WPA to get large-scale works performed. Price's network of professional musicians in Chicago and those on the national and international concert halls made the choice of writing songs, in particular, a logical one. Her songs continued to be in demand; many of them were published as well. In addition to Marian Anderson, Price could count Blanche Thebom, Roland Hayes, Abbie Mitchell, and Lillian Evanti among her coterie of friends and colleagues who regularly performed her music. She wrote about one hundred songs in all: about 75 art songs, 13 popular/commercial songs, and 14 arrangements of spirituals.

Most of Price's art songs are serious-minded and reveal an almost intense glimpse of her inner self. Price chose her texts from a wide variety of poets, many of whom were African Americans. By far, her favorite poets were Langston Hughes and Paul Laurence Dunbar. In addition to the nine settings of Hughes's poems, there are nineteen poems by Dunbar represented. She also set texts by James Weldon Johnson and Georgia Douglas Johnson (one poem each). These songs are intelligent and thoughtful, capturing some of the most passionate poetry written during the Harlem and Chicago Renaissance.

One of Price's most provocative art songs is a setting of Georgia Douglas Johnson's title poem from her collection *The Heart of a Woman* (see example 48). In it a woman's heart is metaphorically compared to a lone bird that wings "forth with the dawn" over "life's turrets and vales." It then "falls back with the night / And enters some alien cage in its plight / And tries to forget it has dreamed of the stars / While it breaks, breaks, breaks on the sheltering bars."

Published in 1918, Johnson's poem is strikingly feminist in its sensibility.[2] Aware of how far women still had to come before they were completely "emancipated," Douglas's poem speaks of the "oppressiveness and pain of the traditional female lot."

Price set the two-verse poem in a modified strophic form. In the opening lines, as the heart/bird wing "restlessly on," so does the music (see example 46). In the entire 25-measure song in E-flat, the tonic is only briefly alluded to (at the penultimate phrase of the poem). The harmony and the vocal line seemingly wander aimlessly, although nowhere is this song really dissonant. At the conclusion of the song ("while it breaks," and so forth) the dominant chord is veiled by a flat 3 (the chord is really a G minor 7), after which the chordal accompaniment slides chromatically into the final tonic E-flat arpeggio. The fluid piano accompaniment and the several meter and tempo changes propel the music forward seamlessly. It is Price's utter intimacy with the poem that qualifies it as one of her most powerful settings.

Price's song is all the more poignant because it is her only setting of a black woman poet. The feelings of a "caged bird," pained in its trapped existence and the confession of broken, shattered dreams is vividly portrayed. Could this be the veiled autobiographical revelation of the composer herself, echoing that of the despaired poet? This inference might give the reader pause to recount Price's childhood ambition of becoming a doctor, following in her father's footsteps. And although she was far more successful in her career than even she anticipated, there were professional aspirations that went unfulfilled, and as a single mother she lived in aloneness.

Price's music was promoted also by composers, including John Alden Carpenter, William Grant Still, and Harry T. Burleigh. Price's relationship with Carpenter proved to be beneficial to both of them. For Price, the sponsorship of her membership in ASCAP by Carpenter was most appreciated. In return, Carpenter asked Price to use her influence with Marian Anderson to get a hearing of some of his music with the concert singer. In 1940, Marian Anderson's career was arguably at its apex (she had just sung before 75,000 at the Lincoln Memorial April 9, 1939, when she was denied the use of Constitution Hall in Washington, D.C., because of her race). In the 1940s, Marian Anderson, along with Roland Hayes, was counted among the top ten concert artists in the United States and her performance of a song meant worldwide exposure to it.

Example 46. "Heart of a Woman," mm. 1–14

In a letter of May 13, 1940, from Carpenter to Price, Carpenter comments on Anderson's reputation before continuing with his request:

> You are certainly to be congratulated on the inclusion of one of your songs in Miss Anderson's programs, for it is undoubtedly, one of the highest goals that any contemporary writer of songs can reach. I have not yet heard her sing your song

but hope to at the first opportunity. [The song to which Carpenter is referring is probably "Songs to the Dark Virgin," which was introduced to the public by Anderson in 1940].

By way of reciprocity, the next time you see Miss Anderson, you might say to her that you know of an American composer by the name of Carpenter who has been one of her sincerest admirers from afar for a long time and who sent her, about a year ago, a group of his songs in the hope that they might interest her.

Price immediately wrote to Marian Anderson with the composer's inquiry. The letter is dated the following day, May 14, 1940:

Dear Miss Anderson:

Receiving compliments has by this time become such a habit that it has become boresome to you, no doubt. Yet I thought you would like to know of something said by a dyed-in-the-wool American (a direct descendant of John Alden), one of America's most outstanding composers, a man without prejudice—altho he is a millionaire quietly exerting far-reaching influence and power in the world of music—a close personal friend of just about all of our major symphony conductors, to say nothing of having through marriage joined his fortune with that of the former Mrs. Borden, herself a patroness of the arts.

He is very decisive and outspoken in his likes and dislikes. I have seen some very important people all in a dither when he is around and about. By this time you probably have guessed that I am referring to the globe-trotter John Alden Carpenter, who today expressed to me all manner of fine things about you, saying that he had been one of your "sincerest admirers from afar for a long time." I was proud and thrilled and felt that I must tell you about it and also quote from a letter of his: "You are certainly to be congratulated on the inclusion of one of your songs in Miss Anderson's programs, for it is undoubtedly one of the highest goals that any contemporary writer of songs can reach." You can imagine how proud and thrilled I was to have him voice my own thoughts. And now my joy would be complete if I could witness his being bowled over by that breathtaking radiation of your poise, unaffected culture and sincerity that "bowls over" all who come in your presence. I would therefore like to present "the great American composer" to "the world's greatest singer" and then stand back and revel in his well-concealed admiration for you. Do you think this can be accomplished on your next visit here? Could you give us a few minutes at your hotel, perhaps?

Sincerely,
Florence B. Price

Price then apprised Carpenter of her letter to Anderson. In a letter written just two days later, May 16, 1940, she mentioned to Carpenter: "I shall certainly bring to Miss Anderson's attentions your songs on her next visit to Chicago. If you would care to also meet Miss Anderson personally, it would give me great pleasure to try and arrange it. Maybe it might be well to then hand her some more of your song manuscripts, just in case the others did not reach her. I have an idea she likes especially to look over new and untried things." Although Anderson did write back to Price suggesting that Carpenter and she meet sometime, it is not known whether an encounter did occur.

Price was in a good position to know about the types of songs Marian Anderson liked to sing because during the 1930s and 1940s several of Price's songs were among Anderson's favorites. Anderson had over 50 of Price's songs in her possession, many of which were premiered by and dedicated to the diva. Two of Price's songs, the spiritual arrangement, "My Soul's Been Anchored in de Lord," and "Songs to the Dark Virgin" were made immediate successes by Anderson's performances of them. Anderson closed many of her concerts with the spiritual arrangement, including the historic Lincoln Memorial concert in 1939.

Anderson was also the first of three concert artists to record the work (Victor LSC 2592).[3] She performed the spiritual on the nationally broadcast "The Bell Telephone Hour," September 14, 1942, a one-half-hour program of commercially sponsored radio (classical and popular music) featuring full orchestra conducted by Donald Voorhees. Although Voorhees arranged much of the music for his program, he also hired other arrangers, including William Grant Still. Price arranged "My Soul's Been Anchored in de Lord" herself for solo voice and orchestra. Concert singer Blanche Thebom mentioned that Anderson sang "My Soul's Been Anchored in de Lord" over one hundred times.[4] That "My Soul's Been Anchored" was a favorite of Anderson's is evident by the fact that she continued to sing it around the world, including her 1957 Russian tour where she closed the spiritual group with it.

Marian Anderson's rendition of "Songs to the Dark Virgin" scored a similar success for the composer (see Example 47). Set to a Langston Hughes text, the art song was highly acclaimed by Eugene Stinson, critic for the *Chicago Daily News*, who wrote, "Songs to the Dark Virgin" as Miss Anderson (Marian) sang it, [was] one of the greatest immediate successes ever won by an American song."[5] This song completely weds Langston Hughes's descriptive text to its piano accompaniment. The sensuous three-verse text is a powerful one and Price has captured the passion vividly.

In verse one, the broken arpeggios in the accompaniment are dark and murky. Textually, the darkness of the body is set against the light of the jewels ("Would that I were a jewel . . . that all my shining brilliants might fall at thy feet"), much the same way that the accompaniment begins to rise out of its darkness only to fall again in reflection of the text. In verse two, the "I" and the "body" are enveloped one with the other ("Would that I were a garment . . . that all my folds might wrap about thy body"). Musically, the piano accompaniment encircles the voice, at times above it, at times they are in unison (sostenuto

Example 47. "Songs to the Dark Virgin," mm. 1–6

markings highlight the duet). The rapture is made complete in the final verse. Price accentuates the text ("Would that I were a flame . . . to annihilate thy body") by lengthening the note values of the music (the rhythms are at least twice as long as the first and second verses). The music sweeps toward a dramatic climax on "annihilate" before the concluding four-bar cadence.

Concert singer and composer Harry T. Burleigh, a longtime friend of Price, was equally supportive of her career. In addition to singing her music, Burleigh tried to help promote Price's music through his own publisher, G. Ricordi & Co. In the fall of 1943, Price sent Burleigh some of her music for his examination. He wrote the following reply, dated October 14, 1943:

823 E. 166th St., NY

My dear Mrs. Price—Thank you so much for sending me your delightful songs; and the beautiful photograph—which I shall cherish *always*. I looked over the songs with genuine interest, and felt that you would like a music publisher to see them; so, I passed them on to the Editors at G. Ricordi and Co, Inc., who have published my compositions over a period of years. I knew that they would give your songs careful attention and every possible consideration.

They commented *very* favorably on your work; regretting that at this time the market for songs is not one that warrants such publications, and this plus the shortage of paper and engravers has caused a temporary retardation of all publishing.

I sincerely hope you will not feel that I took too much liberty in submitting your manuscripts to Ricordi. One of their music Editors is Ruggero Vené—a pupil of Respighi, whose ideas and opinions in music composition I value very highly. Personally, I consider the third song "I know why the caged bird sings" ["Sympathy," text by Paul Laurence Dunbar] a great setting of those words and melodically effective and dramatic and only in one or two spots does it appear too chromatic (perhaps the second verse—and even there it is in the look of the accidentals, rather than the sound).

Oct. 21

Do pardon and overlook the length of time it has taken me to finish this letter and to ask whether you wish me to return the MSS to you? or whether I may keep them? Kindly let me know.

New York has gone "all out" over Paul Robeson as Othello! He, in Ricordi & Co., cannot sell any songs at all. Octavo things are constantly being used.[6]

Sincerely,
H.Burleigh

Price's setting of Paul Laurence Dunbar's "Sympathy" is one of her most powerful songs (see example 48). Dunbar's text, although published in 1895, still speaks to the restlessness and determination of many African Americans. Its descriptive language is so wrought with emotion that poet Maya Angelou used one of its lines as the title of her best-selling autobiography, *I Know Why the Caged Bird Sings*.[7]

I know what the caged bird feels, alas!
When the sun is bright on the upland slopes;
When the wind stirs soft through the springing grass,
And the river flows like a stream of glass;
When the first bird sings and the first bud opens,
And the faint perfume from its chalice steals—
I know what the caged bird feels!
I know why the caged bird beats his wing
Till the blood is red on the cruel bars;
For he must fly back to his perch and cling

When he fain would be on the bough a-swing;
And the pain still throbs in the old, old scars
And they pulse with a keener sting—
I know why he beats his wing!

I know why the caged bird sings, ah me,
When his wing is bruised and his bosom sore,—
When he beats his bars and he would be free;
It is not a carol of joy or glee,
But a pray'r that he sends from his heart's deep core,
But a plea, that upward to Heaven he flings—
I know why the caged bird sings!

Example 48. "Sympathy," mm. 8–20

Since Price usually shared her newest works with her colleagues and friends, "Sympathy" probably dates from mid-1943 when she sent the music to Burleigh for his perusal. Price's setting is in a modified ABA form. In verse one, the lyrical vocal line is gently underscored by an arpeggiated accompaniment. In this verse, the poet seeks to establish a feeling of oneness with the "caged bird" who can only appreciate the warmth and the beauty of nature from his trap. In the key of E-flat major, the low-lying phrases of the opening bars outlining the tonic lead to a descending chromatic line ("When the first bird sings and the first bud opes") through an octave back to the tonic pitch. The closing phrase of the verse contrasts sharply with it. The voice soars upward an octave leap on "I know" to dramatize the solidarity of the poet and the caged bird.

The second verse (B) is delivered in quasi-recitative; the several changes in meter allow for the rapid-fire delivery of the caustic text. The accompaniment is more sparse in this verse. At times it is closely aligned with the voice; at other moments, chords punctuate the most cryptic words, "cruel," "pain," "scars," and "sting." It is this verse that bothered Burleigh visually with all of its accidentals. (Perhaps it bothered publishers as well, which could explain why this song was never published.) This section is not so much dissonant, however, as it is harmonically unstable. The text, describing the agitation of the trapped bird trying to escape while the pain of old pulses within his body anew, is thus set in bold relief. As in Price's setting of Georgia Douglas Johnson's "The Heart of a Woman," the poet evokes the analogy of the obstructed bird and the suffocating self.

At the beginning of verse three, the text continues to depict the entrapped bird desperately trying to escape "when his wing is bruised and his bosom sore." Musically there is a return of the A section (a simple melody accompanied by broken arpeggios on the tonic). However, the second and third verses are elided (the last line of the second verse is set to the A section of music that begins verse three) so that the text and the music are totally at odds here. It is not until the final lines of the poem, when the bird prays for the release of his soul, that the voice and accompaniment are conjoined.

Although Price never asked Burleigh to assist her in securing Ricordi as a publisher for "Sympathy," she was probably grateful to him for initiating that dialogue. Burleigh was hired as a music editor there in 1913 and remained employed by the publisher for over thirty years. It was through Ricordi that almost all of Burleigh's own art songs and spiritual arrangements were published.

Why didn't Price ask Burleigh to use his influence with this prestigious music press? Her unconquerable shyness appears to have worsened as she got older. It hindered her from promoting her music more widely and it inhibited her from asking her friends for professional support. At its worst, her timidity even got in the way of her relationship with friends. Rather than confront a person in a difficult or awkward situation, Price would back away and thereby create a negative situation where there might not have been one. A letter from Price to William Grant Still in the mid-1940s is clear evidence of this.

Price and Still were longtime friends. Their families knew each other in Little Rock, and they socialized on many occasions, since they moved in the same middle-class black circles. After they established their careers, Price in Chicago and Still in New York and Los Angeles, they kept in touch, apprised each other of their accomplishments, and supported each other when they could. Yet at one point in their relationship, something went awry. Apparently, Price tried to contact Still at his hotel when he visited Chicago sometime in the early 1940s. Thinking that Still had received her messages (which he had not) but had not returned her phone calls, Price gave Still a cold shoulder for several years. After playing telephone tag and mail tag for a good while, Price was able to reestablish the relationship, clearly an important one to her. On March 22, 1945, she wrote:

> Dear Mr. Still,
>
> At this moment I am thinking of the curious coincidence of two messages having been undelivered; and how oddly the revelation came about. For these several years I have been unable to understand why you apparently ignored my message and invitation sent to you at the Grand Hotel [the leading black hotel in Chicago]. Although I was not in the city at the time of your last visit to Chicago, I probably would not have had the hardihood to risk a second rebuff.
>
> Believe me, your puzzling behavior (as it then seemed) did not in the least affect my very great admiration for your work. There is no pupil of mine that has not heard from me of the attainments of the race's musical lights including yourself.
>
> I have often wanted to write and ask you for a list of your published compositions so that I might show it to members of the musical staff here at Lincoln Center [where she resided] as well as to other groups. I invariably retreated. Then when I found myself in your city I determinedly put aside my disinclination and phoned you. How glad I am now that I did. You probably were as much irked by what appeared to be indifference or worse on my part in not replying to Mrs. Still's letter—as was I in believing that you were guilty of discourtesy. (You see they told me at the Grand that you have been given my message!)

Price goes on to discuss her address change:

> I am wondering if Mrs. Still's letter was sent to this address (700 E. Oakwood Blvd) or to the old address 647 E. 50th Place from which I moved in the Spring of 1941 for the sole reason that so much of my mail failed to reach my hands. I gave the P.O. my forwarding address but the mail delivery here, especially in certain sections, is most unreliable.
>
> Very sincerely yours
> (signed) Florence B. Price
>
> Apologies for typewriter spacing trouble which I cannot personally repair.[8]

Price and Still were careful not to repeat this unfortunate situation. This letter of 1951, in which Price acknowledges Still's orchestral work, *In Memoriam: The Colored Soldiers Who Died for Democracy*, shows the efforts that Price made to maintain a cordial relationship with him. The *Pittsburgh Courier* article to which she refers is probably Still's "50 Years of Progress in Music," published November 11, 1950. In it, Still not only details the accomplishments of many African American musicians but he recounts the obstacles that most of them, including himself, had to overcome in order to succeed. The message was none too strong: that in spite of the gains made by black classical musicians, racist attitudes prevented many of them from reaching their highest goals. On January 9, 1951, Price wrote:

> Dear Mr. Still—I read and called to the attention of several friends the issue of the PITTSBURGH COURIER containing your article. Re-actions varied but all agreed that it certainly gave food for thought. It was a pleasure to listen to the Chicago Symphony Orchestra's playing of your IN MEMORIAM, a few months ago.[9]
>
> With continued good wishes, I am
> very sincerely yours
> Florence B. Price[10]

* * *

Price's reputation grew steadily to the early 1950s. Her works were being presented throughout the United States and Canada, and she was earning recognition abroad. In 1951, she received a telegram from Sir John Barbirolli, conductor of the Halle Orchestra, Manchester, England, who knew of her work from his time in the States as conductor of the New York Philharmonic Orchestra from 1936–1942. Would she write a concert overture or suite for strings based on black American spirituals for his orchestra? She would indeed and she would go to England for the performance. This is the personal and professional affirmation that had eluded her. She began work on the overture immediately. Further, the *Chicago Defender* noted that Price was to have "a number of works" presented in Paris during the "spring season of 1951."[11]

During Black History Week, February 1951, Price completed a *String Quartet on Negro Themes*, which was premiered at Carey Temple church in the city. This piece may have been the work that she later titled *Five Folksongs in Counterpoint*. Originally titled "Negro Folksongs in Counterpoint," this quartet includes "Calvary," "Clementine," "Drink to Me Only with Thine Eyes," "Shortnin' Bread," and "Swing Low, Sweet Chariot." The reason for the title change is obvious: two of the five folk songs ("Clementine," and "Drink to Me Only") are not of African American origin.[12]

Five Folksongs in Counterpoint is a work for accomplished players (see example 49). Technically challenging, the texture throughout the work is contrapuntal

Example 49. "Shortnin' Bread," from *Five Folksongs in Counterpoint*, mm. 37–46

and conveys to the listener the serious treatment of these songs. The familiar melodies are shared between the instruments equally; between the thematic phrases is freely interpolated material. A convincing interpretation of these folk songs requires a flexible approach to the execution of the rhythms and an understanding of the subtle, but fluid, phrasing (now detached, now slurred even though it may not be marked in the score).

Price finished the concert overture, now lost, and she readied herself for Europe. Barbirolli did perform her work in the spring of 1951, but Price was not there to hear it. She had heart problems that sent her to the hospital occasionally, and it is likely that she was sick and physically unable to travel at this time.[13] There was probably no other reason that would have kept her from this performance. Now that her children were grown and on their own, Price was only responsible to herself. When her children were young and they were sick, Price frequently canceled her plans to be with them. Her daughter Florence remembered, "I had an appendectomy at that time [February 1934]. Mother would never have left me then."[14] Price's disappointment in not being able to hear this special commissioned work must have been great.

The next eighteen months were good ones for Price. In addition to the completion of the second Violin Concerto, she wrote a chamber work, *Sea Gulls*, for women's chorus or quartet with flute, clarinet, violin, viola, cello, and piano, which won first place in the Lake View Musical Society competition. It was premiered May 14, 1951, at a special installation program of the Society's officers.

Even the U.S. Marine Band found something of interest in Price's oeuvre. During the late 1940s and early 1950s, it regularly performed the *Three Negro Dances*, first made popular by the Michigan W.P.A. Concert Band.[15] Price arranged her *Suite of Negro Dances* for orchestra and was delighted to be present when it was performed by members of the Chicago Symphony Orchestra. Led by the orchestra's associate conductor, George Schick, the work was broadcast live on WGN-TV, Channel 9, February 18, 1953, on a television "pops" concert.[16]

In early 1953, Price planned another trip to Europe. She was to receive an award in Paris in the spring and she would combine it with her always hoped for sightseeing vacation in France and England.[17] For this special trip, she would take with her Perry Quinney Johnston, her close friend from Little Rock. They would sail from New York for Le Havre, France, May 26, 1953, and remain in Europe for five weeks.

Price worked assiduously to finish up some work before her trip. She also had personal business to take care of. In particular she needed to apply for her passport. There was one problem: she had no birth certificate to claim U.S. citizenship. She had never needed one before now. The proposed trip to Europe two years earlier was probably never a reality to her, and even now she waited until just weeks before her trip before she filed the paperwork. April 20, she applied for a "delayed birth certificate." A friend of hers claiming to "have full knowledge of family history" signed the affidavit on her behalf. The signature, almost illegible due to the shaking of the signer's hand, appears to be "P.A. Dorman," age 77. Most curious is the response to question #16 concerning her family history. When asked how many children were born to the mother including the "child" in question, the response was "one." Once again Price's brother, Charles, who may well have died before 1953, was obliterated from the record.[18]

Once the passport was in hand, Price oversaw the remaining details of the trip for both her and Perry—tickets, cruise accommodations, and hotel arrangements in Europe. Early May 1953 Price wrote to Perry:

> Dear Perry,
>
> Our tickets have just come; also tags for our baggage which we can attach here or in New York. In New York we will go to the home of a cousin-by-marriage, Mrs. Eddie Coates 596 Edgecombe Ave. and from there on the morning of Tues. May 26 we go to the ship which leaves from Pier 88, North River at [the] foot of West 48th Street at 11 a.m. New York daylight saving[s] time. Passengers must embark between 9 and 10:30 a.m. New York Daylight Saving[s] Time, bound for Havre, France. Your E. bound ticket on the Ile de France is N 110739. We will be

in Cabin 428. (My ticket no. is 110737). The numbers of our return tickets are: (on Liberte)

Yours is 110740 (cabin 576) leaving Southampton, Eng June 30.

Mine "110738 "

Here are some foreign addresses of the FRENCH LINE[:]

Havre, France 89 Boulevard de Strasbourg[;]

London, Eng. 20 Cockspur St. Of course the man with whom I dealt here could furnish any information if called on, about us, after we leave -C. Burli, Mgr. Foreign Travel Dept., Cartan Travel Bureau, 8 South Mich. Ave., Chi 3.

The Travel Co's representative at Paris is Lissone Lindeman[,] 14 Avenue de L'Opera, Paris, France. This [is] information which I think your family should have. I will keep the tickets until I see you.

I wrote you as soon as I received my passport and asked you if you had received yours. Did you get that letter? And did you get your passport, O.K. Everything is now in the finishing-up stage. Whatever you do, dont let your passport out of your possession. It might be well to have the number of your passport copied off on to something. Also leave the number with your family.

The room here is vacant and ready for you any time you want to come. I think you should have a few days rest here, or sight-seeing if you want to but I can't promise to be of any help in taking you around because I am still hoping I can get out of this rush of work I am in and get some rest, too, before leaving.

Yours
F.B.P.[19]

In anticipation of the trip Price asked the Clayton F. Summy Co. to help promote some of her music (piano teaching pieces) abroad. May 14, Kenneth F. Kimes wrote to a European publisher:

To whom it may concern,

Miss Florence Price, one of the most prominent of American composers, has requested that we cooperate in helping to establish a demand for music by American composers in your country.

Her own compositions are among the best sellers in our catalog and any promotion activities you may initiate in her behalf, will be greatly appreciated.

Attached is our Trade Discount Policy which you may find of value in determining your future needs.

Cordially,
Clayton F. Summy Co.
Kenneth F. Kimes[20]

While Price was busy taking care of personal and professional business in preparation for the trip, her friend Perry was less enthusiastic and readied herself unhurriedly. Her daughter, Marion, anxious for her mother to make the trip, helped her to get her wardrobe together but Perry Johnston was apathetic about it all. She had a premonition that she and Price would not make it to Europe, so why get excited about a trip that was not going to take place? Marion did not question her mother about her strong feelings, for her mother, although not really clairvoyant, had correctly predicted events before. Marion Ross explains:

> My mother was one of those people who dreamed a lot and she put a lot of stock in interpreting her dreams. And we grew to at least tolerate it because so many of the things that she said we watched come true. One morning, when I was fairly young, she got up and said, "I really got Mrs. Price on my mind" and she sat down and wrote her a letter and insisted that my dad take it down to the post office and mail it special delivery, which then was a big thing. And in that letter, she told her that she had a dream about her and cautioned her about signing any contracts without reading the fine print. Mrs. Price was living in something we would probably now . . . describe as a commune at that time [the Abraham Lincoln Center]. They managed to get her just before she was leaving one morning and gave her this special delivery letter. She got in the cab on her way to a contract signing and read the letter and indeed there was some things in the contract that would not have been favorable to her. We always kind of marveled at some [of] those experiences.[21]

Mrs. Johnston, of course, never let on to her good friend about her forebodings. The European trip, as she predicted, however did not take place. Her daughter explained why:

> Mrs. Price had never been to Europe and her daughter Florence had always wanted her to have that opportunity. . . . Florence, the daughter, made the arrangements for her to have the European trip and asked Mrs. Price who she would like to have accompany her. And of course she wanted my mother to go along with her. And once again it was some [of] these feelings that my mother had that she really wasn't going any place and we were all excited about it and did quite a lot to encourage her and kinda pushed that she get her passport. And I was doing a lot of sewing at the time and made her this wonderful wardrobe. And we were real excited. The church clubs gave her little handkerchiefs, showers, and whatever for the trip. And on the Monday before they were to have met, before they were to have sailed from New York, my mother called Chicago and the daughter said her mother was in the hospital for a check-up. And when my mother hung up she said, "I don't think so" and she left the next day and went to Chicago. Mrs. Price died that Wednesday, I believe, [actually, it was the following Wednesday] and they had the funeral. She stayed there for her funeral. I was teaching at South Carolina at the time and mother came and spent two weeks with me. She was not at all disappointed because she never felt she was going any place any way.

Price died June 3, 1953, at 12:30 a.m. after a ten-day stay in St. Luke's hospital. She entered the hospital on Sunday, May 24, just two days before she was to leave for Europe, but she had been ailing for the entire week before. Price and her doctors decided against an operation; her heart was failing and her vital signs had deteriorated. She could not have asked for better care at St. Luke's. The doctors were attentive; her primary care physician saw her just hours before she passed away. According to the death certificate, Price died from a cerebral hemorrhage due to hypertensive cardiovascular disease. In simpler terms, her heart was pumping so fast that it caused a vein to burst in her brain. An autopsy was performed confirming the doctor's findings.[22]

Her funeral was held just two days later, June 5, at her church, Grace Presbyterian. There was a "simple and brief" service followed by burial in Lincoln Cemetery.[23]

Postscript

By 1935, Florence Price's accomplishments were such that the *Chicago Defender*, arguably the most widely read black newspaper in the country, began to refer to her as the "Dean of Negro Composers of the Middle West."[1] For the black community, this sobriquet was more than sentimental. It was bequeathed to her not only for her professional accomplishments but also because she wrote music with which African Americans could identify. Price worked at her craft continuously, developing throughout her career as a composer with many voices. Her music was constantly motivated from sources both national and cosmopolitan—African American folk music on the one hand and European traditions on the other.

It was understood by all, including Price, that her honorary title was in deference to William Grant Still, *the* "Dean of American Negro Composers." Still, who was Price's friend from childhood, is credited with bringing concert music by African American composers to the fore. His pioneering career included orchestral music, ballet, and opera. Still's friendship was important to Price and they were very supportive of each other's careers. Even after Price's death, Still maintained a cordial relationship with Price's daughter and he continued to promote Price's music when he could.

For some composers, the title "Dean of Negro Composers" would be problematic, owing to the perception that one's work would be limited to specific ethnic content. For Price, this was not the case. Many of Price's works are in the black musical idiom because she found it to be a very personal expression of her own heritage. She often referred to herself in terms that made clear her African American identity, though of mixed heritage, and stated that her music was in many ways self-expressive. Although much of her music is written with a slant toward black folk idioms, she composed freely, utilizing programmatic associations when they suited her purpose.

The esteem with which most members of the black community held Price was further evident when a third Chicago branch of the National Association of Negro Musicians, the Florence B. Price Music Study Guild, was formed and named after her. Herman Billingsly, known for conducting mass choir concerts, was the Club's first president. Believing that the two older branches of NANM had become too complacent, the Price Music Study Guild formed in February 1940 and had as its mission the elevation of musical standards in performance and composition with the hope of attracting larger audiences to its concerts.[2] Because of the Guild's strong commitment to education, Price donated the first gift toward a scholarship fund. Many Chicagoans thought the Price Study Guild was appropriately named for this musician who stood as a symbol of professional achievement and personal tenacity. The organization was immediately vibrant, promoting the musical activities of black classical artists throughout the Midwest.

From late 1927, the time of Price's arrival in Chicago, to the mid-1940s, her name appears continuously in the *Chicago Defender*. The most important black newspaper in America at the time, the *Chicago Defender* produced local and national editions, and as such, played a huge role in chronicling the whole of Price's career as performer, composer, and teacher. Maude Roberts George, then the music critic of the paper and a tireless advocate of classical music by black composers, is very responsible for elevating Price's career through her reviews of Price's activities, which appeared in her column regularly.

By the late 1940s, Price's name appears less frequently in the *Chicago Defender* as a composer and almost never as a performer. Ill health took its toll and the all-consuming energy that was required of her to promote her music waned. Although she continued to compose (some of her most stunning art songs were written in the mid- to late-1940s), her time was focused now on studio teaching.

In spite of all of her pioneering accomplishments, Florence Beatrice Price was still not satisfied with her career. There were more elusive goals to be attained—more performances in the East and abroad, more acceptance, more happiness. Price had a prohibitively nonaggressive personality, which haunted her all of her life, yet she managed to tread ground no black woman had before her. The resurgence of interest in her music, including performances by major U.S. orchestras and recordings of her music in all genres and the building of the Florence B. Price Elementary School in Chicago (dedicated November 1964) are a living testimony to the accomplishments and legacy of this remarkable woman.[3]

Afterword

CARLENE J. BROWN

In August 2017, my sister, Rae Linda Brown, knew she had little time left to share with me what I needed to know. She said, "My book . . . publish it . . . it's done. It's finished." And without hesitation, I replied, "Of course I will, Rae Linda." She also asked me to enlist the expertise of the one person she knew who could, would, and should oversee the final edits on the book: Dr. Guthrie Ramsey, who has walked alongside Rae Linda not simply as a close colleague, but as a brother. I deeply appreciate that Guy Ramsey said an immediate "Yes!" to writing the Foreword and to offering his scholarly perspective on Rae Linda's book within the context of current popular and scholarly interest on Florence Price. (I would also like to acknowledge Dwight Andrews, William Banfield, Stephen Newby, April Middeljans, and my research assistant, Clarissa Aaron, for supporting this project.)

Many have wondered why Rae Linda did not publish this book years ago. Her dissertation, *Selected Orchestral Music of Florence B. Price (1888–1953) in the Context of Her Life and Work*, was completed at Yale University in 1987. Her contract with the University of Illinois Press to write the book, *A Biography of Florence Beatrice Smith Price*, was offered in 1995, which began years of research, writing, publishing, and "digging" for the distinguished life story of the first black woman composer to have had her composition performed by an American symphony orchestra. And yet, Rae Linda's biography of Florence Price was not to be published until over twenty years later. I once asked her the reason, and in typical Rae Linda fashion she answered, "I've been busy." And that she was.

In surveying Rae Linda's work, it is clear that all of her career has been spent bringing the music and life story of Florence Price to American culture. In fact, she once declared, "My identity has become intertwined with hers." She was deeply inspired by "the power of this unassuming composer and her music, which broke down racial, gender, and economic barriers." And she was compelled by the need to put Price's life and music down on paper for posterity. As she explained in one of her speeches:

> I started thinking about the *invisibility of this black woman*, who grew up in the segregated south, yet went to one of the best music conservatories in the nation, returned to the segregated south, but ended up having her orchestral music performed by leading American orchestras. Who was she? There was a story and I needed to tell it. I needed to bring her from invisibility to visibility and document her life and her music so that her legacy could be a lived legacy. She needed to be included in the history books.

To make the music and story of Florence Price part of a shared, living history, Rae Linda used her own hard-won powers as an administrator, a board member, a chair of committees, and (most important to her) a teacher in the classroom. For example, promoting research, especially at the undergraduate level, was a central mission to Rae Linda's vision of higher education. At each of her administrative university positions, she created and developed Undergraduate Research Symposiums and would use her background, passion, and commitment to research to tell her story on the work of Florence Price.

Her scholarship was not only for college students. Rae Linda lectured and presented on Price at churches, music festivals, and conferences, and gave radio interviews from Los Angeles to New York. She spoke internationally, addressing audiences in Paris, Toronto, and London. She published numerous scholarly articles as well. Her significant contributions include essays in *The International Dictionary of Black Composers* (1999) and *Women Composers: Music through the Ages* (2001); and entries in encyclopedias and dictionaries, such as *The New Grove Dictionary of Music* and *Encyclopedia of African-American Culture and History*.

More important than the lectures and scholarship, Rae Linda sought tirelessly to have Price's music *heard* or as she put it, "to bring Florence Price to life through performance." She offered her editions of Price scores, especially the Symphony in E Minor and Symphony in C Minor, for a very low, $100 rate—and sometimes even for free—to ensemble conductors throughout the United States. As she stated in her replies to requests, "I am most interested in the opportunity for audiences to hear this music."

A poignant moment came for Rae Linda in 2016 when the music director of the Yale Symphony Orchestra requested a copy of her edition of the Price Symphony No. 3 in C Minor. The director also invited Rae Linda to offer a preconcert lecture as well as write the program notes for the piece. This would bring Rae Linda's work full circle, returning her to Yale, where it all started. It would also represent the first full performance of the Symphony on the East Coast. Rae Linda knew that Price had longed for a hearing of her music by an orchestra in the East and Rae Linda had come to share that desire. However, even though she sent the music and wrote the program notes, Rae Linda was not able to attend the concert. The date happened to coincide with her first board of trustees meeting as provost at Pacific Lutheran University. She had deeply mixed feelings of needing and wanting to be at both ends of the country at the same time, but she felt a deep responsibility toward her own new post.

Rae Linda would have truly appreciated two significant moments in solidifying Florence Price's place in American history. Six months from Rae Linda's passing, the *New York Times* made a pronouncement: *Welcoming a Black Female Composer into the Canon. Finally.* (February 9, 2018). And in March 2019, The Boston Symphony Orchestra performed three movements from the Symphony No. 3, eighty-four years after Florence Price had written Serge Koussevitzky, then conductor of the BSO, to argue a case for her work to be considered for a performance. As Rae Linda has written:

> Her orchestral music was being performed by respected musical institutions—the Chicago Symphony, the Chicago Woman's Orchestra, and several local symphonic bands—and by numerous concert singers. Yet Price's ultimate goal was recognition of her large-scale works—symphonies, concertos, and symphonic overtures—by the old-guard East Coast musical establishment: the orchestras of Boston, New York, and Philadelphia. A performance of her music by one of these orchestras would ensure her place in the annals of music history. But this was not to happen in her lifetime (MUSA [*Music of the United States of America*], Ann Arbor, Michigan, xxxv).

While Rae Linda was not to hear Price's work performed by the Boston Symphony Orchestra, she did learn of the lost scores of Florence Price. As the keynote speaker at the Florence Price Music Festival held at the University of Arkansas in 2015, Rae Linda spoke to the audience:

> So what do we make of Florence Price's legacy? From newspaper accounts and from her friends, I knew she was a prolific composer. Titles and dates of performances could be documented but where were the rest of musical scores, I asked? Some of her friends gave me single pages and parts of manuscripts or the instrumental scores with no performing parts or the performing parts with no full scores. They gave me personal photographs. Surely the complete story of Florence Price's life and music could not be fully told without it. Yet, no one could find the missing pieces to the voluminous puzzle.
>
> And then I received an email from Professor Jim Greeson [University of Arkansas] this summer who told me that Special Collections here had some music of Florence Price. I visited here in June and upon first glance, I knew immediately the treasure that resided in the many boxes. It was the lost scores—chamber music, vocal and piano music, orchestral scores and instrumental parts—music lost, now found.

> And so, the end of this story is now really the beginning. And, we have come full circle. My research on the life and music of Florence Beatrice Smith Price started with conversations and visits with Barbara Garvey Jackson and to study the Price archive in the Special Collections. And now we come together to celebrate the expansion of the Price archive in the Special Collections and to hear some of the lost scores, now found. It is, however, for the next generation of music scholars to delve through the music, to study it, to perform, to record it, and to tell the rest of the story. . . . Let us mark this moment in history—this weekend—in which we all contribute to the legacy of Florence Beatrice Price.

Thus, through published books, monographs, book chapters, articles, encyclopedia and dictionary essays, music edition scores edited and published, program notes for concerts, liner notes for recordings, interviews and invited lectures. . . . Rae Linda Brown devoted her scholarly career to a woman composer deserving of her place in American history. The publishing of this book is the final chapter in Rae Linda's career and life story as an extraordinary scholar, who "kept digging."

Notes

Foreword

1. See Douglas Shadle, "Plus Ça Change: Florence B. Price in the #BlackLivesMatter Era," *NewMusicBox* (February 20, 2019). Retrieved March 8, 2019.

Acknowledgments

1. MA thesis, African American Studies, Yale University, 1980. Published as *Music, Printed and Manuscript, in the James Weldon Johnson Collection of Negro Arts and Letters*. New York, Garland Press, 1982.

2. The transcription of my interview with Valter Poole (May 28, 1983) is housed in the archive of the Oral History Program of the Institute on the Federal Theater Project and New Deal Culture. Fairfax, Va.: George Mason University, 1–33.

Introduction

*Cuney, *Opportunity*, 88.

1. hooks, *Feminist Theory*, 15.

2. Gatewood, "The Formative Years," 11.

3. Ibid., 12.

4. Although Du Bois himself did not think of the Talented Tenth as being of necessity light-skinned, the fact is that many of them were. Of the 131 men and 8 women listed in Du Bois's *Who's Who of Colored Americans*, published in 1916, 124 of the men and all of the women were of mixed heritage. Cited in Giddings, *When and Where I Enter*, 186.

5. Gatewood, *Aristocrats of Color*, 153.

6. Hull, *Color, Sex and Poetry*, 11.

7. *Whispers of Love*, 2.

8. I wish to thank Professor Guthrie Ramsey for suggesting this idea to me.

9. Wilson, "Black Music as Art," 8–9. See also Wilson, "Composition from the Perspective of the African American Tradition," 43–51.

Chapter 1. Family Ties

1. Florence Irene Gulliver's birth dates have been listed in various census records as 1854 (1860 and 1870 Indianapolis census), 1857 (1900 Little Rock census), and 1859 (1880 Little Rock census). Her age indicated at the time of the 1860 and 1870 census (age 6 and age 16, respectively) and the 1900 census (age 42) are consistent with the 1854 or 1857 birth dates; however, 1854, is the most plausible date since the 1860 census was taken when she was at a young age.

2. From 1860 to 1900, African Americans of mixed racial heritage were listed in the census records as mulatto. It is well known that the information provided on the census forms was not always accurate. The census takers often based their information on appearances rather than on what was fact. Virtually all light-skinned blacks were classified as "mulatto" and often, for example, long or straight hair was enough to warrant registering someone as "mulatto." After 1900, the term *mulatto* was replaced by *black* or *Negro*. The information on the Gulliver and McCoy families comes from the 1860 Indiana census, Marion County, Indianapolis, Fifth Ward, p. 16, and the 1870 Indianapolis census, p. 47. The 1860 census lists Mary [McCoy] Gulliver's birth date as 1837. The 1870 census lists her birth date as 1835. Her death certificate, which indicates that she was 54 at the time of her death, May 10, 1889 (Certified Record of Death, Marion County, Indianapolis, Indiana) also suggests that she was born in 1835. In all of the census records consulted, women's ages are the least accurate. Women often falsified their ages, perhaps in an effort to appear younger than they actually were. There were distinct advantages to this, particularly if the women were unmarried.

3. Mary McCoy's death certificate indicates that both of her parents, William J. McCoy and Margaret Chambers, were born in North Carolina.

4. Blassingame, *The Slave Community*, 34.

5. *Acts Passed by the General Assembly of the State of North Carolina at the Session of 1830–1831* (Raleigh, 1831), 11. Quoted in Fishel and Quarles, *The Black American*, 115.

6. *Frederick Douglass' Paper*, March 4, 1853. Quoted in Fishel and Quarles, *The Black American*, 143.

7. See entry in James H. Smith, "Prominent Colored Citizens of Central Arkansas," in *Biographical and Historical Memoirs of Pulaski, Jefferson, Saline, Perry, Garland and Hot Springs Counties* (Chicago: Goodspeed Publishing Co., 1889), 807–808. The entry in "Prominent Colored Citizens" indicates that when Mary Gulliver died (May 19, 1889), she left a considerable inheritance to her two daughters. The author has found evidence of only one child, Florence Irene.

8. The information on the Gullivers' finances was obtained from the 1860 and 1870 Indianapolis census records.

9. From the 1874 Indianapolis public school census. I am indebted to Dr. Barbara Garvey Jackson for sharing the information on the Indianapolis public school system with me.

10. Smith entry in "Prominent Colored Citizens," 807–808. The information in this entry contradicts the 1880 and 1900 census, which indicate that Smith and his parents were born in New Jersey. Dr. Smith's obituary (*Arkansas Gazette*, April 17, 1910) states that he was born in Boston. The census records and the obituary are probably incorrect.

Information given in "Prominent Colored Citizens" is fairly detailed and is generally considered reliable.

11. Blassingame, *The Slave Community*, 338, 344.

12. Fishel and Quarles, *The Black American*, 128.

13. The number of black dentists in this country remained miniscule until well after the second decade of this century. Lewis, D.D.S., "The Negro in the Field of Dentistry," 207.

14. *Chicago Defender*, July 11, 1926, 7.

15. Smith, *Maudelle*, 304–306. For a broader historical summary of educating blacks in the years after the Civil War, see Blassingame and Berry, *Long Memory*, 261–294.

16. Smith, *Maudelle*, 306.

17. Marriage license filed in Marion County, Indianapolis, November 15, 1876.

18. The 1900 Little Rock census lists two living children in the Smith household, Charles W. and Beatrice. It is unlikely that Mrs. Smith named two living daughters after herself. Florence Gertrude probably died before Florence Beatrice was born in 1887.

19. Florence Beatrice Smith's birth year is usually cited as 1888, based on her death certificate. Because it was not required by the state of Arkansas, no birth certificate was filed when she was born. A delayed birth certificate, witnessed by a family friend, was filed with the Arkansas Bureau of Vital Statistics on April 20, 1953, less than two months before Florence Beatrice Smith [Price] died. It also carries the date 1888. However, the 1900 Little Rock census records, taken when Price was thirteen, and the information on Edith Price's (Price's daughter) birth certificate, filed when Price was 34, both place her birth date in 1887. The earlier date is probably more accurate given that the information in the 1900 census was reported by her parents and, at 34, Price was more unlikely to falsify her age than in later years.

20. Perhaps Florence Irene and James Smith were so devastated by the loss of their firstborn daughter, Florence Gertrude, that Florence Beatrice was so named to comfort them in their grief. When one child is created to replace the loss of another, and sometimes even given the same name, it is known, psychologically, as "replacement child syndrome."

21. Florence Price Robinson to Mary Hudgins, October 14, 1967. Florence Beatrice Smith Price Materials, University of Arkansas, Mullins Library, Special Collections. Gift of Florence Price Robinson and collected by Mary Dengler Hudgins and Barbara Garvey Jackson, 1974–1975. Includes the Mary Dengler Hudgins Research Files, University of Arkansas, Mullins Library, Manuscript Collections 988. Hereafter cited as Price Materials, University of Arkansas.

22. "Blue baby" refers to the discoloration of the baby's skin if it is born with a heart rate and response that is slower than normal or if the baby's blood circulation is not proper.

Chapter 2. Little Rock

1. Gatewood, "William Grant Still's Little Rock," 10.

2. Information on Little Rock's businesses is taken from Graves, *Town and Country*, 101.

3. Still, "My Arkansas Boyhood," 285–292, and Arvey, *In One Lifetime*, 16.

4. Ibid., 288.

5. Graves, *Town and Country*, 115.

6. Ibid., 117.

7. Kennan, "The First Negro Teacher in Little Rock," 198.

8. Baskett, *Persistence of the Spirit*, 30.

9. Graves, *Town and Country*, 117.

10. Baskett, *Persistence of the Spirit*, 27.

11. Gill, *The Crossroads of Arkansas*, 33–34.

12. Graves, "Negro Disenfranchisement in Arkansas," 201.

13. Baskett, *Persistence of the Spirit*, 27.

14. Gill, "The Crossroads of Arkansas," 35.

15. The following information on Little Rock's black community is taken from: "Prominent Colored Citizens of Central Arkansas," 806 and 808.

16. A daughter, Cora Alice, became a faculty member at Little Rock's Shorter College, her alma mater, and another son, Isaac Jr., became principal of M. W. Gibbs High School.

17. Gatewood, *Aristocrats of Color*, 93. In 1897, Union School, the city's public school for Negroes, was in need of a new principal. A bitter fight developed over the position between Jefferson Ish and J. E. Rector, another of the city's prominent black teachers and community leaders. The *Indianapolis Freeman* described the controversy as a "bitter one—so bitter that the two professors came near having a fist fight"! *Indianapolis Freeman*, October 9, 1897, 1.

18. Graves, *Town and Country*, 125–126.

19. Still, "My Arkansas Boyhood," 286.

20. Gaines, *Racial Possibilities*, 95. See also: *The History of Dentistry in Arkansas*, 45 and note cards of Florence Price Robinson, #40–43, Price Materials.

21. Letter from Florence Price Robinson to Mary D. Hudgins, n.d., Hudgins file, Price Materials.

22. William Grant Still to Mary D. Hudgins, February 3, 1967. Hudgins file, folder 3, Price Materials.

23. Still, "My Arkansas Boyhood," 290. See also Adolphine Fletcher Terry, *Charlotte Stephens*, 112.

24. *Indianapolis Freeman*, January 31, 1891.

25. "Correcting Fred Douglass," 5.

26. "Fred Douglass," 8.

27. Graves, "Negro Disenfranchisement in Arkansas," 190–225.

28. Graves, *Town and Country*, 151.

29. Ibid., 153–154.

30. "They Still Protest," 1; "Senator Tillman's 'Separate Coach' Bill," 4; Kousser, "A Black Protest in the 'Era of Accommodation,'" 161–163.

31. Graves, *Town and Country*, 159.

32. Mary Gulliver died of enteritis and typhoid malarial fever. Certified Copy of Record of Death for Mary Gulliver, Marion County, Indianapolis, Indiana, May 10, 1889.

33. Note cards of Florence Beatrice Price Robinson, numbers 40–43. Further, these note cards reveal that Dr. and Mrs. Smith had a difficult relationship and she speculated that her grandparents should never have married. She added, "He [Dr. Smith] was such a wonderful man," but Mrs. Smith "was a dictator when it came to who should be in society. She made many enemies." Price Materials.

Chapter 3. The Pursuit of Education

1. Letter from Florence Price Robinson to Mary D. Hudgins, n.d., Price Materials.
2. Florence Price Robinson wrote, "The 500 acres became a very busy section later and would have been worth a fortune but my grandmother[,] against everyone's wishes[,] insisted on selling it." Note card #54, Price Materials.
3. This information can be inferred from the "Bill of Sale" for the contents of Florence Smith's household, March 14, 1911. Florence I. Smith to O. Benjamin Jefferson, Little Rock County Court House Deeds (Book 103, p. 636). Bill of Sale 9048.
4. Beginning in 1899, black women were graduated from Meharry Medical College in Tennessee, but most entering classes had only a few female students. Prior to that the three or four black women doctors who had formal training had all matriculated at northern white institutions. In spite of these statistics, black women were the first practicing female physicians in four southern states.
5. Miscellaneous pages of Price's diary. Folder 12, Price Materials.
6. "Composer Wins Noteworthy Prizes for Piano Sonata," 25.
7. Note cards of Florence Price Robinson #4-54, Price Materials. None of this music is extant.
8. In her book, *Black Women Composers*, Green suggests that shortly after Florence Beatrice was born, Dr. Smith moved his family to Chicago where he set up a dental office in the Loop. She writes that Price attended elementary school in Chicago at Forrestville but returned to Little Rock for high school. Green's information came from an interview with Neumon Leighton, a friend of Price's from Cotton Plant, Arkansas. My research, however, does not bear out this information or chronology.
9. Anderson, *The Education of Blacks in the South*, 28.
10. Negro literacy in Arkansas was 43 percent in 1900. *1900 Statistical Abstract of the U.S.* (Bureau of the U.S. Census), 67. I am grateful to Tom Dillard, Director, Torreyson Library, University of Central Arkansas, for bringing to my attention several articles on the education of Negroes in Arkansas and information on Dr. James H. Smith.
11. Mosley, *The History of Higher Education for Negroes in Arkansas*, 11–12.
12. Bullock. *A History of Negro Education in the South*, 177. *1909–1910: 1928–1929*: white students—94 days, white students—152 days; black students—70 days, black students—132 days.
13. The information on Andrews and his daughter, Charlotte Andrews Stephens, is taken from Terry, *Charlotte Stephens*, and Kennan, "The First Negro Teacher in Little Rock," 194–204.
14. Since the 1840s, Oberlin had been accepting black students. Oberlin was one of the schools most aspired to by blacks because, before the war, it had been a station on the underground railroad.

15. Charlotte Andrews Stephens retired from teaching in 1939 at the age of eighty-five, after a tenure of seventy years in the Little Rock public school system.

16. Anderson, *The Education of Blacks in the South*, 28–29.

17. As late as 1915, twenty-three of the nation's largest southern cities (those with a population of 20,000 or more), including Mobile, Montgomery, Atlanta, New Orleans, Charleston, Wilmington, Roanoke, and Jacksonville, had no high school for black children. In Georgia, for example, the number of high schools for white students increased from 4 in 1904 to 122 in 1916 while providing no public high school for black children, who constituted 46 percent of the state's secondary school age population. Mississippi, South Carolina, Louisiana, and North Carolina also had no four-year public high schools for blacks. Anderson, *The Education of Blacks in the South*, 92, 916.

18. Still, "My Arkansas Boyhood," 285–292.

19. Jones, *A Traditional Model of Educational Excellence*, 13.

20. Anderson, *The Education of Blacks in the South*, 30, 199.

21. Note cards of Florence Price Robinson, #44–54. Price Materials. Price's graduation from Capitol Hill school at the age of fourteen is confirmed in a *Chicago Defender* article (July 11, 1936, 7) in which Price's achievements are noted.

Chapter 4. The New England Conservatory of Music

1. Mary Cardwell Dawson, founder and director of the National Negro Opera Company attended the Conservatory just after Price, graduating in 1909.

2. The information on Chadwick and the New England Conservatory has been taken from the following sources: Chadwick, *Memoirs and Diaries*; Yellin, *Chadwick*; Goodrich, *Personal Recollections of the New England Conservatory of Music*; Williams, *Indeed Music*. Wallace Goodrich taught organ at the Conservatory and was its director from 1931–1942. Chester W. Williams was affiliated with the Conservatory for thirty years, 1946–1976, as a member of the theory faculty, twice as dean, and as president.

3. Peabody, founded in 1868, and Oberlin, founded in 1865, modeled themselves exclusively after European conservatories, and their faculties were largely inbred. Trained first at their own institutions, the faculty sought advanced study in Europe and returned to teach at their alma mater. At Peabody, the majority of the faculty had studied in Dutch conservatories or in those of Berlin and Leipzig. Even more than Peabody, Oberlin was considered a preparatory school for further study in Europe, particularly Germany. Most of Oberlin's faculty had an exceptionally strong European conservatory background. In a total of 28 teaching faculty at Oberlin, 21 had been trained at Oberlin. Of these, 15 faculty had advanced training in Europe, most in Berlin or Leipzig. In addition, they studied in Paris, Vienna, Munich, and less frequently in Florence and London. Fitzpatrick, *The Music Conservatory in America*, v. 2, 251–302.

4. Ibid., 370.

5. Chadwick, *Memoirs*, 29 [1897, f. 52v–53r]. Carl Stasny taught piano at the conservatory.

6. Chadwick, "Musical Atmosphere and Student Life," 138–141.

7. See Goodrich, "Personal Recollections," and Williams, *Indeed Music*. For the specifications of the Jordan Hall organ and the smaller organs, see Calvert Johnson, ed., *Music of Florence Beatrice Price: Suite No. 1 for Organ*, x–xi.

8. The information on the Conservatory's library is taken from Goodrich, *Personal Recollections.*

9. Chadwick, *Memoirs*, 21 (1897, f. 40v). Chadwick's harmony book was printed in many editions and was a standard text in many of the nation's leading music schools.

10. Ibid., 27 (1897, f. 50r).

11. Ibid., 27–28 [1897, f. 51r, f. 51v]. Eugene Gruenberg and Emil Mahr both taught violin and viola. Henry M. Dunham taught organ and was chair of the department.

12. Ibid., [March 7, 1902, f. 121r–121v].

13. Yellin, *Chadwick*, 69.

14. Chadwick, *Memoirs*, [1902, f. 122r–123r].

15. Fitzpatrick, *The Music Conservatory*, 371.

16. The *Neume*, 1906, 39.

17. Tick, "Passed Away Is the Piano Girl" in *Women Making Music*, 325–348.

18. Wright, "Black Women in Classical Music in Boston."

19. I am grateful to Chester W. Williams, dean emeritus (correspondence with the author July 24, 1985, and April 19, 1989), Jean A. Morrow, director of libraries (correspondence with the author July 14, 1988), and Marguerite L. Daly, registrar (correspondence with the author June 21, 1989, and July 11, 1989) for their assistance in establishing the curriculum of Florence Beatrice Smith, New England Conservatory, 1903–1906.

20. Johnson, *Music of Florence Beatrice Price*, ix.

21. Note cards of Florence Price Robinson, #44–54, Price Materials.

22. Johnson, *Music of Florence Beatrice Price*, xii.

23. The information in the New England Conservatory catalog, 1903–1904, has been used to glean information on the general music curriculum and it has also been used to speculate on Florence's weekly activities given her course of study.

24. Note cards of Florence Price Robinson, #44–854, Price Materials. This information was confirmed in the *Chicago Defender*, May 4, 1935, July 25 and 11, 1936, 7.

25. Chadwick, *Diary*, [1897, f. 39r].

26. Elson, *The History of American Music*, 133, quoted in Block, "Dvorák's Long American Reach," 168.

27. Chadwick, *Diary*, 27 [1897, f. 50r].

28. *Chicago Defender*, May 4, 1935, 25. Florence Price Robinson note cards #49–50, Price Materials.

29. Johnson, *Music of Florence Beatrice Price*, ix. It is not known which of the two Guilmant D Minor sonatas Price performed, Number 1, op. 42 (1875) or Number 4, op. 61 (1901).

30. For the specifications of the Jordan Hall organ and the other New England Conservatory organs, see Johnson, *Music of Florence Beatrice Price*, x–xi.

31. Fitzpatrick, *The Music Conservatory*, 371.

32. Du Bois, *The Autobiography*, 137.

33. Ibid., 139.

34. Florence Price Robinson, note cards #40–843, Price Materials.

35. The *Neume*, graduating class picture, June 1906.

36. Du Bois, *The Autobiography*, 138.

37. Arvey, *In One Lifetime*, 34.

Chapter 5. Return to Little Rock

1. Gatewood, *Aristocrats of Color*, 265.

2. Smith, *Maudelle.*

3. Ibid., preface.

4. Ibid., 19.

5. Ibid., 18.

6. Ibid., 324–325.

7. Bullock, *A History of Negro Education*, 181. Ten years later, the discrepancy was worse. In 1928–1929, black teachers were paid $69.08 per month while their white colleagues earned substantially more, $96.40.

8. "Site Bought for Negro School," 2. Gibbs remained the Negro high school in Little Rock until 1930 when the curriculum was extended, with the persuasion of Jones and others, to include a two-year college preparatory division. The school was renamed Dunbar High School and Junior College. Jones, *A Traditional Model of Educational Excellence*, 4.

9. Graves, *Town and Country*, 112.

10. Letter from Solar Carethers, piano teacher, to Mary D. Hudgins, November 22, 1967. Hudgins file, Price Materials. See also Green, *Black Women Composers*, 32. It is difficult to confirm Price's employment from 1906–1912 when she was on the faculty of the Cotton Plant—Arkadelphia Academy, Shorter College, and Clark University. Faculty lists, if they existed, cannot be found, and she is not listed among the faculty in the school catalogs. This is not surprising, however, given that most black colleges were small and they required few teachers, and music courses at these schools were considered a supplement to the curriculum. It may be that the faculty that are listed in the catalogs are core faculty in each division. Her appointments, however, are noted in newspaper articles, for example, *Opportunity* 10 (December 1932): 391, and confirmed by former colleagues.

11. Green, *Black Women Composers*, 32.

12. The following information on Shorter College is taken primarily from McSwain, "Shorter College," 81–84.

13. In 1903–1904 Shorter had an enrollment of 280 students and 10 teachers. In 1916, there were 219 students—128 enrolled in the elementary program, 76 in the secondary program, 15 in the college program (theological)—and 18 teachers. "The Shorter University That Was Never Built."

14. McSwain, *Shorter College*, 82–83.

15. Obituary, *Arkansas Gazette*, April 17, 1910; *Chicago Defender*, May 7, 1910, 1. Both newspapers list Smith's age as 56, but the census records and Goodspeed, which were used to establish his date of birth, would place his age closer to 67.

16. Information on the expenses for Dr. Smith's funeral and the following information on his financial status has been taken from the probate records of Dr. Smith located in the Little Rock History Commission [state archives].

17. Note cards of Florence Price Robinson, Price Materials, University of Arkansas, cards #40–43.

Chapter 6. Clark University and Marriage

1. Price's appointment at Clark University was noted in *Opportunity* 10 (December 1932): 391. Her appointment was also verified in correspondence to the author from Florence Crim Robinson, Fuller E. Callaway Professor of Music, Clark College, November 5, 1986; Doris Smith, Administrative Assistant to the President, Clark College, October 21, 1988; and a program announcement from J. de Koven Killingsworth, Professor of Music, Clark College, April 9, 1972.

2. Du Bois, *The Autobiography*, 234–235.

3. In 1910, Du Bois resigned from the university to become the Director of Publications and Research for the newly formed National Association for the Advancement of Colored People.

4. Du Bois, *The Autobiography*, 234–235.

5. Brawley discusses the importance of Negro teachers at Clark University in *The Clark College Legacy*, 303.

6. Ibid., 80.

7. Ibid., 31.

8. Ibid., 51–52.

9. Clark University Catalog, 1910–1911, 34–41.

	Male	Female	Total
College	22	8	30
College Preparatory	55	10	65
Normal	-	137	137
Grade School	69	100	169
Special Students	3	4	7
Printing	29	-	29
Dressmaking	-	65	65
Agriculture	13	27	40
Music (music majors only, 7)	1	39	40
TOTAL	192	390	582
TOTAL, COUNTING NONE TWICE	139	341	479

10. Brawley, *Clark College Legacy*, 178–179.

11. Ibid.

12. The information on Thomas Jewell Price comes from the following sources: Yenser, *Who's Who in Colored America, 1941–1944* and the Little Rock city directories, 1906–1928.

13. Birth certificate for Price's daughter Edith, filed April 2, 1921 (Bureau of Vital Statistics, Little Rock) lists Price's date of birth as 1882 but the *Who's Who* volumes, which place Price's birth in 1884, may be more accurate.

14. The information on Judge Terrell is taken from Gatewood, *Aristocrats of Color*, 43, 60–62.

15. *Ibid.*, 60.

16. Dillard, "Scipio A. Jones." See also *The Messenger* 10/1 (January 1928): 10.

17. Little Rock History Commission, marriage licenses, book 53, 463.

18. Earnest Lamb, radio documentary transcription, "From Spiritual to Symphony." Broadcast on KLRE and KUAR, Little Rock, February 11 and 13, 1993.

19. Gatewood, "The Formative Years of William Grant Still," 8.

20. Lamb interview with Mrs. Judith Finn, Little Rock, transcription, 18–19.

21. *Arkansas Gazette*, July 7, 1914. I am grateful to Tom Dillard, archivist, The University of Central Arkansas, for sharing this information with me.

22. The death certificate for Florence Louise Price [Robinson], filed in Chicago August 25, 1975, indicates that she was born July 6, 1920. *Opportunity* magazine indicates that Florence Louise was born in 1917. No birth certificate was filed, but the earlier date, based on information given to *Opportunity* magazine by Florence Price, is probably correct. The birth certificate for "Edith Sassandra" [*sic*] Price was filed March 29, 1921, with the Bureau of Vital Statistics, Little Rock. References to Edith often include her middle initial as "C," indicating that her middle name was probably Cassandra.

23. Lamb interviews with Mrs. Edith Flakes and Mrs. Judith Finn, transcription, 16.

24. Hudgins, "A Noted Little Rock Composer."

25. Southern, *The Music of Black Americans*, 396. See also: *The Messenger* 9 (1927): 14.

26. *Opportunity* (May 1926): 157.

27. Announcements for the 1927 competition in *Opportunity* (June 1927): 179, 213, and *Opportunity* (July 1927): 204–205, incl. photo. Both of these articles refer to Price's late parents and musical daughters.

28. Notes of Florence Price Robinson, Price Materials. *At the Cotton Gin* was published by G. Schirmer, 1928.

29. Until 1926, Price often used her husband's letterhead to correspond with music publishers and conductors. After the family's move to Chicago, she asserted her independence and wrote professional letters on her own letterhead. This change supports the speculation that Price and her husband were probably separated shortly after their arrival in Chicago.

30. Block, "Arthur P. Schmidt."

31. Correspondence between Price and the Arthur P. Schmidt Co., Boston: Price to Schmidt, June 25, 1926; Price to Schmidt, September 17, 1926; Schmidt to Price, September 20, 1926; Price to Schmidt, September 24, 1926. Obvious typographical errors have been silently corrected. Arthur P. Schmidt file, The Library of Congress, Music Division. I am indebted to Wayne Shirley, Music Division, Library of Congress, for explaining Schmidt's shorthand to me.

32. Transcripts of the Chicago Musical College, summer sessions 1926 and 1927.

33. Lamb interview with Mrs. Finn, transcription, 17.

34. Green, *Black Women Composers*, 32.

35. "Forced to Leave."

36. "Innocent but Lynched."

37. *Cleveland Gazette*, May 14, 1927, 1.

38. Lamb interview with Mrs. Judith Finn, transcription, 18.

39. Telephone conversation with Price's grandson, Lawrence Robinson, November 28, 1994. Examination of the Little Rock City Directory reveals that Florence Price moved to Chicago in late 1927 or early 1928. Thomas Price continued his law practice in Little Rock until sometime in 1928.

Chapter 7. VeeJay and the Black Metropolis

1. Drake and Cayton, *Black Metropolis*, 78.

2. "New Pekin Theater," *History of Negro Music*, Part I, box 84, Vivian Harsh Collection.

3. For a brief overview of jazz's establishment in Chicago, see Travis, "Chicago's Jazz Trail," and Wang, "Jazz in Chicago." See also Samuel Floyd, *The Power of Black Music*. New York: Oxford University Press, 122–126.

4. Dubbed "The Stroll" by the *Chicago Defender*, this street, after Seventh and Lenox Avenues in Harlem in the 1920s, was a center for activity in the African American community. In the evening, the street was active with people attending the jazz clubs; during the day, it was a popular area in which people congregated. See White, "The Stroll," *Electronic Encyclopedia of Chicago*@2005, Chicago Historical Society. http://www.encylopedia.chicagohistory.org/pages/121.html.

5. Spencer, "The Diminishing Rural Residue of Folklore," 32.

6. The most detailed information on black classical music in Chicago in the 1920s–1940s can be found in the files of the Illinois Writers' Project of the WPA, boxes 84–104. See also "The Negro in Illinois," Illinois Writers' Project, box. 38, Vivian Harsh Collection.

7. "Musical and Dramatic," *The Half-Century Magazine* (August 9, 1916).

8. Helen Hagan received her Bachelor of Music degree in piano performance at Yale University in 1912, and between 1912–1914 she studied in France, earning a second diploma from the Schola Cantorum. From 1915, Hagan toured widely throughout the United States and Europe making her New York debut in Aeolian Hall in 1921, the first black pianist to give a solo recital in a New York concert hall.

9. "Musical and Dramatic," *The Half-Century Magazine*. The magazine indicates that Hackney sang Burleigh art songs and spirituals. Burleigh's first spiritual arrangement for solo voice and piano was published in 1917, well after this May 1916 concert. However, Hackney may have sung one of Burleigh's folk-song arrangements included in Henry E. Krehbiel's *Afro-American Folk Songs* collection published in 1914, or perhaps he sang the melody of a Burleigh spiritual arrangement intended for performance by chorus.

10. Spivey, *Union and the Black Musician*, 22, 24.

11. For example, see Dyett, "In the Realm of Music." Program of organ, choral, and solo vocal music at Grace Presbyterian Church.

12. On March 31, 1930, for example, the Metropolitan Community Center Choir and the Mundy Choristers competed in a choral competition in Orchestra Hall. *Chicago Defender*, March 29, 1930, 3.

13. *Chicago Defender*, April 2, 1932, 16.

14. "Music Schools and Teachers," *History of Negro Music*. Illinois Writers Project, part I, box 84 [1939], Vivian Harsh Collection of Afro-American History and Literature, Woodson Regional Library, Chicago.

15. Ibid.

16. Louise Henry. "Normal Vocal Institute," *History of Negro Music*. Illinois Writers Project, part I, box 84 (November 29, 1939).

17. Gatewood, *Aristocrats of Color*, 217.

18. Lovell Jr. *Black Song: The Forge and the Flame*, 251.

19. Ibid., 459.

Chapter 8. "My Soul's Been Anchored in de Lord"

1. *Opportunity* 10 (December 1932): 391. Haake was later to become one of Price's editors.

2. The evidence for this information comes from the *Chicago Defender* ("Florence Price's Work Spotlighted," February 10, 1951, 21), and from Price's daughter, Florence Robinson (notecards #44–54, Price Materials).

3. Earnest Lamb interview with Marion Ross, Little Rock, Arkansas. Radio documentary transcription, "From Spirituals to Symphony: A Portrait of Florence Price," 14. This information was confirmed by Price's grandson, Lawrence Robinson, in a telephone conversation with the author November 28, 1994.

4. Interview with concert singer Helen White, Chicago, September 13, 1988.

5. Though most theaters no longer showed silent films by the Depression, some were still in use. Other theaters hired organists for the entertainment. For example, Chicago theaters owned by Balaban & Katz (B & K) always offered live stage shows as well as movies. Douglas Gomery writes, "B & K so carefully nurtured local talent that, by the middle 1920s, it had become more famous for its impressive stage attractions, orchestras, and organists than for the movies. Shows celebrated fads and heroes, from Lindbergh to the Charleston to 'Jazz and Opera' week." Douglas Gomery, "Movie Palaces," in the *Electronic Encyclopedia of Chicago*@2005, Chicago Historical Society. http://www.encyclopedia.chicagohistory.org/pages/850.html.

6. Spivey, *Union and the Black Musician*, 100.

7. All of the information on Florence Price's divorce is from the divorce file, *Florence B. Price vs. Thomas J. Price*, Circuit (Superior) Court of Cook County, August 26, 1930–January 19, 1931. The papers include the summons on Thomas Price, "Bill for Divorce" (Florence Price's deposition), a transcript of the divorce proceedings, and the Decree for Divorce.

8. The information on Price's marriage to Arnett is taken from their marriage license (dated February 11, 1931) and the certificate (dated February 14, 1931). Cook County Clerk, Office of vital Records, Chicago. I am indebted to Suzanne Flandreau, librarian, Center for Black Music Research, for bringing Price's second husband, Pusey Dell Arnett, to my attention. She also helped identify Price's addresses during the turbulent years of the 1930s.

9. Quoted in notecards #14–16 of Florence Price Robinson, Price Materials, University of Arkansas.

10. *The Crisis* 41, no. 2 (February 1932): 60.

11. Maude Roberts George, "Music News." *Chicago Defender*, September 24, 1932, 15; George, *Chicago Defender*, "Wanamaker Awards Given in Music," October 1, 1932, 2; *Chicago Defender*, "Music News," October 15, 1932, 15.

12. There is no title for Cadman's work in the *Defender* article. The composition was probably *South in Sonora*, a three-movement operetta completed in 1932.

13. The *Fantasie Negre No. 4* was premiered June 15, 1937, at the Composers Forum of the Federal Music Project (WPA) with pianist Marion Hall.

Chapter 9. Black Satin Clothes at the Fair

1. Epstein, "Frederick Stock and American Music," 29.

2. Ibid., 22.

3. Ibid., 24.
4. Ibid., 29.
5. George, "Music News," *Chicago Defender*, December 17, 1932, 15.
6. Ibid.
7. George, *Chicago Defender*, April 16, 1932, 15.
8. *Ibid.*, October 15, 1932, 15.
9. Bonds, "A Reminiscence," 191.
10. Spady, *William L. Dawson*, 16.
11. By the early 1930s, Dawson had become an internationally known arranger of spirituals, such as *King Jesus Is a 'Listening*, *My Lord What a Morning*, and *Talk about a Child That Do Love Jesus*, which were sung by the Ebenezer A.M.E. church choir where he was music director. As a performer, Dawson was active as well. He became first trombonist with the Chicago Civic Orchestra. In addition, he was first trombonist in Charles "Doc" Cooke's jazz band, the 15 Doctors of Syncopation and, in June 1927, he recorded four tunes with them. Among those on the set were Jimmy Noone, clarinet, and Johnny St. Cyr, banjo. Both born in New Orleans, Noone and St. Cyr were considered two of the finest jazz musicians in the city. While in Chicago, Dawson also played with clarinetist Johnny Dodds, pianist Earl Hines, and other top jazz artists.
12. George, *Chicago Defender*, February 11, 1933, 15, and February 18, 1933, 15. Bonds was a recipient of a Rosenwald Fellowship in 1933, which enabled her to pursue a Master's Degree in piano performance at Northwestern University (MM 1934).
13. *Ibid.*, March 25, 1933, 15. The spiritual "Sinner, Please Don't Let This Harvest Pass" was used by Price in a concert overture, in an arrangement for two pianos and in the solo piano work, *Fantasie Negre* in E Minor.
14. George, *Chicago Defender*, February 11, 1933, 15.
15. Interview with Helen White, Chicago, September 13, 1988.
16. George, *Chicago Defender*, March 18, 1933, 15.
17. Ibid., April 22, 1932, 15.
18. Bonds, "A Reminiscence," 192.
19. George, *Chicago Defender*, April 13, 1993, 15.
20. *Ibid.*, May 13, 1933, 15; June 17, 1933, 15.
21. The information on Roland Hayes has been gathered from two articles: Woolsey, "Conversation with Roland Hayes"; and Marr, "Roland Hayes."
22. Graham, "Spirituals to Symphonies."
23. The first black soloist with the Chicago Symphony was singer George R. Garner, tenor, who appeared with the orchestra under Frederick Stock in 1924 or 1925. Holly, "Black Concert Music," 6.
24. "Black Satin Clothes Seen at Symphony."

Chapter 10. Spirituals to Symphonies

1. Robert Abbot, *Chicago Defender*, June 24, 1933, 11.
2. Nahum Daniel Brascher, "Roland Hayes Concert Shows Progress of Race in Music," *Chicago Defender*, June 24, 1933, 11.
3. Gatewood, *Aristocrats of Color*.

4. "Music, Gender, and 'Uplift' in *The Chicago Defender*, 1927–1937," *The Musical Quarterly*. 81, no. 3 (Fall 1997): 344–370.

5. George, "Noted Tenor and Miss Margaret Bond [*sic*] Star with Symphony."

6. Glenn Dillard Gunn, *Chicago Herald & Examiner*, June 16, 1933; *Winnetka Talk*, Winnetka, Ill., June 16, 1933.

7. Herman Devries, *Chicago Evening American*, June 16, 1933; E.H.B., *Music News*, June 16, 1933. A review also appeared the following week, June 22, 1933, in the *Musical Leader*. It read, "A symphony in E minor by Florence Price was most favorably received. It contains interesting material in the way of themes, characteristic rhythms and pleasing orchestration."

8. Eugene Stinson, *Chicago Daily News*, June 16, 1933, 1.

9. Graham, "Spirituals to Symphonies."

10. Harry Lawrence Freeman (1866–1954) completed fourteen operas. He produced his first opera, *The Martyr*, in 1893 in Denver, Colorado; in 1900 scenes from his second opera, *Nada* (1898) were performed by the Cleveland Symphony in 1900. To earn a living, however, Freeman wrote stage music and served as musical director for vaudeville companies. Southern, *The Music of Black Americans*, 272.

11. Mueller, *The American Symphony Orchestra*, 276–278.

12. Dvořák, "Music in America," 432.

13. For further discussions of Dvořák's views on American nationalism, see Block, "Dvořák's Long American Reach." For a fuller discussion of Dvořák's New World Symphony, see Horowitz, *Classical Music in America*, and Beckerman, *New Worlds of Dvořák*.

14. A. Walter Kramer, "H. T. Burleigh: Composer by Divine Right and the American Coleridge-Taylor," *Musical America* 23, no. 26 (April 29, 1916): 25, quoted in Snyder, "A Great and Noble School of Music," 132.

15. Hare, *Negro Musicians and Their Music*, 57.

16. James Creelman, "Dvořák's Negro Symphony," *Pall Mall Budget* (June 21, 1894): 31–32, cited in lecture materials by Michael Beckerman, "The Real Author of 'Real Value of Negro Melodies,'" August 5, 1993, Iowa Centennial Symposium, Cedar Rapids, Iowa. Although Creelman finds the "New World Symphony" a well-crafted work, the article is tinged with racism. The author, while stating that black students should be admitted to the nation's conservatories, reveals that Dvořák's aspirations are naive and the composer's "enthusiasm is almost pathetic." Creelman adds, "I fear that he does not yet appreciate the limitations of the Negro race."

17. Du Bois, *The Souls of Black Folk*, 378.

18. Farwell, *A Letter to American Composers*, xvii–xix.

19. In the early years of his career, composer John Powell was a known racist. He sponsored and helped to write the Virginia antimiscegenation laws, and in the notes to his Rhapsodie Negré, he referred to Negroes as "savages" and "the child among the peoples."

20. Mason, *Music in My Time*, 366. And yet, Mason to the contrary, Debussy did respond to African American folk materials in "Golliwog's Cakewalk" from the *Children's Corner* suite for piano and in other works.

21. Copland, *Music and Imagination*, 103.

22. Ibid., 104.

Chapter 11. The Symphony in E Minor

1. Smith, "African American Music," 46.

2. For a full discussion of the relationship between these three symphonies, see the author's article, "William Grant Still, Florence Price, and William Dawson." Much of the analysis of Price's symphony appears in this article.

3. Price's score has not been published or recorded. Performances of the symphony include the Camellia Symphony (Sacramento), the American Symphony Orchestra (New York), the Women's Philharmonic (San Francisco), and the orchestra of the Plymouth Music Series of Minnesota. Editor's note: Since this time, interest in Price's music has soared. See, for example, Florence Price, Symphonies Nos. 1 and 4, Fort Smith Symphony, conducted by John Jeter, recorded May 13–14, 2018, Naxos 8.559827, 2019, compact disc; and Florence B. Price, *Concerto in One Movement* and Symphony in E Minor, New Black Music Repertory Ensemble, conducted by Lester B. Dunner with Karen Walwyn, piano, Albany Records 1295, 2011, compact disc. See, also Rae Linda Brown, "Symphony in E Minor" in *Music of the United States of America*, Vol. 16, Middleton, Wisconsin: A-R Editions, 2008. A documentary of Price's life by James Greeson titled *The Caged Bird: The Life and Music of Florence B. Price* was released in 2015.

4. It is not known what Price means by "wind whistle." Whistles, however are not uncommon in African traditional music. The instruments can be made of a variety of material including cane and wood. Many of them sound much like flutes.

5. Paine was neither a slaveholder nor an abolitionist. He was imprisoned for aiding a slave in escape. Paine, "Six Years in a Georgia Prison," 1851, quoted in Southern, *Readings*, 89.

6. Solomon Northup, "Twelve Years a Slave," 1853, quoted in Southern, *Readings*, 100. Northup was born a free man and then was kidnapped into slavery. Born in Saratoga Springs, New York, he was a dance fiddler of some repute. Northup was lured to the South, where he was sold into slavery by traveling entrepreneurs who had engaged his professional services as a musician.

7. Florence B. Price, letter to Frederick L. Schwass, Allen Park, Michigan, October 22, 1940. Price Archive, University of Arkansas.

8. Dett's suite, published by Clayton F. Summy, was given its premiere in Chicago in 1913 by Fanny Bloomfield-Zeisler, a distinguished pianist of the day.

9. Locke, *The Negro and His Music*, 114.

10. Ibid., 115.

11. Dett, Introduction, *In the Bottoms*, 33.

12. One exception to Locke's attitude toward women was his support of writer Zora Neale Hurston. But even Hurston found his demeanor cause to label him "a malicious, spiteful little snot," who "lends out his patronage. . . . And God help you if you get on without letting him represent you." Quoted in Hull, *Color, Sex and Poetry*, 7–8.

13. Floyd, "Toward a Philosophy of Black Music Scholarship," 83.

14. Moore, "Negro in Music Given Place."

Chapter 12. O Sing a New Song

1. In addition to teaching at the conservatory from 1925–1962, Sowerby was organist and choirmaster at the Episcopal Church of St. James (1927–1962). In a letter from

Florence Price Robinson to Mildred Denby Green dated June 20, 1973, Price's daughter states that her mother studied with Sowerby, but there is no evidence of this. See Green, *Black Women Composers*, 33. However, the Price Materials has general correspondence between the two composers.

2. George, *Chicago Defender*, June 24, 1933: 15.

3. The original manuscript is in four movements with no subtitles, thus indicating that the *Dances* were substantially revised over a period of time. In 1953, William Grant Still orchestrated the published version of the *Dances*. I do not know whether Still's score was ever performed.

4. The information on Price's activities from summer 1933 to early 1934 are taken from George, "Music News," *Chicago Defender*, July 8, 1933, 15; July 15, 15; July 29, 15; August 12, 15; September 9, 15; September 30, 15; October 7, 6; October 28, 12; November 5, 12; November 11, 12; and January 20, 1934, 12.

5. The information on Riverwood is from Marion Quinney Ross, Perry Quinney's daughter, interview, Little Rock, August 25, 1991. See also George, *Chicago Defender*, September 9, 15.

6. Price was the only black member of the Illinois Federation of Music Clubs until the 1950s.

7. Price to Helen Armstrong Andrews, October 24, 1933. Price Materials, University of Arkansas. Five letters from Andrews to Price have survived. In these letters, Andrews often expresses her support for the composer (June 19, 1933; October 24, 1933; March 12, 1934; May 3, 1934). In a letter of February 10, 1934, Andrews gives her negative news of a lecture she heard by Roy D. Welsh, chair of the music department at Smith College, in which he played contemporary music, including Schoenberg. Presumably, Andrews was implying to Price that she should maintain her conservative compositional style.

8. Diary entry, December 5, 1933. MS. 8p. on 4L. Price Materials.

9. Ibid., December 7, 1933.

10. Eric DeLamarter to Florence B. Price, February 6, 1934. Price Materials.

11. Helen Armstrong Andrews to Price, October 24, 1933. MS. 2p. on 1 L. Price Materials.

12. No extant transcript of Price's study at the Chicago Musical College during the 1930s exists. When the Chicago Musical College merged with Roosevelt College in 1954, many of the school's records were lost. However, the lengthy review of Price's Concerto in the *Chicago Musical Leader* 66, no.23 (July 14, 1934): 9, and the *Chicago Tribune*, June 25, 1934, establish her residency at the school. It is likely that Price continued her study of composition and orchestration with Carl Busch and Wesley LaViolette, respectively, with whom she studied in 1926 and 1927.

13. *Chicago Tribune*, June 25, 1934.

14. *Pittsburgh Sun Telegraph*, August 31, 27; *Pittsburgh Press*, August 31, 1934, 27. The early performances of the concerto were reviewed also in *The California Eagle*, June 29, 1934, 8, and *The Chicago Defender*, September 18, 1934, 2.

15. National Auditions Annual: A Century of Progress Souvenir Edition of Afro-American Pageant, Inc. Soldiers Field, August 25, 1934.

16. Although Price may have conducted other orchestral works of her own during her career, this is the only documented occasion of her doing so.

17. Earl Hines's band played at the Grand Terrace Ballroom from 1928–1938.

18. For a longer discussion of the relationship between the Castles dance team and James Reese Europe, see Badger's *A Life in Ragtime*, 78–127. I am grateful to Wayne Shirley for pointing out this source to me.

Chapter 13. The Piano Concerto in One Movement

1. Many articles and books have reprinted the picture of Margaret Bonds's performance of Price's concerto with the Woman's Symphony Orchestra of Chicago, which appears in Bonds's article, "A Reminiscence." The conductor in the photograph, often misidentified as Price, is Ebba Sundstrom.

2. In the mid-1920s, as Carol Neuls-Bates points out, while women constituted the majority of the nation's music students, and women were primarily responsible for raising funds to ensure a concert season, they were barred from the professional mainstream in performance, excluding choral and solo concert work. Neuls-Bates, "Women's Orchestras," 349. After the war, most of the women's symphony orchestras folded. The war depleted orchestras of men in large numbers, thereby causing major orchestras for the first time to hire women in significant numbers.

3. "Brief History of the Woman's Symphony Orchestra of Chicago," *Women's Symphony Orchestra Programs*, Chicago Public Library, 1936–1940 (Chicago: n.p., n.d.). For more information on the history of the Woman's Symphony Orchestra of Chicago, see the author's article, "The Woman's Symphony Orchestra of Chicago." Much of the analysis of the concerto is taken from that article. See also Linda Dempf, "The Woman's Symphony Orchestra of Chicago," *Notes* 62, no. 4 (June 2006): 857–903.

4. Eleanor Everest Freer, *Musical Leader* 66, no. 26 (October 13, 1934): 22.

5. Gunn, here, mistakenly refers to Price's Symphony in E Minor, which was performed by the Chicago Symphony, June 1933. *Chicago Herald and Examiner*, October 12, 1934.

6. The concerto was played at later dates by the Chicago Symphony and in 1940 with the Michigan WPA Orchestra with Price as soloist. It was performed also on numerous occasions in the two-piano arrangement.

7. Notecards of Florence Price Robinson, #36–38, Price Materials.

8. Many of the manuscript orchestral parts have been located in the private collection of Mrs. Eugenia Anderson, a Chicago piano teacher and former President of the Chicago Club of Women Organists. Still missing are the violin I and II, viola, trumpet, and oboe parts. The solo piano and orchestral reduction, however, contain instrumental indications.

9. I thank Wayne Shirley, music librarian, Library of Congress, for bringing the similarities in Clara Schumann's concerto to my attention.

10. *Century of Progress Exhibition: The Official Guide Book of the Fair*, 1934, 114. Century of Progress Papers, Chicago Public Library Special Collections.

11. "169,179 Attend Fair: Day Is 3d Biggest in 1934," *Chicago Tribune* (special edition), August 19, 1934. Century of Progress Papers, Chicago Public Library Special Collections.

Chapter 14. Performing Again

1. This information can be garnered from tracking Florence Price's addresses in phone directories and on copyright records.

2. Pusey Dell Arnett died in Chicago on July 8, 1957, at the age of 81. His death certificate states that he was "widowed," implying that he and Florence Price never divorced. Medical Certificate of Death, Bureau of Statistics, Illinois Department of Public Health.

3. *Chicago Defender*, February 20, 1932, 7.

4. Bonds, "A Reminiscence," 192.

5. Conversation with concert singer Helen White, Chicago, September 13, 1988.

6. Bonds, "A Reminiscence," 192.

7. Letter from Price to William Grant Still, March 22, 1945, in which she implies that a letter of Still's wife never reached her. I am indebted to Judith Anne Still for a copy of this letter. Price wrote, "I am wondering if Mrs. Still's letter was sent to this address (700 E. Oakwood Blvd) or to the old address 647 E. 50th Place from which I moved in the Spring of 1941 for the sole reason that so much of my mail failed to reach my hands. I gave the P.O. my forwarding address but the mail delivery here, especially in certain sections, is most unreliable."

8. Quoted in Rampersad, *The Life of Langston Hughes*, v. 1, 320–321.

9. The information on the transition from Gibbs High School to Dunbar High School is taken from Anderson, *The Education of Blacks in the South*, 186–237, and Jones, *A Traditional Model of Educational Excellence*, 1–17.

10. Dunbar remained the only public high school for blacks in Little Rock from 1930–1955.

11. *Arkansas Democrat*, Sunday, February 17, 1935, 6; "Around the City," *Arkansas Democrat*, Tuesday, February 19, 1935, 7; "City News," *Arkansas Gazette*, February 19, 1935.

12. Hudgins, "A Noted Little Rock Composer—Florence B. Price."

13. Letters from Florence Price Robinson to Mary Hudgins (Hot Springs, Arkansas), September 22, 1967, and from Solar M. Carethers (Little Rock, Arkansas) to Mary Hudgins, November 3, 1967.

14. Florence Price Robinson to Mary D. Hudgins, September 22, 1967.

15. *Arkansas Survey-Journal*, February 19, 1935. Hudgins File, Price Materials. According to Price's daughter, Florence Price Robinson, at one time, Price's husband, Thomas Price, owned stock in this newspaper and was one of its editors. Notecards #44–54, Price Materials.

16. I am grateful to Calvert Johnson for providing me with the information on Price's activities with the Chicago Club of Women Organists. Their archives are located at the Chicago Historical Society.

17. Jackson, "Florence Price, Composer," 40.

18. Edited by Calvert Johnson, the *Suite No. 1* for organ was published by ClarNan Editions, 1993.

19. "Thomas Price," *Who's Who in Colored America, 1941–1944*, Thomas Yenser, ed., 6th edition.

Chapter 15. Professional Recognition

1. Henry S. Sawyer (Philadelphia) to Price, March 5, 1933. TS. 1p. Price Materials.

2. Henry S. Sawyer (Philadelphia) to FBP, September 20, 1937. TS. 2p. Price Materials.

3. John Alden Carpenter (Chicago) to FBSP, November 16, 1934. TS. 1p.; Carpenter to FBSP, December 18, 1934. TS. 1p.; Gene Buck (ASCAP, New York) to FBSP, November 26, 1934, TS. 1p.

4. FBSP to American Society of Composers, Authors and Publishers, Inc. (New York). July 27, 1940. Proc/TS. 1 p. Price Materials.

5. Helen D. Gillespie (New York) to FBSP, February 26, 1940. Proc./TS. 1 p. Price Materials.

6. Paul Berthoud (New York) to FBSP, September 24, 1940. TS. 1p. Price Materials.

7. Florence Price to Claude A. Barnett, March 4, 1940. TS 1p. Claude A. Barnett to Florence Price, March 9, 1940. TS. 1p. Claude Barnett Papers, Chicago Historical Society. For a brief overview of the contents of the Barnett papers, see Day, "Black Musicians in the Claude Barnett Papers."

8. Betty Jackson King, a widely performed Chicago-born composer and an active member of NANM, became the second black woman to join the Musicians Club of Women. In a letter to Barbara Garvey Jackson (February 22, 1974), King wrote, "Mrs. Price was the only woman of color to my knowledge to be a member of the Musicians Club of Women in Chicago, Ill. in 1950." Price Materials.

9. Letter from Anamay Owen Wales to Barbara Garvey Jackson, October 17, 1974. Price Materials.

10. Fishel and Quarles, *The Black American*, 449–452.

11. Walden, "Keep Ideals in Front of You."

12. Hull, *Color, Sex and Poetry*, 12.

13. Ibid.

14. Tick, "Passed Away Is the Piano Girl," 336–337.

15. The letters between Price and Koussevitzky are as follows: August 8, 1935 (4611 Wabash Ave., Apt. 5C); September 18, 1941 (Lincoln Center, 700 Oakwood Blvd.); July 5, 1943 (700 East Oakwood Blvd.); November 6, 1943; Secretary to Dr. Koussevitzky to FBSP, November 17, 1943; FBSP to Koussevitzky, May 22, 1944, with a handwritten message at the bottom of the letter "sent back June 7, 1944"; FBSP to Koussevitzky, October 23, 1944; Secretary to Dr. Koussevitzky to FBSP October 31, 1944.

16. This is probably a reference to the myriad of compositions written during the early part of the century, primarily by white Americans, which include African American folk themes as their basis. Chadwick's Symphony No. 2 may also be included here.

17. More puzzling is that one of her scores was lost en route to Koussevitzky. Apparently, the Overture, the work Price most wanted him to review, was never received in his office.

18. Hall Johnson's arrangement was published in 1930 by the Robbins Music Corporation. Price's arrangement probably dates from the late 1930s–1940s.

Chapter 16. The WPA Years

1. The Federal Music Project was discontinued in 1939, and the WPA continued the music project of Federal One (Federal One included the professional arts projects, music, art, theater, and writer) under the WPA Music Program, 1939-1943.

2. Faxio, "The Music Program of the Works Progress Administration," 242. See also "WPA Music Project Positions Open," in *The Keynote, Detroit Federation of Music*, October 1939.

3. Advertisement in *The Keynote, Detroit Federation of Music*, October 1939. In WPA files, Detroit Public Library.

4. "WPA Orchestras Preserve Living Music, Says Director." See also Holmes, "Sokoloff Praises WPA Music Work in Michigan." Under the direction of Nikolai Sokoloff, the Cleveland Orchestra, which he led from its founding in 1918 to 1933, became one of the outstanding orchestras in the country.

5. Much of the information on the Composers' Forum-Laboratory comes from Pettis, "The WPA and the American Composer."

6. Ellison, *Going to the Territory*, 204–205.

7. The "WPA Music Project of Detroit."

8. All of the information on Poole is taken from the author's interview with Valter Poole, May 28, 1983. Transcription in the Archive of the Oral History Program of the Institute on the Federal Theatre Project and New Deal Culture (Fairfax, Va., George Mason University, 1984), 1–33.

9. J. D. Callahan, *The Detroit Free Press*, November 7, 1940. See also "Chicagoan Guest Artist of Michigan Symphony Orchestra," *Chicago Defender*, November 16, 1940.

10. Malvina C. Thompson (Washington, D.C.) to FBSP, November 20, 1940. TS. 1 p. Price Materials.

11. Personal notes included with the Symphony No. 3 added to press materials. Misc. Price Materials.

12. Florence Price Robinson to Mary D. Hudgins, Hudgins papers, Price Archive. There is no date on this letter but from the context of the whole letter, it appears to have been written after 1963.

Chapter 17. The Chicago Renaissance

1. The information on the Abraham Lincoln Center is from the interview with Eleanor Price, who began the kindergarten program there in the 1940s (telephone conversation, September 12, 1988), Edna Oates, director of the after-school program in the 1940s and 1950s (telephone conversation, September 12, 1988, and Helen White, September 13, 1988).

2. "Local Artist [*sic*] to Honor Florence B. Price," *Chicago Defender*, April 3, 1948, 9. See also Holt, "Chicago Woman Composer's Works Heard," 15.

3. The information on Richard Wright and the Chicago Renaissance is taken from Bone, "Richard Wright and the Chicago Renaissance."

4. "The History of Negro Music and Musicians in Chicago" of the Illinois Writers' Project. See also the two-volume *The Negro in Chicago: 1779–1927*.

5. There was an earlier effort to provide an overview of black Chicago, the two-volume *The Negro in Chicago: 1779–1927*, but it was essentially a listing of churches, organizations (including music), physicians, and so forth with no interpretation of the data.

6. Bone, "Richard Wright and the Chicago Renaissance."

7. Arna Bontemps, "Famous WPA Authors," *Negro Digest* (June 1950): 46–47, quoted in Bone, "Richard Wright and the Chicago Renaissance," 447.

8. Bone, "Richard Wright," 452.

9. Quoted in Rampersad, *The Life of Langston Hughes*, vol. 1, 387.

10. Many of Price's art songs are undated, but stylistically they fall into the 1935–1945 time period.

11. Langston Hughes (Hollow Hills Farm, Monterey, California) to Arna Bontemps (Chicago), November 8, 1941. In Nichols, ed., *Arna Bontemps–Langston Hughes Letters: 1925–1967*, 95.

12. Rampersad, *The Life of Langston Hughes*, 386–387.

13. Ibid., 132.

Chapter 18. The Symphony No. 3

1. Florence B. Price to Frederick L. Schwass (Allen Park, Michigan), October 22, 1940. TS copy. 1 p. Price Materials.

2. In the score, the rhythms of the percussion are notated precisely, but it is up to the individual percussionist to decide which instrument(s) is used where.

3. Florence B. Price to Dr. Serge Koussevitzky, October 18, 1941. Koussevitzky Collection, Library of Congress.

Chapter 19. Final Years

1. Lovell, *Black Song*, 421.

2. For a discussion of Georgia Douglas Johnson's collection of poetry, see Hull, *Color, Sex and Poetry*, 156–159.

3. It was later recorded by opera singers Ellabelle Davis (Victor 1799 and London LPS-182) and Leontyne Price (*Swing Low, Sweet Chariot: Fourteen Spirituals*, RCA-LSC 2600).

4. Blanche Thebom to Barbara Garvey Jackson, June 29, 1974. Personal materials of BGJ, University of Arkansas.

5. Reprinted in the *Musical Courier*, December 1, 1952.

6. It is not clear from the context of this letter to what Burleigh is referring with reference to Paul Robeson's relationship with Ricordi & Co.

7. Angelou, *I Know Why the Caged Bird Sings*.

8. FBSP to William Grant Still, March 22, 1945. TS, 1 p. William Grant Still Music. Courtesy of Judith Anne Still.

9. Still's *In Memoriam: The Colored Soldiers Who Died for Democracy* was first performed by the New York Philharmonic, January 1944, with Arthur Rodzinski conducting.

10. Price to William Grant Still, January 9, 1951. TS 1p. William Grant Still Music. Courtesy of Judith Anne Still.

11. Price's friend, Neumon Leighton, explained to Mildred Denby Green that he was present when Price received the cable from England. See Green, *Black Women Composers*, 34. The Paris trip is also mentioned in: "Florence Price's Work Spotlighted," *Chicago Defender*, February 10, 1951, 21. Also, "Noted Composers' Works to Spark Circle Concert," *Chicago Defender*, January 20, 1951, 24.

12. Price wrote two string quartets on American themes. The other quartet, which has not survived, was based entirely on spirituals: "Go Down, Moses," "Lil' David Play on Your Harp," "Somebody's Knockin' at Your Door," and "Joshua Fit de Battle of Jericho."

13. In an undated letter, presumably to Mary Hudgins, to whom she was corresponding, Florence Price Robinson wrote, "One time my mother was in the hospital. She had a coronary thrombosis attack. (She always had a bad heart even as a child)." Price Materials.

14. Florence Price Robinson to [Mary] Hudgins, September 22, 1967. Hudgins File, Price Materials.

15. The *Three Negro Dances* received high visibility in July 1953 when it was programmed over the American Broadcast Company network in a program dedicated to the American band movement.

16. Information from Florence Price Robinson, miscellaneous notes to Mary D. Hudgins, Hudgins file, Price Materials. The information is verified in several press releases.

17. Earl Calloway, in "Florence B. Price, a Chicagoan Who Was an Acclaimed Composer," *Chicago Defender*, November 5, 1988, 47, wrote: "While preparing to go to Paris, France to receive the Grand Prize of France, she suffered a heart attack and died shortly thereafter." Calloway knew Price in the 1950s so this information is likely correct.

18. Delayed Birth Certificate filed April 20, 1953, Arkansas State Board of Health—Bureau of Vital Statistics. Certified copy of the original document. Although I cannot prove that Price applied for the birth certificate in order to obtain a passport, it is a reasonable assumption given the proximity of her planned trip to Europe a few weeks later.

19. Letter from Price to Perry [Quinney Johnson] dated May, no year. Price Materials. Barbara Garvey Jackson correctly established the year as 1953. The date was confirmed by Marion Quinney Ross, Johnston's daughter.

20. Kenneth F. Kimes, Clayton F. Summy Co. (Chicago, IL), May 14, 1953. TLS. 1p. Price Materials.

21. Marion Ross radio interview. "From Spirituals to Symphony: A Portrait of Florence Price." Interviewed by Earnest Lamb (Little Rock), March 1993. Mrs. Ross shared the information on her mother's premonitions with the author as well.

22. Medical Certificate of Death, State of Illinois. Filed June 3, 1953.

23. "Florence Price, Noted Composer, Buried Here," *Chicago Defender* (City Edition), June 11, 1953. Her obituary was also carried in: *Etude* 71 (August 1953): 56; *Musical Courier* 147 (July 1953): 7; *Musical America* 73 (July 1953): 19.

Postscript

1. See *Chicago Defender* articles on Price and reviews of her music from 1935 to 1953.

2. "Music News," *Chicago Defender*, February 10, 1940, 17; February 17, 1940, 18; and May 25, 1940, 15.

3. There are several articles and photos that document the dedication of the Florence B. Price Elementary School. See *Chicago Defender*, March 1, 1963; District Thirteen Newsletter, Chicago Public Schools, March 27, 1963. Also: Dedication Program of the Florence B. Price School (November 24, 1964); Letter from Florence Price Robinson to Mary D. Hudgins (September 1967) in Hudgins File, Price Papers, University of Arkansas. Hudgins, "Chicago School Named for State Composer."

Selected Bibliography

Collections: Public and Private That Hold Materials of or about Florence B. Price

Marian Anderson Collection, University of Pennsylvania.

Chicago Historical Society, Papers of the Woman's Symphony Orchestra of Chicago.

Chicago Public Library, Music Division and Special Collections.

Detroit Public Library, Papers of the Michigan WPA Symphony.

E. Azalia Hackley Memorial Collection of Negro Music, Drama, and Dance. Detroit Public Library.

Frederick D. Hall, Atlanta, Georgia. Private Collection.

Vivian Harsh Collection of Afro-American History and Literature, Chicago Public Library.

James Weldon Johnson Memorial Collection of Negro Arts and Letters. Beinecke Rare Book and Manuscript Library, Yale University.

Moorland-Spingarn Research Center. Howard University, Washington, D.C.

New York Public Library at Lincoln Center. Performing Arts Research Center, Music Division.

Schmitt Collection, Library of Congress, Music Division.

Schomburg Center for Research in Black Culture, New York Public Library.

Sibley Library, Eastman School of Music, University of Rochester.

Bernice Skooglund, Chicago, Illinois. Private Collection.

Judith Anne Still, Flagstaff, Arizona. Papers of William Grant Still.

Florence Stith, Chicago, Illinois. Private Collection.

University of Arkansas, Mullins Library Special Collections, Florence Beatrice Smith Price Materials, Access No. 195. Gift of Florence Price Robinson and collected by Mary Dengler Hudgins and Barbara Garvey Jackson, 1974–1975. The papers consist of correspondence of Price and that of her daughter, Florence Price Robinson; diary fragments; programs; photographs; and scores. The collection also includes the Mary Dengler Hudgins Research Files. Hereafter referred to as the Price Materials.

Helen White, Chicago, Illinois. Private Collection Articles and Books.

* * *

Abdul, Raoul. *Blacks in Classical Music: A Personal History.* New York: Dodd, Mead, 1977.

———. "Florence Price's Huge, Untapped Musical Output." *Amsterdam News*, April 19, 1986, 26.

Ammer, Christine. *Unsung, A History of Women in American Music.* Westport, Conn.: Greenwood Press, 1980.

Anderson, James D. *The Education of Blacks in the South, 1860–1935.* Chapel Hill: The University of North Carolina Press, 1988.

Angelou, Maya. *I Know Why the Caged Bird Sings.* New York: Random House, 1970.

"Any Old Iron or Rubber? Come and See WPA Show." *Detroit News*, April 24, 1942.

Arvey, Verna. *In One Lifetime.* Fayetteville: The University of Arkansas Press, 1984.

———. "Outstanding Achievements of Negro Composers." *Etude* 60 (March 1942): 171, 210.

ASCAP Biographical Dictionary of Composers, Authors, and Publishers. Comp. and ed. by the Lynn Farnol Group. New York: American Society of Composers, Authors, and Publishers, 1966.

ASCAP Biographical Dictionary. Fourth ed. Comp. by Jaques Catell Press. New York: R. R. Bowker Co., 1980.

ASCAP Symphonic Catalog. Third ed. New York: R. R. Bowker and Co., 1977.

"Attend Dance, Band Concert, Buy War Bonds, Stamps Tonight." *Edmore Times*, May 7, 1942.

"Awards—Florence B. Price." *Opportunity* 10 (December 1932): 391.

Badger, Reid. *A Life in Ragtime: A Biography of James Reese Europe.* New York: Oxford University Press, 1995.

Baskett, Tom, Jr. *Persistence of the Spirit: The Black Experience in Arkansas.* Little Rock: Exhibition Booklet, Resource Center, Arkansas Endowment for the Arts, 1986.

Beckerman, Michael. *New Worlds of Dvořák.* New York: Norton, 2003.

Biographical and Historical Memoirs of Pulaski, Jefferson, Ionoke, and Faulkner, Grant, Saline, Perry, Garland, and Hot Springs Counties, Arkansas. Chicago: Goodspeed, 1889.

"Black Satin Clothes Seen at Symphony." *Chicago Daily Tribune*, June 16, 1933, 1.

Blassingame, John W. *The Slave Community: Plantation Life in the Antebellum South.* New York: Oxford University Press, 1979.

Blassingame, John W., and Mary Francis Berry. *Long Memory: The Black Experience in America.* New York: Oxford University Press, 1982.

Block, Adrienne Fried. "Arthur P. Schmidt, Music Publisher and Champion of American Women Composers." In vol. 2 of *The Musical Woman: An International Perspective*, edited by Judith Lang Zaimont, 145–176. Westport, Conn.: Greenwood Press, 1987.

———. "Dvořák's Long American Reach," in *Dvořák in America: 1892–1895*, ed. John C. Tibbetts. Portland, Ore.: Amadeus Press, 1993, 157–181.

Block, Adrienne Fried, and Carol Neuls-Bates., comp. and ed. *Women in American Music: A Bibliography of Music and Literature.* Westport, Conn.: Greenwood Press, 1979.

Bonds, Margaret. "A Reminiscence." In *International Library of Negro Life and History: The Negro in Music and Art.* Comp. and ed. by Lindsay Patterson under the auspices of the Association for the Study of Negro Life and History. New York: Publishers Co., 1967.

Bone, Robert. "Richard Wright and the Chicago Renaissance." *Callaloo* 9, no. 3 (Summer 1986): 446–468.

Bowers, Jane, and Judith Tick, eds. *Women Making Music: The Western Art Tradition, 1150–1950*. Urbana: University of Illinois Press, 1986.

Brascher, Nahum Daniel, "Roland Hayes Concert Shows Progress of Race in Music." *Chicago Defender*, June 24, 1933, 11.

Brawley, James P. *Clark College Legacy: An Interpretive History of Relevant Education, 1869–1975*. Atlanta: Clark College, 1977.

Brown, Ernest J. *An Annotated Bibliography of Selected Solo Music Written for the Piano by Black Composers*. DMA Dissertation, University of Maryland, 1976.

Brown, Rae Linda. "Florence B. Price and Margaret Bonds: The Chicago Years." *Black Music Research Bulletin* 12, no. 2 (Fall 1990): 11–14.

———. *Selected Orchestral Music of Florence B. Price (1888–1953) in the Context of Her Life and Work*. PhD dissertation, Yale University, 1987.

———. "William Grant Still, Florence B. Price, and William Dawson: Echoes of the Harlem Renaissance." In *Black Music in the Harlem Renaissance: A Collection of Essays*, ed. Samuel A. Floyd Jr.. Westport, Conn.: Greenwood Press, 1990, 71–86.

———. "The Woman's Symphony Orchestra of Chicago and Florence B. Price's Piano Concerto in One Movement." *American Music* 11, no. 2 (Summer 1993): 185–205.

Bullock, Henry Allen. *A History of Negro Education in the South: From 1916 to the Present*. Cambridge: Harvard University Press, 1967.

Butcher, Margaret Just. *The Negro in American Culture*. 1956. Reprint. New York: Alfred A. Knopf, 1966.

Calloway, Earl. "Florence B. Price, a Chicagoan Who Was an Acclaimed Composer." *Chicago Defender*, November 5, 1988, 47.

Chadwick, George Whitefield. *Harmony*. Boston: B. F. Wood Music Co., 1897, rev. 1922.

———. *Memoirs and Diaries*. Unpublished manuscript. Edited and transcribed by Steven Ledbetter (unpublished typescript).

———. "Musical Atmosphere and Student Life." *New England Conservatory Magazine* IX/4 (May 1903): 138–141.

Cohen, Aaron I. *International Encyclopedia of Women Composers*. New York: R. R. Bowker Co., 1981.

"Composer Wins Noteworthy Prizes for Piano Sonata." *Chicago Defender*, May 4, 1935, 25.

Copland, Aaron. *Music and Imagination*. Cambridge Press: Harvard University Press, 1952.

"Correcting Fred Douglass: Arkansas Not the First to Refuse Him Admission to a Public Dining Room." *Arkansas Gazette*, February 8, 1889, 5.

Cuney, Waring. *Opportunity* 4, no. 180 (June 1926): 88. Copyright 1926 by The National Urban League.

Day, Otha. "Black Musicians in the Claude Barnett Papers." *Black Music Research Bulletin* 12, no. 2 (Fall 1990): 15–17.

Dett, R. Nathaniel. *In the Bottoms: Characteristic Suite for the Piano*. Chicago: Clayton F. Summy, [1913] 1973.

Dietrich, Fred W., D.D.S., comp. *The History of Dentistry in Arkansas: A Story of Progress.* Little Rock: Arkansas State Dental Association, 1957.

Dillard, Tom W. "Scipio A. Jones: Fought Mobs, Climbed Rungs of GOP Politics." *Arkansas Gazette*, January 30, 1979, 4B.

Drake, St. Clair, and Horace R. Cayton. *Black Metropolis: A Study of Negro Life in a Northern City*. New York: Harcourt, Brace, and World, 2nd ed., 1962.

Du Bois, W. E. B. *The Autobiography of W. E. B. Du Bois*. New York: International Publishers, 1968. Reprint 1973.

———. *The Souls of Black Folk*. Chicago, 1903. Reprinted in *Three Negro Classics*. New York: Avon, 1965.

Dvořák, Antonin. "Music in America." *Harper's New Monthly Magazine* (February 1895): 429–434.

Dyett, Neota McCurdy. "In the Realm of Music." *Chicago Defender*, June 29, 1935, 4.

Ellison, Ralph. *Going to the Territory*. New York: Random House, 1986.

Epstein, Dena. "Frederick Stock and American Music." *American Music* 10, no. 1 (Spring 1992): 20–52.

Ewen, David. *All the Years of American Popular Music: A Comprehensive History*. Englewood Cliffs, N.J.: Prentice Hall, 1977.

Farwell, Arthur. *A Letter to American Composers*. Newton Center, Mass.: Wa-Wan Press, 1903.

———, ed. *The Wa-Wan Press*. Reprint. New York: Arno Press and The New York Times, 1970.

Faxio, Lorraine M. "The Music Program of the Works Progress Administration: A Documentation and Description of Its Activities with Special Reference to Afro-Americans" in *More Than Dancing: Essays on Afro-American Music and Musicians*. ed. by Irene V. Jackson. Prepared under the auspices of the Center for Ethnic Music, Howard University. Westport: Greenwood Press, 1985.

Fischel, Leslie H., Jr., and Benjamin Quarles. *The Black American: A Documentary History*. Glenview, Ill.: Scott, Foresman & Co., 1970.

Fitzpatrick, Edward John, Jr. *The Music Conservatory in America*. DMA dissertation, Boston University, 1963.

Floyd, Samuel A., Jr. "Black American Music and Aesthetic Communication." *Black Music Research Journal* (1980): 1–17.

———. "On Black Music Research." *Black Music Research Journal* (1983): 46–57.

———. "Toward a Philosophy of Black Music Scholarship." *Black Music Research Journal* 2 (1982): 72–93.

"Forced to Leave." *Cleveland Gazette*, March 17, 1928, 2.

Franklin, John Hope. *Reconstruction after the Civil War*. Chicago: University of Illinois Press, 1967.

"Fred Douglass." *Arkansas Gazette*, February 6, 1889, 8.

Gaines, D. B., D.D.S. *Racial Possibilities as Indicated by the Negroes of Arkansas*. Little Rock: Philander Smith College, 1898.

Gatewood, Willard B. *Aristocrats of Color: The Black Elite, 1880–1920*. Bloomington: Indiana University Press, 1990.

———. "The Formative Years of William Grant Still: Little Rock, Arkansas, 1895–1911," in Catherine Parsons Smith, *William Grant Still: A Study in Contradictions*. Berkeley: University of California Press, 2000.

———. "William Grant Still's Little Rock." In *William Grant Still Studies at the University of Arkansas: A 1984 Congress Report*. Fayetteville: University of Arkansas Department of Music, 1984.

George, Maude Roberts. "Music News." *Chicago Defender*. George, a singer and columnist, documented Chicago's black classical music scene in this column from the 1920s to the early 1930s.

———. "Noted Tenor and Miss Margaret Bond [*sic*] Star with Symphony." *Chicago Defender* (City Edition), June 17, 1933, 33.

George, Zelma Watson. *A Guide to Negro Music: An Annotated Bibliography of Negro Folk Music and Art Music by Negro Composers or Based on Negro Thematic Material*. PhD dissertation, New York University, 1953.

Giddings, Paula. *When and Where I Enter: The Impact of Black Women on Race and Sex in America*. Toronto: Bantam Books, 1984.

Gill, John P. *The Crossroads of Arkansas*. Little Rock: Old Statehouse Museum Associates, 1990.

Goodrich, Wallace. *Personal Recollections of the New England Conservatory of Music*. Boston: New England Conservatory, 1947.

Graham, Shirley. "Spirituals to Symphonies." *Etude* 54 (November 1936): 692.

Graves, John William. "Negro Disenfranchisement in Arkansas." *Arkansas Historical Quarterly* 26 (1967): 190–225.

———. *Town and Country: Race Relations in an Urban-Rural Context, Arkansas 1865–1905*. Little Rock: University of Arkansas Press, 1990.

Green, Mildred. *Black Women Composers: A Genesis*. Boston: G. K. Hall, 1983.

Haas, Robert Bartlett. *William Grant Still and the Fusion of Cultures in American Music*. Los Angeles: Black Sparrow Press, 1975.

Hare, Maud Cuney. *Negro Musicians and Their Music*. Washington, D.C.: Associated Publishers, 1936.

Hildreth, John. *Keyboard Works of Selected Black Composers*. PhD dissertation, Northwestern University, 1978.

"The History of Dentistry in Arkansas: A Story of Progress," Arkansas State Dental Association, 1957.

History of Negro Music. Illinois Writer's Project of the Works Progress Administration, boxes 84–104. Vivian Harsh Collection of Afro-American History and Literature, Carter G. Woodson Regional Library, Chicago.

Holly, Ellistine Perkins. "Black Concert Music in Chicago, 1890 to the 1930s. *Black Music Research Newsletter* 9, no. 2 (Fall 1987): 3–7.

Holmes, Ralph. "Sokoloff Praises WPA Music Work in Michigan." *The Detroit Times*, May 20, 1938.

Holt, Nora. "Chicago Woman Composer's Works Heard in Concert" *New York Amsterdam News*, May 22, 1948.

"Honored" [Clyde Winkfield]. *Michigan Chronicle (Negro Weekly)*, March 5, 1938.

hooks, bell. *Feminist Theory: From margin to center*. Boston: South End Press, 1984.

Horowitz, Joseph. *Classical Music in America: A History of Its Rise and Fall.* New York: Norton, 2004.

Hudgins, Mary D. "Chicago School Named for State Composer." *Arkansas Gazette*, June 30, 1968, E-5.

———. "A Noted Little Rock Composer—Florence B. Price." Unpublished manuscript, Hudgins file, Price Materials, University of Arkansas.

Hull, Gloria T. *Color, Sex and Poetry*. Bloomington: Indiana University Press, 1987.

"Innocent but Lynched." *Cleveland Gazette*, September 10, 1927, 4.

Jackson, Barbara. "Florence Price: Composer." *The Black Perspective in Music* 5, no. 1 (September 1977): 30–43.

Jackson, Raymond. *The Evolution of Piano Music as Seen in Works of Four Black Composers.* DMA Dissertation, Juilliard School of Music, 1973.

Johnson, Calvert, ed. *Music of Florence Beatrice Price: Suite 1 for Organ*. Fayetteville, Ark.: ClarNan Editions, 1993.

Jones, Faustine Childress. *A Traditional Model of Educational Excellence: Dunbar High School of Little Rock, Arkansas*. Washington, D.C.: Howard University Press, 1981.

Kennan, Clara B. "The First Negro Teacher in Little Rock." *Arkansas Historical Quarterly* 9 (1950): 194–204.

Kousser, J. Morgan. "A Black Protest in the 'Era of Accommodation': Documents." *Arkansas Historical Quarterly* 34/2 (Summer 1975): 161–163.

Krummel, D. W., Jean Geil, Doris Dyen, Deane Root, eds. *Resources of American Music History: A Directory of Source Materials from Colonial Times to World War II.* Urbana: University of Illinois Press, 1981.

Lamb, Earnest. "From Spiritual to Symphony: A Portrait of Florence Price." Radio broadcast transcript dated February 1993. In Price Materials.

Laurence, Anya. *Women of Notes: 1000 Women Composers Born before 1900*. New York: Richard Rosen Press, 1978.

Levy, Alan Howard. *Musical Nationalism: American Composers' Search for Identity*. Westport, Conn.: Greenwood Press, 1983.

Lewis, Stephen J. "The Negro in the Field of Dentistry." *Opportunity* 2 (July 1924): 207–212.

Locke, Alain. *The Negro and His Music*. New York: Arno Press and The New York Times, 1969, c. 1936.

———. "Toward a Critique of Negro Music." *Opportunity* (November-December 1934): 328+.

Lovell, John, Jr. *Black Song: The Forge and The Flame (How the Negro Spiritual Was Hammered Out)*. New York: Macmillan, 1972.

Marr, Warren, II. "Roland Hayes." *The Black Perspective in Music* 2, no. 2 (Fall 1974): 186–190.

Mason, Daniel Gregory. *Music in My Time*. New York: Macmillan Co., 1938.

McSwain, Bernice Lamb. "Shorter College: Its Early History." *Pulaski County Historical Review*, xxx (Winter 1982): 81–84.

Meggett, Joan M. *Keyboard Music by Women Composers: A Catalog and Bibliography.* Westport, Conn.: Greenwood Press, 1981.

Moore, Edward. "Negro in Music Given Place in Concert of Century of Progress Series." *Chicago Tribune*, June 16, 1933, 1.

Mosley, Ellis Greenlee. *The History of Higher Education for Negroes in Arkansas*. MA thesis, University of Texas, 1944.

Mueller, John H. *The American Symphony Orchestra: A Social History of Musical Taste*. Bloomington: Indiana University Press, 1951.

"Musical and Dramatic." *The Half-Century Magazine* (August 9, 1916).

The Negro in Chicago: 1779–1927. Chicago: The Washington Intercollegiate Club of Chicago. Vol. 1 [1927], Vol. 2 [1929]. Carter G. Woodson Library (Branch) of the Chicago Public Library.

Neuls-Bates, Carol, ed. "Women in the Orchestral Field from the 1920s to the 1940s." In *Women in Music: An Anthology of Source Readings from the Middle Ages to the Present*. New York: Harper and Row, 1982.

Nichols, Charles, ed. *Arna Bontemps-Langston Hughes Letters: 1925–1967*. New York: Dodd, Mead, 1980.

Northrup, Solomon. "Twelve Years a Slave," 1853, in Eileen Southern, ed., *Readings in Black American Music*, Second Edition. New York: W. W. Norton, 1983.

Osgood, Marion G. "America's First Ladies Orchestra." *Etude* 58 (October 1940): 713+.

Paine, Lewis. "Six Years in a Georgia Prison," in Eileen Southern, ed., *Readings in Black American Music*, 2nd ed. New York: W. W. Norton, 1983.

Pettis, Ashley. "The WPA and the American Composer." *Musical Quarterly* (January 1940): 101–112.

Poole, Valter, Dr. Interview by Rae Linda Brown, May 28, 1983. Transcription in the Archive of the Oral History Program of the Institute on the Federal Theater Project and New Deal Culture. Fairfax, Va.: George Mason University, 1–33.

Rampersad, Arnold. *The Life of Langston Hughes: I, Too, Sing America*, vol. 1. New York: Oxford University Press, 1986.

Roosevelt, Eleanor. "My Day . . . First Lady Describes Detroit Stay." *Detroit Free Press*, November 15, 1940.

"Save the Music Project." *Detroit Free Press*, March 22, 1940.

Sawyer, Lisa Lee. *Unpublished Songs of Florence B. Price*. University of Missouri-Kansas City, DMA dissertation, 1990.

Schenbeck, Lawrence. "Music, Gender, and 'Uplift' in *The Chicago Defender*, 1927–1937." *The Musical Quarterly* 81, no. 3 (Fall 1997): 344–370.

"Scipio A. Jones." *The Messenger* 10/11 (January 1928): 10.

"Senator Tillman's Separate Coach Bill." *Arkansas Gazette*, January 20, 1891, 4.

"The Shorter University That Was Never Built." *Arkansas Mirror*, July 17, 1969, 7.

Sicherman, Barbara, and Carol Hurd Green, ed. *Notable American Women: The Modern Period*. Cambridge: The Belknap Press of Harvard University Press, 1980.

"Site Bought for Negro School." *Arkansas Gazette*, August 1, 1907, 2.

"Sixteen-Piece Colored Dance Band Will Play in Edmore May 7" [LeRoy Smith's Dance Band, the Detroit WPA 'Stamp Stompers']. *Edmore Times*, April 30, 1942.

Smith, Catherine Parsons. *William Grant Still: A Study in Contradictions*. Berkeley: University of California Press, 2000.

Smith, Hale. "African-American Music: The Hidden Tradition." Chicago Symphony Orchestra *Stagebill* (Spring 1995): 8–14, 46–48.

Smith, James H., Dr. *Maudelle: A Novel Founded on Facts Gathered from Living Witnesses*. Boston: Mayhew Publishing Co., 1906.

Snyder, Jean E. "A Great and Noble School of Music: Dvorák, Harry T. Burleigh, and the African American Spiritual." In *Dvorák in America: 1892–1895*, ed. John C. Tibbetts. Portland, Ore.: Amadeus Press, 1993, 123–148.

Southern, Eileen. "Afro-American Musical Materials." *The Black Perspective in Music* 1 (1973): 24–32.

———. "America's Black Composers of Classical Music." *Music Educators Journal* 62/3 (November 1975): 46–59.

———. *The Music of Black Americans: A History*. 2nd ed. New York: W. W. Norton, 1983.

———. "Music Research and the Black Aesthetic." *Black World* (November 1973): 4–13.

———. *Readings in Black American Music*. 2nd ed. New York: W. W. Norton, 1983.

Spady, James G., ed. *William L. Dawson: A Umum Tribute and a Marvelous Journey*. Philadelphia: Creative Artists' Workshop, 1971.

Spencer, Jon Michael. "The Diminishing Rural Residue of Folklore in City and Urban Blues, Chicago 1915–1950." *Black Music Research Journal* 12, no. 1 (Spring 1992): 25–41.

Spivey, Donald. *Union and the Black Musician: The Narrative of William Everett Samuels and Chicago Local 208*. Lanham, Md.: University Press of America, 1984.

"The Spotlight: Florence Price." *Opportunity* (July 5, 1927): 204–205, 213.

Spradling, Mary Mace, ed. *In Black and White: Afro-Americans in Print—A Guide to Magazine Articles, Newspaper Articles, and Books*, 1971. 3rd ed. Detroit: Gale Research, 1980.

Still, William Grant, as told to Verna Arvey. "Fifty Years of Progress in Music." *The Courier* (November 11, 1950): 15.

———. "My Arkansas Boyhood." *Arkansas Historical Quarterly* 26 (1967): 235–290.

———. "Symphony Orchestra Greatly Enjoyed in Concerts Tuesday [Michigan WPA Symphony]." *Cass City* paper, February 20, 1942.

Terry, Adolphine Fletcher. *Charlotte Stephens: Little Rock's First Black Teacher*. Little Rock: Academic Press of Arkansas, 1973.

Tibbetts, John C., ed. *Dvořák in America: 1892–1895*. Portland, Ore.: Amadeus Press, 1993.

Tick, Judith. "Passed Away Is the Piano Girl: Changes in American Musical Life, 1870–1900." In *Women Making Music: The Western Art Tradition, 1150–1950*, eds. Jane Bowers and Judith Tick. Urbana: University of Illinois Press, 1986.

"They Still Protest: Colored Citizens at War on the Tillman Bill." *Arkansas Gazette*, January 28, 1891, 1.

Travis, Dempsey J. "Chicago's Jazz Trail: 1893–1950." *Black Music Research Newsletter* 9, no. 2 (Fall 1987): 1–3.

Walden, Goldie M. "Keep Ideals in Front of You: They Will Lead to Victory, Says Mrs. Florence B. Price." *Chicago Defender*, July 11, 1936, 7.

Wang, Richard. "Jazz in Chicago: A Historical Overview." *Black Music Research Bulletin* 12, no. 2 (Fall 1990): 8–11.

Westlake, Neda, and Otto Albrecht, eds. *Marion Anderson: A Catalog of the Collection at the University of Pennsylvania Library*. Philadelphia: University of Pennsylvania Press, 1981.

Whispers of Love: A History of the R. Nathaniel Dett Club of Music and Allied Arts, 1922–1987. Unpublished typescript.

Williams, Chester. *Indeed Music: My Years at the New England Conservatory*. Boston: New England Conservatory of Music, 1989.

Williams, Ora. *American Black Women in the Arts and Social Sciences*. 1973. Rev. ed. Metuchen, N.J.: The Scarecrow Press, 1978.

Willis, Sharon Joyce. *A Musical Analysis of the Works of Florence Price*. MA thesis, Georgia State University, 1986.

Wilson, Olly. "Black Music as an Art Form." *Black Music Research Journal* (1983): 1–22.

———. "Composition from the Perspective of the African American Tradition." *Black Music Research Journal* 16, no. 1 (Spring 1996): 43–51.

———. "The Black American Composer." *The Black Perspective in Music* (Spring 1973): 33–36.

———. "The Significance of the Relationship between Afro-American and West African Music." *The Black Perspective in Music* 2/1 (Spring 1974): 3–22.

Winter, Marian Hannah. "Juba and American Minstrelsy," in Paul Magriel, ed. *American Dance*. New York: Da Capo Press, 1948, 1978.

Woolsey, F. W. "Conversation with Roland Hayes." *The Black Perspective in Music* 2, no. 2 (Fall 1974): 179–185.

"The WPA Music Project of Detroit." *The Keynote*. Published by the Detroit Federation of Musicians (October-November 1938): 5.

"WPA Orchestras Preserve Living Music, Says Director." *The Detroit News*, May 10, 1938.

Wright, Josephine. "Black Women in Classical Music in Boston during the Late Nineteenth Century: Profiles of Leadership." In *New Perspectives on Music: Essays in Honor of Eileen Southern*, ed. Josephine Wright with Samuel A. Floyd Jr. Warren, Mich.: Harmonie Park Press, 1992.

Yellin, Victor Fell. *Chadwick: Yankee Composer*. Washington, D.C.: Smithsonian Institution Press, 1990.

Yenser, Thomas, ed. *Who's Who in Colored America*. n.p., Thomas Yenser. 4th ed. (1933–37), 5th ed. (1938–40), 6th Ed. (1941–44).

Yuhasz, Sister Marie Joy, O.P. "Florence B. Price." *American Music Teacher* 19 (February-March 1970): 24–26.

Discography

Anderson, Marian. "My Soul's Been Anchored in the Lord." *Go Down Moses / My Soul's Been Anchored in the Lord.* Victor Red Seal 1799. 1937. Shellac 78 RPM.

Anderson, Marian. "My Soul's Been Anchored in the Lord." *Go Down Moses / My Soul's Been Anchored in the Lord.* Victor Red Seal 1799. 1939. Shellac 78 RPM.

Anderson, Marian. "My Soul's Been Anchored in the Lord." *Songs and Spirituals.* RCA Victor Red Seal M 986. 1942. Shellac 78 RPM.

Davis, Ellabelle. "My Soul's Been Anchored in the Lord." *Recital of Negro Spirituals.* Greenslade, Hubert. Olof, Victor. Decca LM 4504. 1950. Vinyl LP.

Davis, Ellabelle. "My Soul's Been Anchored in the Lord." *Ellabelle Davis Sings Negro Spirituals.* Greenslade, Hubert, and Olof, Victor. London Records LPS 182. 1950. Vinyl LP.

Anderson, Marian. "My Soul's Been Anchored in de Lord." *He's Got the Whole World in His Hands and 18 Other Spirituals.* RCA 09026-61960-2. 1962. Vinyl LP.

Anderson, Marian. "I Am Bound for de Kingdom." *He's Got the Whole World in His Hands and 18 Other Spirituals.* RCA 09026-61960-2. 1962. Vinyl LP.

Price, Leontyne. "My Soul's Been Anchored in de Lord." *Were You There?* Decca DFE 8618. 1965. Vinyl 45 RPM.

Roberts, Richard, and Roberts, Patti. "Let Not Your Heart Be Troubled." *A Quiet Place.* Light Records LS-5578-LP. 1972. Vinyl LP.

The Renaissance. "Let Not Your Heart Be Troubled." *Renaissance II.* Tempo R-7097. 1974. Vinyl LP.

Jeffrys, Jerome. "My Soul's Been Anchored in the Lord." *Negro Spirituals.* Vogue LDM. 30172. 1974. Vinyl LP.

Dorsey, Leroy O. "Song to the Dark Virgin." *Music at the Church of St. Katherine of Alexandria.* Parker, Clyde. Louis J. Wright Memorial Concert Series. Vol. 1. KM-1702. 1977. Vinyl LP.

Harris, Hilda. "Night." *Art Songs by Black American Composers.* University of Michigan SM-0015. 1980. Vinyl LP.

Price, Leontyne. "My Soul Has Been Anchored in the Lord." *Leontyne Price Live! (At the Historic Opening of the Ordway Music Theatre)*. Pro-Arte Digital PAD 231. 1985. Vinyl LP.

Price, Leontyne. "My Soul Has Been Anchored in the Lord." Garvey, David. *Leontyne Price Live! (At the Historic Opening of the Ordway Music Theatre)*. Pro Arte CDD 231. 1985. Compact Disc.

Marshall, Kimberly. "Suite no. 1 for Organ." *Divine Euterpe*. Loft CD-1021. 1987. Compact Disc.

Waites, Althea. "Sonata in E minor." *Althea Waites Performs the Piano Music of Florence Price*. Cambria C-1027. 1987. Vinyl LP. Compact Disc.

Waites, Althea. "The Old Boatman." *Althea Waites Performs the Piano Music of Florence Price*. Cambria C-1027. 1987. Vinyl LP. Compact Disc.

Waites, Althea. "Cotton Dance." *Althea Waites Performs the Piano Music of Florence Price*. Cambria C-1027. 1987. Vinyl LP. Compact Disc.

Waites, Althea. "Dances in the Canebrakes." *Althea Waites Performs the Piano Music of Florence Price*. Cambria C-1027. 1987. Vinyl LP. Compact Disc.

Field, Lucille. "Travel's End." *Lucille Field Sings Songs by American Women Composers*. Cambria CD 1037. 1987/1990. Compact Disc.

Field, Lucille. "To My Little Son." *Lucille Field Sings Songs by American Women Composers*. Cambria CD 1037. 1987/1990. Compact Disc.

Field, Lucille. "Night." *Lucille Field Sings Songs by American Women Composers*. Cambria CD 1037. 1987/1990. Compact Disc.

Field, Lucille. "To the Dark Virgin." *Lucille Field Sings Songs by American Women Composers*. Cambria CD 1037. 1987/1990. Compact Disc.

Macoulescou-Stern, Yolanda. "Night." *Art Songs by American Composers*. Phillabaum, Katja. Cambria GSCD-287. 1991. Compact Disc.

Macoulescou-Stern, Yolanda. "Song to the Dark Virgin." *Art Songs by American Composers*. Phillabaum, Katja. Cambria GSCD-287. 1991. Compact Disc.

Waites, Althea. "Sonata in E Minor." *Black Diamonds*. Cambria CD-1097. 1993. Compact Disc.

Waites, Althea. "Dances in the Canebrakes." *Black Diamonds*. Cambria CD-1097. 1993. Compact Disc.

Videmus: Dillard, Pamela. Hamilton, Ruth. Honeysucker, Robert. Taylor, Vivian. "My Dream." *Watch and Pray: Spirituals and Art Songs by African-American Women Composers*. Koch International Classics 3-7247-2HI. 1994. Compact Disc.

Videmus: Dillard, Pamela. Hamilton, Ruth. Honeysucker, Robert. Taylor, Vivian. "My Soul's Been Anchored in de Lord." *Watch and Pray: Spirituals and Art Songs by African-American Women Composers*. Koch International Classics 3-7247-2HI. 1994. Compact Disc.

Videmus: Dillard, Pamela. Hamilton, Ruth. Honeysucker, Robert. Taylor, Vivian. "Night." *Watch and Pray: Spirituals and Art Songs by African-American Women Composers*. Koch International Classics 3-7247-2HI. 1994. Compact Disc.

Hoy, Patricia J. "Rabbit Foot." *Works for Symphonic Band: William Grant Still, Flor-*

ence Price. Northern Arizona University Wind Symphony Ensemble. Cambria 1156. NAUWS-003. 1995. Compact Disc.

Hoy, Patricia J. "Hoe Cake." *Works for Symphonic Band: William Grant Still, Florence Price.* Northern Arizona University Wind Symphony Ensemble. Cambria 1156. NAUWS-003. 1995. Compact Disc.

Hoy, Patricia J. "Ticklin' Toes." *Works for Symphonic Band: William Grant Still, Florence Price.* Northern Arizona University Wind Symphony Ensemble. Cambria 1156. NAUWS-003. 1995. Compact Disc.

Sterrett-Bryant, James. "Night." *How the Spirit Moves Me.* JaanSin Productions DIDX 031339 22302. 1995. Compact Disc.

Walker-Hill, Helen, and Walker, Gregory. "Fantasie Negré." *Kaleidoscope: Music by African-American Women.* Leonarda LE 339. 1995. Compact Disc.

Johnson, Calvert. "A Pleasant Thought." *Chicago Renaissance Woman: Florence B. Price Organ Works.* Calcante CAL-014. 1997. Compact Disc.

Johnson, Calvert. "Adoration." *Chicago Renaissance Woman: Florence B. Price Organ Works.* Calcante CAL-014. 1997. Compact Disc.

Johnson, Calvert. "Allegretto." *Chicago Renaissance Woman: Florence B. Price Organ Works.* Calcante CAL-014. 1997. Compact Disc.

Johnson, Calvert. "Festal March." *Chicago Renaissance Woman: Florence B. Price Organ Works.* Calcante CAL-014. 1997. Compact Disc.

Johnson, Calvert. "In Quiet Mood." *Chicago Renaissance Woman: Florence B. Price Organ Works.* Calcante CAL-014. 1997. Compact Disc.

Johnson, Calvert. "Little Melody." *Chicago Renaissance Woman: Florence B. Price Organ Works.* Calcante CAL-014. 1997. Compact Disc.

Johnson, Calvert. "Offertory." *Chicago Renaissance Woman: Florence B. Price Organ Works.* Calcante CAL-014. 1997. Compact Disc.

Johnson, Calvert. "Retrospection." *Chicago Renaissance Woman: Florence B. Price Organ Works.* Calcante CAL-014. 1997. Compact Disc.

Johnson, Calvert. "Sonata, Organ, No. 1, D Minor." *Chicago Renaissance Woman: Florence B. Price Organ Works.* Calcante CAL-014. 1997. Compact Disc.

Johnson, Calvert. "Suite, Organ, No. 1." *Chicago Renaissance Woman: Florence B. Price Organ Works.* Calcante CAL-014. 1997. Compact Disc.

Johnson, Calvert. "The Hour Glass." *Chicago Renaissance Woman: Florence B. Price Organ Works.* Calcante CAL-014. 1997. Compact Disc.

Johnson, Calvert. "Peter Go Ring dem Bells." *Chicago Renaissance Woman: Florence B. Price Organ Works.* Calcante CAL-014. 1997. Compact Disc.

Schiff, Zina, and Grant, Cameron. "The Deserted Garden." *Here's One.* 4 Tay Inc. 4TAY-CD-4005. 1997. Compact Disc.

Anderson, Marian. "My Soul's Been Anchored in de Lord." *Rare and Unpublished Recordings, 1936–1952.* VAI Audio VAIA 1168. 1998. Compact Disc.

Nobert, Frances. "Peter Go Ring dem Bells." *Music She Wrote: Organ Compositions by Women.* Ravel OAR-550. 1998. Compact Disc.

Pons, Monica. "Cotton Dance." *Compositio.* Ars Harmonica AH307. 1998. Compact Disc.

Pons, Monica. "Tropical Noon." *Compositio.* Ars Harmonica AH307. 1998. Compact Disc.

Pons, Monica. "Nimble Feet." *Compositio.* Ars Harmonica AH307. 1998. Compact Disc.
Brown, William, and Sears, Ann. "Night." *Fi-yer! A Century of African-American Song.* Albany TROY. 1999. Compact Disc.
Toppin, Louise. "Hold Fast to Dreams." *Ah! Love, but a Day: Songs and Spirituals of African American Women.* O'Brien, John. Albany TROY 385. 1999. Compact Disc.
Toppin, Louise. "Sympathy." *Ah! Love, but a Day: Songs and Spirituals of African American Women.* O'Brien, John. Albany TROY 385. 1999. Compact Disc.
Toppin, Louise. "The Glory of the Day Was in Her Face." *Ah! Love, but a Day: Songs and Spirituals of African American Women.* O'Brien, John. Albany TROY 385. 1999. Compact Disc.
Amaize, Odekhiren. "Night." *The Negro Speaks of Rivers: Art Songs by African-American Composers.* Korevaar, David. Musician's Showcase MS 1011. 2000. Compact Disc.
Amaize, Odekhiren. "Songs to the Dark Virgin." *The Negro Speaks of Rivers: Art Songs by African-American Composers.* Korevaar, David. Musician's Showcase MS 1011. 2000. Compact Disc.
Barnes, Sebronette, and Auerbach, Elise. "An April Day." *You Can Tell the World: Songs by African-American Women Composers.* Senrad Records. 2000. Compact Disc.
Barnes, Sebronette, and Auerbach, Elise. "Out of the South Blew a Wind." *You Can Tell the World: Songs by African-American Women Composers.* Senrad Records. 2000. Compact Disc.
Barnes, Sebronette, and Auerbach, Elise. "Songs to the Dark Virgin." *You Can Tell the World: Songs by African-American Women Composers.* Senrad Records. 2000. Compact Disc.
Hsu, Apo. "Songs of the Oak." *Florence Price: The Oak, Mississippi River Suite, and Symphony No. 3.* The Women's Philharmonic. Koch 3-7518-2HI. 2001. Compact Disc.
Hsu, Apo. "Mississippi River." *Florence Price: The Oak, Mississippi River Suite, and Symphony No. 3.* The Women's Philharmonic. Koch 3-7518-2HI. 2001. Compact Disc.
Hsu, Apo. "Symphony No. 3 in C minor." *Florence Price: The Oak, Mississippi River Suite, and Symphony no. 3.* The Women's Philharmonic. Koch 3-7518-2HI. 2001. Compact Disc.
Moses, Oral. "Night." *Amen!; African-American Composers of the 20th Century.* Albany TROY. 2001. Compact Disc.
Taylor, Darryl. "Songs to the Dark Virgin." *Dreamer: A Portrait of Langston Hughes.* Warfield, William. Naxos 8.559136. 2002. Compact Disc.
Brunelle, Phillip. "Moon Bridge." *Witness: Got the Saint Louis Blues—Classical Music in the Jazz Age.* VocalEssence Ensemble Singers and Chorus. Clarion CLR 907. 2004. Compact Disc.
Brunelle, Phillip. "Song for Snow." *Witness: Got the Saint Louis Blues—Classical Music in the Jazz Age.* VocalEssence Ensemble Singers and Chorus. Clarion CLR 907. 2004. Compact Disc.
Nyaho, William Chapman. "Dances in the Canebrakes." *Asa: Piano Music by Composers of African Descent.* MSR Classics MS 1242. 2008. Compact Disc.
Dunner, Leslie B. *Florence B. Price: Concerto in One Movement and Symphony in E minor.*

Walwyn, Karen. New Black Music Repertory Ensemble. Albany TROY 1295. 2011. Compact Disc.

Martin, James, and Boriskin, Michael. "Gonna Wake Up Singin'." *Wake Up Singin' (A Copland House Celebration of Songs, Hymns, and Spirituals).* Copland House Blend CHB-CD-101. 2013. Compact Disc.

Downes, Lara. "Fantasie Negre." *America Again.* Sono Luminus DSL 92207. 2016. Compact Disc.

Kahng, Er-Gene, and Cockerman, Ryan. *Florence B. Price: Violin Concertos Nos 1 (D major—1939) and 2 (D minor—1952).* Janáček Philharmonic Orchestra. Albany TROY 1706. 2018. Compact Disc.

Downes, Lara. "Memory Mist." *Holes in the Sky.* Portrait 19075920792. 2019. Compact Disc.

Chen, Mei-Ann. "Dances in the Canebrakes: Nimble Feet / Tropical Noon / Silk Hat and Walking Cane." *Project W—Works by Diverse Women Composers.* Chicago Sinfonietta. Cedille Records CDR 90000 185. 2019. Compact Disc.

Jeter, John. "Symphony No. 1 in E Minor (1932)." *Symphony Nos. 1 and 4.* Fort Smith Symphony Orchestra. Naxos 8.559827. 2019. Compact Disc.

Jeter, John. "Symphony No. 4 in D Minor (1945)." *Symphony Nos. 1 and 4.* Fort Smith Symphony Orchestra. Naxos 8.559827. 2019. Compact Disc.

Harris, Inetta. "My Soul's Been Anchored in the Lord." *My Heritage Sings: A Selection of Spirituals & Hymns.* Lippodt, Scott. Compact Disc. Year and Label Unknown.

For Further Reading

Absher, Amy. *The Black Musician and the White City: Race and Music in Chicago, 1900–1967*. Urbana: University of Illinois Press, 2017.

Berg, Gregory. "My Dream: Art Songs and Spirituals by Florence Price." *Journal of Singing*, 69, no. 3 (January 2013): 385–386.

Broadbent, Amy Arlene. "The Piano Teaching Pieces of Florence B. Price: A Pedagogical and Theoretical Analysis of 11 Late Elementary Piano Teaching Pieces." MA thesis, Western Illinois University, 2016.

David, Farrah Scott. "Signifyin(g): A Semiotic Analysis of Symphonic Works by William Grant Still, William Levi Dawson and Florence B. Price." PhD dissertation, The Florida State University, 2007.

Hayes, Eileen M., and Linda F. Williams, eds. *Black Women and Music: More than the Blues*. Urbana: University of Illinois Press, 2007.

Hobbs, Erin. "Rehearing Florence Price: A Closer Look at Her Symphony in E Minor." MA thesis, California State University, Long Beach, 2017.

Mashego, Shana Thomas. "Music from the Soul of Woman: The Influence of the African American Presbyterian and Methodist Traditions on the Classical Compositions of Florence Price." DMA dissertation, The University of Arizona, 2010.

Ross, Alex. "New World: The Rediscovery of Florence Price." *The New Yorker* (February 5, 2018).

Shadle, Douglas. "Plus Ça Change: Florence B. Price in the #BlackLivesMatter Era," *NewMusicBox* (February 2019).

Index

Page numbers in italic refer to illustrations.

RAE LINDA BROWN was a professor at the University of Michigan and a professor and Robert and Marjorie Rawlins Chair of the Department of Music at the University of California, Irvine. She was the author of *Music, Printed and Manuscript, in the James Weldon Johnson Memorial Collection of Negro Arts and Letters: An Annotated Catalog*. She died in 2017.

GUTHRIE P. RAMSEY JR. is the Edmund J. and Louise W. Kahn Term Professor of Music at the University of Pennsylvania. He is the author of *Race Music: Black Cultures from Bebop to Hip-Hop* and *The Amazing Bud Powell: Black Genius, Jazz History, and the Challenge of Bebop*.

Music in American Life

Only a Miner: Studies in Recorded Coal-Mining Songs *Archie Green*
Great Day Coming: Folk Music and the American Left *R. Serge Denisoff*
John Philip Sousa: A Descriptive Catalog of His Works *Paul E. Bierley*
The Hell-Bound Train: A Cowboy Songbook *Glenn Ohrlin*
Oh, Didn't He Ramble: The Life Story of Lee Collins, as Told to Mary Collins *Edited by Frank J. Gillis and John W. Miner*
American Labor Songs of the Nineteenth Century *Philip S. Foner*
Stars of Country Music: Uncle Dave Macon to Johnny Rodriguez *Edited by Bill C. Malone and Judith McCulloh*
Git Along, Little Dogies: Songs and Songmakers of the American West *John I. White*
A Texas-Mexican *Cancionero*: Folksongs of the Lower Border *Américo Paredes*
San Antonio Rose: The Life and Music of Bob Wills *Charles R. Townsend*
Early Downhome Blues: A Musical and Cultural Analysis *Jeff Todd Titon*
An Ives Celebration: Papers and Panels of the Charles Ives Centennial Festival-Conference *Edited by H. Wiley Hitchcock and Vivian Perlis*
Sinful Tunes and Spirituals: Black Folk Music to the Civil War *Dena J. Epstein*
Joe Scott, the Woodsman-Songmaker *Edward D. Ives*
Jimmie Rodgers: The Life and Times of America's Blue Yodeler *Nolan Porterfield*
Early American Music Engraving and Printing: A History of Music Publishing in America from 1787 to 1825, with Commentary on Earlier and Later Practices *Richard J. Wolfe*
Sing a Sad Song: The Life of Hank Williams *Roger M. Williams*
Long Steel Rail: The Railroad in American Folksong *Norm Cohen*
Resources of American Music History: A Directory of Source Materials from Colonial Times to World War II *D. W. Krummel, Jean Geil, Doris J. Dyen, and Deane L. Root*
Tenement Songs: The Popular Music of the Jewish Immigrants *Mark Slobin*
Ozark Folksongs *Vance Randolph; edited and abridged by Norm Cohen*
Oscar Sonneck and American Music *Edited by William Lichtenwanger*
Bluegrass Breakdown: The Making of the Old Southern Sound *Robert Cantwell*
Bluegrass: A History *Neil V. Rosenberg*
Music at the White House: A History of the American Spirit *Elise K. Kirk*
Red River Blues: The Blues Tradition in the Southeast *Bruce Bastin*
Good Friends and Bad Enemies: Robert Winslow Gordon and the Study of American Folksong *Debora Kodish*
Fiddlin' Georgia Crazy: Fiddlin' John Carson, His Real World, and the World of His Songs *Gene Wiggins*
America's Music: From the Pilgrims to the Present (rev. 3d ed.) *Gilbert Chase*
Secular Music in Colonial Annapolis: The Tuesday Club, 1745–56 *John Barry Talley*
Bibliographical Handbook of American Music *D. W. Krummel*
Goin' to Kansas City *Nathan W. Pearson Jr.*

"Susanna," "Jeanie," and "The Old Folks at Home": The Songs of Stephen C. Foster from His Time to Ours (2d ed.) *William W. Austin*
Songprints: The Musical Experience of Five Shoshone Women *Judith Vander*
"Happy in the Service of the Lord": Afro-American Gospel Quartets in Memphis *Kip Lornell*
Paul Hindemith in the United States *Luther Noss*
"My Song Is My Weapon": People's Songs, American Communism, and the Politics of Culture, 1930–50 *Robbie Lieberman*
Chosen Voices: The Story of the American Cantorate *Mark Slobin*
Theodore Thomas: America's Conductor and Builder of Orchestras, 1835–1905 *Ezra Schabas*
"The Whorehouse Bells Were Ringing" and Other Songs Cowboys Sing *Collected and Edited by Guy Logsdon*
Crazeology: The Autobiography of a Chicago Jazzman *Bud Freeman, as Told to Robert Wolf*
Discoursing Sweet Music: Brass Bands and Community Life in Turn-of-the-Century Pennsylvania *Kenneth Kreitner*
Mormonism and Music: A History *Michael Hicks*
Voices of the Jazz Age: Profiles of Eight Vintage Jazzmen *Chip Deffaa*
Pickin' on Peachtree: A History of Country Music in Atlanta, Georgia *Wayne W. Daniel*
Bitter Music: Collected Journals, Essays, Introductions, and Librettos *Harry Partch; edited by Thomas McGeary*
Ethnic Music on Records: A Discography of Ethnic Recordings Produced in the United States, 1893 to 1942 *Richard K. Spottswood*
Downhome Blues Lyrics: An Anthology from the Post–World War II Era *Jeff Todd Titon*
Ellington: The Early Years *Mark Tucker*
Chicago Soul *Robert Pruter*
That Half-Barbaric Twang: The Banjo in American Popular Culture *Karen Linn*
Hot Man: The Life of Art Hodes *Art Hodes and Chadwick Hansen*
The Erotic Muse: American Bawdy Songs (2d ed.) *Ed Cray*
Barrio Rhythm: Mexican American Music in Los Angeles *Steven Loza*
The Creation of Jazz: Music, Race, and Culture in Urban America *Burton W. Peretti*
Charles Martin Loeffler: A Life Apart in Music *Ellen Knight*
Club Date Musicians: Playing the New York Party Circuit *Bruce A. MacLeod*
Opera on the Road: Traveling Opera Troupes in the United States, 1825–60 *Katherine K. Preston*
The Stonemans: An Appalachian Family and the Music That Shaped Their Lives *Ivan M. Tribe*
Transforming Tradition: Folk Music Revivals Examined *Edited by Neil V. Rosenberg*
The Crooked Stovepipe: Athapaskan Fiddle Music and Square Dancing in Northeast Alaska and Northwest Canada *Craig Mishler*

Traveling the High Way Home: Ralph Stanley and the World of Traditional Bluegrass Music *John Wright*
Carl Ruggles: Composer, Painter, and Storyteller *Marilyn Ziffrin*
Never without a Song: The Years and Songs of Jennie Devlin, 1865–1952 *Katharine D. Newman*
The Hank Snow Story *Hank Snow, with Jack Ownbey and Bob Burris*
Milton Brown and the Founding of Western Swing *Cary Ginell, with special assistance from Roy Lee Brown*
Santiago de Murcia's "Códice Saldívar No. 4": A Treasury of Secular Guitar Music from Baroque Mexico *Craig H. Russell*
The Sound of the Dove: Singing in Appalachian Primitive Baptist Churches *Beverly Bush Patterson*
Heartland Excursions: Ethnomusicological Reflections on Schools of Music *Bruno Nettl*
Doowop: The Chicago Scene *Robert Pruter*
Blue Rhythms: Six Lives in Rhythm and Blues *Chip Deffaa*
Shoshone Ghost Dance Religion: Poetry Songs and Great Basin Context *Judith Vander*
Go Cat Go! Rockabilly Music and Its Makers *Craig Morrison*
'Twas Only an Irishman's Dream: The Image of Ireland and the Irish in American Popular Song Lyrics, 1800–1920 *William H. A. Williams*
Democracy at the Opera: Music, Theater, and Culture in New York City, 1815–60 *Karen Ahlquist*
Fred Waring and the Pennsylvanians *Virginia Waring*
Woody, Cisco, and Me: Seamen Three in the Merchant Marine *Jim Longhi*
Behind the Burnt Cork Mask: Early Blackface Minstrelsy and Antebellum American Popular Culture *William J. Mahar*
Going to Cincinnati: A History of the Blues in the Queen City *Steven C. Tracy*
Pistol Packin' Mama: Aunt Molly Jackson and the Politics of Folksong *Shelly Romalis*
Sixties Rock: Garage, Psychedelic, and Other Satisfactions *Michael Hicks*
The Late Great Johnny Ace and the Transition from R&B to Rock 'n' Roll *James M. Salem*
Tito Puente and the Making of Latin Music *Steven Loza*
Juilliard: A History *Andrea Olmstead*
Understanding Charles Seeger, Pioneer in American Musicology *Edited by Bell Yung and Helen Rees*
Mountains of Music: West Virginia Traditional Music from *Goldenseal* *Edited by John Lilly*
Alice Tully: An Intimate Portrait *Albert Fuller*
A Blues Life *Henry Townsend, as told to Bill Greensmith*
Long Steel Rail: The Railroad in American Folksong (2d ed.) *Norm Cohen*
The Golden Age of Gospel *Text by Horace Clarence Boyer; photography by Lloyd Yearwood*

Aaron Copland: The Life and Work of an Uncommon Man *Howard Pollack*
Louis Moreau Gottschalk *S. Frederick Starr*
Race, Rock, and Elvis *Michael T. Bertrand*
Theremin: Ether Music and Espionage *Albert Glinsky*
Poetry and Violence: The Ballad Tradition of Mexico's Costa Chica *John H. McDowell*
The Bill Monroe Reader *Edited by Tom Ewing*
Music in Lubavitcher Life *Ellen Koskoff*
Zarzuela: Spanish Operetta, American Stage *Janet L. Sturman*
Bluegrass Odyssey: A Documentary in Pictures and Words, 1966–86 *Carl Fleischhauer and Neil V. Rosenberg*
That Old-Time Rock & Roll: A Chronicle of an Era, 1954–63 *Richard Aquila*
Labor's Troubadour *Joe Glazer*
American Opera *Elise K. Kirk*
Don't Get above Your Raisin': Country Music and the Southern Working Class *Bill C. Malone*
John Alden Carpenter: A Chicago Composer *Howard Pollack*
Heartbeat of the People: Music and Dance of the Northern Pow-wow *Tara Browner*
My Lord, What a Morning: An Autobiography *Marian Anderson*
Marian Anderson: A Singer's Journey *Allan Keiler*
Charles Ives Remembered: An Oral History *Vivian Perlis*
Henry Cowell, Bohemian *Michael Hicks*
Rap Music and Street Consciousness *Cheryl L. Keyes*
Louis Prima *Garry Boulard*
Marian McPartland's Jazz World: All in Good Time *Marian McPartland*
Robert Johnson: Lost and Found *Barry Lee Pearson and Bill McCulloch*
Bound for America: Three British Composers *Nicholas Temperley*
Lost Sounds: Blacks and the Birth of the Recording Industry, 1890–1919 *Tim Brooks*
Burn, Baby! BURN! The Autobiography of Magnificent Montague *Magnificent Montague with Bob Baker*
Way Up North in Dixie: A Black Family's Claim to the Confederate Anthem *Howard L. Sacks and Judith Rose Sacks*
The Bluegrass Reader *Edited by Thomas Goldsmith*
Colin McPhee: Composer in Two Worlds *Carol J. Oja*
Robert Johnson, Mythmaking, and Contemporary American Culture *Patricia R. Schroeder*
Composing a World: Lou Harrison, Musical Wayfarer *Leta E. Miller and Fredric Lieberman*
Fritz Reiner, Maestro and Martinet *Kenneth Morgan*
That Toddlin' Town: Chicago's White Dance Bands and Orchestras, 1900–1950 *Charles A. Sengstock Jr.*
Dewey and Elvis: The Life and Times of a Rock 'n' Roll Deejay *Louis Cantor*

Come Hither to Go Yonder: Playing Bluegrass with Bill Monroe *Bob Black*
Chicago Blues: Portraits and Stories *David Whiteis*
The Incredible Band of John Philip Sousa *Paul E. Bierley*
"Maximum Clarity" and Other Writings on Music *Ben Johnston, edited by Bob Gilmore*
Staging Tradition: John Lair and Sarah Gertrude Knott *Michael Ann Williams*
Homegrown Music: Discovering Bluegrass *Stephanie P. Ledgin*
Tales of a Theatrical Guru *Danny Newman*
The Music of Bill Monroe *Neil V. Rosenberg and Charles K. Wolfe*
Pressing On: The Roni Stoneman Story *Roni Stoneman, as told to Ellen Wright*
Together Let Us Sweetly Live *Jonathan C. David, with photographs by Richard Holloway*
Live Fast, Love Hard: The Faron Young Story *Diane Diekman*
Air Castle of the South: WSM Radio and the Making of Music City *Craig P. Havighurst*
Traveling Home: Sacred Harp Singing and American Pluralism *Kiri Miller*
Where Did Our Love Go? The Rise and Fall of the Motown Sound *Nelson George*
Lonesome Cowgirls and Honky-Tonk Angels: The Women of Barn Dance Radio *Kristine M. McCusker*
California Polyphony: Ethnic Voices, Musical Crossroads *Mina Yang*
The Never-Ending Revival: Rounder Records and the Folk Alliance *Michael F. Scully*
Sing It Pretty: A Memoir *Bess Lomax Hawes*
Working Girl Blues: The Life and Music of Hazel Dickens *Hazel Dickens and Bill C. Malone*
Charles Ives Reconsidered *Gayle Sherwood Magee*
The Hayloft Gang: The Story of the National Barn Dance *Edited by Chad Berry*
Country Music Humorists and Comedians *Loyal Jones*
Record Makers and Breakers: Voices of the Independent Rock 'n' Roll Pioneers *John Broven*
Music of the First Nations: Tradition and Innovation in Native North America *Edited by Tara Browner*
Cafe Society: The Wrong Place for the Right People *Barney Josephson, with Terry Trilling-Josephson*
George Gershwin: An Intimate Portrait *Walter Rimler*
Life Flows On in Endless Song: Folk Songs and American History *Robert V. Wells*
I Feel a Song Coming On: The Life of Jimmy McHugh *Alyn Shipton*
King of the Queen City: The Story of King Records *Jon Hartley Fox*
Long Lost Blues: Popular Blues in America, 1850–1920 *Peter C. Muir*
Hard Luck Blues: Roots Music Photographs from the Great Depression *Rich Remsberg*
Restless Giant: The Life and Times of Jean Aberbach and Hill and Range Songs *Bar Biszick-Lockwood*

Champagne Charlie and Pretty Jemima: Variety Theater in the Nineteenth Century *Gillian M. Rodger*
Sacred Steel: Inside an African American Steel Guitar Tradition *Robert L. Stone*
Gone to the Country: The New Lost City Ramblers and the Folk Music Revival *Ray Allen*
The Makers of the Sacred Harp *David Warren Steel with Richard H. Hulan*
Woody Guthrie, American Radical *Will Kaufman*
George Szell: A Life of Music *Michael Charry*
Bean Blossom: The Brown County Jamboree and Bill Monroe's Bluegrass Festivals *Thomas A. Adler*
Crowe on the Banjo: The Music Life of J. D. Crowe *Marty Godbey*
Twentieth Century Drifter: The Life of Marty Robbins *Diane Diekman*
Henry Mancini: Reinventing Film Music *John Caps*
The Beautiful Music All Around Us: Field Recordings and the American Experience *Stephen Wade*
Then Sings My Soul: The Culture of Southern Gospel Music *Douglas Harrison*
The Accordion in the Americas: Klezmer, Polka, Tango, Zydeco, and More! *Edited by Helena Simonett*
Bluegrass Bluesman: A Memoir *Josh Graves, edited by Fred Bartenstein*
One Woman in a Hundred: Edna Phillips and the Philadelphia Orchestra *Mary Sue Welsh*
The Great Orchestrator: Arthur Judson and American Arts Management *James M. Doering*
Charles Ives in the Mirror: American Histories of an Iconic Composer *David C. Paul*
Southern Soul-Blues *David Whiteis*
Sweet Air: Modernism, Regionalism, and American Popular Song *Edward P. Comentale*
Pretty Good for a Girl: Women in Bluegrass *Murphy Hicks Henry*
Sweet Dreams: The World of Patsy Cline *Warren R. Hofstra*
William Sidney Mount and the Creolization of American Culture *Christopher J. Smith*
Bird: The Life and Music of Charlie Parker *Chuck Haddix*
Making the March King: John Philip Sousa's Washington Years, 1854–1893 *Patrick Warfield*
In It for the Long Run *Jim Rooney*
Pioneers of the Blues Revival *Steve Cushing*
Roots of the Revival: American and British Folk Music in the 1950s *Ronald D. Cohen and Rachel Clare Donaldson*
Blues All Day Long: The Jimmy Rogers Story *Wayne Everett Goins*
Yankee Twang: Country and Western Music in New England *Clifford R. Murphy*
The Music of the Stanley Brothers *Gary B. Reid*
Hawaiian Music in Motion: Mariners, Missionaries, and Minstrels *James Revell Carr*

Sounds of the New Deal: The Federal Music Project in the West *Peter Gough*
The Mormon Tabernacle Choir: A Biography *Michael Hicks*
The Man That Got Away: The Life and Songs of Harold Arlen *Walter Rimler*
A City Called Heaven: Chicago and the Birth of Gospel Music *Robert M. Marovich*
Blues Unlimited: Essential Interviews from the Original Blues Magazine *Edited by Bill Greensmith, Mike Rowe, and Mark Camarigg*
Hoedowns, Reels, and Frolics: Roots and Branches of Southern Appalachian Dance *Phil Jamison*
Fannie Bloomfield-Zeisler: The Life and Times of a Piano Virtuoso *Beth Abelson Macleod*
Cybersonic Arts: Adventures in American New Music *Gordon Mumma, edited with commentary by Michelle Fillion*
The Magic of Beverly Sills *Nancy Guy*
Waiting for Buddy Guy *Alan Harper*
Harry T. Burleigh: From the Spiritual to the Harlem Renaissance *Jean E. Snyder*
Music in the Age of Anxiety: American Music in the Fifties *James Wierzbicki*
Jazzing: New York City's Unseen Scene *Thomas H. Greenland*
A Cole Porter Companion *Edited by Don M. Randel, Matthew Shaftel, and Susan Forscher Weiss*
Foggy Mountain Troubadour: The Life and Music of Curly Seckler *Penny Parsons*
Blue Rhythm Fantasy: Big Band Jazz Arranging in the Swing Era *John Wriggle*
Bill Clifton: America's Bluegrass Ambassador to the World *Bill C. Malone*
Chinatown Opera Theater in North America *Nancy Yunhwa Rao*
The Elocutionists: Women, Music, and the Spoken Word *Marian Wilson Kimber*
May Irwin: Singing, Shouting, and the Shadow of Minstrelsy *Sharon Ammen*
Peggy Seeger: A Life of Music, Love, and Politics *Jean R. Freedman*
Charles Ives's *Concord*: Essays after a Sonata *Kyle Gann*
Don't Give Your Heart to a Rambler: My Life with Jimmy Martin, the King of Bluegrass *Barbara Martin Stephens*
Libby Larsen: Composing an American Life *Denise Von Glahn*
George Szell's Reign: Behind the Scenes with the Cleveland Orchestra *Marcia Hansen Kraus*
Just One of the Boys: Female-to-Male Cross-Dressing on the American Variety Stage *Gillian M. Rodger*
Spirituals and the Birth of a Black Entertainment Industry *Sandra Jean Graham*
Right to the Juke Joint: A Personal History of American Music *Patrick B. Mullen*
Bluegrass Generation: A Memoir *Neil V. Rosenberg*
Pioneers of the Blues Revival, Expanded Second Edition *Steve Cushing*
Banjo Roots and Branches *Edited by Robert Winans*
Bill Monroe: The Life and Music of the Blue Grass Man *Tom Ewing*
Dixie Dewdrop: The Uncle Dave Macon Story *Michael D. Doubler*
Los Romeros: Royal Family of the Spanish Guitar *Walter Aaron Clark*

Transforming Women's Education: Liberal Arts and Music in Female Seminaries *Jewel A. Smith*

Rethinking American Music *Edited by Tara Browner and Thomas L. Riis*

Leonard Bernstein and the Language of Jazz *Katherine Baber*

Dancing Revolution: Bodies, Space, and Sound in American Cultural History *Christopher J. Smith*

Peggy Glanville-Hicks: Composer and Critic *Suzanne Robinson*

Mormons, Musical Theater, and Belonging in America *Jake Johnson*

Blues Legacy: Tradition and Innovation in Chicago *David Whiteis*

Blues Before Sunrise 2: Interviews from the Chicago Scene *Steve Cushing*

The Cashaway Psalmody: Transatlantic Religion and Music in Colonial Carolina *Stephen A. Marini*

Earl Scruggs and Foggy Mountain Breakdown: The Making of an American Classic *Thomas Goldsmith*

A Guru's Journey: Pandit Chitresh Das and Indian Classical Dance in Diaspora *Sarah Morelli*

Unsettled Scores: Politics, Hollywood, and the Film Music of Aaron Copland and Hanns Eisler *Sally Bick*

Hillbilly Maidens, Okies, and Cowgirls: Women's Country Music, 1930–1960 *Stephanie Vander Wel*

Always the Queen: The Denise LaSalle Story *Denise LaSalle with David Whiteis*

Artful Noise: Percussion Literature in the Twentieth Century *Thomas Siwe*

The Heart of a Woman: The Life and Music of Florence B. Price *Rae Linda Brown, edited by Guthrie P. Ramsey Jr.*

The University of Illinois Press
is a founding member of the
Association of University Presses.

University of Illinois Press
1325 South Oak Street
Champaign, IL 61820-6903
www.press.uillinois.edu